Lights and Shadows

Studies in International Criminal Law

Editor-in-Chief

VOLUME 7

The titles published in this series are listed at *brill.com/sicl*

Lights and Shadows

The Ongwen *Case at the International Criminal Court*

Edited by

Juan-Pablo Perez-Leon-Acevedo
Fabio Ferraz de Almeida

BRILL | NIJHOFF

LEIDEN | BOSTON

Originally published, in part, as vol. 23, nos. 5–6 (2023) and vol. 24, no. 1 (2024) of Brill's journal *International Criminal Law Review*.

This work was supported by the Research Council of Finland (project number 325535).

Cover illustration: Untitled watercolour, 2011, Edward Matwijkiw (1937–2012), reproduced with kind permission of the family.

Library of Congress Cataloging-in-Publication Data

Names: Perez-Leon-Acevedo, Juan-Pablo editor | Ferraz de Almeida, Fabio editor
Title: Lights and shadows : the Ongwen case at the International Criminal Court / Juan-Pablo Perez-Leon-Acevedo, Fabio Ferraz de Almeida.
Description: Leiden ; Boston : Brill/Nijhoff, 2026. | Series: Studies in international criminal law, 2666-903X ; volume 7 | Includes index.
Identifiers: LCCN 2025040907 (print) | LCCN 2025040908 (ebook) | ISBN 9789004743373 hardback | ISBN 9789004743380 ebook
Subjects: LCSH: International Criminal Court | Victims of crimes (International law) | Child soldiers (International law) | War criminals | Victims of crimes—Legal status, laws, etc—Uganda | International crimes—Law and legislation—Uganda | Genocide—Law and legislation—Uganda | War crimes—Uganda
Classification: LCC KZ7495 .L54 2025 (print) | LCC KZ7495 (ebook) | DDC 345/.0122--dc23/eng/20250903
LC record available at https://lccn.loc.gov/2025040907
LC ebook record available at https://lccn.loc.gov/2025040908

Typeface for the Latin, Greek, and Cyrillic scripts: "Brill". See and download: brill.com/brill-typeface.

ISSN 2666-903X
ISBN 978-90-04-74337-3 (hardback)
ISBN 978-90-04-74338-0 (e-book)
DOI 10.1163/9789004743380

This book is printed on acid-free paper and produced in a sustainable manner.

Contents

Foreword: Lights, Shadows, and Dialogue

> The idea of a conversation is, as we will show, critical to what we understand doing research to be about. Producing knowledge, as we see it, is fundamentally about participating in one amongst the many conversations that are now taking place within the social and human sciences. The main goal of this book, then, is to provide a guide to participating in the conversations about language that matter to you.[1]

∴

Conversation analysis, a praxiological approach to interaction and intersubjectivity that emerged from the sociological imagination of the late Harold Garfinkel, has long maintained that conversation is the bedrock of all sociality. It is in and through mundane interaction with relevant others in our immediate environment that we are socialized into languaged beings, and this mundaneity is the starting point for our subsequent engagements in the many specialized and particularized forms of communication that characterize adult society.[2] The literary scholar Mikhail Bakhtin pointed out that little of what we say is truly original, and that our words make sense only in relation to, or in dialogue with, the words of others who have spoken before or after us.[3] Research in the humanities and social sciences is an activity conducted in and through language, and as such it is no exception to this dialogical principle. Dialogicity, in turn, is closely related to interdisciplinarity. Alessandro Duranti, in a commentary on the history of linguistic anthropology (the tradition in which I was socialized), pointed out that Dell Hymes's project of re-founding the study of language in the context of anthropology was dramatically reinvigorated once it no longer imagined itself as exclusively centered on a "discrete dimension" of social life (the ways in which members of particular society or community use language), but reinvented itself as a *dialogical* enterprise aimed at bringing out

---

1 M. Heller, S. Pietikäinen, and J Pujolar, *Critical Sociolinguistic Research Methods: Studying Language Issues That Matter* (Routledge, New York, 2017).

2 *See* J. Heritage and P. Drew (eds.), *Talk at Work: Interaction in Institutional Settings* (Cambridge University Press, Cambridge, 1992).

3 *See* M. Bakhtin, *The Dialogic Imagination: Four Essays* (University of Texas Press, 1981).

the interactional underpinnings of issues raised in adjacent disciplines in the humanities and social sciences.[4]

The collection of articles that you are holding in your hands today originated in the context of the project *Negotiating International Criminal Law: A courtroom ethnography of trial performance at the International Criminal Court*, funded by the Research Council of Finland and hosted by the University of Jyväskylä from 2019 to 2023. The project was a prime example of a dialogical enterprise as outlined above, in which insights from interactional analysis, linguistic anthropology, and sociolinguistics were combined to address (and in the process reformulate) research questions that were essentially (socio-)legal in nature. Its point of departure was the eminently novel character of the International Criminal Court (ICC) as a transnational justice setting. In contrast to the vast majority of domestic criminal justice systems, the ICC does not (yet) have a long tradition or deeply entrenched routines. Both its substantive law and its courtroom procedures are not yet fully clarified, and the Court is therefore still in the process of consolidating itself. This is a unique opportunity for linguistic anthropologists not only to better understand this consolidation process, but also to make a wider scholarly audience aware of the unique contribution our discipline can make to a better understanding of how international criminal justice is implemented. In this spirit, the project set itself the ambitious goal of offering a fresh perspective on the many internal and external challenges facing the Court, ranging from procedural uncertainty to various challenges to its legitimacy. It did so by opening the black box of trial performance, something all too often kept under the radar of doctrinal scholarship, and examining how trial actors navigate these tensions in everyday courtroom practice, in the minutiae of examining witnesses and challenging the other party's testimony and in the pointed exchanges over the interpretation of this or that rule. As such, the project did not pretend to "correct" doctrinal scholarship, but rather to offer a different perspective, one that does not denigrate the practice of law but emphasizes its embedding in concrete practical circumstances, and that views adjudication not as the disembodied formal application of rules but as rule-based reasoning done by real people in real time in real-life settings—in this case, lengthy trial hearings that took place in one of the three superimposed courtrooms of the central tower of the ICC's premises in The Hague.[5]

---

4 *See* A. Duranti, 'Language as Culture in US Anthropology: Three Paradigms', 44(3) *Current anthropology* (2003) 323–347, doi: 10.1086/368118.

5 The fact that such a praxiological perspective transcends the dichotomy between "internal" and "external" approaches to law has been most clearly articulated by ethnomethodologists.

A project like this is dialogical not only because it addresses questions formulated in adjacent disciplines, but also because such an ambitious agenda can only be successfully implemented if scholars from different disciplines are willing to pool their expertise and analytical resources. Thus, at the outset of the project, a bold decision was made to hire not a linguist but a scholar of international criminal law. As a result, in March 2020, the jurist Juan-Pablo Pérez-León-Acevedo joined the research team. In October of the same year, Fabio Ferraz de Almeida, who had graduated in Law but had done his Ph.D. in the field of Conversation Analysis, came on board. Another person who deserves special mention is Elena Barrett, who joined the project first as a research assistant and data manager, and later as a Ph.D. student. Finding a common language and negotiating shared working practices proved to be a bit of a bumpy road at first, partly because the start of our collaboration coincided with the first wave of the pandemic. But we soon arrived at what Celia Roberts and Srikant Sarangi call *joint problematization*,[6] in which linguists and lawyers each brought their specific expertise to the table and worked together to identify the most pressing issues that needed to be addressed. The result was a fascinating journey that led us to explore topics such as the ambiguity of victim participation in ICC proceedings and the tension between the witness and victim roles;[7] the interactive format in which cultural evidence is elicited during courtroom examinations and its subsequent recontextualization and evaluation by the judges;[8] or the ways in which ICC judges navigate the tension between the hybrid inquisitorial-civil law and accusatorial-common law legacies of ICC courtroom procedure when questioning witnesses.[9]

See B. Dupret, M. Lynch, and T. Berard (eds.), *Law at Work: Studies in Legal Ethnomethods*. (Oxford University Press, New York, 2015).

6 *See* C. Roberts and S. Sarangi, 'Uptake of Discourse Research in Interprofessional Settings: Reporting from Medical Consultancy', 24(3) Applied Linguistics (2003) 338–359, doi: 10.1093/applin/24.3.338.

7 *See* S. D'hondt, J.P. Peréz-León-Acevedo and E. Barrett, 'The Indeterminacy of Precedent: Negotiating the Admissibility of Victim Participant Testimony before the International Criminal Court', 22(5–6) *International Criminal Law Review* (2022) 1068–1093, doi: 10.1163/15718123-bja10082; S. D'hondt, J.P. Peréz-León-Acevedo, F. Ferraz de Almeida and E. Barrett, 'Evidence About Harm: Dual Status Victim Participant Testimony at the International Criminal Court and the Straitjacketing of Narratives About Suffering', 33(3) *Criminal Law Forum* (2022) 191–232, doi: 10.1007/s10609-022-09442-8.

8 *See* S. D'hondt, J.P. Peréz-León-Acevedo, F. Ferraz de Almeida and E. Barrett, 'Trajectories of spirituality: Producing and assessing cultural evidence at the International Criminal Court', *Language in Society* (forthcoming), doi: 10.1017/S0047404523001008.

9 *See* F. Ferraz de Almeida and E. Barrett, 'The Ambivalence of Judicial Interventions at the International Criminal Court'. In T. Grieshofer and K. Haworth (eds.) *Communication and Legal Practice* (Cambridge University Press, forthcoming).

Of course, such dialogues are never limited to only the members of the project team. On October 28–29, 2021, still under COVID restrictions, the University of Jyväskylä hosted a webinar on dialogical and interdisciplinary approaches to the ICC trial of Ahmad Al Faqi Al Mahdi, a Malian jihadist found guilty of destroying cultural heritage in Timbuktu. Inspired by Max Gluckman's extended-case method (which he used to identify the various tensions and dilemmas of colonial society as they played out in a bridge-opening ceremony in 1940s South Africa), the webinar sought to develop a new perspective on the tensions and dilemmas of international criminal justice through the prism of a single trial. The result was a small event, in which linguistic anthropologists and discourse analysts interacted with legal scholars, historians, political scientists, and ethnomethodologists. The experience was refreshing. The participants may have been isolated in front of their laptops and faced the challenge of navigating different zones, but a sense of intimacy and camaraderie quickly developed as common interests emerged and new opportunities for collaboration presented themselves.

It was in the wake of this workshop that Juan-Pablo and Fabio approached me with a proposal to organize a similar event around the trial of Dominic Ongwen. The rest is history, and eventually led to the present collection of articles. In this sense, the volume you are now holding in your hands is not only the result of dialogue. It is also the product of trust, and of a growing understanding that, as a principal investigator, you sometimes need to take a step back and give others around you the space to pursue their own projects. This book is proof that that trust was justified.

Sigurd D'hondt

Notes on Contributors

Juan-Pablo Perez-Leon-Acevedo
is pursuing a second doctoral degree: the DPhil in Law at the University of Oxford, UK. He has also been a tutor in international law and tort law and a moot court coach at the University of Oxford plus a tutor in the Stanford in Oxford programme. He holds a PhD from Åbo Akademi University (Finland), an LLM from Columbia University (USA), and an LLB from Catholic University of Peru. He has also served in different capacities at, among others, the International Criminal Court, the International Criminal Tribunal for the Former Yugoslavia, the United Nations, the University of Jyvaskyla (Finland) and the University of Oslo.

Fabio Ferraz de Almeida
is a lecturer in criminology at the University of Lincoln, UK. His work focuses on social interactions in police and judicial settings. He has conducted research in a variety of criminal justice settings, including Brazilian criminal courts, police interviews in England and, more recently, the International Criminal Court.

Giovanna Frisso
is a senior lecturer at the University of Lincoln—UK, where she coordinates the LLM module on International Criminal Justice. Her areas of interest are theories of international law, international criminal law and international human rights law.

Fangyi Li
is a PhD candidate at Edinburgh Law School, researching on local conceptions of harm, victimhood, and redress in post-conflict Cambodia and Timor-Leste as alternatives to liberal understandings of transitional justice. Her research interests include transitional justice, international criminal law, critical theory, and sensory approaches to law.

Kathleen M. Maloney
is a visiting law professor at Lewis & Clark Law School, teaching international criminal law, human trafficking, international human rights, and public international law for almost 15 years. She was part of a global feminist collective as amicus curiae to ensure gender justice in the ICC *Ongwen* case on appeal.

As a visiting professional in the ICC's Appeals Chamber, she drafted opinions for Chief Judge Navi Pillay on multiple appeals regarding child soldiers, sexual and gender-based violence, and other atrocities. Her recent publications in law reviews and on legal blog posts concern forced marriage in armed conflicts and other grave gender-based crimes. She is a graduate of Stanford University (MA, BA), the University of Arizona's College of Law (JD), and Oxford University (MSt, LLM equiv.) and has taught at Willamette University's School of Law's International Human Rights Clinic.

Christelle Molima Bameka
is a scientific coordinator of the Law and Society Initiative of the University of Lausanne (Switzerland). She is the author of *Enfants soldats et reinsertion socio- communautaire. Questions de responsabilité pénale en droit international et national congolais* (2022) and co- editor of *Children and Violence. Agency, Experience, and Representation in and beyond Armed Conflict* (with Jastine C. Barrett, Mohamed Kamara, Karl Hanson, and Mark A. Drumbl, 2025).

Linda Mushoriwa
is a researcher at the African Centre for Transnational Criminal Justice (ACTCJ), Faculty of Law, University of the Western Cape. She teaches the International Criminal Law module in the LLM in Transnational Criminal Justice programme. She is Associate Editor for the African Student Law Journal published by the University of the Western Cape. She obtained her PhD degree in international criminal law from the University of KwaZulu Natal in South Africa in 2019.

Adina-Loredana Nistor
is a lecturer in criminology in the Faculty of Law at Vrije Universiteit Amsterdam, Netherlands. She is also a PhD candidate in International Criminal Law at the University of Groningen, Netherlands. Her research explores how cultural differences impact international trials throughout their proceedings, with a particular focus on the International Criminal Court.

Windell Nortje
is an associate professor in the Department of Criminal Justice and Procedure at the Faculty of Law, University of the Western Cape, and an advocate of the High Court of South Africa. He was a former recipient of the German Academic Exchange Service (DAAD) LLM and PhD scholarships. His research interests focus on criminal procedure, international criminal law and the decolonisation of the education landscape in the Global South.

Melanie O'Brien
is Associate Professor of International Law and Deputy Head of School (Research) at UWA Law School, and President of the International Association of Genocide Scholars. Recognised for her expertise in international criminal law, her work on forced marriage has been cited by the International Criminal Court, and she has advised multiple UN bodies, conducted research across six continents, and is frequently consulted by global media. Her publications include *From Discrimination to Death.*

Valerie Oosterveld
is the Western Research Chair in International Criminal Justice and a full Professor at the Faculty Law, University of Western Ontario (Canada). She has published widely on gender-based international crimes, and on gender-sensitive investigation and prosecution of these crimes. She is the co-editor of the award-winning book, Gender and International Criminal Law (OUP, 2022). Previously, she served in the Global Affairs Canada Legal Bureau, focussing on international criminal law and the International Criminal Court.

Noëlle Quénivet
is Professor in International Law and Director of Research and Enterprise at the Bristol Law School of the University of West of England (UK). She has published extensively in the fields of international humanitarian law, international criminal law, and human rights law, primarily on issues concerning children and women in armed conflict.

Silvina Sanchez Mera
is a lecturer in law at Robert Gordon University where she teaches law and criminology. She holds a PhD from La Trobe University. Her research focuses on the International Criminal Court's practice regarding intra party crimes and engages with feminist and criminological theories. She has previously worked as a tutor at La Trobe and as a Lecturer in Public International Law and Human Rights Law in Argentina. Her professional experience also includes working as legal officer at a State Juvenile Court, as a researcher for the Defence Counsel at the ICTY and interned at the ECCC. She is a Chevening alumni and an Endeavour Scholar.

Demetra Sorvatzioti
is a professor of law at the University of Nicosia and a trial lawyer with expertise in both common and continental criminal justice systems. She holds two

PhDs, the most recent in international criminal evidence law from Queen's University, Canada. She serves on the advisory board of Fair Trials International and collaborates with the Clooney Foundation for Justice and the University of Montreal. Her work appears in the *Canadian Criminal Law Review* and *International Criminal Law Review*.

Raghavi Viswanath
is a postdoctoral researcher and teaching fellow at the SOAS School of Law, Gender, and Media Studies as well as Law and Humanities Fellow of the Institute of Advanced Legal Studies in London. She holds a doctorate in international law from the European University Institute in Florence. Her areas of interest are epistemic injustice, cultural rights, sensory approaches to international law, racism, and international criminal justice.

CHAPTER 1

Lights and Shadows of the *Ongwen* Case at the International Criminal Court: An Overview

Juan-Pablo Perez-Leon-Acevedo and Fabio Ferraz de Almeida

The Prosecutor v. Dominic Ongwen has arguably been the most complex case adjudicated at the International Criminal Court (ICC).[1] Ongwen was the Commander of the Sinia Brigade of the Lord's Resistance Army (LRA), responsible for a series of crimes against humanity and war crimes perpetrated after 1 July 2002 in Northern Uganda. On 8 July 2005, the ICC issued an arrest warrant, but Ongwen was captured only 10 years later, in early 2015. His trial began on 6 December 2016 at the ICC, where the Prosecution and the Defence presented their respective evidence, and the Legal Representatives of Victims called their witnesses to appear before the Trial Chamber IX. On 12 December 2019, the Presiding Judge declared the closure of evidence submission in the case, and three months later, between 10 and 12 March 2020, the closing statements were delivered.

On 4 February 2021, Trial Chamber IX found the defendant guilty of a total number of 61 crimes comprising crimes against humanity and war crimes, perpetrated in Northern Uganda from 1 July 2002 to 31 December 2005. Subsequently, he was sentenced to 25 years of imprisonment on 6 May 2021. These decisions have been confirmed by the ICC Appeals Chamber on 15 December 2022. Ongwen remained in the ICC detention centre and, then, he was transferred to Norway (December 2023) to serve his sentence of imprisonment. In turn, on 28 February 2024, the ICC Trial Chamber set Ongwen's financial liability to €52,429,000 EUR. It granted collective community-based reparations focused on symbolic measures, rehabilitation, and satisfaction, plus a symbolic award of €750 EUR for victims as well as other community symbolic measures.

The novel and problematic issues underlying the *Ongwen* Case have attracted a large amount of attention from a wide array of actors, including policymakers, lawyers, activists, journalists, and academics. First, Ongwen was convicted of a record number of charges in the ICC's history. Second, he was sentenced to 25 years in prison, which is the second largest prison sentence

1 For official information on the *Ongwen* Case, see: ICC, 'Ongwen Case—The Prosecutor v. Dominic Ongwen ICC-02/04-01/15', at https://www.icc-cpi.int/uganda/ongwen.

 | DOI:10.1163/9789004743380_002

imposed by the ICC. Third, Ongwen holds a double status: a former child soldier abducted by the LRA who rose in rank to be one of the top commanders of this armed group.[2] Fourth, this case required and enabled the ICC to engage with facts concerning diverse acts of sexual and gender-based violence, which has led to the development of novel jurisprudence. Fifth, spirituality related to duress and mental health illness were invoked by the defence as grounds for exoneration of criminal liability, which required the ICC to tackle these matters for the first time in its proceedings and jurisprudence. Sixth, there has been a strong presence of a series of cultural elements, such as the *sui generis* nature of the LRA led by the messianic and despotic Joseph Kony, which underlies diverse issues addressed by the ICC such as witness testimony and victim participation.[3] Seventh, this case reveals in a particularly intense manner the tensions and dilemmas between a ('western'-led) international criminal justice project and the potential or even advisability of local/regional transitional justice initiatives, which in turn powerfully illustrates the ongoing legitimacy crisis of the ICC.[4] Finally, a great deal of media spotlight has been put on this case and, more broadly, on the atrocities committed by the LRA as exemplified by the documentary 'Kony 2012' and attention among diverse personalities (politicians, international media journalists, celebrities, etc.).

Although there have been scholarship pieces dealing with some of these issues in the *Ongwen* Case (or more generally the *Situation in Uganda* at the ICC),[5] there is not a collective book to discuss them in a systemic,

---

2 *See* I. Steflja, J. Trisko Darden and A. Wintersieck, 'Breaking Through the Legal Binary: Media Labelling of Dominic Ongwen as a Victim—Perpetrator', *Social & Legal Studies* (2023), doi.org/10.1177/096466392311953; W. Nortje, 'Victim or Villain: Exploring the Possible Bases of a Defence in the Ongwen Case at the International Criminal Court', 17(1) *International Criminal Law Review* (2017) 186–207, doi.org/10.1163/15718123-01701002.

3 *See* S. D'hondt, J.P. Peréz-León-Acevedo, F. Ferraz de Almeida and E. Barrett, 'Trajectories of spirituality: Producing and assessing cultural evidence at the International Criminal Court', *Language in Society* (forthcoming); A.L. Nistor, A. Merrylees and B. Hola, Spellbound at the International Criminal Court: The intersection of spirituality & international criminal law. In J. Fraser, and B. McGonigle Leyh (eds.), *Intersections of Law and Culture at the International Criminal Court* (Edward Elgar Publishing Limited, 2020), pp. 147–168.

4 *See* L.G. Minkova, 'Expressing what? The stigmatization of the defendant and the ICC's institutional interests in the Ongwen case', 34(1) *Leiden Journal of International Law* (2021) 223–245, doi:10.1017/S0922156520000539.

5 In addition to the publications indicated in the previous footnotes, among others, the following academic pieces can also be of interest: Annie Bunting, 'Gender politics and geopolitics of international criminal law in Uganda', 8(3) *Global Discourse* (2018) 422–437; Filip Strandberg Hassellind, 'The International Criminal Trial as a Site for Contesting Historical and Political Narratives: The Case of Dominic Ongwen', 30(5) *Social & Legal Studies* (2021) 790–809, doi.org/10.1177/0964663920971836; Pascale Chifflet and Ian Freckelton, 'The Mental Incapacity Defence in International Criminal Law: Ramifications from the Ongwen Trial Judgment',

interdisciplinary and multidisciplinary fashion. This book, whose contents correspond to a double special issue published in the *International Criminal Law Review* volumes 23(5–6) (2023) and 24(1) (2024), draws from a selection of papers presented at a two-day conference organised in the context of the project 'Negotiating International Criminal Law'[6] at the University of Jyväskylä (Finland), in which we brought together a large number of scholars whose research addressed issues arising from or related to the *Ongwen* Case. By having the *Ongwen* Case as a case study or 'centre of gravity', the authors contributing to this collection have comprehensively examined those issues listed above in the light of law, anthropology, sociology and other disciplines. We aimed that each contribution identified and discussed both the strengths and weaknesses of the ICC and other actors when dealing with relevant matters in the *Ongwen* Case, namely, the 'lights and shadows' of this pivotal case.

In addition to this introduction and a conclusion piece by us, this edited collection consists of a total of nine chapters. The first chapter is titled 'Fertile or Futile Grounds for Excluding Criminal Responsibility? A Critical Analysis of the Ongwen Judgment in Relation to the Claim of Coercive Environment' authored by Windell Nortje and Noëlle Quénivet. In this chapter, the authors remark that: i) the Defence focused on the coercive environment to which Ongwen was subjected from his abduction as a boy until his surrender as an adult; and ii) the ICC rejected duress as a ground for exonerating criminal responsibility in the scenario of a past and present coercive environment. Thus, the authors discuss the manner in which the ICC interpreted and applied duress in the *Ongwen* Case to then assess whether a coercive environment may be regarded

---

22(4) *International Criminal Law Review* (2022) 751–779, doi.org/10.1163/15718123-bja10138; Lee Hiromoto and Landy F. Sparr, 'Ongwen and Mental Health Defenses at the International Criminal Court', 51(1) *The Journal of the American Academy of Psychiatry and the Law Online* (2023) 61–71, doi.org/10.29158/jaapl.220034-21. It must be also mentioned the articles published in the double special issue of the *International Criminal Law Review* (indicated later in this introduction) that corresponds to the chapters of the present book. After the publication of the case special issue, another special issue related to the *Ongwen* Case has been published in the *Journal of International Criminal Justice*.

6 The project was funded by the Academy of Finland between 2019 and 2023, and it was led by Sigurd D'hondt (University of Jyväskylä). Drawing upon linguistic anthropology and interaction analysis, the research was focused on investigating the discursive production of legitimacy, the interactional negotiation of trial procedure, and the ICC's response to cultural diversity and the plurality of normative orders. *See* S. D'hondt, J.P. Peréz-León-Acevedo, F. Ferraz de Almeida and E. Barrett, 'Evidence About Harm: Dual Status Victim Participant Testimony at the International Criminal Court and the Straitjacketing of Narratives About Suffering', 33(3) *Criminal Law Forum* (2022) 191–232, doi.org/10.1007/s10609-022-09442-8; S. D'hondt, J.P. Peréz-León-Acevedo and E. Barrett, 'The Indeterminacy of Precedent: Negotiating the Admissibility of Victim Participant Testimony before the International Criminal Court', 22(5–6) *International Criminal Law Review* (2021) 1068–1093, doi.org/10.1163/15718123-bja10082.

as a unique defence under the Rome Statute. The chapter proceeds with a scrutiny of whether a coercive environment has been invoked as a defence at the national level. Finally, this contribution evidences that domestic courts have not recognised such a specific defence tailored to atrocities perpetrated in a coercive environment and concludes that the defendants cannot invoke the said defence at the ICC.

The second chapter is 'Forced Marriage as the Crime Against Humanity of "Other Inhumane Acts" in the International Criminal Court's *Ongwen* Case' by Kathleen Maloney , Melanie O'Brien, and Valerie Oosterveld. By highlighting that Ongwen was convicted of a gender-based crime that had never been adjudicated at the ICC, namely, forced marriage, this piece sustained that the judicial consideration of forced marriage in the *Ongwen* Case has settled relevant supranational case law in the following manners. First, the ICC clarified the categorization of forced marriage as an 'other inhumane act'. Second, it recognised and solidified the criminal conduct and resulting harm encapsulated by the term 'forced marriage', differentiating it from other crimes against humanity. Finally, the ICC confirmed that prosecution of forced marriage is consistent with the *nullum crimen sine lege* principle. The authors claim that the said outcomes will play a fundamental role in international criminal justice for forced marriage. Moreover, they argue that the next step is to add forced marriage to the catalogue of acts constitutive of crime against humanity in both the Rome Statute and the draft Crimes Against Humanity Convention.

The third chapter is entitled '*The Prosecutor v Dominic Ongwen*: An Examination of the Role of Traditional Justice Mechanisms in International Criminal Justice' authored by Linda Mushoriwa. By focusing on the ICC's approach to the *Ongwen* Case and bearing in mind that the ICC rejected to incorporate the *mato oput* traditional justice mechanism of the Acholi people of Northern Uganda, it investigates whether traditional justice mechanisms have a place in international criminal justice settings as for the commission of international crimes. This chapter claims that while concerns have been raised concerning the application of traditional justice mechanisms in the aftermath of mass atrocities, the said mechanisms can still play a significant role alongside prosecutions for core international crimes at international criminal tribunals and courts, including the ICC. The author explores manners whereby traditional justice mechanisms may be incorporated into ICC proceedings. She concludes that should the Court aim to be a truly universal court as originally conceived, it must take into account the issues brought before it, particularly from the Global South and in a holistic manner.

The fourth chapter is 'Proportionality and Moral Blameworthiness in Ongwen's ICC Sentencing Decision' by Demetra Sorvatzioti. The author provides an in-depth analysis of sentencing decisions in the *Ongwen* Case and argues that ICC judges failed to address the defendant's unique individual circumstances, i.e., that he was a formed abducted child soldier, and the historical and cultural context in which the crimes occurred. According to Sorvatzioti, although the ICC framework combines continental and common law features, the judges in the *Ongwen* Case sentenced the defendant in a pure continental fashion, ignoring the principle of proportionality that should have governed sentencing determination.

The fifth chapter corresponds to 'Fighters, Not Victims: On Victimhood Recognition and Gender Representations in the Enslavement Charges in the *Ongwen* Case' by Silvina Sánchez Mera. The author remarks that: i) according to the ICC's Office of the Prosecutor (OTP) in the *Ongwen* Case, women were abducted to become wives and men to be soldiers, women were coerced into working and men were obliged to fight; ii) the OTP brought enslavement charges for some of these crimes. Yet, forced fighting of men was not included in. Based on a doctrinal analysis and a feminist approach, the chapter examines the crime of enslavement in the *Ongwen* Case and endeavours to demonstrate how gender representations emerge when international criminal law is applied in detriment of men's victimhood. It is sustained that the application of the law responds to gender representations in armed conflicts. Thus, male soldiers are not regarded as victims and women are continuously considered as non-fighters and victims of armed conflicts. All of this results in a reinforcement of the said representations as well as a lack of acknowledgment of victimhood for men and a reduced recognition of the experiences of women.

In the sixth chapter, titled 'Constructing a sensory alternative to the Ongwen judgement', Raghavi Viswanath and Fangyi Li offer a powerful and original critique of international criminal law in general and the Ongwen judgement in particular. Drawing upon socio-legal scholarship that highlight the reparative values of senses and affect for international criminal justice, the authors argue that the purely textual format of the judgement resulted in epistemic and material injuries on the victims and decontextualized evidence. In response to that, Viswanath and Li make a case for a jurisprudence of senses and show how the current toolboxes of the ICC can be channelled to reimagine judgments in order to provide direct outlets for the voices/faces of the unheard local communities and achieve a more reparative and reconstructive justice.

In the seventh chapter, titled 'Culture and the Illusion of Self-Evidence: Spiritual Beliefs in the Ongwen Trial', Adina-Loredana Nistor sheds light into the way in which culture broadly, and spiritualism in particular, were introduced and assessed by the parties during the Ongwen trial. By analysing transcripts, submissions and other trial documents, the author discusses the complications of introducing an anthropological concept into the terrain of international criminal law. In her analysis, Nistor demonstrates that in the construction of the legal truth, cultural evidence undergoes a process of rationalisation, through which beliefs turn into patterns, and then into certainties. The chapter poses a series of questions about the way in which culture as evidence impacts the delivery of justice in the case of international criminal proceedings.

The eighth chapter is 'The Post-*Ongwen* Case Period and the Reconciliation Process in Northern Uganda: Local Communities as a Site of Knowledge', by Christelle Molima. Drawing upon a series of focus groups conducted with former abducted child soldiers and their parents in Northern Uganda, the author examines the construction of different narratives about child soldiers and ideas about human rights, before exploring how these representations may forge future transitional justice mechanisms around the world. According to the author, these narratives illustrate, for example, the different ways in which child soldiers are perceived by members of their communities: they can be either victims or perpetrators. The author concludes that, in view of these multiple forms of comprehending criminal responsibility in the context of the events in Northern Uganda, restorative peace initiatives should move away from offering a one-size-fits-all solution to all those involved in that conflict.

The final piece is 'Children born of war: the recognition of children born of war as victims in the *Ongwen* case' by Giovanna Frisso. The author investigates the manner in which the experiences of children born of war were approached in the *Ongwen* Case by drawing special attention to their recognition as direct victims. However, the chapter sustains that the recognition of children born of war as direct victims demands to translate one's moral intuition concerning the wrongful act committed against these children into an international crime under the ICC's jurisdiction. The chapter further argues that, if the Rome Statute is not amended, the said process may be very difficult because tackling issues long contested in scholarship on procreative wrongfulness will be necessary.

To conclude, we would like to extend our gratitude to Brill Publishers as well as the *International Criminal Law Review*, in particular to its editor-in-chief, Caroline Fournet, for providing us with the opportunity to publish this book and (previously) the above-mentioned double special issue, for the respective re-publication authorizations, and for the unwavering support throughout the process of organising this collection. Our appreciation also goes to the authors, for their original and thought-provoking contributions, and to the reviewers, whose meticulous feedback enhanced the quality of the published chapters. We hope that this book 'Lights and Shadows of the *Ongwen* Case at the International Criminal Court' will stimulate those interested in understanding this unique case and its complexities from various angles. Enjoy your reading!

CHAPTER 2

Fertile or Futile Grounds for Excluding Criminal Responsibility? A Critical Analysis of the *Ongwen* Judgment in Relation to the Claim of Coercive Environment

Windell Nortje and Noëlle Quénivet

Abstract

Dominic Ongwen was convicted and sentenced for numerous atrocities by the International Criminal Court (ICC) in 2021. The Defence focused on the coercive environment that Ongwen was subjected to from his abduction as a boy until his surrender as an adult. The ICC rejected the claim of duress as a ground for excluding criminal responsibility in the context of a past and present coercive environment. This article examines how the ICC interpreted and applied duress in the *Ongwen* case and evaluates whether a coercive environment can be categorised as a unique defence in the ICC Statute. This is done by scrutinising whether a coercive environment has been raised as a defence in domestic jurisdictions. This paper shows that national courts have not recognised a defence specific to crimes committed in a coercive environment and thus concludes that no such defence can be used by defendants before the ICC.

Keywords

child soldiers – coercive environment – *Ongwen* – grounds for excluding responsibility – duress – ICC Statute

1 Introduction

Children growing up in a war context suffer immensely and child soldiers even more as they must learn to survive amongst the violence and terror inflicted

 | DOI: 10.1163/9789004743380_003

upon, around and by them. The recent judgment[1] and sentencing[2] by the International Criminal Court (ICC) of Dominic Ongwen, a former child soldier turned warlord in the LRA in Uganda, has put a face on this myriad of child soldiers. Assuredly, he might not be representative of all child soldiers, but he certainly is one of them. He was found guilty of 61 crimes comprising crimes against humanity and war crimes and sentenced to 25 years imprisonment. Judgment and sentencing were confirmed on appeal.[3] Throughout the trial, his Defence argued that he should not be held responsible for these crimes. Yet, none of the grounds for excluding responsibility advanced by the Defence—duress and mental defect—were accepted.

Duress, a ground for excluding responsibility listed in Article 31(1)(d) ICC Statute,[4] was used to absolve Ongwen of his crimes whilst his Defence team repeatedly and unsuccessfully stressed the coercive environment in which he grew up and lived: 'throughout the turns and twists in the armed conflicts between the government of Uganda and the LRA, [Ongwen] lived his life under *duress*',[5] 'the environment of *duress* never dissipated as Dominic remained in the rebel group. His so-called promotions in the rebel ranks were demonstrative of one thing; development of a higher survival instinct than others while under *duress* in the bush.'[6] The central aspect of such characterisations was that Ongwen had carried out these acts because he had no choice; external factors were forcing him to act in such a manner.

One of the basic tenets of criminal justice is *actus me invito factus non est meus actus*, an act done by me against my will is not my act.[7] Ongwen argued

1 ICC, *Prosecutor* v. *Ongwen*, ICC -02/04-01/15, Trial Chamber, Judgment, 4 February 2021 (ICC *Ongwen* Judgment).

2 ICC, *Prosecutor* v. *Ongwen*, ICC -02/04-01/15, Trial Chamber, Sentencing Judgment, 6 May 2021 (ICC *Ongwen* Sentencing).

3 ICC, *Prosecutor* v. *Ongwen*, ICC -02/04-01/15, Appeals Chamber, Judgment on the Appeal of Mr Ongwen against the Decision of Trial Chamber IX of 4 February 2021 Entitled "Trial Judgment", 15 December 2022 (ICC *Ongwen* Appeal Judgment); ICC, *Prosecutor* v. *Ongwen*, ICC -02/04-01/15, Appeals Chamber, Judgment on the Appeal of Mr Dominic Ongwen against the Decision of Trial Chamber IX of 6 May 2021 entitled "Sentence", 15 December 2022 (ICC *Ongwen* Appeal Sentencing).

4 Rome Statute of the International Criminal Court, 1998, 2187 UNTS 90 (ICC Statute).

5 ICC, *Prosecutor* v. *Ongwen*, ICC -02/04-01/15-T-22-ENG, Transcript of the Confirmation of Charges, 57, lines 3–4 (emphasis added).

6 *Ibid.*, lines 19–22 (emphasis added).

7 R.L.A. Pangalangan, 'Dominic Ongwen and the Rotten Social Background Defense: The Criminal Culpability of Child Soldiers Turned War Criminals', 33(3) *American University International Law Review* (2018) 605–635, p. 608. *See* D. Byrd, *Islam in a Post-Secular Society: Religion, Secularity and the Antagonism of Recalcitrant Faith* (Brill, Leiden, 2017) p. 297.

that he did not choose a life of crime; rather life chose it for him. The Defence provided ample evidence of the coercive environment that he endured, noting that the same harsh environment with devastating long-term effects on child soldiers had been previously acknowledged by the ICC. Yet, the Court dismissed the defence of duress on the basis of a coercive environment and its long-term effects.

This paper argues that the Court rejected the defence correctly because duress cannot be applied in a coercive environment. As Article 31(3) ICC Statute does not expressly recognise a coercive environment-related defence, albeit that it considers the possibility of using other defences, this article scrutinises alternative defences grounded in national law. Whilst not claiming to be representative of defences worldwide, this unprecedented overview reveals that it is highly unlikely that such an alternative defence exists. The article contends that, even if the Court had been creative, it would not have been able to fathom an accepted coercive environment-related defence.

Using the example of Ongwen, after sketching the coercive environment in which child soldiers grow up and live, this article analyses the ICC's decision to reject duress as a ground for excluding responsibility in *Ongwen*. After contending that the ICC Statute allows for broadening the range of grounds for excluding responsibility, it offers an *aperçu* of alternative defences found in national law, first focusing on defences based on the fact that the criminal act was caused by external factors and then examining defences in a detention context. It concludes that presently no ground for excluding responsibility is available to (former) child soldiers like Ongwen.

2 Child Soldiers, Ongwen and Coercive Environments

Child soldiers undergo a process of brutalisation and indoctrination that ensures their obedience and normalises violence as a method of interaction. Trapped in that coercive environment, they are obliged to act in a certain manner. Even as adults, they suffer from their experiences. Taking Dominic Ongwen as an example of a child soldier, this section defines the concept of a 'coercive environment' in the context of child soldering and sets out the long-term consequences of child soldiering.

2.1 *Child Soldiers, Coercive Environments and Ongwen, the 'Child' Soldier*

Child soldiers live in a coercive environment from the moment they enter the group until they leave it. The ICC has recognised this situation in relation to child soldiers as victims. Their experience remains extremely traumatic and violent.[8] Besides, 'the … serious trauma that can accompany recruitment including separating children from their families, interrupting or disrupting their schooling and exposing them to an environment of violence and fear,'[9] children are confronted with physical and mental violence. First, they are threatened that they will be killed if they try to flee,[10] and such threats are executed.[11]

Second, military training is carried out brutally. The Prosecution in *Lubanga* explained that children 'were beaten, whipped, imprisoned and inadequately fed, and young girls were raped.'[12] If they disobey orders, they are punished,[13] beaten,[14] and violence is exercised in full view of others[15] for deterrence purposes. In *Ntaganda*, the ICC refers to the acts committed in the training camps for child (and other) soldiers as 'acts … alleged to have been committed in the *institutionalised coercive environment* of the UPC/FPLC'.[16] The Court adds that 'with regard specifically to these children, Mr Ntaganda [and commanders] … were taking advantage of the *coercive environment* in which they were at the time.'[17] Although this statement is limited to a specific context, the conditions described in the camps in *Ntaganda* are typical of those to which child soldiers are subjected. The Prosecution in *Lubanga* acknowledged the existence of this coercive environment, referring to the omnipresent 'environment of terror'.[18] 'The children were terrorised', said Chief Prosecutor Moreno-Ocampo in his opening statement of the *Lubanga* trial.[19]

Third, their young age and underdeveloped morality make them susceptible to indoctrination and other psychological abuse aimed at turning them into

8 *See* R. Brett, 'Adolescents Volunteering for Armed Forces or Armed Groups', 85(852) *International Review of the Red Cross* (2003) 857–866.

9 ICC, *Prosecutor* v. *Lubanga Dyilo*, ICC -01/04-01/06, Trial Chamber I, Judgment Pursuant to Article 74 of the Statute, 14 March 2012, para. 605 (ICC *Lubanga* Judgment).

10 ICC, *Prosecutor* v. *Ntaganda,* ICC -01/4-02/06, Trial Chamber VI, Judgment, 8 July 2019, para. 376 (ICC *Ntaganda* Judgment).

11 *Ibid.*, para. 376.

12 ICC *Lubanga* Judgment, *supra* note 9, para. 32.

13 ICC *Ntaganda* Judgment, *supra* note 10, para. 377. *See also ibid.*, paras 883–889.

14 ICC *Ntaganda* Judgment, *supra* note 10, para. 377.

15 *Ibid.*, para. 818.

16 *Ibid.*, para. 1112 (emphasis added).

17 *Ibid.*, para. 1195 (emphasis added).

18 ICC, *Prosecutor* v. *Ongwen*, ICC -01/04-01/06, Opening Statement of Moreno-Ocampo, 26 January 2009, p. 6, lines 8–11.

19 *Ibid.*, p. 7, line 10.

killers.[20] In *Ntaganda*, the ICC found that child soldiers, as 'vulnerable soldiers were subjected to conditions of living and training which could only have the impact of increasing their vulnerability and making them even more docile and submissive to their commanders.'[21] It observed that such 'conditions of living, training and service' 'were, beyond reasonable doubt, of such a nature that the soldiers reliably acted in complete obedience in the execution of orders', further adding that 'the will of the individual soldiers was irrelevant for the execution of a given order.'[22] Even, if they do not adhere to the values of the group, they see no choice but to comply.[23] Research reveals that child soldiering does not destroy *per se* the capacities of moral agency, but creates considerable risks of harm to moral development in the sense that child soldiers apply moral concepts in a problematic way, i.e. consistent with the values and the notions of right and wrong as known in the group.[24]

Fourth, violence becomes normal, child soldiers being 'empty vessels into which the capacity for violence has been poured'[25] and they, willingly, partake in the commission of crimes.[26]

Ongwen was brutally abducted on his way to school in 1987 when he was nine years old.[27] During the first four days of his abduction, he was initiated, taught how to assemble and fire a gun and witnessed the killing of recaptured escapees.[28] LRA members were forced to obey the rules, as they were placed in constant surveillance, and closely monitored, making it hard to escape.[29]

---

20 J. Kwik, 'The Road to Ongwen: Consolidating Contradictory Child Soldiering Narratives in International Criminal Law', 1 *Asia-Pacific Journal of International Humanitarian Law* (2020) 135–163, pp. 154–155. *See also* SCSL, *Prosecutor* v. *Brima, Kamara and Kanu*, SCSL-2004-16-T, Trial Chamber II, Judgment, 20 June 2007, para. 1275 and SCSL, *Prosecutor* v. *Sesay, Kallon and Gbao*, SCSL-04-15-T, Trial Chamber I, Judgment, 2 March 2009, para. 1616.

21 ICC *Ntaganda* Judgment, *supra* note 10, para. 818.

22 *Ibid.*, para. 819.

23 *See* G. Kan, 'The Prosecution of a Child Victim and a Brutal Warlord: The Competing Narrative of Dominic Ongwen', 5 *SOAS Law Journal* (2018) 70–86, p. 80–81.

24 R.N. Souris, 'Child Soldiering on Trial: An Interdisciplinary Analysis of Responsibility in the Lords' Resistance Army', 13(3) *International Journal of Law in Context* (2017) 316–335, pp. 323–324.

25 A. Honwana, 'Innocent and Guilty: Child-Soldiers as Interstitial and Tactical Agents', in A. Honwana and F. de Boeck (eds.), *Makers and Breakers: Children and Youth in Postcolonial Africa* (Africa World Press, Trenton, NY, 2005) pp. 31–52, p. 48.

26 *See* Souris, *supra* note 24, p. 320.

27 ICC *Ongwen* Sentencing, *supra* note 2, para. 67.

28 *Ibid.*, para. 72.

29 ICC, *Prosecutor* v. *Ongwen*, ICC -02/04-01/15, Appeals Chamber, Defence Appeal Brief Against the Convictions in the Judgment of 4 February 2021, 21 July 2021, paras 556 and 595 (ICC *Ongwen* Defence Appeal Brief).

Ongwen felt permanently watched.[30] The ICC avowed that the LRA adopted 'a disciplinary system to ensure compliance, and it noted that its effect was heightened by the living conditions to which its members were subjected.'[31] This compounded the suffering and emotional strain Ongwen was under owing to living in a coercive environment based on apprehension and constant fear making him susceptible to the authority of Kony who was able to control him.[32] The Defence argued that Kony created a coercive environment where survival depended on following the rules of the LRA.[33] Moreover, indoctrination and constant death threats for disobeying the rules created a coercive environment in which any pre-LRA teachings were suppressed.[34] This type of abuse was compounded by the 'use of witchcraft to intimidate recruits and to magnify perception of the group's power throughout the indoctrination process.'[35] As the Defence claimed, Ongwen 'held his ranks under duress through a methodological process of spiritual indoctrination.'[36]

2.2 *Long-Term Effects of Child Soldiering and Ongwen, the 'Adult' Soldier*

Although the crime of enlisting and conscripting children 'ends only when the child reaches 15 years of age or leaves the force or group',[37] child soldiering has long-term effects. In brief, former child soldiers suffer from a lack of education and social upbringing, PTSD, physical and mental disabilities and disorders, ongoing aggressiveness, depression and dissociation, social stigmas, etc.[38] The ICC in *Lubanga* upheld testimonies by expert witnesses who emphasised the 'devastating long-term consequences' of child soldiers who have 'experienced or witnessed acts of violence'.[39] The Prosecutor, commenting on Lubanga's

30 *Ibid.*, para. 595.

31 *Ibid.*, para. 689.

32 *See* Kan, *supra* note 23, p. 79.

33 ICC, *Prosecutor* v. *Ongwen*, ICC -02/04-01/15, Trial Chamber IX, Defence Closing Brief, 24 February 2020, para. 475 (ICC *Ongwen* Defence Closing Brief).

34 *Ibid.*, para. 576.

35 J.T.D. Kelly, L. Branham and M.R Decker, 'Abducted Children and Youth in Lord's Resistance Army in Northeastern Democratic Republic of the Congo (DRC): Mechanisms of Indoctrination and Control', 10 *Conflict and Health* (2016) 11, p. 4.

36 ICC, *Prosecutor* v. *Ongwen*, ICC -02/04-01/15, Trial Chamber II, Defence Brief for the Confirmation of Charges Hearing, 18 January 2016, para. 106 (ICC *Ongwen* Defence Brief Confirmation of Charges).

37 ICC *Lubanga* Judgment, *supra* note 9, para. 618.

38 *See* Kwik, *supra* note 20, pp. 153–154; ICC, *Prosecutor* v. *Lubanga Dyilo*, ICC -01/04-01/06, Trial Chamber I, Decision on Sentence Pursuant to Article 76 of the Statute, 10 July 2012, paras 40–41 referring to Schauer (expert witness) (ICC *Lubanga* Sentencing).

39 *Ibid.*, para. 39. *See* Kan, *supra* note 23, p. 77.

sentencing, also stressed the physical and psychological scars of child soldiering.[40] In Ongwen the ICC repeated that '[i]t is clear that the impact of the crime on the victims was devastating'.[41] The long-term consequences of child soldiering have thus been acknowledged by the Court.

It can thus be safely stated that Ongwen, as a child soldier, suffered the same fate and that his life after he reached the age of 15 years old, even if he had left the group, was still affected by his experience. Whilst the physicality of the coercive environment might have disappeared once child soldiers have left the group, the group's values and beliefs linger: 'Ongwen's values and beliefs were moulded by his environment while he was a child soldier'.[42] As Drumbl explains, such an environment 'rendered the children as victims damaged for life, with their reality today as deriving from their previous suffering. Once a child soldier in fact, always a child soldier in mind, body, and soul.'[43] As Aguiling Pangalangan poignantly states, 'Ongwen, the Brigadier General, carries with him the same traumas and values formed by Ongwen the child soldier.'[44] The Defence maintained that although Ongwen was an adult when he committed the offences, the ICC should have contemplated the long-term effects of living in a coercive environment where his mental, physical and emotional development was severely impeded.[45]

If child soldiers who have left the group suffer from such devastating effects, one might assume that staying in the group has an even more pervasive effect on them. When child soldiers stay in the group as adults, the coercive environment might seem 'normal' to them as they have integrated all the values, principles, and habits of the group. The physical coerciveness might at times be felt though it has been internalised.[46] To the outsider, it does not seem that the former child soldier is coerced. Yet, as the Defence essentially argued that Kony created a permanent coercive environment. We agree that Ongwen

40 Statement of the Office of the Prosecutor, ICC Prosecutor's Address on the Sentencing of Thomas Lubanga (13 June 2012), available online at www.icc-cpi.int/news/icc-prosecutors-address-sentencing-thomas-lubanga (accessed 2 May 2023).

41 ICC *Ongwen* Sentencing, *supra* note 2, para. 366.

42 Pangalangan, *supra* note 7, p. 629.

43 M.A. Drumbl, *Shifting Narratives: Ongwen and Lubanga on the Effects of Child Soldiering* (20 April 2016), available online at justiceinconflict.org/2016/04/20/shifting-narratives-ongwen-and-lubanga-on-the-effects-of-child-soldiering/ (accessed 2 May 2023).

44 Pangalangan, *supra* note 7, p. 629.

45 ICC *Ongwen* Defence Appeal Brief, *supra* note 29, para. 697.

46 *See* E. Benyera, 'Child Victim, Loyal War Spirit Medium or War Criminal: Shifting the Geography and Logic of Historical Accountability in Dominic Ongwen's ICC Trial', *African Identities* (2021) 1–16, p. 12.

remained under the apprehension of fear of imminent death throughout his entire stay in the LRA as the constant environment of duress or, better phrased, the coercive environment never dissipated.[47]

3 Use of Duress as a Ground for Excluding Responsibility in Relation to a Coercive Environment

Ongwen's Defence raised several times the issue of the coercive environment in which he grew up and lived, even as an adult. To this effect, it used duress as a ground for excluding responsibility for crimes Ongwen committed as an adult; yet the Court rejected this ground. After briefly explaining duress as a ground for excluding criminal responsibility under the ICC Statute and case law, the following sections examine in detail its application in *Ongwen*.

3.1 *Duress as a Ground for Excluding Criminal Responsibility under the ICC Statute*

Article 31 ICC Statute lists admissible 'grounds for excluding criminal responsibility'[48] that can be classed as grounds relating either to the individual's qualities (affecting the capacity to act autonomously) or the circumstances of the act (impeding the freedom of choice): mental disease or defect, intoxication, self-defence, and duress.[49]

Article 31(1)(d) ICC Statute identifies duress as a ground for excluding responsibility and specifies that three requirements must be met for this ground to be successful.[50] First, the defendant must prove that he committed the crime because of a threat of imminent death or of continuing or imminent or serious bodily harm.[51] Moreover his criminal conduct 'must have been in response to a threat of death or serious bodily harm that was aimed at either

47 ICC *Ongwen* Defence Brief Confirmation of Charges, *supra* note 36, para. 4.

48 ICC Statute, *supra* note 4, Articles 31–33.

49 As a non-exhaustive list, other grounds include abandonment (Article 25(3)(f)), exclusion of jurisdiction because the individual is under the age of 18 years old (Article 26), mistake of fact or mistake of law (Article 32), and superiors order and prescription of law (Article 33).

50 ICC *Ongwen* Judgment, *supra* note 1, para. 2581. Prior to the case, some scholars (authors included) considered that there were four requirements. *See* C.F. Moran, 'A Perspective on the Rome Statute's Defence of Duress: The Role of Imminence', 18 *International Criminal Law Review* (2018) 154–177, p. 155; W. Nortje and N. Quénivet, *Child Soldiers and the Defence of Duress in International Criminal Law* (Palgrave, Cham, 2020), p. 50.

51 ICC Statute, *supra* note 4, Article 31(1)(d). *See also* Nortje and Quénivet, *supra* note 50, p. 52.

the actor herself or a third party'[52] and the threat 'may either be: (1) made by other persons or (ii) constituted by other circumstances beyond that person's control'.[53] Further it is not the threat to his life or body that must be immediate but rather the harm itself that is imminent (in case of death) and continuing or imminent (in case of serious bodily harm).[54] 'When imminence is mentioned in duress, the question dealt with by the court or tribunal is really whether the individual had any freedom to choose.'[55] The threat must also be considered real since an elevated probability of danger or a mere abstract danger would not suffice.[56] There must be an 'actual bona fide belief' on the defendant's part that a threat existed at the time, which requires the court to determine whether the defendant subjectively foresaw that the harm was immediate and present.[57] A causal link between the threat and the conduct must be established to determine how the threat impacted the defendant's conduct.[58]

The second requirement is that the defendant must prove that he intended to avert the threat and acted necessarily and reasonably in doing so.[59] This is a subjective and objective test. It is subjective because it determines whether the defendant, in his unique position, showed some resistance to avert the danger, taking into account 'the totality of the circumstances in which the person found themselves'.[60] It also adopts an objective approach 'which includes the question whether a reasonable person would have given in to the threat.'[61] This objective test determines whether a person in a similar position to the defendant's would have acted in the same manner:[62] 'whether others in comparable circumstances were able to necessarily and reasonably avoid

52 ICC *Ongwen* Judgment, *supra* note 1, para. 2581. See J. Bond and M. Fougere, 'Omnipresent Threats: A Comment on the Defence of Duress in International Criminal Law', 14 *International Criminal Law Review* (2014) 471–512, p. 492.

53 ICC *Ongwen* Judgment, *supra* note 1, para. 2581.

54 *Ibid.*, para. 2582.

55 Moran, *supra* note 50, p. 175.

56 ICC *Ongwen* Judgment, *supra* note 1, para. 2582. See A. Eser, 'Article 31: Grounds for Excluding Criminal Responsibility', in O. Triffterer and K. Ambos (eds), *The Rome Statute of the International Criminal Court: A Commentary*, 3rd edn (Beck, Munich, 2016), pp. 1125–1160, at pp. 1149–1150. *See also* Nortje and Quénivet, *supra* note 50, p. 54.

57 Nortje and Quénivet, *supra* note 50, p. 54.

58 *Ibid.*, p. 54.

59 ICC Statute, *supra* note 4, Article 31(1)(d).

60 ICC *Ongwen* Judgment, *supra* note 1, para. 2583.

61 *See* K. Ambos, *Treatise on International Criminal Law: Volume I: Foundations and General Part* (Oxford University Press, Oxford, 2013); Nortje and Quénivet, *supra* note 50, p. 64.

62 B. Krebs, 'Justification and Excuse in Article 31(1) of the Rome Statute', 2(3) *Cambridge Journal of International and Comparative Law* (2013) 382–410, pp. 408–409; Nortje and Quénivet, *supra* note 50, p. 64.

the same threat'.[63] If he had any reasonable opportunity to remove himself from the coercive situation, such as escaping or resisting the coercer, then the defence is unsupportable.[64]

The final requirement is that the defendant 'does not intend to cause a greater harm than the one sought to be avoided.'[65] As the Court explained, '[t]his is a subjective element—it is not required that the person actually avoided the greater harm, only that he/she intended to do so.'[66] To determine whether the harm is greater, the Court is obliged to compare the harms and in doing so it examines the character of the harms.[67]

3.2 *Duress as a Ground for Excluding Criminal Responsibility in the* Ongwen *Case*

Duress was analysed and applied in both the judgment and appeal judgments and was dismissed accordingly. From the outset, it should be noted that the Court did not apply the above-mentioned requirements in a rigorous manner. In the Judgment it boldly ascertained that since 'the first element of duress [...] is not met [...] it is not necessary, or even possible, to consider its remaining elements',[68] eventually concluding 'that there is no basis in the evidence to hold that Dominic Ongwen was subjected to a threat of imminent death or imminent or continuing serious bodily harm to himself or another person at the time of his conduct underlying the charged crimes.'[69] Although the Court was right to reject Ongwen's defence of duress as a ground to exclude criminal responsibility, it is submitted that it should have applied all the Article 31(1)(d) requirements.[70] Concentrating on the first element, given it considered the two other elements irrelevant,[71] the Court focused on some pertinent issues which included (1) Ongwen's position in the hierarchy of the LRA; (2) the execution of Ongwen's fellow commanders; (3) the possibility of escape; (4) Kony's alleged spiritual powers; (5) loyalty and career advancement; and (6) private acts.

63 ICC *Ongwen* Judgment, *supra* note 1, para. 2583.

64 Eser, *supra* note 56, p. 1150; Nortje and Quénivet, *supra* note 50, pp. 58–59.

65 ICC Statute, *supra* note 4, Article 31(1)(d). *See also,* Nortje and Quénivet, *supra* note 50, p. 64.

66 ICC *Ongwen* Judgment, *supra* note 1, para. 2584.

67 *Ibidem.*

68 *Ibid.*, para. 2585.

69 *Ibid.*, para. 2668.

70 Ongwen's situation as a former child soldier turned warlord remains poorly understood and subject to simplistic thinking. M.A. Drumbl, 'Victims', 4 *London Review of International Law* (2016) 217–246, p. 217; Kan, *supra* note 23, p. 77.

71 ICC *Ongwen* Judgment, *supra* note 1, para. 2669.

First, the Court held that, as a senior commander in the LRA, Ongwen did not receive the same threats to his life as low-level commanders[72] and, in fact, personally made death threats to low-level commanders and abductees.[73] The Trial Chamber also heard and accepted numerous witness testimonies explaining that Ongwen was a confident commander who made his own decisions, hence negating the Defence's argument that Ongwen religiously followed Kony's orders or was threatened to do so.[74] The Court held 'that the relationship between Joseph Kony and Dominic Ongwen was not characterised by the complete dominance of the former and subjection of the latter',[75] a point echoed by the Appeals Chamber that claimed that the LRA was a functioning hierarchy with several layers and should not be equated to Kony.[76] The ICC also rejected for lack of evidence the Defence's argument that Ongwen and others were forced to participate in sexual acts.[77]

Second, the Court rejected the Defence's claim that the killings by Kony of other high-ranking commanders like Otti Lagony and Okello Can Odonga were indicative of a threat to Ongwen's life.[78] The Court retorted that Lagony and Odonga were killed for politically challenging Kony's rule,[79] which Ongwen was not.[80] The Appeals Chamber held that Kony at most demoted or threatened to demote commanders not executing his orders.[81] To illustrate this, the Appeals Chamber noted that Ongwen was once reprimanded by Kony for being a weak commander and threatened to demote him.[82] The Appeals Chamber accepted the Prosecution's argument that the commanders were killed for attempting to overthrow Kony.[83]

Third, the Court investigated whether Ongwen could escape.[84] The Court held that various other high-ranking officials escaped between 2002 and 2004, yet Ongwen remained.[85] The Appeals Chamber further accepted the evidence that several senior commanders, in a similar position as Ongwen, were able

72 *Ibid.*, para. 2591.
73 *Ibid.*, para. 2591.
74 *Ibid.*, paras 2594 and 2602.
75 *Ibid.*, para. 2602.
76 ICC *Ongwen* Appeal Judgment, *supra* note 3, para. 735.
77 ICC *Ongwen* Judgment, *supra* note 1, para. 2608.
78 *Ibid.*, para. 2609.
79 *See* ICC *Ongwen* Appeal Judgment, *supra* note 3, para. 735.
80 ICC *Ongwen* Judgment, *supra* note 1, paras 2613 and 2614.
81 ICC *Ongwen* Appeal Judgment, *supra* note 3, paras 1488–1489.
82 *Ibid.*, para. 1489.
83 *See* ICC *Ongwen* Appeal Judgment, *supra* note 3, para.1487.
84 *Ibid.*, para. 2619.
85 *See ibid.*, paras 2621–2628.

to escape the LRA.[86] Low-level LRA officials also testified that they managed to escape.[87] The ICC agreed with the Prosecution's argument that, because of Ongwen's high-ranking position, he was in a better position to escape as opposed to a low-ranking official.[88] The Prosecution further maintained that 'Dominic Ongwen's claim that he could have never escaped are an insult to the thousands of adults and children who showed great courage and resilience in braving the escape from the LRA captors.'[89] Moreover, approximately 21,000 LRA rebels took Uganda's offer for an amnesty in 2000.[90] Ongwen failed to take that opportunity. The Court held that escaping was a realistic option for Ongwen. Since he did not take this option, it meant he was under no serious threat from Kony.[91] The Appeals Chamber held that it was not unreasonable for the Trial Chamber to determine that Ongwen had various opportunities to escape.[92] The Defence, moreover, criticised the Trial Chamber by averting that it cherry-picked several cases of escape based on opportunity and by selecting commanders apparently on the same level as Ongwen,[93] a claim the Appeals Chamber dismissed.[94] This narrative is, however, an oversimplification of the situation. The fear and shame of returning to his community and the fact that he already bought into the ideologies of the LRA through indoctrination and brainwashing further complicates any agency to flee.[95] That he could not have run away is not argued, but such a decision was more difficult to take than presented by the Court.

Fourth, the Court probed the role of Kony's 'spiritual powers'. The Defence asserted that '[t]he indoctrination into Kony's perverted version of spiritualism created a coercive environment .... [that] compelled people to follow rules by preying on their fears of death or severe punishment.'[96] The Court dismissed such an account and, instead, accepted the testimony of other LRA members maintaining that Kony did not possess spiritual powers, and evidence indicating that Ongwen defied Kony's orders at times, all refuting

86 ICC *Ongwen* Appeal Judgment, *supra* note 3, para. 1531.
87 *Ibid.*, para. 2632.
88 *Ibid.*, para. 2634.
89 ICC, *Prosecutor* v. *Ongwen*, ICC -02/04-01/15, Pre-Trial Chamber II, Confirmation of Charges, Open Session, 25 January 2016, p. 35.
90 *See ibid.*, p.35.
91 ICC *Ongwen* Judgment, *supra* note 1, para. 2635.
92 ICC *Ongwen* Appeal Judgment, *supra* note 3, para.1520.
93 *Ibid.*, para. 1530.
94 *Ibid.*, para. 1531.
95 *See* Kan, *supra* note 23, p. 80.
96 ICC *Ongwen* Defence Closing Brief, *supra* note 33, para. 477.

Kony's spiritual influence on Ongwen.[97] On Appeal, the Defence argued, *inter alia*, that spiritualism in the LRA was 'inextricably interwoven' with duress and that the Trial Chamber did not consider its effects on abducted child soldiers.[98] It held further that the assessment of spiritualism required an in-depth analysis of the subjective belief of Ongwen *at the time*.[99] The Appeals Chamber disagreed and held that the Trial Chamber did not err in holding that the evidence showed that spiritualism subsided once the abducted child grew older.[100] Put simply, only children are susceptible to these beliefs and as an adult, it was not possible that Ongwen held such beliefs.

Fifth, in analysing Ongwen's career advancement and his positions in the LRA, the Court whilst acknowledging that these were held for having followed many of Kony's orders, also submitted that much of Ongwen's conduct resulted from his own initiative, free from any fear or threats.[101] The Trial Chamber noted that Ongwen's conduct was regularly praised by Kony and held that Ongwen resembled 'a commander in control of his unit, directing its organisation and its actions according to his own planning.'[102] The Appeals Chamber dismissed the Defence's argument that the Trial Chamber erred in its assessment of intercepted LRA communications since the Defence did not provide any evidence of this.[103]

Last but not least, to hammer in the point that Ongwen was not under duress when committing the crimes, the Court examined his behaviour in private, i.e., away from all external pressures. The Trial Chamber held that Ongwen never told the young girls he raped in his tent that they could simply pretend to have sex, thereby pleasing Kony's orders for them to have sex.[104] Ongwen never protected the girls from sex, and this was enough evidence for the Trial Chamber to hold that Ongwen could have prevented sexual offences from occurring in private. On Appeal, the Defence held that the Trial Chamber erred in holding that the commission of sexual offences was 'in private' and 'indicative' of the fact that Ongwen was not under duress when he committed these offences.[105] The Appeals Chamber agreed that Ongwen committed

---

97 ICC *Ongwen* Judgment, *supra* note 1, para. 2658.
98 *Ibid.*, para. 1540.
99 *Ibid.*
100 *Ibid.*, para. 1554.
101 *Ibid.*, para. 2665.
102 *Ibid.*
103 ICC *Ongwen* Appeal Judgment, *supra* note 3, para. 1529.
104 ICC *Ongwen* Judgment, *supra* note 1, paras 2666–2667.
105 ICC *Ongwen* Appeal Judgment, *supra* note 3, para. 1563.

sexual offences in his sleeping place where no threats made to him could have any effect.[106]

3.3 *Duress and the Coercive Environment*

Applying duress to Ongwen as a possible ground for excluding criminal responsibility was always going to be challenging for the Defence. The problem, we submit, is that the past coercive environment of child soldiers (and especially their experience) and the present coercive environment of former child soldiers who stayed in the armed forces or group cannot *as such* be equated with duress. This is obvious when examining how the Trial and Appeals Chambers deal with the Defence's reliance on (1) Ongwen's past status as a victim of child soldiering growing up in a coercive environment and (2) the continuous spiritualism, ingrained indoctrination and a continuous coercive environment within the LRA, which it argued created an environment conducive to duress.[107]

The Trial and Appeals Chambers stressed on numerous occasions that his experience as a victim of child soldiering himself could not exclude his criminal accountability as an adult.[108] No doubt simply being a former child soldier does not absolve one from crimes committed later in life. However, it is the link between the experience as a child soldier growing up in a coercive environment and the adult that ought to be examined carefully. In *Ongwen* the ICC clearly illustrated the fact that duress is an unsuitable ground for excluding criminal responsibility when an individual has grown up in a coercive environment. To the Defence's argument that Ongwen's childhood abduction and death threats he received as a child were central to the duress defence, the ICC responded that those threats were too far removed from his conduct as an adult.[109] At the Appeal, the Defence insisted that a human cannot be separated from his past and that it was 'pathetic, insensitive and factually and legally erroneous' for the Trial Chamber to focus solely on Ongwen's situation as a commander and mostly ignoring his history as a child soldier.[110] The Defence contended that the Trial Chamber should have considered (1) Ongwen's 'childhood immediately before and after his abduction'; (2) the 'vicissitudes and vacillations of his life under the coercive environment'; and (3) the special attention he was given

---

106 ICC *Ongwen* Judgment, *supra* note 1, para. 1570.
107 *See* ICC *Ongwen* Appeal Judgment, *supra* note 3, para. 1396.
108 *See, e.g.*, ICC *Ongwen* Appeal Judgment, *supra* note 3, paras 706, 708, 1383, 1471.
109 ICC *Ongwen* Appeal Judgment, *supra* note 3, para. 2592.
110 *Ibid.*, para. 1466.

leading to his expedited rise in rank.[111] The ICC entertained, but dismissed, the claim that there was a link between Ongwen, the child soldier, and Ongwen, the defendant. Both chambers held that the lack of evidence by the Defence to prove that this coercive environment as a child soldier led to him being in a state of duress as an adult, was one of the main reasons why the defence could not apply in this context.[112] In particular, the Appeals Chamber held that there was no evidence that the indoctrination and childhood experience of Ongwen had the effect of bringing about the circumstances identified in Article 31(1)(d).[113] The Appeals Chamber added that the Trial Chamber had 'considered his childhood experiences in its holistic assessment of the evidence relevant to [...] mental disease or defect'.[114] From the perspective of duress as a ground excluding criminal responsibility, the ICC rightfully dismissed Ongwen's dreadful and tragic past, background and experience and the devastating consequences this had on his behaviour as an adult.

The ICC also correctly did not accept that duress covered situations of a continuing, implied, latent coercive environment. The Defence averred that Ongwen, throughout his entire time in the LRA, 'was always under apprehension of continuing imminent serious bodily harm',[115] arguing 'that the threat should be interpreted to include a threat to be killed at a later point in time, and that the threat may emanate from the "perpetual hostile and violent environment" which ruled Mr Ongwen's life at the relevant time of the charges.'[116] The Defence essentially contended that Ongwen should have been able to claim duress due to the coercive environment and that the immediacy of the harm was interpreted too strictly by the Trial Chamber. The Appeals Chamber, however, held that the threat must be present and real at the time of the commission of the offence and 'cannot lie too far in the future.'[117] The Appeals Chamber confirmed the assessment by the Trial Chamber by agreeing that duress is not available where the defendant is threatened with serious bodily harm that is not materialising sufficiently soon.[118] This is one of the main reasons why the Defence failed in raising duress in such a coercive environment which Ongwen found himself in—at the time of the commission

111 *Ibid.*, para. 1467.
112 *See* ICC Ongwen Judgment, *supra* note 1, paras 2606, 2614, 2658, 2668; ICC Ongwen Appeal Judgment, *Ibid.*, paras 1389, 1414, 1434,
113 ICC *Ongwen* Appeal Judgment, *supra* note 3, para. 1434.
114 *Ibid.*, para. 1472.
115 *Ibid.*, para. 1398.
116 *Ibid.*, para. 1422.
117 *Ibid.*, para. 1423.
118 *Ibid.*, para. 1423.

of the offences the coercive environment was simply not dangerous and immediate enough to excuse his abhorrent conduct. The Appeals Chamber also agreed with the Trial Chamber's decision that Ongwen was not under an immediate threat of death considering that he made his own decisions and even spared the lives of some victims.[119]

In conclusion, duress, as a ground for excluding criminal responsibility, cannot be raised in relation to a person's past, background and experience in a coercive environment nor in the situation of a coercive environment where the harm is not immediate or continuing and/or based on a defendant's (real or perceived) apprehension based on their past experience.

4 Broadening the Range of Grounds for Excluding Responsibility in a Coercive Environment

Since the defence of duress is inadequate to exclude responsibility for crimes committed in a coercive environment, a defendant might seek to explore alternative defences.

According to Article 31(3) ICC Statute, the ICC is not limited to the defences expressly listed therein but can also use other defences: 'where such a ground is derived from applicable law as set forth in Article 21.' Article 21(1) in particular specifies the order in which the Court ought to use the applicable law. First, the Court must refer to the 'Statute, Elements of Crimes and its Rules of Procedure and Evidence'.[120] As seen, the Statute and the Rules of Procedure and Evidence are not useful. Second, the Court should turn towards 'applicable treaties and the principles and rules of international law, including the established principles of the international law of armed conflict'.[121] As there are no treaties on grounds for excluding responsibility and the established principles and rules of international law are limited to referring to duress, this source is again of limited use. The third and last resort potential source of ICC law[122] is

> general principles of law derived by the Court from national laws of legal systems of the world including, as appropriate, the national laws of States

---

119 *Ibid.*, para. 1452.

120 ICC Statute, *supra* note 4, Article 21(1)(a).

121 *Ibid.*, Article 21(1)(b).

122 *See* M. Boumghar, 'Quelques utilisations des principes généraux du droit international et des principes généraux de droit en droit international pénal', *African Yearbook of International Law* (2012) 97–137, pp. 117–119.

> that would normally exercise jurisdiction over the crime, provided that those principles are not inconsistent with this Statute and with international law and internationally recognized norms and standards.[123]

Whilst the ICC can thus use alternative defences grounded in national legal systems, several caveats must be stressed. As Ambos explains, any such principle 'must be based on comparative criminal law and not on one legal tradition alone' and 'must be comprehensible and accessible not only to those limited experts from a specific legal tradition but also to lawyers from all legal traditions'.[124] Cognizant of the difficulty to undertake such a comparative survey[125] within the constraints of this paper, its focus is on the most relevant national defences mentioned in English-language literature and then on ascertaining whether they were used in other jurisdictions. Moreover, it must be stressed that defences are fundamentally value-laden; they irresistibly depend on which acts society condemns, permits and tolerates.[126] Also, in importing national law into international criminal law the specificity, context and scope of international crimes, in contrast to 'common' crimes, must be given due consideration.

Whether specific national defences might be suitable to the situation of individuals in a coercive environment and, more specifically, to (former) child soldiers, must be determined on the basis that defendants (1) claim that external factors were at play and (2) they have engaged in unlawful activities against the general public and not against the person who has established and is maintaining the coercive environment.[127] Consequently, the following defences are considered: the rotten social background defence and the brainwashing or indoctrination defence. The reasons for focusing on these defences are that they have already been suggested by academics (see below) and whilst it is acknowledged that they all or mostly stem from the American legal system (a legal system that allows for a wider range of defences to be mounted) they have been chosen for explorative purposes rather than to

123 ICC Statute, *supra* note 4, Article 21(1)(c).

124 K. Ambos, 'Remarks on the General Part of International Criminal Law', 4 *Journal of International Criminal Justice* (2006) 660–673, p. 662. *See also* Boumghar, *supra* note 122, p. 126.

125 *See* O. Quirico, 'General Principles of International Criminal Law and their Relevant to Africa', *African Yearbook of International Law* (2012) 139–163, p. 160.

126 M.C. Bassiouni, *Introduction to International Criminal Law*, 2nd edn. (Martinus Nijhoff, Leiden, 2013), p. 285.

127 This sets aside defences relating to victims of abuse at home who commit crimes against their abusers, and the battered woman's syndrome.

provide a full picture of all potential alternative defences available worldwide. Moreover, mindful of the context in which international crimes are committed and the specificity of such crimes as well as the need to understand better the impact of the coercive environment on an individual through the prism of detention which is *per se* a coercive environment, defences raised in two specific situations are scrutinised: the prosecution of (1) individuals held as prisoners in the context of an armed conflict and (2) 'Kapos' of concentration and labour camps during WWII. It should also be borne in mind that this paper cannot provide an exhaustive analysis of all the cases where these defences were raised and thus uses the most prominent and representative (in relation to a coercive environment) cases for illustrative purposes.

5 Defences Based on Criminal Acts Caused by External Factors

Duress is a ground for excluding responsibility based on individuals claiming that external factors constrained their choice to such a level that they had no choice. The defences of rotten social background (that has only been raised in US courts) and brainwashing/indoctrination work on a similar basis as in both instances the defendants' criminal behaviour is caused by external factors beyond their control.[128] They are thus defences that could be reckoned with by the ICC, should they meet the requirements of being recognised as defences and general principles of law.

5.1 *The Rotten Social Background Defence*

The rotten social background defence recognises 'the relationship between environmental adversity and criminal propensity,'[129] thus acknowledging that an individual's criminal behaviour might be explained by environmental, external factors. Consequently, 'when environmental tensions create a predisposition to commit a crime, it would be an injustice to adjudge culpability'.[130] As Harris bluntly enounces, '[i]f society has failed to be responsible to its citizens, those citizens cannot justly be held "responsible" for their crimes against that society.'[131] The possibility of using this defence

---

128 Pangalangan, *supra* note 7, p. 627.

129 *Ibid.*, p. 609.

130 *Ibid.*

131 A.P. Harris, 'Rotten Social Background and the Temper of the Times', 2(1) *Alabama Civil Rights & Civil Liberties Law Review* (2011) 131–146, p. 134.

in relation to child soldiers has already been mounted by Pangalangan[132] and Brown[133] and was used, though not expressly, by Ongwen's Defence[134] and flatly rejected by the Court.[135]

This defence emerged for the first time in the dissenting opinion of Judge Bazelon in *US v. Alexander*, a case that dealt with Murdock who had shot and killed a Marine who called him a 'black bastard'. Judge Bazelon explained that the rotten social background evidence should not have been dismissed and that '[t]he thrust of Murdock's defense was that the environment in which he was raised—his "rotten social background"- conditioned him to respond to certain stimuli in a manner most of us would consider flagrantly inappropriate. Because of his early conditioning, he argued, he was denied any meaningful choice when the racial insult triggered the explosion in the restaurant.'[136] Delgado championed that defence, maintaining that external factors create a propensity to perpetrate crimes; he argues that persons who grow grown up 'in socially deprived environments do not have the same chances to absorb the majority's legal and moral norms'.[137] The defence appears best acknowledged in relation to children who have grown up in such an environment,[138] notably because developmental psychology supports the view that 'developmental trajectories are established in early childhood'.[139]

---

132 Pangalangan, *supra* note 7, p. 605.

133 J. Brown, 'When Children Are Trained to Kill: A Look at the Victim-Perpetrator Debate in the United States and Uganda', 38(3) *Arizona Journal of International & Comparative Law* (2022) 375–401, p. 375.

134 ICC, *Prosecutor* v. *Ongwen*, ICC -02/04-01/15, Pre-Trial Chamber II, Further Redacted Version of "Defence Brief for the Confirmation of Charges Hearing", filed on 18 January 2016, 3 March 2016, paras 36–49. *See* also discussion above.

135 ICC, *Prosecutor* v. *Ongwen*, ICC -02/04-01/15, Pre-Trial Chamber II, Decision on the Confirmation of Charges against Dominic Ongwen, 23 March 2016, para. 150 (ICC *Ongwen* Confirmation of Charges).

136 *U.S.* v. *Alexander*, 471 F.2d 923, 960 (D.C. Cir. 1973). *See* M.A. Jayaraman, 'Rotten Social Background Revisited', 14(2) *Capital Defence Journal* (2002) 327–348, pp. 327–329.

137 R. Delgado, 'Rotten Social Background: Should the Criminal Law Recognize a Defense of Severe Environmental Deprivation?', 3 *Law and Inequality* (1985) 9–90, pp. 55–56. *See also* E. Luna, 'Spoiled Rotten Social Background', 2 *Alabama Civil Rights & Civil Liberties Law Review* (2011) 23–51, p. 45.

138 P. Robinson, 'Are we Responsible for Who we Are? The Challenge for Criminal Law Theory in the Defenses of Coercive Indoctrination and "Rotten Social Background"', 2 *Alabama Civil Rights & Civil Liberties Law Review* (2011) 53–77, pp. 54 and 69–74 referring to Cabarga, a boy who suffered abuse and indoctrination at the hands of a sexual predator after a rather disturbed youth and helped his abuser groom children.

139 M. Tonry, *Doing Justice, Preventing Crime* (Oxford University Press, Oxford, 2020), p. 81.

Using this defence is undoubtedly controversial since many issues can be raised at a practical, theoretical and policy level. First, the defence has never been successfully pleaded as a stand-alone defence in American courts[140] and 'has failed utterly to gain any real world traction'.[141] If a person's social background was used to negate legal responsibility, it was linked to a defence of insanity.[142] In other jurisdictions such as Australia and Canada, it was only raised as a mitigating factor.[143] Second, as Delgado himself avows, the relationship between deprivation and criminal responsibility 'while intuitive and compelling, still has yet to be determined'.[144] Moreover, many people with a rotten social background do not become criminals.[145] Third, as Morse explains, 'all environments affect choice, making some choices easy and others hard'.[146] And whilst there might be a correlation (though not necessarily a causal relationship[147]) between the environment and a propensity to commit a crime, an element of personal choice remains.[148] Furthermore, as Jayaraman explains, 'the cognitive requirement of "knowledge" or right and wrong will usually be met as well because, despite a rough childhood, the defendant usually knows that killing is wrong'.[149] Fourth, as the defence works on the basis of social determinism, an entire class of individuals could be viewed as criminals or at least viewed in the same brushstroke. Whilst criminologists involved in international criminal justice have argued that 'certain social environments may be inherently "criminogenic", producing cultures of criminality',[150] accepting such social determinism would at a policy level open

140 Jayaraman, *supra* note 136, p. 330; Brown, *supra* note 133, p. 386.

141 E.W. Lambert, 'A Way out of the "Rotten Social Background" Stalemate: "Scarcity" and Stephen Morse's Proposed Generic Partial Excuse', 21 *University of Pennsylvania Journal of Law and Social Change* (2018) 297–338, p. 299.

142 P. Arenella, 'Demystifying Abuse Excuse: Is There One?', 19 *Harvard Journal of Law & Public Policy* (1996) 703–710, p. 704.

143 *See* Tonry, *supra* note 139, p. 93.

144 R. Delgado, 'The Wretched of the Earth', 2 *Alabama Civil Rights & Civil Liberties Law Review* (2011) 1–22, 5. *See also* Luna, *supra* note 137, p. 45; Robinson, *supra* note 138, pp. 58–59.

145 Robinson, *supra* note 138, p. 75; S. Morse, 'The Twilight of Welfare Criminology: A Reply to Judge Bazelon', 49 *Southern California Law Review* (1976) 1247–1268, pp. 1252 and 1259.

146 Morse, *supra* note 145, p. 1252.

147 *See* Robinson, *supra* note 138, p. 59.

148 Morse, *supra* note 145, p. 1259. *See also* Tonry, *supra* note 139, pp. 80–84.

149 Jayaraman, *supra* note 136, p. 343. *See also*, S. Kadish, 'Excusing Crime', 75 *California Law Review* (1987) 257–289, pp. 284–285; and J. Dressler, 'Some Very Modest Reflections on Excusing Criminal Wrongdoers', 42 *Texas Tech Law Review* (2009) 247–258, p. 253.

150 P. Roberts and N. McMillan, 'For Criminology in International Criminal Justice', 1 *Journal of International Criminal Justice* (2003) 315–338, p. 323.

the floodgates and, as Aguiling Pangalangan explains, would, in line with ICC *ratio decidendi* in relation to duress, 'provide blanket immunity to members of criminal organisations which have brutal systems of ensuring discipline as soon as they can establish that their membership was not voluntary.'[151]

Overall, the rotten social background defence does not work as an alternative defence because (1) it is not established as a defence in (US) national law and there is no evidence that it has been used in other jurisdictions; thus it cannot be considered as a general principle of law, and (2) it suffers from several critical flaws at theoretical and policy level.

5.2 *Brainwashing and Indoctrination*

The defences of brainwashing and indoctrination[152] work on the basis that individuals' minds have been influenced to such a level that their acts are not theirs anymore. Whilst they are 'free' in their decision-making, including the possibility to leave the coercive environment, that freedom has been withdrawn from them by an elaborate manipulation mechanism. Defendants 'argue that they should not be held responsible because their criminal actions were a consequence of mind control'.[153] The appositeness of this defence for child soldiers has been highlighted by Brown[154] and was used by Ongwen's Defence[155] as it referred to the impact of the LRA's spiritual indoctrination on the child soldiers whose beliefs and perceptions of right and wrong were shaped by such indoctrination.

Brainwashing works on the basis that an individual is 'a relatively passive subject under the control of all-powerful ... external agents who use coercive

---

151 ICC *Ongwen* Confirmation of Charges, *supra* note 109, para. 153. The California Supreme Court also stated: 'If duress is recognized as a defense to the killing of innocents, then a street or prison gang need only create an internal reign of terror and murder can be justified'. *People* v. *Anderson,* 50 P.3d 368, 374 (Cal. 2002).

152 Several concepts, some overlapping, are used to describe this defence (*see* A. Penners Wrosch, 'Undue Influence, Involuntary Servitude and Brainwashing: A More Consistent, Interests-Based Approach', 25 *Loyola of Los Angeles Law Review* (1992) 499–554, p. 501, fn 20).

153 A.D. Renteln, 'Criminal Defenses' in N.J. Smelser and P.B. Baltes (eds.), *International Encyclopedia of the Social & Behavioral Sciences* (Elsevier, Amsterdam, 2001) 2945–2948.

154 Brown, *supra* note 133, p. 375.

155 ICC, *Prosecutor* v. *Ongwen*, ICC -02/04-01/15, Pre-Trial Chamber II, Further Redacted Version of "Defence Brief for the Confirmation of Charges Hearing", Filed on 18 January 2016, 3 March 2016, paras 36–49. *See* also discussion above.

and manipulative techniques'.[156] Delgado explains that individuals have undergone 'a forcible indoctrination process designed to induce the subject to abandon existing political, religious, or social beliefs in favor of a rigid system imposed by the indoctrinator.'[157] Not only the individuals' identity is disrupted but they also appear to have surrendered their will and autonomy and lost their ability to think independently.[158] The intent to commit the crime is superimposed by another person.[159]

In contrast, indoctrination aims to instil a 'doctrine and an ideology, a vision and a programme on how to create a better world'.[160] As such, indoctrination is a social process by which an individual's beliefs are altered, one step at a time.[161] '[I]ndoctrination is not an on-off switch rather a continuum of depth and control. Even after one is initially indoctrinated, a well-organized program will continue to work to deepen and "consolidate" the indoctrination.'[162] Eventually, individuals are unable to resist or even question the demands and orders of the indoctrinators. The grave impact brainwashing and indoctrination have on children has been highlighted on many occasions: 'There is a common view among psychologists that children's minds are so impressionable that merely teaching youth a certain ideology can steer their later intentions and motivations towards that ideology.'[163]

---

156 I.-G. Warburton, 'The Commandeering of Free Will: Brainwashing as a Legitimate Defense', 16(1) *Capital Defence Journal* (2003) 73–97, p. 77 quoting D.G. Bromley and J.T. Richardson (eds), *The Brainwashing/Deprogramming Controversy: Sociological, Psychological, Legal and Historical Perspectives* (Mellen Press, New York, NY, 1983) 6. Brainwashing consists of three stages namely 'breaking down the self, introducing the possibility of salvation, and rebuilding the self.' R. Emory, 'Losing Your Head in the Washer—Why the Brainwashing Defense Can Be a Complete Defense in Criminal Cases', 30(4) *Pace Law Review* (2010) 1337–1359, p. 1340.

157 R. Delgado, 'Ascription of Criminal States of Mind: Toward a Defense Theory for the Coercively Persuaded ("Brainwashed") Defendant', 63(1) *Minnesota Law Review* (1979) 1–33, p. 1.

158 R. Delgado, 'Religious Totalism: Gentle and Ungentle Persuasion under the First Amendment', 51(1) *Southern California Law Review* (1977) 1–98, pp. 21–22.

159 Warburton, *supra* note 156, p. 75.

160 A. Smeulers, 'Punishing the Enemies of All Mankind', 251 *Leiden Journal of International Law* (2008) 971–993, p. 978.

161 *Ibid.*, p. 977.

162 P.H. Robinson and L. Holcomb, 'Indoctrination and Social Influence as a Defense to Crime: Are We Responsible for Who we Are', 85(3) *Missouri Law Review* (2020) 739–801, p. 783. There are four stages: softening up, compliance, internalisation and consolidation. R.S. Baron, 'Arousal, Capacity, and Intense Indoctrination', 4(3) *Journal of Personality and Social Psychology* (2000) 238–254, pp. 240–241.

163 Brown, *supra* note 133, p. 384.

These defences appear particularly relevant in international criminal law. After all, as '[p]eople are social beings and conformity research has shown how susceptible people are to social influence such as peer pressure and how eager they are to show that they are good group members',[164] indoctrination is far more successful in a collective setting, a point to remember in the context of international crimes as they are committed by obedient masses.[165] As Stahn articulates, '[c]rimes are part of group dynamics, conformity pressures and reward schemes that create incentives to follow and "obey"'[166] and so indoctrination has an important role to play in the commission of crimes.

Brainwashing and indoctrination seem *prima facie* useful defences for those who commit crimes having been subjected to a coercive environment. However, two issues must be underlined. First, those defences are essentially deployed in relation to 'new' religious groups or cults.[167] Penners Wrosch warns against comparing brainwashing in religious cults and in other contexts such as criminal defendants and prisoners of war, pointing out that since the latter's behaviour significantly deviates from acceptable social norms, there must be further compelling reasons, such as (threats of) the use of physical violence, to excuse such acts.[168] Recent discussions suggesting that brainwashing and indoctrination are normal processes of socialisation, albeit in a more controlling environment,[169] warrant such a cautious approach. Second, these defences were used successfully in civil cases but not in criminal ones. In fact, they have never been raised in criminal cases as standalone defences. Remarkably, many such cases involved young adults or children, the most famous case being *U.S. v. Hearst* which dealt with a teenage girl who had been kidnapped, ill-treated and then embraced the views of her captors and eventually took part in a bank

164 A. Smeulers and L. Hoex, 'Studying the Microdynamics of the Rwandan Genocide', 50 *British Journal of Criminology* (2010) 435–454, p. 447.

165 Smeulers, *supra* note 160, p. 974.

166 C. Stahn, *A Critical Introduction to International Criminal Law* (Cambridge University Press, Cambridge, 2019), p. 129.

167 Warburton, *supra* note 156, p. 74; J.T. Richardson, 'Cult/Brainwashing Cases and Freedom of Religion', 33 *Journal of the Church State* (1991) 55–74, p. 57. *See* cases in Penners Wrosch, *supra* note 152.

168 Penners Wrosch, *supra* note 152, p. 547.

169 D.D. Coates, 'Life Inside a Deviant "Religious" Group: Conformity and Commitment as Ensured through "Brainwashing" or as the Result of Normal Processes of Socialisation', 44 *International Journal of Law Crime & Justice* (2016) 103–121.

robbery.[170] Her lawyers did not raise the defence of brainwashing *per se*,[171] but relied on the coercion theory which failed.[172] Cases from the 1980s to nowadays show that even in combination with a defence of insanity, indoctrination has not been accepted as a defence.[173]

In conclusion, indoctrination and brainwashing do not work as alternative defences because (1) they are not well established in (US) national law and certainly not in criminal law; and (2) resultantly cannot be viewed as general principles of law.

6 Detention and Coercive Environment

Probably the most incisive way to understand the defences related to coercive environment is to investigate those raised by detainees—since detention is *per se* a coercive environment—in a situation where international crimes are rife. When detention occurs between groups opposing each other or looking to subjugate one another, the animosity leads to a heightened level of coerciveness driving detainees into committing crimes against their peers.

6.1 *Prisoners in Armed Conflict*

In some instances, prisoners of war associate with their captors and engage in unlawful activities, some of them of a criminal nature. Throughout history, the defence most raised in such cases was coercion.[174] Later, the terms 'coercive

---

170 *U.S.* v. *Hearst,* 466 F. Supp. 1068, 1071 (N.D. Cal. 1978).

171 *See* Delgado, *supra* note 137, p. 4 fn 11.

172 *U.S.* v. *Hearst,* 563 F.2d. 1331, 1336–1337; *U.S.* v. *Hearst, supra* note 170, paras 1071–1072.

173 *See, e.g.*, a Court, noting that a 17-year-old member of a cult was able to distinguish right from wrong, was convicted of murder having raised an insanity defence combined with indoctrination (*People* v. *Hoover,* 187 Cal. App. 3d 1074 (1986), p. 1080.) In *Ryan* which involved a 15-year-old who had tortured and killed a member of the cult of his father who had ordered the crimes, brainwashing was pleaded as part of an insanity defence as he was 'totally under the domination of his father' (*State* v. *Ryan,* 226 Neb. 59, 409 N.W.2d 579 (1987), p. 72). The Court found he understood the nature of his acts and willingly and enthusiastically participated in the murder. Malvo, a 17-year-old sniper, raised the defence of indoctrination, claiming to be under the control of his elder companion (*see* T.D. Nolan III, 'The Indoctrination Defense: From the Korean War to Lee Boyd Malvo', 11 *Virginia Journal of Social Policy & Law* (2003–2004) 435–465, pp. 451–455).

174 No author, 'Misconduct in the Prison Camp: A Survey of the Law and an Analysis of the Korean Cases', 56 *Columbia Law Review* (1956) 709–794, p. 722.

persuasion',[175] 'brainwashing',[176] and 'thought reform'[177] gained traction in academic circles, especially concerning the experience of American, British, and French soldiers in East Asia.

During the Korean War, American POWs were subjected to what can be described as highly sophisticated methods of coercive indoctrination to the effect that 'the subject does not feel manipulated and comes to truly hold the beliefs of his captors'.[178] Korean prison camps and conditions were so set up that many POWs collaborated with their captors,[179] some staying behind.[180] British POWs in Korea[181] and French soldiers in Indochina[182] were also indoctrinated though it is unclear whether they collaborated with their captors and mistreated their fellow prisoners.[183] In Vietnam, American POWs were subjected to similar treatment.[184] Several individuals were prosecuted in the US for acts committed in Korea[185] though much fewer for acts perpetrated during the Vietnam War.[186]

Much can be learned from these cases about alternative defences.[187] The defence of individual mental and psychological duress was only successfully

---

175 See E. Schein, *Coercive Persuasion: A Socio-Psychological Analysis of the 'Brainwashing' of American Civilian Prisoners by the Chinese Communists* (W.W. Norton, New York, NY, 1961); V. Merton and R. Kinscherff, 'Coercive Persuasion and the "Culpable Mind"', 11(3) *Hastings Center Report* (1981) 5–8, p. 6.

176 *See* E. Hunter, *Brainwashing: From Pavlov to Power* (The Bookmailer, New York, NY, 1956).

177 See R. Lifton, *Thought Reform and the Psychology of Totalism: A Study of 'Brainwashing' in China* (W.W. Norton, New York, NY, 1963).

178 Robinson, *supra* note 138, p. 66.

179 *See supra* note 174, pp. 725–733.

180 33 American POWs originally refused to be repatriated, then 20 stayed behind (*supra* note 174, pp. 734–735). All but two returned to the US (G.S. Moakley, *U.S. Army Code of Conduct Training: Let the POWs Tell their Stories,* MMAS Thesis (Command and General Staff College, Fort Leavenworth, KS, 1976), p. 97).

181 M. Felton, 'War Zone—PoW Camp, Korea 1952', *Military History Matters* (15 August 2012); H. Kim, 'The Korean War (1950–1953) and the Treatment of Prisoners of War', in S. Linton, T. McCormack and S. Sivakumaran (eds.), *Asia-Pacific Perspectives on International Humanitarian Law* (Cambridge University Press, Cambridge, 2019) pp. 356–365, pp. 363–366.

182 M.-C. Villatoux, 'Traitement psychologique, endoctrinement, contre-endoctrinement en guerre d'Algérie: le cas des camps de détention', 4(208) *Guerres Mondiales et Conflits Contemporains* (2002) 45–54, pp. 47–50.

183 Our research did not yield any results.

184 No author, 'Garwood Trial Offers Lok (sic) at Harsh Life of P.O.W.'s', *New York Times* (23 November 1980).

185 Robinson, *supra* note 138, p. 67.

186 G.D. Solis, *Marines and Military Law in Vietnam: Trial by Fire* (US Marine Corps, Washington, DC, 1989), pp. 218 and 221.

187 *See supra* note 174, pp. 769–771.

used by Schwable (Korea) because he tried to resist as much as he could.[188] All other cases were dismissed.[189] General duress raised in many cases relating to Korean camps was only accepted on a perjury charge.[190] Many tried to fit what they had endured into an insanity plea but failed.[191] The defence of indoctrination was completely rejected by military courts in cases arising from the Korean and Vietnam conflicts.[192] Garwood's (Vietnam) defence essentially centred upon his lack of mental responsibility owing to the brutality of his initial captivity,[193] contending that as 'a victim of coercive persuasion [he] could not be held responsible for [the acts]'.[194] Reference was made to the rotten social defence, explaining that, when enlisted, Garwood was 'a shy and immature teenager temporarily placed in a detention home for juveniles' and that, as a 19-year-old person, he was particularly vulnerable to indoctrination.[195] Dubbed the White VC, he had not only participated in the guarding, indoctrination and questioning of American POWs[196] but also taken part in combat against American forces.[197] Even when allowed to leave, he did not. His trial revealed the long-lasting effects of coercive persuasion in such settings.[198]

However, these cases are of limited use to drafting a new coercive-environment-based defence in international criminal law. First, the majority of cases did not involve criminal acts of the type found in international criminal law.[199] Only two POWs[200] held in Korea were prosecuted for such types of

188 *See ibid.*, p. 770. Nolan III however explains that this case 'was not a judicial ruling'. Nolan III, *supra* note 173, p. 440, fn 27.

189 *See supra* note 174, pp. 769–770 and Merton and Kinscherff,, *supra* note 175, p. 8. *See, e.g., U.S.* v. *Fleming*, 19 C.M.R. 438 (1955), aff'd, 23 C.M.R. 7 (1957), pp. 20–21.

190 *See supra* note 174, pp. 770–771.

191 Merton and Kinscherff, *supra* note 175, p. 5.

192 Nolan, *supra* note 173, pp. 439–440 and fns. 27–28. The brainwashing defence was raised for the first time in *U.S.* v. *Dickenson,* 17 C.M.R. 438, 443 (C.M.A. 1954). *See* F.L. Borch, 'The Trial of a Korean War "Turncoat": The Court-Martial of Corporal Edward S. Dickenson', *Army Law* (January 2013) 1–4.

193 Solis, *supra* note 186, p. 228.

194 Merton and Kinscherff, *supra* note 175, p. 5.

195 *Ibid.*, p. 7. *See also* Pasley's study of the background of the 21 American POWs who stayed in Korea. V. Pasley, *21 Stayed: The Story of the American GIs who Chose Communist China: Who they Were and Why they Stayed* (Farrar, Straus and Cuhahy, New York, NY, 1955).

196 Solis, *supra* note 186, p. 224.

197 *Ibid.*, p. 226.

198 Merton and Kinscherff, *supra* note 175, p. 6.

199 For Korea, *see supra* note 174, pp. 709–794; for Vietnam, *see* Solis, *supra* note 186, pp. 218–230.

200 One could add Batchelor who at a trial in the POW camp had recommended another POW to be shot. He was however only charged with collaboration and sentenced to 20 years. *U.S.* v. *Batchelor*, 19 C.M.R. 452 (1955), aff'd, 22 C.M.R. 144 (1956), 7 USCMA 354.

crimes: Gallagher was found guilty of mistreating two fellow prisoners but acquitted on another similar charge,[201] and Floyd was found guilty of assaulting fellow prisoners but acquitted of the murder of another prisoner.[202] Garwood was convicted of communicating with the enemy and assaulting a POW,[203] the assault being 'a backhanded slap to the ribs of one man'.[204] Second, the great variety of defences attempted (and rejected)[205] does not enable ascertaining the contour of a single defence. Moreover, the common denominator would be close to the defence of mental disease as most defendants seemed to rely solely on the mental element of the coercive environment. Third, even in the case of Garwood, the coercive persuasion defence was not accepted either as a standalone defence or in combination with a plea of insanity.

In conclusion, as the coercive persuasion defence did not work for American prisoners who perpetrated crimes against their fellow prisoners, it cannot be classed as an established defence under national law, let alone a general principle of law.

6.2 *Kapos*

Another potential source for a defence against criminal acts committed in coercive environments is the trials of Kapos[206] who were prisoners in concentration or labour camps and given supervisory functions by the Nazi administration of the camps.[207] They were given various tasks, including taking part in the 'selection of prisoners for extermination, beatings, theft,

201 *Supra* note 174, p. 758.

202 *See supra* note 174, p. 761 (referring to *U.S.* v. *Floyd*, 18 C.M.R. 362 (1954); *U.S.* v. *Floyd*, 19 C.M.R. 413 (1955)).

203 Solis, *supra* note 186, p. 228.

204 Merton and Kinscherff, *supra* note 175, p. 7.

205 *E.g.*, 'mental psychosis induced by Communist pressures and propaganda' (*U.S.* v. *Batchelor*, *supra* note 200, p. 360), 'induced political psychosis', 'atypical dissociative reaction' and 'post-traumatic stress syndrome' (Merton and Kinscherff, *supra* note 175, pp. 5 and 8).

206 Singer explains that these judgments are 'a valuable source for customary international law and international criminal law jurisprudence'. I.M. Singer, '*Reductio ad absurdum:* The *Kapo* Trial Judgements' Contribution to International Criminal Law Jurisprudence and Customary International Law', 24 *Criminal Law Forum* (2013) 235–258, p. 240.

207 *See* M.J. Bazyler and J.Y. Scheppach, 'The Strange and Curious History of the Law Used to Prosecute Adolf Eichmann', 34 *Loyola Los Angeles International & Comparative Law Review* (2012) 417–461, p. 419. Individuals who collaborated with the Nazis in the ghettos or in other circumstances are not examined here.

humiliation',[208] 'escorting condemned prisoners to execution sites, or killing them',[209] in exchange for which they received increased portions of food, better accommodation and warmer clothes.[210] Even in that 'privileged' position, they were under immense pressure.[211] Whilst some mistreated their fellow prisoners as a survival strategy, others used their position to help them.[212]

After World War II, several Kapos were prosecuted in various States.[213] Israel's 1950 Nazi and Nazi Collaborators (Punishment) Law Israel allowed for the prosecution of Jews accused of persecution of their Jewish brethren,[214] allegations mostly 'concern[ing] the excessive use of violence and cruelty in exercising their disciplinary functions',[215] though no one was charged with or found guilty of causing death.[216] For example, Tarnek who hit female inmates with her hands and forced prisoners to kneel was found guilty of assault and battery.[217] Enigster who was violent towards inmates[218] was charged with grave and deliberate bodily harm.[219] His claim for duress, based on Article 10 of the Law,[220] was rejected because there was no threat of immediate death, the position had not been forced upon him and the judges found it difficult to believe that he thought he was averting more serious consequences.[221] As

208 M.J. Bazyler and F.M. Tuerkheimer, *Forgotten Trials of the Holocaust* (New York University Press, New York, NY, 2015), p. 197.

209 N. Wachsmann, *KL. A History of the Nazi Concentration Camps* (Little, Brown, London, 2015), p. 513.

210 Bazyler and Scheppach, *supra* note 207, pp. 419–420.

211 A. Brown, *Judging 'Privileged' Jews. Holocaust Ethics, Representation and the 'Grey Zone'* (Berghahn, New York, NY, 2018), p. 12; B. Akinrinade, 'Judging the Impossible: Kapos and Justice after the Holocaust', *Reflections—Auschwitz Jewish Center Annual Alumni Journal* (2017) 9–17, pp. 14–15.

212 R.A. Alija-Fernández, 'Justice for No-Land's Men? The United States Military Trials against Spanish Kapos in Mauthausen and Universal Jurisdiction' in K. Heller and G. Simpson (eds.), *The Hidden Histories of War Crimes Trials* (Oxford University Press, Oxford, 2013) 103–121, p. 105. Drumbl, *supra* note 70, p. 219.

213 Akinrinade, *supra* note 211, pp. 10–11.

214 Bazyler and Scheppach, *supra* note 207, p. 418; Drumbl, *supra* note 70, p. 229. Very little is known about these trials as the records are sealed (Bazyler and Scheppach, *supra* note 207, p. 429). One of the few cases available is the trial of Demjanjuk but, as he was acquitted based on incorrect charges, this paper does not discuss his case.

215 O. Ben-Naftali and Y. Tuval, 'Punishing International Crimes Committed by the Persecuted', 4 *Journal of International Criminal Justice* (2006) 128–178, p. 153.

216 Bazyler and Tuerkheimer, *supra* note 208, p. 209.

217 *Ibid.*, pp. 211–212.

218 *Ibid.*, pp. 212–213.

219 *Ibid.*, p. 213.

220 Ben-Naftali and Tuval, *supra* note 215, p. 138. For a discussion on the defence of duress under Article 10(a) and 10(b), *see* Singer, *supra* note 181, p. 253.

221 Drumbl, *supra* note 70, p. 232; Singer, *supra* note 181, p. 253.

Segev explains, judges 'had to decide whether a man could refuse to accept the post of *kapo* and to what extent the job required cruelty. They tended not to punish a person for simply being a k*apo,* only for not having been a decent one.'[222] The court stressed that Tarek was placed in charge, did not volunteer[223] and did not identify with the Germans;[224] she was, in Ben-Naftali and Yuva's words, a 'reasonable kapo'.[225] Even in the case of Enigster, who had not been coerced into the post,[226] the court found that, as he did not identify with the Nazis,[227] a line had to be drawn between the Germans and the Jewish prison-functionary.[228] Whether other defences were used in these trials is unknown.

Other States also prosecuted Kapos but information on defences raised is very sparse.[229] One of the few publicly available trials is that of five Spanish Kapos taken prisoners by Germany.[230] All were accused of a range of instances of ill-treatment of prisoners, often leading to the death of their fellow prisoners.[231] Their defences included denying being present or having committed the said acts[232] and having themselves suffered ill-treatment.[233] The latter could be understood as a form of defence relating to the coercive environment. Alija-Fernández states that the judgment did not contemplate the fact that 'their conduct was arguably the result of a combination of self-preservation and brutalization'.[234]

In conclusion, Kapo trials do not uncover much about alternative defences relating to crimes committed in a coercive environment.

---

222 T. Segev, *The Seventh Million: The Israelis and the Holocaust* (Farrar, Straus and Giroux, New York, NY, 2019), p. 262.

223 Bazyler and Tuerkheimer, *supra* note 208, p. 211.

224 *Ibid.*, p. 212.

225 Ben-Naftali and Tuval, *supra* note 215, p. 170.

226 Bazyler and Tuerkheimer, *supra* note 208, p. 213.

227 Ben-Naftali and Tuval, *supra* note 215, p. 155; J.M. Wenig, 'Enforcing the Lessons of History: Israel Judges the Holocaust', in G.J. Simpson and T. McCormack (eds), *The Law of War Crimes: National and International Approaches* (Kluwer Law International, The Hague, 1997) 103–122, p. 119.

228 Bazyler and Tuerkheimer, *supra* note 208, p. 213.

229 *See ibid.*, p. 199 and cases in Akinrinade, *supra* note 211, pp. 12–13.

230 Alija-Fernández, *supra* note 212, p. 104.

231 General Military Government Court, *U.S.A.* v. *Navas et al.*, Review and Recommendations, 000-50-5-25, 14 January 1948; General Military Government Court, *U.S.A.* v. *Espinosa*, Review and Recommendations, US National Archives M-1217 RG 0338 No. 00003, 000-Mauthausen-19, 29 January 1948.

232 U.S.A. v. *Espinosa, supra* note 231, p. 5; U.S.A. v. Navas et al., supra note 231.

233 *U.S.A.* v. *Espinosa, supra* note 231, p. 5.

234 Alija-Fernández, *supra* note 212, p. 120.

7 Conclusion

As much as it is well recognised that child soldiers grow up and live in a coercive environment and that child soldiering has long-term effects on them, the crimes they commit cannot be exculpated on the ground of duress under the ICC Statute. It is clear that a person's traumatic experience in a coercive environment cannot be raised as a ground for excluding criminal responsibility. Further, situations of a 'general' coercive environment where the harm is not immediate or continuing and/or based on a defendant's (real or perceived) apprehension based on their past experience do not constitute duress either.

Moreover, the analysis of alternative defences indicates that none of them is well-anchored in national law, notably because they are highly controversial in society. This brief survey reveals that neither the law nor society excuses or justifies crimes committed in such a situation. The law only allows a defence that falls within a clearly defined category in which choice is virtually inexistent. It is expected that, when faced with adverse conditions, humans will stand by the society's principles and moral precepts. They cannot flinch. Some form of heroism is demanded as the bar has been set rather high. One would have expected some understanding (i.e., an excuse) for crimes perpetrated in a coercive environment like a POW or a concentration camp when individuals are at the hands of the enemy and the survival rate is very low. Yet, none was shown. These alternative defences are not accepted as defences in law and thus cannot even be considered to qualify as general principles of law to become eventually a source of ICC law. Whether explicitly or implicitly, the ICC Statute does not recognise a defence for crimes committed in a coercive environment.

Nonetheless, this article has importantly highlighted the fact that defendants have put forward such claims, often in conjunction with established claims such as duress and insanity and that courts have grappled and even struggled with such claims. Verdicts often squirm with disquiet about the task given to judges. The crime cannot be excused or justified but at the same time, human frailty is acknowledged. Feeling somehow uncomfortable with the situation, national courts have pushed the discussion into the realm of mitigation. And that is probably where claims relating to the coercive environment sit better in international criminal law too.

Acknowledgements

The authors would like to thank Prof James Green and Christian Dadomo for their comments on various versions of this paper.

CHAPTER 3

Forced Marriage as the Crime against Humanity of 'Other Inhumane Acts' in the International Criminal Court's *Ongwen* Case

Kathleen M. Maloney, Melanie O'Brien and Valerie Oosterveld

Abstract

The *Ongwen* case, concluded in December 2022 at the International Criminal Court (ICC), convicted the defendant of a gender-based act that had never been litigated by the ICC: forced marriage. This article argues that the judicial consideration of forced marriage in *Ongwen* has settled the international jurisprudence in three important ways. First, it clarified the classification of forced marriage as an 'other inhumane act'. Second, it recognised and solidified the conduct and harms captured by the term 'forced marriage', distinguishing it from other crimes against humanity. Finally, it confirmed that prosecution of forced marriage does not contravene *nullum crimen sine lege* principles. These outcomes will play a key role in future recognition and prosecutions of forced marriage in international criminal law. This article suggests that the logical next step is to explicitly list forced marriage as a crime against humanity in the Rome Statute and the draft Crimes Against Humanity Convention.

Keywords

armed conflict – forced marriage – International Criminal Court – sexual and gender-based violence

1 Introduction

The case of *Prosecutor v Ongwen*, concluded in December 2022 at the International Criminal Court (ICC),[1] is replete with ground-breaking

1 ICC, *Prosecutor* v. *Dominic Ongwen*, Case No. ICC-02/04-01/15-422-Red [93], Pre-Trial Chamber, Decision on the confirmation of charges against Dominic Ongwen, 23 March

 | DOI: 10.1163/9789004743380_004

developments. These include charging and convicting a defendant for a gender-based act that had never been litigated by the ICC: forced marriage.[2] While this case represented the first such prosecution in the ICC, forced marriage had been previously prosecuted by the Special Court for Sierra Leone (SCSL) and the Extraordinary Chambers in the Courts of Cambodia (ECCC). This article argues that the ICC Trial and Appeal Chambers' discussion of forced marriage in *Ongwen* has settled the international jurisprudence in three important ways. First, it clarified the classification of forced marriage as an 'other inhumane act'. Second, it recognised and solidified the conduct and harms captured by the term 'forced marriage', distinguishing it from other crimes against humanity. Finally, it confirmed that prosecution of forced marriage does not contravene *nullum crimen sine lege* ('no crime without law') principles. These outcomes from *Ongwen* will play a key role in future recognition and prosecutions of forced marriage in international criminal law.

This article begins by introducing forced marriage as committed by the Lord's Resistance Army (LRA) in Uganda and describes the conviction of LRA commander Dominic Ongwen for forced marriage. It then turns to international courts' and tribunals' use of the crimes against humanity category of 'other inhumane acts' to assess why this category is relevant and necessary, and examines how these courts have used 'other inhumane acts' to prosecute forced marriage. The article then explores the conduct and harms encapsulated by the phrase 'forced marriage' and examines how the ICC Appeals Chamber dealt with Ongwen's argument that the Prosecutor's approach to forced marriage violated one of the principles of legality, *nullum*

---

1 2016 (hereafter *Ongwen* Confirmation of Charges); ICC, *Prosecutor* v. *Dominic Ongwen*, Case No. ICC-02/04-01/15, Trial Chamber IX, Judgment, 4 February 2021 (hereafter *Ongwen* Trial Judgment); ICC, *Prosecutor* v. *Dominic Ongwen*, Judgment on the appeal of Mr Ongwen against the decision of Trial Chamber IX of 4 February 2021 entitled "Trial Judgment", Case No. ICC-02/04-01/15 A, Appeals Chamber, Judgment, 15 December 2022 (hereafter *Ongwen* Appeals Judgment).

2 Women's Initiatives for Gender Justice, *Trailblazing ICC Judgment on SGBC—Ongwen verdict advances international accountability for forced marriage and forced pregnancy* (4 February 2021), available online at 4genderjustice.org/trailblazing-icc-judgment-on-sgbc-ongwen-verdict/ (accessed 22 May 2023). Other 'firsts' include prosecuting and convicting forced pregnancy, distinguishing between enslavement and sexual slavery of girls, and prosecuting a former child soldier for international crimes, some of which he, too, had suffered from the age of nine years to adulthood.

3 This article focuses on these issues because they were repeatedly raised by Ongwen and his counsel throughout the case. Other defence arguments regarding forced marriage, such as those relating to modes of liability, are outside the scope of this article.

crimen sine lege.[3] This article concludes that, despite the clarity brought by the ICC's findings regarding forced marriage in armed conflict in the *Ongwen* case, it would be wise to explicitly enumerate forced marriage as a crime against humanity both in the Rome Statute and in the draft Crimes Against Humanity Convention, to avoid continual relitigation of the classification, definition, and status of this act.

2 Forced Marriages Imposed by the LRA and Ongwen's Related Conviction

Throughout the most recent Ugandan civil war (1986–2006), members of the LRA, led by Joseph Kony, forced girls and young women to serve as 'wives' of its fighters. The *Ongwen* case detailed many facts regarding LRA forced marriages.[4] Dominic Ongwen was a high-ranking soldier in the LRA's Sinia brigade.[5] Girls and women were abducted by members of the brigade, forcibly assigned as 'wives', required to undertake various forms of domestic labour, childbearing, and childcare duties, beaten regularly until their bodies were swollen and/or they were unconscious, and routinely raped by their 'husbands'.[6]

Strict control was imposed on every aspect of the girls' and women's lives in the forced marriages through brutal disciplinary measures. The 'wives' were subject to violent discipline for 'disobedience, resistance, not conceiving [a child], talking together unsupervised, having blank expressions on their faces, looking miserable, allegedly planning an escape, or breaking rules or taboos of the fighting group'.[7] 'Husbands' could have more than one 'wife', but punishment was meted out to any 'wife' suspected of or engaging in infidelity, confirming each 'wife' as belonging exclusively to her allocated 'husband'.[8]

4 *Ongwen* Trial Judgment, *supra* note 1, paras 205–437, 2009–2309.

5 *Ibid.*, paras 134–138. The Sinia Brigade was active in Uganda, Sudan, Central African Republic, and Democratic Republic of Congo. The ICC's jurisdiction over LRA actions relates only to Uganda, although the judges did draw on testimony relating to crimes committed in other states as background: *ibid.*, paras 310, 314, 579, 609–610, 624, 876, 925, 941, 984, 1009.

6 *Ibid.*, paras 2256–2270, 2289–2308.

7 H. Baumeister, *Sexualised Crimes, Armed Conflict and the Law* (Routledge, Abingdon, 2018), p. 51.

8 *Ibid.*

The ICC Trial Chamber found a 'coordinated and methodical effort' by Dominic Ongwen, the brigade leadership, and the LRA's leader Joseph Kony, relying on the LRA soldiers under their control, to engage in forced marriage.[9] Dominic Ongwen was therefore convicted as a direct perpetrator for forcing girls and women to be his 'wives' and as an indirect perpetrator for enforcing and sustaining this system of forced marriage within the Sinia brigade.[10]

3 The Crime against Humanity of 'Other Inhumane Acts'

The ICC's Prosecutor charged Ongwen with directly and indirectly committing forced marriage as the crime against humanity of 'other inhumane acts', charges which were confirmed by the Pre-Trial Chamber.[11] The Prosecutor classified forced marriage in this manner for two reasons: first, the category of 'other inhumane acts' has historically been used to incorporate unenumerated acts deemed by the prosecution to be serious; and second, this category has been utilised by previous tribunals to classify forced marriage.[12] Given that this categorisation was the subject of numerous defence arguments in *Ongwen*, it is necessary to review the residual crime of 'other inhumane acts' to understand why this is presently the appropriate provision under which to prosecute forced marriage.

International and national tribunals have identified numerous types of conduct as falling within the crimes against humanity residual category of 'other inhumane acts' since World War II. 'Other inhumane acts' were first instituted in 1945 as a crime against humanity through the international legal instruments governing the International Military Tribunals at Nuremberg and

---

9 *Ongwen* Trial Judgment, *supra* note 1, paras 212, 3089; *see also Ongwen* Confirmation of Charges, *supra* note 1, para. 137.

10 *Ongwen* Trial Judgment, *supra* note 1, paras 2098–2142, 3097, 3100.

11 *Ongwen* Confirmation of Charges, *supra* note 1, paras 87, 117, 124. In particular, the relevant counts were Count 50 (direct participation) and Count 61 (indirect co-perpetration and ordering).

12 ICC, *Prosecutor* v. *Domenic Ongwen*, Case No. ICC-02/04-01/15, Appeals Chamber, Public Redacted Version of 'Prosecution Response to "Defence Appeal Brief Against the Convictions in the Judgment of 4 February 2021"', 19 November 2021, paras 561–565 (hereafter *Ongwen* Prosecution Appeals Brief).

Tokyo,[13] and this category was repeated in the laws governing post-World War II prosecutions of European Axis war criminals.[14]

In 1950, the United Nations International Law Commission (ILC) adopted the Nuremberg Principles, further codifying and establishing 'other inhuman acts done against any civilian population' as a crime against humanity.[15] In 1993 and 1994, the United Nations Security Council incorporated 'other inhumane acts' as a crime against humanity into the Statutes for the International Criminal Tribunals for the former Yugoslavia (the ICTY)[16] and for Rwanda (the ICTR).[17]

By 1996, the International Law Commission adopted the Draft Code of Crimes Against the Peace and Security of Mankind, which prohibited '[o]ther inhumane acts which severely damage physical or mental integrity, health or human dignity, such as mutilation and severe bodily harm', acknowledging the impossibility of creating 'an exhaustive list of the inhumane acts which might constitute crimes against humanity'.[18] Two years later, the Rome Statute codified 'other inhumane acts' as a distinct crime against humanity to be investigated and prosecuted at the ICC.[19] In 2000, the Statute for the SCSL

13 United Kingdom of Great Britain and Northern Ireland, United States of America, France and Union of Soviet Socialist Republics, *Charter of the International Military Tribunal* in *Agreement for the Prosecution and Punishment of the Major War Criminals of the European Axis* (London Agreement) (82 U.N.T.S. 280), 8 August 1945, Article 6(c); Supreme Commander for the Allied Powers in Occupied Japan, *Charter of the International Military Tribunal for the Far East*, 19 January 1946 (TIAS No. 1589, 4 Bevans 20) (as amended April 26, 1946, 4 Bevans 27), Article 5(c).

14 *Control Council Law No. 10, Punishment of Persons Guilty of War Crimes, Crimes Against Peace and Against Humanity of 20 December 1945*, (3 Official Gazette Control Council for Germany 1946), pp. 50–55, Article II.1(c): 'Atrocities and offenses, including but not limited to murder, extermination, enslavement, deportation, imprisonment, torture, rape, or other inhumane acts'.

15 UN General Assembly, *Principles of International Law Recognized in the Charter of the Nürnberg Tribunal and in the Judgment of the Tribunal*, (A/RES/95), 11 December 1946, Principle VI.3.

16 Statute of the International Criminal Tribunal for the Former Yugoslavia (UN Doc. S/RES/827, amended by S/RES/1877), Article 5(i).

17 Statute of the International Criminal Tribunal for Rwanda (UN Doc. S/RES/955, amended by S/RES/1901), Article 3(i).

18 International Law Commission (ILC), 'Draft Code of Offences against the Peace and Security of Mankind with Commentaries', *Yearbook of the International Law Commission*, 1996, Vol. II, Part Two, p. 50, Commentary (17) on Article 18(k).

19 ICC, *Rome Statute of the International Criminal Court* (UN Doc A/CONF.183/9), Article 7(1)(k) (hereafter Rome Statute).

did the same,[20] and shortly thereafter, the Law on the Establishment of the ECCC also followed suit.[21] The SCSL's Appeals Chamber observed that, given this history, the materially distinct category of 'other inhumane acts' had crystallised into customary international law.[22] The existence and legitimacy of 'other inhumane acts' as a category is therefore well-settled in international criminal law.

The jurisprudence of these tribunals developed the parameters of 'other inhumane acts', with the ICTY in particular analysing this residual clause. In the *Čelebići* case, the ICTY drew on 'inhumane treatment' from the Geneva Conventions and human rights law, determining this to be consistent with the crime against humanity of 'other inhumane acts'.[23] The Tribunal held that the prohibition on 'inhumane treatment' is prohibited under 'conventional and customary law'.[24] The ICTY assessed 'other inhumane acts' in several cases, and ultimately identified the basic characteristics of 'other inhumane acts' in its *Karadžić* Trial Judgment:

> (i) there was an act or omission of similar seriousness to the other enumerated acts under Article 5; (ii) the act or omission caused serious mental or physical suffering or injury or constituted a serious attack on human dignity; and (iii) the act or omission was committed with the intent to inflict serious physical or mental suffering or to commit a serious

20 Statute of the Special Court for Sierra Leone, annexed to the Agreement Between the United Nations and the Government of Sierra Leone on the Establishment of a Special Court for Sierra Leone (16 January 2022), Article 2(i).

21 Law on the Establishment of the Extraordinary Chambers, with inclusion of amendments as promulgated on 27 October 2004 (NS/RKM/1004/006), Article 5.

22 SCSL, *Prosecutor* v. *Brima, Kamara and Kanu*, Case No. SCSL-2004-16-A, Appeals Chamber, Judgment, 22 February 2008 (hereafter *AFRC Brima* Appeals Judgment), paras 198, 200, citing ICTY, *Prosecutor* v. *Stakić*, Case No. IT-97-24-A, Appeals Chamber, Judgment, 22 March 2006, para. 315 (hereafter *Stakić* Appeals Judgment); ICTY, *Prosecutor* v. *Blagojević and Jokić*, Case No. IT-02-60-T, Judgment, Trial Chamber, 17 January 2005, para. 624 (hereafter *Blagojević and Jokić* Trial Judgment).

23 ICTY, *Prosecutor* v. *Delalić et al.*, Case No. IT-96-21-T, Trial Chamber, Judgment, 16 November 1998, paras 516–542 (*Čelebići*). The ICTY also referred to international humanitarian law, international human rights law and international criminal law (including the ICC Rome Statute) in *Prosecutor* v. *Kupreškić et al.*, Case No. IT-95-16-T, Trial Chamber, Judgment, 14 January 2000, paras 562–566.

24 *Čelebići*, supra note 23, para. 517. Despite the extensive use of different sources of international law, the approach to 'other inhumane acts' has not been without criticism; *see* G. MacNeil, *Legality Matters: Crimes Against Humanity and the Problems and Promise of the Prohibition on Other Inhumane Acts* (T.M.C. Asser Press, The Hague, 2021), particularly p. 131 *et seq.*

attack on the human dignity of the victim(s), or with the knowledge that this act or omission was likely to cause such suffering or a serious attack upon human dignity.[25]

In similar wording, but without the intent requirement, the ICC Elements of Crimes mandate that 'other inhumane acts' must fulfil two material elements:

1. The perpetrator inflicted great suffering, or serious injury to body or to mental or physical health, by means of an inhumane act.
2. Such act was of a character similar to any other act referred to in Article 7, paragraph 1, of the Statute.[26]

In the *Katanga* Confirmation of Charges decision, the ICC Pre-Trial Chamber held that 'inhumane acts are to be considered as serious violations of international customary law and the basic rights pertaining to human beings, drawn from the norms of international human rights law, which are of a similar nature and gravity to the acts referred to in Article 7(1) of the Statute'.[27] Thus, the ICC's perspective on such 'inhumane acts' is that it is appropriate for courts to conclude that 'other inhumane acts' constitute crimes against humanity fulfilling Article 22's *nullum crimen sine lege* criteria.[28]

The residual criminal category of 'other inhumane acts' has been used by international courts to delineate numerous acts, including sexual and gender-based violations. For example, the ICTR recognised forced public nudity and sexual and physical mutilation of corpses as 'other inhumane acts'.[29]

25 ICTY, *Prosecutor v Radovan Karadžić*, Case No. IT-95-5/18-T, Trial Chamber, Judgment, 24 March 2016, para. 494.

26 The second requirement was added to appease state concerns about any imprecision in this category of crime: D. Robinson, 'Defining "Crimes against Humanity" at the Rome Conference', 93(1) *American Journal of International Law* (1999) 43–57, at p. 56. For more detail on this crime, *see* R. Dubler and M. Kalyk, *Crimes Against Humanity in the 21st Century: Law, Practice and Threats to International Peace and Security* (Brill, Leiden, 2018) 942–958.

27 ICC, *Prosecutor v Germain Katanga,* Case No. ICC-01/04-01/07-717, Pre-Trial Chamber, Decision on the Confirmation of Charges, 30 September 2008, paras 441, 448.

28 J.-P. Pérez-León Acevedo, 'The Close Relationship Between Serious Human Rights Violations and Crimes Against Humanity: International Criminalization of Serious Abuses', 17 *Anuario Mexicano de Derecho Internacional* (2017) 145–186 at p. 163.

29 ICTR, *Prosecutor* v. *Akayesu*, Case No. ICTR-96-4-T, Trial Chamber, Judgment, 2 September 1998, para. 697; ICTR, *Prosecutor* v. *Kayishema and Ruzindana*, Case No. ICTR-95-1-T, Trial Chamber, Judgment, 21 May 1999, para. 730; ICTR, *Prosecutor* v. *Niyitegeka*, Case No. ICTR-96-14-T, Trial Chamber, Judgment, 16 May 2003, paras 303–313, 465–467; ICTR, *Prosecutor* v. *Kajelijeli*, Case No. ICTR-98-44A-T, Trial Chamber, Judgment and Sentence, 1 December 2003, para. 936.

The ICTY, ICTR, and SCSL held that serious physical and mental injuries,[30] beatings and cruel treatment,[31] forcible transfer,[32] forced prostitution,[33] 'forced disappearance, beatings, torture, sexual violence, humiliation, harassment, psychological abuse, and confinement in inhumane conditions', and 'mutilation and other types of severe bodily harm, beatings and other acts of violence'[34] also amount to 'other inhumane acts'.

To allow some heinous crimes to go unpunished simply because they are not explicitly enumerated, when they clearly comprise harmful conduct as grave as other crimes against humanity, creates a legal absurdity—an absurdity the residual category of 'other inhumane acts', like the residual war crime category of 'outrages against personal dignity', seeks to counter. As the ICTY stated:

> The phrase 'other inhumane acts' was deliberately designed as a residual category, as it was felt to be undesirable for this category to be exhaustively enumerated. An exhaustive categorization would merely create opportunities for evasion of the letter of the prohibition.[35]

Likewise, the ICC Trial Chamber acknowledged the necessity of the residual clause, noting the 'impossibility of exhaustively enumerating every inhumane act which could constitute a crime'.[36]

The crime against humanity of 'other inhumane acts' has existed in international law for many decades, and has been defined in myriad sources.

---

30 ICTR, *Prosecutor* v. *Niyitegeka*, Case No. ICTR-96-14-A, Appeals Chamber, Judgment, 9 July 2004, para. 271; ICTY, *Prosecutor* v. *Vasiljević*, Case No. IT-98-32-T, Trial Chamber, Judgment, 29 November 2002, paras 239–240; ICTY, *Prosecutor* v. *Blaškić*, Case No. IT-95-14-T, Trial Chamber, Judgment, 3 March 2000, para. 239; ICTY, *Prosecutor* v. *Tadić*, Case No. IT-94-1, Trial Chamber, Opinion and Judgment, 7 May 1997, paras 730, 737, 744.

31 *AFRC Brima* Appeals Judgment, *supra* note 22, paras 184–185.

32 *Stakić* Appeals Judgment, *supra* note 22, para. 317; *Blagojević and Jokić* Trial Judgment, *supra* note 22, para. 629; ICTY, *Prosecutor* v. *Krstić*, Case No. IT-98-33-T, Trial Chamber, Judgment, 2 August 2001, para. 523.

33 ICTY, *Prosecutor* v. *Prlić et al.*, Case No. IT-04-74, Trial Chamber, Judgment, 29 May 2013, para. 79; ICTY, *Prosecutor* v. *Kupreškić et al.*, Case No. IT-95-16-T, Trial Chamber, Judgment, 14 January 2000, para. 566.

34 ICTY, *Prosecutor* v. *Kvočka et al.*, Case No. IT-98-30/1-A, Appeals Chamber, Judgment, 28 February 2005, para. 435.

35 *Kupreškić et al.*, *supra* note 33, para. 563. *See also Prosecutor v Blaskic*, IT-95-14-T, Trial Chamber Judgment, 3 March 2000, para 237.

36 *Ongwen* Trial Judgment, *supra* note 1, para. 2745.

It is rooted in the core concepts of humanity and human dignity.[37] This is why it is appropriate to prosecute forced marriage, which deprives its direct and indirect victims of basic human dignity, under 'other inhumane acts'; the next sections will explore how international courts have done so.

4 Forced Marriage as an 'Other Inhumane Act'

Prior to the ICC's *Ongwen* case, the SCSL and the ECCC both held that forced marriage constitutes an inhumane act distinct from other crimes against humanity and therefore squarely falls within the 'other inhumane acts' category.[38] These determinations were crucial to, and helped to shape, the ICC's subsequent consideration of forced marriage.

4.1 *The SCSL and ECCC's Determinations on Forced Marriage*

Examining the widespread phenomenon of forced marriage in the brutal armed conflict in Sierra Leone in the 1990s, the SCSL Appeals Chamber specifically determined in 2008 in *Prosecutor* v. *Brima, Kamara and Kanu* (*Brima et al.*) that forced marriage met 'other inhumane acts' requirements.[39] In particular, the act causes 'great suffering, or serious injury to body or to mental or physical health',[40] and was 'of similar gravity to several enumerated crimes against humanity including enslavement, imprisonment, torture, rape, sexual slavery and sexual violence'.[41] The Appeals Chamber emphasised the gravity of long-lasting and stigmatising harms to forced marriage victims, especially given their young ages, stating that many 'were children themselves'.[42] It

37 B. Kuschnik, 'Humaneness, Humankind and Crimes against Humanity', 2(2) *Goettingen Journal of International Law* (2010) 501–530.

38 *AFRC Brima* Appeals Judgment, *supra* note 22, para. 198; SCSL, *Prosecutor* v. *Sesay, Kallon and Gbao*, Case No. SCSL-04-15-T, Trial Chamber, Judgment, 2 March 2009, paras 1464, 1473 (hereafter *RUF Sesay Trial Judgment*); SCSL, *Prosecutor* v. *Sesay, Kallon and Gbao*, Case No. SCSL-04-15-A, Appeals Chamber, Judgment, 26 October 2009, paras 726, 849, 861–862 (hereafter *RUF Sesay* Appeals Judgment); ECCC, *Co-Prosecutors* v. *Nuon Chea and Khieu Samphân*, Case No. 002/19-09-2007/ECCC/TC, Trial Chamber, Judgment, 16 November 2018, paras 741,4172, 4198, 4303–4305 (hereafter *Case 002/02* Trial Judgment).

39 *AFRC Brima* Appeals Judgment, *supra* note 22, para 198.

40 *Ibid.*, para. 200.

41 *Ibid.*

42 *Ibid.*, para. 199.

also concluded that forced marriage was not subsumed by the crime against humanity of sexual slavery.[43]

One year later, the SCSL's Appeals Chamber upheld the first-ever conviction for forced marriage as an 'other inhumane act' crime against humanity in *Prosecutor v Sesay, Kallon and Gbao* (*Sesay et al.*),[44] agreeing with the Appeals Chamber in *Brima et al.* on this legal characterisation of forced marriage.[45] Additionally, the Appeals Chamber confirmed that the only elements of forced marriage the Prosecutor must prove are the *mens rea* and *actus reus* of 'other inhumane acts'.[46]

In 2018, the ECCC Trial Chamber charged and convicted top-ranking former Khmer Rouge leaders, Nuon Chea and Khieu Samphân, for forced marriage as 'other inhumane acts',[47] finding that this category of crime was prohibited under customary international law at the relevant time, and that the 'other inhumane acts' category is not restricted to a specifically-elaborated list of conduct.[48] Moreover, the ECCC found that forced marriage need not have been explicitly recognised as part of the category by 1975.[49] The Trial Chamber clarified that since 'other inhumane acts' is *in itself* a distinct crime against humanity, it is not necessary to prove that each constituent act was recognised as a separate crime because *nullum crimen sine lege* requirements attach only to the entire category 'other inhumane acts,' not to the different subcategories

43 *Ibid.*, paras 190, 195. It declined to enter a conviction because 'it is convinced that society's disapproval of the forceful abduction and use of women and girls as forced conjugal partners as part of a widespread or systematic attack against the civilian population, is adequately reflected by recognising that such conduct is criminal and that it constitutes an "Other Inhumane Act" capable of incurring individual criminal responsibility in international law', at *ibid.*, paras 202, 713. For an analysis of this reasoning, *see* V. Oosterveld, 'Forced Marriage: Terminological Coherence and Dissonance in International Criminal Law', 27(4) *William & Mary Bill of Rights Journal* (2019) 1263–1282 at 1266–1267 (hereafter Oosterveld, 'Terminological Coherence').

44 *RUF Sesay* Appeals Judgment, *supra* note 38, paras 726, 849; *RUF Sesay* Trial Judgment, *supra* note 38, paras 168, 1464, 1473.

45 *RUF Sesay* Appeals Judgment, *supra* note 38, para. 2307.

46 *Ibid*, paras 740 (Sesay), 861 (Kallon) and 972 (Gbao), confirming *RUF Sesay* Trial Judgment, *supra* note 38, para. 168. Note that, in a subsequent case in which forced marriage was not charged, *Prosecutor* v. *Taylor*, the Trial Chamber opined in *obiter dicta* that forced marriage should not be pursued under 'other inhumane acts' but rather as 'conjugal slavery': *Prosecutor* v. *Charles Taylor*, Case No. SCSL-03-01-T, Trial Chamber, Judgment,18 May 2012, paras 422, 424, 427–428, 1101, 1700 (hereafter *Taylor* Trial Judgment). This is discussed in Section 5 below.

47 *Case 002/02* Trial Judgment, *supra* note 38, paras 4172, 4198, 4303–4305.

48 *Ibid.,* para. 741.

49 *Ibid.*

thereof.[50] The ECCC found that forced marriage satisfied both requirements for 'other inhumane acts' as it 'caused serious mental or physical suffering or injury' or 'constituted a serious attack on human dignity' and it was of a similar gravity to the enumerated crimes against humanity.[51]

The ECCC Trial Chamber further distinguished forced marriage from other crimes against humanity due to its unique violation of the international human right to consensually marry.[52] Like the SCSL did in its analysis of marriage in Sierra Leonean society,[53] the ECCC differentiated traditional or arranged marriages in Cambodian society from the non-consensual marriages being prosecuted.[54] The Trial Chamber found that genuine consent was impossible in Khmer Rouge-enforced marriages given the regime's coercive environment, in which victims were threatened with death or other punishments for non-compliance.[55] Victims of forced marriage under the Khmer regime were thereby denied agency to enter into marriage with the free and full consent of both partners.

On 22 September 2022, the Supreme Court Chamber rejected defendant Khieu Samphân's appeal challenging his conviction on forced marriage under 'other inhumane acts'.[56] In dismissing the defendant's contention that it was not foreseeable and accessible to him that forced marriage specifically constituted a crime against humanity, the Supreme Court Chamber clarified that the requirements of foreseeability and accessibility within the principle of legality are only applicable to the general category of 'other inhumane acts'.[57] The Appeals Judgment also dismissed the defendant's argument that his conduct must be specifically prohibited in human rights instruments for it be judged an inhumane act. The Supreme Court Chambers instead found

50 ECCC, *Co-Prosecutors* v. *Ieng Sary*, Case No. 002/19-09-2007-ECCC/OCIJ (PTC75), Pre-Trial Chamber, Decision on Ieng Sary Appeal on Closing Order, 11 April 2011, para. 378 (emphasis in original).

51 *Case 002/02* Trial Judgment, *supra* note 38, para. 746.

52 *Ibid.*, para. 743.

53 *See e.g.*, *AFRC Brima* Appeals Judgment, *supra* note 22, para. 127; SCSL, *Prosecutor* v. *Brima, Kamara and Kanu*, Case No. SCSL-04-16-T, Trial Chamber, Judgment, 20 June 2007, para. 11 (Sebutinde J., concurring) (hereafter *AFRC Brima* Trial Judgment).

54 *Case 002/02* Trial Judgment, *supra* note 38, para. 3688.

55 *Ibid.*, paras 3620–3625, 3648–3666, 3694, 3688 (sexual intercourse consummating the 'marriage' was compulsory and monitored, with refusal leading to rape by militia or 'husbands').

56 ECCC, Co-Prosecutors v. Khieu Samphân, Case No. 002/19-09-2007-ECCC/SC, Supreme Court Chamber, Appeal Judgment, 23 December 2022, paras 1171–1195 (hereafter *Case 002/02* Appeals Judgment).

57 *Ibid.*, para. 93.

that 'other inhumane acts' comprised 'conduct infringing basic human rights appertaining to human beings, as identified under international legal instruments'.[58] Moreover, the particular conduct need not be expressly criminalised by international law to qualify as an 'other inhumane act'; requiring otherwise would defeat the necessity of this residual crime against humanity category.[59]

4.2 *The ICC Confirms Forced Marriage as a Distinct Crime against Humanity*

In *Ongwen*, the Prosecutor charged forced marriage as an 'other inhumane act', while the defence claimed that this categorization was invalid because the acts described are subsumed by the charges for sexual slavery.[60] The Chamber indicated that, in order to qualify as an 'other inhumane act' under Article 7(1)(k) of the Rome Statute, the alleged acts of forced marriage—forcing women and girls to serve as 'conjugal partners' to Ongwen and other LRA fighters in the Sinia brigade—must satisfy statutory requirements.[61] As outlined in Section 3 above, these must be acts which intentionally caused great suffering or serious injury to body or to mental or physical health, and must be of a character similar to any other acts listed in the Article 7(1) crimes against humanity provision.[62] Additionally, given the defence argument, forced marriage must be distinguishable from sexual slavery (and, by extension, any other crime against humanity).[63] The Pre-Trial Chamber concluded that all of these requirements were met: 'forcing another person to serve as a conjugal partner may, *per se*, amount to an act of a similar character to those explicitly enumerated by Article 7(1) of the Statute and may intentionally cause great suffering, and … forced marriage may, in the abstract, qualify as "other inhumane acts" under Article 7 of the Statute rather than being subsumed by the crime of sexual slavery'.[64] The Pre-Trial Chamber concluded 'forced marriage as an other inhumane act differs from the other crimes with which Dominic Ongwen is charged, and notably from the crime of sexual slavery, in terms of conduct, ensuing harm, and protected interests' due to its core and distinct feature: a forced conjugal exclusive union.[65] This approach to forced marriage was confirmed by the

58 *Ibid.*, para. 1131.
59 *Ibid.*, para. 1130.
60 *Ongwen* Confirmation of Charges, *supra* note 1, para. 87.
61 *Ibid.*, para. 88.
62 *Ibid.*
63 *Ibid.*
64 *Ibid.*, para. 91.
65 *Ibid.*, paras 92–93.

Trial and Appeals Chambers' holdings that forced marriage is similar in nature and gravity to the other acts listed in Article 7(1) of the Rome Statute, but also comprises a course of conduct which differs from those acts.[66]

Given the similar and sustained reasoning stemming from the SCSL's *Brima et al.* appeals judgment and the *Sesay et al.* trial and appeals judgments, as well as decisions of the ECCC and ICC, it is now clear that forced marriage qualifies as an 'other inhumane act' within the crimes against humanity category under international criminal law. The clarity provided by the *Ongwen* case helps to answer the questions raised by the SCSL's *Brima et al.* and *Taylor* trial judgments about categorizing forced marriage in this manner.

5 Clarification of the Conduct Constituting Forced Marriage and Associated Harms

While there was strong agreement among the SCSL, ECCC, and ICC that forced marriage amounts to an 'other inhumane act', there was initially less clarity on the exact conduct and precise harms encompassed by the term. This lack of clarity stemmed from the evolving case law of the SCSL and ECCC. The SCSL's first trial judgment to consider the conduct and harms of forced marriage—*Brima et al.*—dismissed the forced marriage charges as being subsumed by the sexual slavery charges.[67] This flattening of forced marriage into solely a sexual crime was reversed on appeal.[68] The Appeals Chamber defined forced marriage as a 'forced conjugal association' which encompassed two types of harm to victims: injuries, including stigmatisation, stemming from forcibly having the status of 'wife' imposed upon them; and maltreatment stemming from being compelled to carry out 'conjugal duties' including forced domestic labour, submitting to rape, and bearing and rearing children of the 'marriage'.[69] This approach to the conduct of forced marriage was subsequently reinforced

66 *Ongwen* Trial Judgment, *supra* note 1, paras 2747–2748; *Ongwen* Appeal Judgment, *supra* note 1, para. 1022.

67 *AFRC Brima* Trial Judgment, *supra* note 53, para 712.

68 *AFRC Brima* Appeals Judgment, para. 195. For a critique of this flattening, *see* V. Oosterveld, 'The Special Court for Sierra Leone's Consideration of Gender-based Violence: Contributing to Transitional Justice?', 10(1) *Human Rights Review* (2009) 73–98 at p. 86.

69 *AFRC Brima* Appeals Judgment, *supra* note 22, paras 190–193 and 199–200. *See also* V. Oosterveld, 'Forced Marriage and the Special Court for Sierra Leone: Legal Advances and Conceptual Difficulties', 2(2) *Journal of International Humanitarian Legal Studies* (2011) 127–158 at p. 135 (hereafter Oosterveld, 'Legal Advances').

by the Trial Chamber in *Prosecutor* v. *Sesay, Kallon and Gbao*.[70] In particular, the trial judgment indicated that the imposition of the status of 'wife' led to the psychological manipulation of victims, instilled fear in their communities, destroyed families, and undermined Sierra Leonean society.[71] This growing clarity on the conduct and harms of forced marriage was undermined by the SCSL's final trial judgment in *Prosecutor* v. *Taylor*, which opined in *obiter dicta* that the term 'conjugal slavery' was more appropriate than 'forced marriage' and that the illegal conduct is a combination of sexual and domestic enslavement.[72] The Appeals Chamber did not discuss this view, thus missing the opportunity to clarify or reconcile the jurisprudence in this regard.

The ECCC, as the second tribunal to prosecute forced marriage, agreed that the illegal conduct involved forcing victims to enter into conjugal relationships in coercive circumstances.[73] The ECCC identified two types of harm: the damage done to male and female victims who had the status of 'spouse' forcibly imposed upon them through Khmer Rouge-organised marriage ceremonies lacking traditional rituals or customs, and the resulting rape.[74] The ECCC's approach demonstrated that the specific conduct captured by the term 'forced marriage' is not uniform.[75] The SCSL relied heavily on forced domestic and sexual labour, and the use of the term 'wife' without legal marriage, as integral parts of the illegal conduct.[76] On the other hand, the ECCC emphasised lack of consent to actual marriage under Khmer Rouge law and the rape after marriage.[77] These differences indicate both the flexibility of the term 'forced marriage', and potentially that the exact conduct comprising the term was undertheorised.[78]

The *Ongwen* trial and appeals judgments deepened and solidified the understanding of the conduct and harms captured by the term 'forced marriage'. The Pre-Trial, Trial, and Appeals Chambers indicated that conduct charged as

---

70 RUF Sesay Trial Judgment, *supra* note 38 at paras 1154–1155, 1211–1213, 1293, 1295–1296, 1348–1349, 1412–1413, 1466–1472.

71 *Ibid.*, paras 1348–1349, 1466.

72 *Taylor*, *supra* note 46, paras 425, 427–430.

73 ECCC, *Co-Prosecutors* v. *Nuon Chea and Khieu Samphân*, Case No. 002/19-09-2007/ECCC/OCIJ, Closing Order, 15 September 2010, para. 1443.

74 *Case 002/02* Trial Judgment, *supra* note 38, paras 3670–3701.

75 *See* Oosterveld, 'Terminological Coherence', *supra* note 43, p. 1277.

76 *See, for example*, *AFRC Brima* Appeals Judgment, *supra* note 22, paras 190, 199.

77 *Case 002/02* Trial Judgment, *supra* note 38, paras 3670–3701.

78 Oosterveld, 'Terminological Coherence', *supra* note 43, p. 1277. *See also* M. O'Brien, '"Don't Kill them, Let's Choose them as Wives": the Development of the Crimes of Forced Marriage, Sexual Slavery and Enforced Prostitution in International Criminal Law', 20(3) *International Journal of Human Rights* (2016) 386–406 at pp. 391–392.

forced marriage involves at least two types of unique harm: the violation by the accused of the victim's relational autonomy (including social ostracisation), and a constellation of human rights violations.[79] Arguably, this approach more precisely elucidates the 'central element' of forced marriage: 'the imposition, regardless of the will of the victim, of duties that are associated with marriage, as well as of a social status' of being the perpetrator's 'spouse'.[80] This imposition of a 'spousal' status creates 'exclusivity', under which the victim cannot have any other conjugal relationships. The Pre-Trial Chamber noted that the forced conjugal association plus the exclusivity are 'characteristic aspect[s] of forced marriage' which are 'absent from any other crime with which Dominic Ongwen is charged'.[81] The Pre-Trial Chamber articulated the value protected by the charge—'the independently recognised basic right to consensually marry and establish a family'—which is 'distinct from e.g. physical or sexual integrity, or personal liberty'.[82] This right is recognised under international human rights treaties.[83] The Trial Chamber agreed that marriage, or a situation akin to marriage, 'creates a status based on a consensual and contractual relationship—it is an institution and also an act or rite' that is undermined when it is forced.[84] This was reinforced by the Appeals Chamber.[85]

The denial of relational autonomy involves the assignment of 'spousal' status to the victim.[86] Ongwen's defence counsel argued that 'there was no conjugal union between the perpetrators and the victims, since one of the requirements of marriage in the Acholi culture was not fulfilled and that their

79 *Ongwen* Confirmation of Charges, *supra* note 1, paras 92–94; *Ongwen* Trial Judgment, *supra* note 1, paras 2748–2751; *Ongwen* Appeals Judgment, *supra* note 1, paras 1022–1024.

80 *Ongwen* Confirmation of Charges, *supra* note 1, para. 93. This was also accepted by the trial and appellate levels: *Ongwen* Trial Judgment, *supra* note 1, paras 2748–2749; *Ongwen* Appeals Judgment, *supra* note 1, paras 1022–1024. *See also* AFRC *Brima* Appeals Judgment, *supra* note 22, para. 195.

81 *Ongwen* Confirmation of Charges, *supra* note 1, para. 93.

82 *Ibid.*, para. 94.

83 The ICC Appeals Chamber referred to two treaties: *Ongwen* Appeals Judgment, *supra* note 1, para. 1021, referring to UN General Assembly, *International Covenant on Civil and Political Rights*, (999 UNTS 171) (1966), Article 23(3) (hereafter ICCPR) and UN General Assembly, *Convention on the Elimination of All Forms of Discrimination Against Women*, (1249 UNTS 13) (1979) Article 16(1)(b), as well as the *Universal Declaration of Human Rights*, (UN Doc. 217 A (III)) (1948), Article 16(2). *See also* African Union, *Protocol to the African Charter on Human and People's Rights on the Rights of Women in Africa*, Maputo, 11 July 2003, Article 6.

84 *Ongwen* Trial Judgment, *supra* note 1, para. 2748.

85 *Ongwen* Appeals Judgment, *supra* note 1, para. 1024.

86 *Ongwen* Confirmation of Charges, *supra* note 1, para. 93. This was also accepted by the trial and appellate levels: *Ongwen* Trial Judgment, *supra* note 1, paras 2748–2749; *Ongwen* Appeals Judgment, *supra* note 1, paras 1022–1024.

relationship was[,] in substance, "mere cohabitation".'[87] In answer to this, all levels of the Court stressed that the fact that the 'marriage' was illegal or not recognised by the laws or customs of the country or society in which the events occurred is irrelevant.[88] The Appeals Chamber stated that the conjugal union's existence 'may be established on the facts of the case including the nature of the relationship between the perpetrator and the victim, as well as the subjective view of the victim, third parties and the perpetrator'.[89] In other words, '[w]hat matters is whether or not a conjugal union was factually imposed on the victims'.[90] As the *nullum crimen sine lege* analysis below demonstrates, it also matters that '[t]he perpetrator was aware of the factual circumstances that established the character of the act.'[91]

The Pre-Trial, Trial, and Appeals Chambers commented on the consequences of being deprived of relational autonomy: victims suffer social stigma, mental trauma, and a serious attack on their dignity.[92] Stigmatisation may result in victims being rejected from their communities.[93] They may also suffer trauma because they bore children as a result of their forced marriage, and their children may also be affected. As the Trial Chamber observed, '[t]o the extent forced marriage results in the birth of children, this creates even more complex emotional and psychological effects on the victim and their children beyond the obvious physical effects of pregnancy and childbearing'.[94]

The second unique type of harm caused by forced marriage is a range of human rights violations experienced by victims, which differ from context to context. Here again, the ICC added more detail, indicating that these harms are connected with various 'duties that are associated with marriage' and 'socially constructed gendered expectations and roles attached to [being a

87 *Ongwen* Appeals Judgment, *supra* note 1, para. 1025.

88 *Ongwen* Confirmation of Charges, *supra* note 1, para 93; *Ongwen* Trial Judgment, *supra* note 1, para. 2748; *Ongwen* Appeals Judgment, *supra* note 1, para. 1025. *See also* ICC, *Prosecutor* v. *Al Hassan Ag Abdoul Aziz Ag Mohamed Ag Mahmoud*, Case No. ICC-01/12-01/18-461-Corr-Red, Pre-Trial Chamber, Rectificatif à la Décision Relative à la Confirmation des Charges Portées Contre Al Hassan Ag Abdoul Aziz Ag Mohamed Ag Mahmoud, 13 November 2019, para. 555 (hereafter *Al Hassan* Confirmation of Charges); *AFRC Brima* Appeals Judgment, *supra* note 22, para. 195.

89 *Ongwen* Appeals Judgment, *supra* note 1, para. 1025.

90 *Ibid.*

91 *Ibid.*, para 1015.

92 *Ongwen* Confirmation of Charges, *supra* note 1, para. 93; *Ongwen* Trial Judgment, *supra* note 1, paras 2748–2749.

93 *Ongwen* Trial Judgment, *supra* note 1, paras 2748–2749.

94 *Ibid.*, para. 2748.

forced] "wife" or "husband"'.[95] Many of these human rights violations are crimes unto themselves. For example, the SCSL referred to abduction, rape, sexual slavery, enforced exclusivity in the sexual relationship, inability to leave the conjugal union for fear of violent retribution, non-consent to being placed in a polygamous conjugal situation, forced pregnancy, forced childbearing and childrearing, physical violence, forced domestic labour such as cooking and cleaning, and forced portering.[96] Similarly, the *Ongwen* Pre-Trial Chamber listed as indicators of forced marriage, situations in which the victim is 'sexually or otherwise enslaved by the perpetrator', is restricted in freedom of movement, or is subjected to repeated sexual abuse, forced pregnancy, or forced labour such as forced performance of domestic duties.[97] The Trial Chamber also referred to serial rape and birth of children, physical violence, forced beating and killing of other abductees, and, for those who were Ongwen's 'wives', forced 'domestic duties, including cooking, working in the garden, doing laundry, fetching and chopping wood, carrying Dominic Ongwen's dishes, fetching water, washing, nursing Dominic Ongwen when he was injured and taking things to him'.[98] The Appeals Chamber added that victims were 'placed under heavy guard', 'threatened with death if they tried to escape',[99] raped, and subjected to physical and psychological violence.[100] However, these duties, roles, and consequences do not, in themselves, amount to forced marriage, as the denial of relational autonomy is also required.[101]

The Trial Chamber in *Ongwen* found that it is acceptable that these forced marriage human rights violations may also 'compris[e] acts falling under one or more of the enumerated crimes' in the Rome Statute: indeed, it is this overlap that indicates that forced marriage is 'nonetheless "similar" in character in terms of nature and gravity, to those enumerated crimes.'[102] At the same time, the forced assignment of the status of 'spouse' is not reflected in the other enumerated acts, creating the required differentiation from those other crimes.[103]

---

95 *Ongwen* Confirmation of Charges, *supra* note 1, para. 93; *Ongwen* Trial Judgment, *supra* note 1, para. 2748; *Ongwen* Appeals Judgment, *supra* note 1, para. 1024.

96 AFRC *Brima* Appeals Judgment, *supra* note 22, para. 190. *See also* RUF *Sesay* Trial Judgment, *supra* note 38, paras 460, 1154–1155, 1211–1213, 1293, 1295, 1408–1411, 1413, 1460, 1468, 1472, 1553.

97 *Ongwen* Confirmation of Charges, *supra* note 1, para. 92.

98 *Ongwen* Trial Judgment, *supra* note 1, paras 205, 208, 209–210, 215, 218, 220, 2748, 2750.

99 *Ongwen* Appeals Judgment, *supra* note 1, para. 1027.

100 *Ibid.*, paras 1027–1028.

101 *Ongwen* Confirmation of Charges, *supra* note 1, paras 92–93.

102 *Ongwen* Trial Judgment, *supra* note 1, para. 2747.

103 *Ibid.*, para. 2748.

In response to defence arguments, the Pre-Trial, Trial and Appeals Chambers commented on the ways in which forced marriage differs from sexual slavery and rape as crimes against humanity, such that the presence of one does not negate the ability to consider and convict for the other. For example, sexual slavery involves 'the perpetrator's restriction or control of the victim's sexual autonomy while held in a state of enslavement', including 'the exercise of ownership over a person'.[104] In contrast, 'the other inhumane act of forced marriage penalises the perpetrator's imposition of "conjugal association" with the victim', a 'relationship of exclusivity' and 'disciplinary consequences for breach of this exclusive relationship'.[105] Therefore 'exclusivity of ownership is not an element of forced marriage' as a form of 'other inhumane acts'.[106] Similarly, 'the crime of rape does not penalise the imposition of the "marital status" on the victim' of forced marriage and, even though serial rape is often a part of forced marriage, 'victims suffer trauma and stigma beyond that caused by being a rape victim alone'.[107] Given these differences, the Trial Chamber concluded that the 'conduct underlying forced marriage—as well as the impact it has on victims—are not fully captured by other crimes against humanity'.[108]

Not all of the human rights violations associated with forced marriage constitute international crimes. 'This is particularly so with human rights violations such as the inability to leave the conjugal union for fear of violent retribution, and non-consent to being placed in a polygamous conjugal situation'.[109] Others include the violation of the right to health, loss of education, and interruption of family ties.[110] The ICC recorded evidence of associated human rights violations that may not amount to international

104 *Ongwen* Trial Judgment, *supra* note 1, para. 2750. *See also AFRC Brima* Appeals Judgment, *supra* note 22, para. 195; *RUF Sesay* Trial Judgment, *supra* note 38, para. 2307.

105 *Ongwen* Confirmation of Charges, *supra* note 1, para. 93; *Ongwen* Trial Judgment, *supra* note 1, para. 2750; *Ongwen* Appeals Judgment, *supra* note 1, para. 1026. *See also, AFRC Brima* Appeals Judgment, *supra* note 22, para. 195; *RUF Sesay* Trial Judgment, *supra* note 38, para. 2307.

106 *Ongwen* Appeals Judgment, *supra* note 1, para. 1026.

107 *Ongwen* Trial Judgment, *supra* note 1, para. 2750. *See also AFRC Brima* Appeals Judgment, *supra* note 22, para. 199. The SCSL Trial Chamber noted the 'lasting social stigma' attached to the 'bush wives', 'which hampers their recovery and reintegration into society': *RUF Sesay* Trial Judgment, *supra* note 38, para. 1296.

108 *Ongwen* Trial Judgment, *supra* note 1, para. 2750.

109 ICC, *Prosecutor* v. *Ongwen*, Case No. No. ICC-02/04-01/15 A A2, Appeals Chamber, *Amici Curiae* Brief on Forced Marriage, 22 December 2021, note 52.

110 ICCPR, *supra* note 83, Article 17; UN General Assembly, *International Covenant on Economic, Social and Cultural Rights*, (993 UNTS 3) (1996), Articles 10, 12, 13.

crimes.[111] While the Chambers' forced marriage analysis overlooked certain gross violations of fundamental and non-derogable human rights of girls—as children and as female child soldiers — despite their *jus cogens* and criminal status,[112] the Court's delineation of the conduct and harms of forced marriage refined and solidified international criminal law's understanding of this type of inhumane act.

6 Forced Marriage and the Legality Principle of *Nullum Crimen Sine Lege*

Throughout his case, Ongwen argued that the charge of forced marriage violated one of the international principles of legality, in particular *nullum crimen sine lege* (*nullum crimen*). This principle is widely viewed as reflecting a general principle of international law, if not customary international law.[113] The principle of *nullum crimen* has two aspects: non-retroactivity and clarity of the law.[114] Both are reflected in Article 22 of the Rome Statute. The first aspect is found in Article 22(1), which states that '[a] person shall not be criminally responsible under this Statute unless the conduct in question constitutes, at the time it takes place, a crime within the jurisdiction of the Court'. The second aspect is reflected in the fact that crimes are specifically defined in the Rome Statute, the elements of the crimes are set out in the Element of Crimes document, and Article 22(2) requires strict construction of the Rome Statute crimes.[115]

Ongwen raised a *nullum crimen* argument following the Confirmation of Charges decision, arguing that a strict construction of the Rome Statute, which does not list forced marriage as a cognisable act, required the Court to dismiss

111 *See, e.g.*, *Ongwen* Trial Judgment, *supra* note 1, paras 2030–2033; ICC, *Prosecutor* v. *Ongwen*, Case No. ICC-02/04-01/15, Trial Chamber, Sentence, 6 May 2021, para. 166; ICC, *Prosecutor* v. *Ongwen*, Case No. ICC-02/04-01/15 A2, Appeals Chamber, Judgment on the appeal of Mr Dominic Ongwen against the decision of Trial Chamber IX of 6 May 2021 entitled 'Sentence', 15 December 2022, para. 363.

112 K.M. Maloney, 'Ending Impunity for Forced Marriage in Conflict Zones: The Need for Greater Judicial Emphasis on the Human Rights of Girls', 19(2) *Journal of International Criminal Justice* (2021) 327–358 at pp. 331–332, 342–343, 348, 357–358.

113 A. Cassese, *International Criminal Law*, 2nd edn. (Oxford University Press, Oxford, 2008), pp. 40–41; A. Grabert, *Dynamic Interpretation in International Criminal Law: Striking a Balance between Stability and Change* (Herbert Utz Verlag, München, 2015), p. 11.

114 R. Cryer, D. Robinson and S. Vasiliev, *An Introduction to International Criminal Law and Procedure*, 4th edn. (Cambridge University Press, Cambridge, 2019), p. 18.

115 ICC, *Elements of Crimes* (UN Doc PCNICC/2000/1/Add.2) (2000).

the charges.[116] The Trial Chamber found that the defence was untimely in its motion but that it would consider arguments on the legal content of forced marriage in its trial judgment.[117] Ongwen therefore again raised a *nullum crimen* argument at the conclusion of trial using the same reasoning.[118] The Trial Chamber rejected this argument, finding 'other inhumane acts' to be a legitimate and established category of crime, for example in the case law of the ICTY and ICTR (indicating non-retroactivity).[119] It evaluated the acts of forced marriage against the requirements of the elements of 'other inhumane acts', finding that forced marriage satisfied the requirement of 'great suffering, or serious injury to body or to mental or physical health' and was of a character similar to, but distinct from, the other enumerated crimes against humanity (indicating clarity of law).[120]

Ongwen appealed, again raising a *nullum crimen* argument that his convictions for forced marriage would amount to punishment for a crime which did not exist at the time of the events in question.[121] The Prosecution's Appeals Brief argued that *nullum crimen* requirements were fulfilled since it was sufficiently foreseeable and accessible to Ongwen that his inhumane acts were of similar nature and gravity as other statutorily-listed crimes against

116 ICC, *Prosecutor* v. *Ongwen*, Case No. ICC-02/04-01/15, Trial Chamber, Defence Motion on Defects in the Confirmation of Charges Decision: Defects in the Charged Crimes (Part IV of the Defects Series), 1 February 2019, para. 41. Earlier, he had argued that the forced marriage charges were subsumed by the sexual slavery charges: ICC, *Prosecutor* v. *Ongwen*, Case No. ICC-02/04-01/15, Pre-Trial Chamber, Third Public Redacted Version of 'Defence Brief for the Confirmation of Charges Hearing filed on 18 January 2016 as ICC-02/04-01/15-404-Conf', 25 May 2016, paras 128–130.

117 ICC, *Prosecutor* v. *Ongwen*, Case No. ICC-02/04-01/15, Trial Chamber, Decision on Defence Motions Alleging Defects in the Confirmation Decision, 7 March 2019, paras 31–35, 37. This was confirmed by the Appeals Chamber: ICC, *Prosecutor* v. *Ongwen*, Case No. ICC-02/04-01/15, Appeals Chamber, Judgment on the Appeal of Mr. Dominic Ongwen against Trial Chamber IX's 'Decision on Defence Motions Alleging Defects in the Confirmation Decision', 17 July 2019, paras 155–158, 161.

118 ICC, *Prosecutor* v. *Ongwen*, Case No. ICC-02/04-01/15, Trial Chamber, Public Redacted Version of 'Corrected Version of "Defence Closing Brief", filed on 24 February 2020', 13 March 2020, para. 471.

119 *Ongwen* Trial Judgment, *supra* note 1, para. 2744.

120 *Ibid.*, paras 2743–2751.

121 ICC, *Prosecutor* v. *Ongwen*, Case No. ICC-02/04-01/15, Appeals Chamber, Public Redacted Version of 'Defence Appeal Brief Against the Convictions in the Judgment of 4 February 2021' filed on 21 July 2021 as ICC-02/04-01/15-1866-Conf, 19 October 2021, paras 147–148, 978 (*Ongwen* Defence Appeal Brief).

humanity.[122] The Appeals Chamber responded that the relevant criminal category against which to measure *nullum crimen* was 'other inhumane acts' and not the subcategory of forced marriage.[123] The Chamber found that Article 7(1)(k) sufficiently delimited 'the action constituting an inhumane act and the consequence required as a result of that action', such that the crime was sufficiently clear and precise.[124] It then evaluated whether acts of forced marriage qualify as 'other inhumane acts'. The Appeals Chamber stated that 'forced marriage describes a situation in which a person is compelled to enter into a conjugal union with another person by the use of physical or psychological force, or threat of force, or by taking advantage of a coercive environment ... [which] violates a person's right to ... freely choose one's spouse and consensually establish a family'.[125] It determined that the Trial Chamber did not err in finding forced marriage to be a form of 'other inhumane acts'.[126] The Appeals Chamber also reiterated that '[t]he perpetrator was aware of the factual circumstances that established the character of the act',[127] thereby fulfilling the applicable *nullum crimen* criteria.

Ongwen's awareness of the factual circumstances establishing the inhumane character of his forced marriage acts was inescapable, since they encompassed crimes against humanity firmly established by longstanding customary international law and treaties—enslavement, imprisonment or other severe deprivation of physical liberty, torture, rape, sexual slavery, and other forms of servitude. These well-settled crimes against humanity already meet *nullum crimen* requirements, thereby imputing commensurate notice of the wrongfulness and criminal character of such conduct. Additionally, the serious nature of the human rights violations underlying forced marriage, some of which are *jus cogens*, combined with the ICC's statutory duty to apply and interpret the law so that it is consistent with internationally recognised human rights and without adverse distinction,[128] also militate in favour of a finding that *nullum crimen* is satisfied.

Despite the jurisprudence both prior to and within the *Ongwen* case, these ICC Trial and Appeals Chamber judicial conclusions on *nullum crimen* were

---

122 ICC, *Prosecutor* v. *Ongwen*, Case No. ICC-02/04-01/15-1882-Conf, Appeals Chamber, Prosecution Response to Defence Appeal Brief, 21 October 2021, paras 562–564 (hereafter *Ongwen* Prosecution Response to Defence Appeal Brief).

123 *Ongwen* Appeals Judgment, *supra* note 1, para. 1019.

124 *Ibid.*

125 *Ibid.*, para. 1024.

126 *Ibid.*

127 *Ongwen* Appeals Judgment, *supra* note 1, para. 1015.

128 Rome Statute, *supra* note 19, Article 21(3).

not necessarily pre-ordained. Numerous international criminal law experts concur with jurisprudential holdings that forced marriage as an 'other inhumane act' fulfils the relevant *nullum crimen* criteria.[129] Others disagree, contending that 'other inhumane acts' prosecutions violate or jeopardise defendants' due process rights.[130] Still others do not view forced marriage as a distinct harm, arguing that it is subsumed in enslavement, for example.[131] This debate is not surprising: courts struggle to balance concerns regarding 'fair warning' or 'reasonable foreseeability' in the criminalisation of specific acts, the subjectivity of an accused's understanding of the content or scope of even explicit criminal provisions, legislative and judicial interpretation of the 'essence of the offense', and the importance of weighing interests and harms vis-a-vis the accused and the victims.[132]

While acknowledging the perils of international courts' application of evolving contemporary norms to past criminal conduct, experts and human rights courts have observed that even relatively novel applications of legality standards by international criminal judges 'have not infringed the higher-order

129 *See, e.g.*, M. Frulli, 'Advancing International Criminal Law: The Special Court for Sierra Leone Recognizes Forced Marriage as a "New" Crime against Humanity', 6(5) *Journal of International Criminal Justice* (2008) 1033–1042 at pp. 1039–1040, DOI: 10.1093/jicj/mqn063; M.P. Scharf and S. Mattler, 'Forced Marriage: Exploring the Viability of the Special Court of Sierra Leone's New Crime Against Humanity', *Case Research Paper Series in Legal Studies Working Paper-05-35* (October 2005), p. 6; Oosterveld, 'Legal Advances', *supra* note 69, pp. 143–148; S. Wharton, 'The Evolution of International Criminal Law: Prosecuting "New" Crimes before the Special Court for Sierra Leone', 11(2) *International Criminal Law Review* (2011) 217–239 at p. 232, DOI: 10.1163/157181211X559662; M.A. Wetherill, *Judicial Interpretation and Nullum Crimen Sine Lege at the International Criminal Court: An Exercise in Utilizing 'Other Inhumane Acts' under Crimes Against Humanity*, PhD thesis (University of Kent, Canterbury, 2019) pp. 56–100, https://kar.kent.ac.uk/81863/.

130 *See, e.g.*, M.C. Bassiouni, *Crimes Against Humanity: Historical Evolution and Contemporary Application* (Cambridge University Press, Cambridge, 2011), p. 262; J. Lincoln, '*Nullum Crimen Sine Lege* in International Criminal Tribunal Jurisprudence: The problem of the residual category of crime', 7(1) *Eyes on the ICC* (2010) 137–155.

131 *See, e.g.*, N.A. Goodfellow, 'The Miscategorization of "Forced Marriage" as a Crime against Humanity by the Special Court for Sierra Leone', 11(5) *International Criminal Law Review* (2011) 831–867 at pp. 866–867; P. Viseur Sellers, 'Wartime Female Slavery: Enslavement?', 44 *Cornell International Law Journal* (2011) 115–142 at p. 135; H. Zawati, *Fair Labelling and the Dilemma of Prosecuting Gender-Based Crimes at the International Criminal Tribunals* (Oxford University Press, Oxford, 2014) at p. 129.

132 *See* A. Rychlewska, 'The *Nullum Crimen Sine Lege* Principle in the European Convention of Human Rights: the Actual Scope of Guarantees', 36 *Polish Yearbook of International Law* (2016) 163–208, DOI: 10.7420/pyil2016h.

principles underlying the [*nullum crimen*] prohibition'.[133] As one such scholar, Van Schaack, argues:

> Today's defendants were on sufficient notice of the foreseeability of ICL jurisprudential innovations in light of extant domestic penal law, universal moral values expressed in international human rights law, developments in international humanitarian law and the circumstances in which this law has been invoked, and other dramatic changes to the international order and to international law brought about in the postwar period ... [Any] lingering concerns about the rights of the defendants can and should be mitigated by sentencing practices.[134]

Other scholars express reservations about the validity of this approach in safeguarding defendants' rights, calling for 'predictability, not interpretive adventurism' and cautioning the ICC to avoid 'victim-focused teleological reasoning' which may result in overly-wide crime definitions.[135]

Ongwen pressed the question of *nullum crimen* for forced marriage as an inhumane act multiple times, and each time the relevant Chamber of the Court found the answer to be straightforward. ICC trial and appeal judges concluded that forced marriage satisfies the *nullum crimen* requirements applicable to the 'other inhumane acts' category of crimes against humanity.[136] The jurisprudence of international criminal tribunals is therefore coalescing around the legality of charging, prosecuting, and convicting forced marriage.

7 Conclusion

The existing enumerated crimes against humanity do not fully capture either the conduct comprising forced marriage or its harmful impacts on victims.[137] Forced marriage is greater than the sum of its common components—deprivation of relational autonomy and myriad human rights

133 B. Van Schaack, '*Nullum Crimen Sine Lege*: Judicial Lawmaking at the Intersection of Law and Morals', 97 *Georgetown Law Journal* (2008) 119–192 at p. 120.
134 *Ibid.*
135 *See* P. Akhavan, 'The Perils of Progressive Jurisprudence: The *Nullum Crimen Sine Lege* Principle in International Criminal Law', 75(1) *Current Legal Problems* (2022) 45–70 at p. 68 (*see also* pp. 66, 69–70); D. Robinson, 'The Identity Crisis of International Criminal Law', 21(4) *Leiden Journal of International Law* (2008) 925–963 at p. 938 (*see also* pp. 925, 930–931, 937).
136 *Ongwen* Trial Judgment, *supra* note 1, paras 2743–2751; *Ongwen* Appeals Judgment, *supra* note 1, para. 1019.
137 *Ongwen* Trial Judgment, *supra* note 1, para. 2750.

abuses—because of the harms flowing from forced conjugal relationships and the children attached to them. The open-ended category of 'other inhumane acts' constitutes the crime against humanity that best encapsulates the myriad contours, diversified contexts, intersectional abuses, and multi-dimensional harms characterising forced marriage. The authors argue that it is now settled jurisprudence that forced marriage falls under this crime, a view supported by various international criminal courts and tribunals, including the ICC in the *Ongwen* Trial and Appeals judgments.

The clarification of international criminal law on forced marriage stemming from the *Ongwen* case will be helpful for the forthcoming judicial reasoning in the ICC's *Al Hassan* case.[138] It will also inform the consideration by states of the International Law Commission's draft Crimes Against Humanity Convention.[139] That draft Convention replicates the Rome Statute's crimes against humanity provision, including the listing of 'other humane acts' as a residual category.[140] In the April 2023 interactive discussions within the Sixth Committee of the United Nations on the draft convention, the United Kingdom recommended that forced marriage be considered for explicit inclusion in the list of enumerated crimes against humanity as a result of the *Ongwen* judgments.[141] Canada similarly recommended that forced marriage be considered for direct listing as a crime against humanity.[142] The authors also support such an amendment to the draft treaty, given the preponderance of case law on the distinct nature and harms of forced marriage. Explicit recognition would help to overcome continued submissions, such as those from the defence in the *Ongwen* case, contesting the existence of the crime of forced marriage as an 'other inhumane act' and raising *nullum crimen* arguments. While it is acknowledged that there is a significant debate among countries about the viability and content of such a treaty,[143] this type of amendment may be among the most palatable, given the strength of the jurisprudence.

138 *Al Hassan* Confirmation of Charges, *supra* note 88.

139 International Law Commission, *Draft Articles on Prevention and Punishment of Crimes Against Humanity*, in International Law Commission, *Report on the Work of its Seventy-First Session*, (UN Doc A/74/10) (2019).

140 *Ibid.*, Article 2(1)(k).

141 United Nations, *Delegates Grapple with Definition of Crimes against Humanity That Supports Future Development, Has Legal Certainty, as Sixth Committee Continues Resumed Session* (UN Doc. GA/L/3680, 11 April 2023), available online at https://press.un.org/en/2023/gal3680.doc.htm (accessed 20 May 2023).

142 *Ibid.*

143 L. Sadat and M. George, 'An Analysis of State Reactions to the ILC's Work on Crimes Against Humanity: a Pattern of Growing Support' 6(2) *African Journal of International Criminal Justice* (2020) 162–190 at pp. 165–187.

This recommendation also raises the question of whether the Rome Statute should be amended to explicitly include 'forced marriage' as a crime against humanity and war crime, positioned with the other listed sexual and gender-based crimes. The definition of 'forced marriage' could be drawn from the *Ongwen* jurisprudence, namely the compulsion 'of a person to enter into a conjugal union with another person by the use of physical or psychological force, or threat of force, or by taking advantage of a coercive environment'.[144] Such a definition should be gender-neutral and encompass different circumstances of forced marriage. Implementing this amendment would help to more directly reflect the gravity and widespread nature of the crime of forced marriage.

As Stacey Hynd has written, '[f]orced marriage corrupts and perverts the social institution of marriage, creating a form of conjugal disorder that threatens society'.[145] This was confirmed in a February 2023 report by the Office of the High Commissioner for Human Rights on the adverse impact of forced marriage on girls and women: 'In all contexts, the essential drivers of forced marriage are patriarchal ideologies and structures, which subjugate women and girls and violate their human dignity and rights'.[146] Victims of forced marriage, used to maintain and prolong conflicts and oppressive regimes, suffer most from this continuing crime that has life-long effects on them and their children. The consideration of and reasoning on forced marriage within the *Ongwen* case has demonstrated the importance of addressing this egregious offence, the breadth of the long-lasting and devastating harms resulting from it, and the legal arguments that underpin its prohibition and associated enforceability.

Acknowledgements

The authors served as *amici curiae* on forced marriage to the ICC Appeals Chamber in the *Ongwen* case. The authors wish to thank Nicole Dotson

144 *Ongwen* Appeals Judgment, *supra* note 1, para. 1024.

145 S. Hynd, '"To Be Taken as a Wife is a Form of Death": The Social, Military, and Humanitarian Dynamics of Forced Marriage and Girl Soldiers in African Conflicts, c. 1990–2010', in A. Bunting, B.N. Lawrence and R.L. Roberts (eds.), *Marriage by Force? Contestation over Consent and Coercion in Africa* (Ohio University Press, Athens, OH, 2016) pp. 292–312 at p. 297. *See also* M. O'Brien, 'Gender Dimensions of Forced Marriage in International Criminal Law' in I. Rosenthal, V. Oosterveld and S. SáCouto (eds.), *Gender and International Criminal Law* (Oxford University Press, Oxford, 2022), pp. 212–222 at pp. 227–229.

146 Office of the High Commissioner for Human Rights, *Adverse impact of forced marriage on the full and effective enjoyment of all human rights by all women and girls* (A/HRC/52/50) (2 February 2023) p. 1.

and Allison Hardy for their research assistance on the manuscript. Valerie Oosterveld wishes to thank the Social Sciences and Humanities Research Council of Canada for its funding to support this research through the Canadian Partnership for International Justice.

CHAPTER 4

The Prosecutor v Dominic Ongwen: An Examination of the Role of Traditional Justice Mechanisms in International Criminal Justice

Linda Mushoriwa

Abstract

This paper examines whether traditional justice mechanisms have a place in international trials where the accused has committed core international crimes; through the lens of The International Criminal Court's approach in the *Ongwen* case. Trial Chamber IX declined to incorporate the *mato oput* traditional justice mechanism of the Acholi people of Northern Uganda. The paper argues that although concerns have been raised regarding the application of traditional justice mechanisms in the aftermath of mass atrocities, they can still play a significant role alongside prosecutions for international crimes before international criminal tribunals and the International Criminal Court. It recommends ways in which traditional justice mechanisms can be incorporated into proceedings before the ICC and concludes that if the Court is to be a truly universal Court as was envisaged at its inception it ought to holistically consider the issues brought before it, particularly from the Global South.

Keywords

International Criminal Court – *mato oput* – *Ongwen* – traditional justice mechanisms

1 Introduction

This paper examines whether traditional justice mechanisms have a place in international criminal justice, particularly in international trials where the accused has committed core international crimes. This is done through the lens of Trial Chamber (TC) IX's approach in the case of *The Prosecutor* v *Dominic Ongwen* before the International Criminal Court (ICC or 'the Court'). Ongwen was convicted of 61 charges of war crimes and crimes against humanity in

 | DOI: 10.1163/9789004743380_005

February 2021, for his role in the crimes perpetrated by the Lord's Resistance Army (LRA) in Northern Uganda between 1 July 2002 and 31 December 2005.[1] Ongwen was one of the top 5 commanders of the LRA, referred to as the Control Altar of the LRA.[2] The crimes which Ongwen was convicted of include torture as a crime against humanity and war crime; forced marriage as an inhumane act constituting a crime against humanity; forced pregnancy as a crime against humanity and war crime; and conscription of children under the age of 15 into an armed group as a war crime.[3] In May 2021, Ongwen was sentenced to 25 years imprisonment, pending the outcome of an appeal lodged by his legal team against both conviction and sentence.[4] The Appeals Chamber of the ICC heard the appeal and rendered its decision in December 2022, which confirmed both the conviction and sentence.[5]

The trial of Ongwen ignited significant debate amongst scholars, even before the commencement of proceedings. Scholars have commented on Ongwen's dual status as both a victim and perpetrator, as he was abducted when he was about 10 years old, on his way to school from his home, and conscripted into the LRA.[6] There has also been discussion on the mental incapacity and duress

1 Situation in Uganda in the case of *The Prosecutor v Dominic Ongwen* Public Redacted Trial Judgment ICC-02/04-01/15-1762-Red (hereinafter ICC *Ongwen* Trial Judgment). For background on the Lord's Resistance Army see A. Cascais, *The last throes of Uganda's Lord's Resistance Army*, available online at www.dw.com/en/uganda-lord-resistance-army-final-days/a-60535944 (accessed 28 August 2023).

2 Open Society Justice Initiative December 2016 Briefing Paper, *The Trial of Dominic Ongwen at the International Criminal Court*, available online at www.justiceinitiative.org/publications/trial-dominic-ongwen-international-criminal-court (accessed 28 August 2023).

3 ICC *Ongwen* Trial Judgment, *supra* note 1, paras 35–36.

4 ICC, Situation in Uganda, *Prosecutor v Dominic Ongwen,* Case no ICC-02/04-01/15-1819-Red, Public Redacted Sentence (hereinafter ICC *Ongwen* Sentencing Judgment).

5 ICC, Situation in Uganda, *Prosecutor v Dominic Ongwen,* Case no ICC -02/04-01/15-2023, Judgment on the appeal of Mr Dominic Ongwen against the decision of Trial Chamber IX of 6 May 2021 entitled "Sentence" (hereinafter ICC *Ongwen* Appeal Judgment).

6 *See, for example,* N.E. Pieters and T.R. Kirabira, 'The Ongwen Judgement at the ICC: A Missed Opportunity for Former Child Soldiers?', *International Law Blog* (22 June 2021), available online at internationallaw.blog/2021/06/22/the-ongwen-judgement-at-the-icc-a-missed-opportunity-for-former-child-soldiers/#_ftn24 (accessed 28 August 2023); L. Issa, 'Avoiding the third Tragedy: Evaluating Criminal Responsibility of Child Soldiers Under International Law', 34(1) *Temple International and Comparative Law Journal* (2019) 61–93 at 70; I. Roestenburg-Morgan, 'Bringing the Cultural Defences of Dominic Ongwen into Practice at the ICC, *Culture and Human Rights Blog* (21 June 2021), available online at 'culture-human-rights.blogspot.com/2021/06/bringing-cultural-defences-of-dominic.html (accessed 28 August 2023); J.M. Mas and K. Zilionyte, 'Child soldiers and the Case of Dominic Ongwen', *Centre for African Justice, Peace and Human Rights* (2021), available online at centreforafricanjustice.org/child-soldiers-and-the-case-of-dominica-ongwen/ (accessed 28 August 2023).

defences raised by Ongwen's Defence team, from a cultural and religious perspective.[7] Before the conclusion of the trial, Lubaale commented on the appropriateness of traditional justice mechanism in international criminal justice, from a legal pluralism perspective.[8] The innovation that this paper seeks to make to the available knowledge is to give a critical appraisal of the appropriateness of traditional justice mechanisms in international criminal justice; in light of TC IX's refusal to incorporate the *mato oput* traditional justice mechanism of the Acholi people during the sentencing proceedings.

As the Appeals Chamber has confirmed Ongwen's guilt and the sentence imposed on him, this appraisal seeks to highlight that both TC IX and the Appeals Chamber arguably missed an opportunity to clarify the role of traditional justice mechanisms in international criminal justice. Notwithstanding that the Chamber's hands were tied as traditional justice mechanisms are not provided for in the Rome Statute, a discussion on the suitability of traditional justice mechanisms and how they can possibly be incorporated into the legal framework of the ICC could have immensely contributed to the jurisprudence of the Court.

TC IX explained that the Chamber's refusal to incorporate the Acholi traditional justice mechanisms as requested by the Defence did not mean that it disregarded the cultural values of the Acholi people.[9] Notwithstanding this explanation, the paper argues that the Chamber's approach in this regard points to the Eurocentric nature of international criminal law, particularly when one considers that the Rome Statute of the International Criminal Court (Rome Statute) does not have a provision for incorporating traditional justice mechanisms. The paper concludes that if the Court is to be a truly universal

7 *See, for example*, M. Kersten and M.A. Drumbl, 'Getting an Unforgettable Gettable: The Trial of Dominic Ongwen', *Justice in Conflict* (5 February 2021), available online at justiceinconflict .org/2021/02/05/getting-an-unforgettable-gettable-the-trial-of-dominic-ongwen/ (accessed 28 August 2023); A. Nistor, A. Merrylees and B. Hola, 'Spellbound at the ICC: the Intersection of spirituality and international criminal law', in J. Fraser and B.M. Leyh (eds), *Intersections of Law and Culture at the International Criminal Court* (Edward Elgar, Cheltenham, 2020), pp. 147–168, doi: 10.4337/9781839107306.00016; S. D'hondt, J Perez-Leon-Acevedo and F. Ferraz-de-Almeida, 'Spirituality and Duress: Local Culture Beliefs and the International Criminal Court', *Opinio Juris* (15 February 2022), available online at opiniojuris .org/2022/02/15/spirituality-and-duress-local-culture-beliefs-at-the-international-criminal -court/ (accessed 28 August 2023).

8 E.C. Lubaale, 'Legal Pluralism as a lens through which to understand the role and place of TJMs in international criminal justice' 52(2) *Journal of Legal Pluralism and Unofficial Law* (2020) 180–202, doi: 10.1080/07329113.2020.1780387.

9 ICC *Ongwen* Sentencing, *supra* note 4, para 27.

mechanism of justice and accountability, it ought to holistically consider the issues brought before it, particularly from the Global South.

This paper is divided into 5 sections. Section 2 gives a brief overview of the *mato oput* traditional justice mechanism as applied in Northern Uganda by the Acholi people. It also highlights that the implementation of traditional justice mechanisms following periods of conflict is not unique to Uganda, by giving an overview of Rwanda's *gacaca* courts, and examples of traditional justice practices from Sierra Leone, Burundi and Mozambique. Section 3 examines TC IX's approach to the request by Ongwen's defence team to incorporate traditional justice mechanisms at the sentencing stage. Section 4 examines whether traditional justice mechanisms have a place in international criminal justice, and Section 5 makes some concluding remarks.

2 Traditional Justice Mechanisms: A Brief Overview

Before examining the approach by TC IX to the request by Ongwen's Defence team to incorporate traditional justice mechanisms at the sentencing stage, it is pertinent to provide a brief overview of the application of traditional justice mechanisms in Africa. This will highlight how some African countries emerging from conflict have applied traditional justice mechanisms in an attempt to ensure healing and forgiveness. Examples include:

- The reconciliation rituals of *mato oput* and nyono *tong gweno* 'stepping of eggs' practiced by the Acholi people in Northern Uganda.[10]
- The establishment of the *gacaca* courts in Rwanda.[11]
- The role of *magamba* spirits following the civil war in Gorongosa, Central Mozambique.[12]

10 M. Lacey, 'Victims of Uganda Atrocities Choose a Path of Forgiveness', *New York Times* (18 February 2005), available online at www.nytimes.com/2005/04/18/world/africa/atrocity-victims-in-uganda-choose-to-forgive.html. (accessed 28 August 2023).

11 B. Ingelaere, 'The Gacaca courts in Rwanda', in L. Huyse and M. Salter (eds), *Traditional Justice and Reconciliation after Violent Conflict: Learning from African Experiences* (International Idea, Stockholm, 2008), pp. 25–59.

12 V. Igreja and B. Dias-Lambrace, 'Restorative justice and the role of magamba spirits in post-civil war Mozambique', in L. Huyse and M. Salter (eds), *Traditional Justice and Reconciliation after Violent Conflict: Learning from African Experiences* (International Idea, Stockholm, 2008), pp. 61–82.

- The *bashingantahe* mechanism in Burundi.[13]
- The *Fambul Tok*[14] and *Kpaa Mende*[15] practices in Sierra Leone.

2.1 *Mato Oput and Nyono Tong Gweno: Northern Uganda*

The Ugandan government and the LRA entered into a peace agreement brokered by the then Vice President, Riek Machar, in June 2007. This agreement, known as the Juba Peace Agreement on Reconciliation (Juba Peace Agreement),[16] incorporated traditional justice mechanisms including the *mato oput*. The agreement stated that although traditional justice mechanisms would be applied, criminal prosecutions were envisaged, to bring those who committed gross human rights violations to account.[17] Article 3.1 of the Juba Agreement provides as follows,

> Traditional justice mechanisms, such as Culo Kwor, Mato Oput, Kayo Cuk, Ailuc and Tonu ci Koka and others as practiced in the communities affected by the conflict, shall be promoted, with necessary modifications, as a central part of the framework for accountability and reconciliation.[18]

Article 4.1 of the Agreement provided as follows,

> Formal criminal and civil justice measures shall be applied to any individual who is alleged to have committed serious crimes or human rights violations in the course of the conflict. Provided that, state actors shall be

13 A. Kaburahe, 'The institution of bashingantahe in Burundi', in L. Huyse and M.Salter (eds) *Traditional Justice and Reconciliation after Violent Conflict: Learning from African Experiences* (International Idea, Stockholm, 2008), pp. 149–178.

14 A. Ilif, 'Root and Branch: Discourses of Tradition in Grassroots Transitional Justice', 6(2) *International Journal of Transitional Justice* (2012) 253–273.

15 J. Alie, 'Reconciliation and traditional justice: Tradition-based practices of the Kpaa Mende in Sierra Leone', in L. Huyse and M. Salter (eds), *Traditional Justice and Reconciliation after Violent Conflict: Learning from African Experiences* (International Idea, Stockholm, 2008), pp. 123–146.

16 Agreement for Peace and Reconciliation between the Government of the Republic of Uganda and the Lord's Resistance Army/Movement, Juba,Sudan,29 June 2007 (Juba Agreement), available online at ucdp.uu.se/downloads/fullpeace/Uga%2020070629.pdf (accessed 28 August 2023).

17 Lubaale, *supra* note 8, p.188.

18 Juba Agreement, *supra* note 16, Article 3.

> subjected to existing criminal justice processes and not to special justice processes under this Agreement.[19]

The government of Uganda later backtracked from its earlier self-referral of the Uganda situation with government officials travelling to the Hague to ask the ICC to withdraw charges against LRA leaders including Ongwen, expressing concern that prosecutions at the ICC would impede the peace process underway in Northern Uganda.[20] The Ugandan President Yoweri Museveni said referring to the Juba Agreement,

> what we have said in the agreement is that instead of using this formal Western type of justice we are going to use the traditional justice, a traditional blood settlement mechanism.[21]

It has been observed that the ICC indictments and arrest warrants against LRA leaders were one of the major impediments to the signing of a final peace agreement between the LRA and the Ugandan government.[22] Saether has asserted that the Ugandan government's concerns were unjustified as it was inconceivable that the LRA leaders would be subjected to traditional justice mechanisms only, because the Juba Peace Agreement clearly stated that these would be applied alongside prosecution for gross human rights violations.[23]

The *mato oput* tradition is based on the belief of the Acholi people on the sacredness of human life, and the strict prohibition of the killing of human beings by their religion.[24] According to Latigo,

---

19 *Ibid*, Article 4.1.

20 Lubaale, *supra* note 8, p. 188.

21 A. Croft, 'Uganda offers blood settlement to LRA rebels', *Reuters* (11 March 2008), available online at www.reuters.com/article/idUSL11891647 (accessed 28 August 2023).

22 S. Nouwen, 'The International Criminal Court: A Peacebuilder in Africa?', in D. Curtis and G. Dzinesa (eds), *Peacebuilding, Power, and Politics and Africa* (Ohio University Press, Athens, OH, 2012), pp. 171–194, p.181; K.M. Clarke, 'Peace and 'Justice' Sequencing in Management of Violence in the Malabo Protocol for the African Court', in C.C. Jalloh, K.M. Clarke and V.O. Nmehielle (eds), *The African Court of Justice and Human and Peoples' Rights in Context: Developments and Challenges* (Cambridge University Press, Cambridge, 2019), 109–146, p.114.

23 G. Saether, 'The Complementarity of ICC and other Instruments in Transitional Justice- the case of Northern Uganda, 27(4) *Nordic Journal of Human Rights* (2009) 467–486, p.475.

24 J.O. Latigo, 'Northern Uganda: Tradition-based practices in the Acholi region', in L. Huyse and M. Salter (eds), *Traditional Justice and Reconciliation after Violent Conflict: Learning from African Experiences* (International Idea, Stockholm, 2008), pp. 85–119, at 103.

> The community was enjoined to observe this strictly by worshipping the same supreme deity, Nyarubanga, through an intermediary deity, known as the jok-ker, which meant 'the ruling deity'. Within such a community, if one person happened to kill another person(s) from the same or a different clan, the killing would provoke the anger of the deities and ancestral spirits of the victim(s) … such killings automatically create a supernatural barrier between the clan of the killer and the clan of the person(s) who has/have been killed. As soon as the killing happens, the members of the two clans immediately stop eating and drinking from the same bowl or vessel, and engaging in social interaction of any form. This supernatural barrier remains in force until the killing is atoned for and a religious rite of reconciliation has been performed, to cleanse the taint.[25]

The reconciliation ritual is performed where an individual has killed accidentally or on purpose. Prior to the reconciliation ritual being performed, the killer is not allowed to visit other homesteads as it is feared that he/she will contaminate the homestead's soil with the taint (*ujabu*). An impartial mediator is appointed by the Council of elders to mediate between the two clans, and to oversee the arrangements for the payment of 'blood money'. The reconciliation ritual is performed in an uncultivated field between the villages of the two clans involved.[26] The killer provides a bull, and the relatives of the deceased provide a goat for the reconciliation ceremony. Members of the two clans drink from the same vessel for the first time following the killing and the bull and goat meat alongside other cooked food is given to elders from both clans, signalling that they can now interact freely with one another.[27] The *oput* (bitter root) which the clan representatives drink symbolizes the bitterness in the clans brought about by the killing, and the drinking represents that the clans have 'washed away' that bitterness.[28]

The Acholi people also practice a ritual known as *nyono tong gweno* (stepping on the egg) to cleanse family members who have not been at home for a long time. This is based on the belief that these family members might have come into contact with bad spirit which would in turn bring bad luck to

25 *Ibid.*
26 *Ibid*, p. 104.
27 *Ibid*, p. 105.
28 Z. Tiberindwa, *The hidden truth: A critical examination of Uganda's transitional justice legal and policy reforms on truth seeking*, LLM mini thesis (University of the Western Cape, Bellville, 2021), p. 36.

their kinsmen if they are allowed to return home without being cleansed.[29] This ritual is also performed in respect of those who may have left home following a misunderstanding or a fight.[30] Although Acholi traditional experts have said that it is meant to be performed at the level of the clan or family,[31] the 'stepping of the egg' ritual has been practiced collectively at the community level in northern Uganda for former child soldiers.[32]

Other rituals performed by the Acholi people include *moyo kum* ('cleansing the body'), *moyo piny* ('cleansing of an area') and *gono tong* ('bending the spear'). Neighbouring ethnic communities also practice reconciliation rituals, including *kayo cuk* ('biting of charcoal') perfomed by the Langi, *tonu ci koka* performed by the Madi and *ailuc* perfomed by the Iteso.*Kayo cuk, tonu ci koka* and *ailuc* are practiced after full accountability.[33]

The Acholi jurisprudence, as observed by Latigo, aligns accountability and reconciliation, and does not accept or promote impunity.[34] The counter-factual investigations into the past and present to promote healing and moving on to the future have the potential to identify the root causes of human rights violations and better understand the impact of violations on victims.[35] Notwithstanding this, the Acholi traditional justice mechanisms have been criticized for a number of reasons which will be discussed below. Despite this criticism, this author is of the view that the Acholi traditional justice mechanisms, like other traditional justice mechanisms practiced by other African societies, remain relevant in addressing atrocities in communities transitioning from periods of conflict to peace.

2.2 *The Gacaca Courts in Rwanda*

The use of traditional justice mechanisms to deal with atrocities is not unique to Uganda. In the aftermath of the 1994 Rwandan genocide, the government of Rwanda established the *gacaca* courts, which were traditional courts established as an alternative to the retributive model of justice offered by the International Criminal Tribunal for Rwanda (ICTR). According to Ingelaere,

29 Latigo, *supra* note 24, pp.105–106.
30 *Ibid*, p. 106.
31 *Ibid.*
32 *Ibid.*
33 *Ibid.*
34 Ibid, p. 110.
35 *Ibid.*

> … the word *gacaca* means 'justice on the grass' … the name Gacaca is derived from the word 'umugaca', the Kinyarwandan word referring to a plant that is so soft to sit on that people preferred to gather on it.[36]

The practice of *gacaca* can be traced back to around the 17th century when Rwanda consisted of smaller territories which were governed by kings. The king (*mwami*) was assisted by guardians of tradition (*abiru*) in adjudicating matters brought before him. Before a matter could be heard by the king however, it had to be deliberated upon by the lineage heads, in gacaca gatherings.[37] After independence the gacaca evolved into a semi-formal or semi-administrative body with procedures being prescribed by local authorities, notes of meetings were recorded, and meetings were held on fixed dates.[38] In the aftermath of the genocide, some communities spontaneously started resorting to the ancient gacaca practice, and this partly paved the way for the government to formally support the communities and establish the gacaca courts.[39] The *gacaca* courts were therefore based on a traditional, community based-tribunals model which was guided by legislation.

The *gacaca* courts were established in June 2002 and run by an institution which later came to be known as the National Service of Gacaca Jurisdictions.[40] This was part of the transitional justice process to enable the people of Rwanda to move on from the conflict period of the civil war between the Hutu and Tutsi ethnic groups, which had led to the genocide campaign against the Tutsis by the Hutu-led government in 1994.[41] From 2002 to 2004, the courts operated in 12 pilot areas, compiling files based on accounts given by the local people, of the events that had transpired from 1990 to 1994.The first *gacaca* trials were held in 2005. The initial deadline was late 2007 but the deadlines were repeatedly extended until mid-July 2010.[42]

---

36 Ingelaere, *supra* note 11, p. 33.

37 *Ibid.*

38 *Ibid*, p. 34.

39 *Ibid*, p. 35.

40 Human Rights Watch Report, 'Justice Compromised: The Legacy of Rwanda's community-based gacaca courts', *Human Rights Watch* (31 May 2011), available at www.hrw.org/report/2011/05/31/justice-compromised/legacy-rwandas-community-based-gacaca-courts (accessed 28 August 2023).

41 E. Barth, 'Rwanda's gacaca courts: Looking back on an innovative mechanism of transitional justice', *African Legal Studies Blog* (22 October 2020), available online at africanlegalstudies.blog/2020/10/22/rwandas-gacaca-courts-looking-back-on-an-innovative-mechanism-of-transitional-justice/ (accessed 18 March 2023).

42 Human Rights Watch Report, *supra* note 40.

Like the Truth and Reconciliation Commission hearings in South Africa, the *gacaca* hearings were held in public, and allowed the people of Rwanda to openly discuss what had happened during the civil war and the ensuing genocide. The gacaca courts were considered to be a cost effective and time efficient model which would foster accountability and reconciliation in a nation which was affected by overcrowding in prisons, and was lacking in resources, including financial resources, due to past conflict.[43]

The gacaca courts have been criticized on the basis that they did not conform to the international standards of fair trial. As noted by Barth,

> In noncompliance with the accused right to a competent and impartial judiciary (Art.14 (1) ICCPR), the judges were not required to have attained any level of education nor qualification in law. Due to the courts' embedding in the local communities and the lack of monetary compensation, they were particularly sensitive to local power structures and bribery.[44]

The *gacaca* courts were also criticized for promoting victors' justice. Rwandan Patriotic Front soldiers which had ended the genocide and became the governing party, were exempted from the *gacaca* processes. The Rwandan President Paul Kagame

> cautioned against confusing crimes committed by RPF soldiers with genocide and explained that RPF crimes were merely isolated incidents of revenge, despite evidence to the contrary.[45]

In addition, the *gacaca* laws were amended in 2004 to exclude war crimes from the jurisdiction of gacaca courts, in a move apparently aimed at protecting the RPF soldiers who had reportedly killed more than 10 000 people during and after the genocide.[46]

Clapham has asserted that notwithstanding the criticism levelled against the *gacaca* courts, they did play a significant part in addressing the problem of overcrowding of genocide-related prisoners awaiting trial in Rwandan prisons;

43 Barth, *supra* note 41.
44 *Ibid.*
45 Human Rights Watch Report, *supra* note 40.
46 *Ibid.*

and a lack of skilled legal experts to deal with the cases.[47] The *gacaca* courts also offered the victims' families the opportunity to know the truth about where their relatives' remains were buried, which is an important step towards healing and closure.[48] Some people in Rwanda have expressed satisfaction at the work of the *gacaca* courts, saying that apart from revealing the truth about what happened during the genocide, the courts have also helped to ease the tensions between the Hutus and the Tutsis.[49]

The prevalence of the use of traditional justice mechanisms to address gross human rights violations in African countries is evidence that these traditional practices are part of the lived realities of the African people. In this vein, the next section will discuss whether traditional justice mechanisms have a place in proceedings before the ICC.

3 Traditional Justice Mechanisms at the International Criminal Court: *The Prosecutor v Dominic Ongwen*

The *Prosecutor v Ongwen* judgment ignited significant debate in international criminal law, particularly because of the many important precedents arising out of this case. For the first time, the Court was faced with a victim turned perpetrator as Ongwen himself had been abducted by the LRA at an early age. The Court also had to deal with mental incapacity and duress defences for the first time since its inception, and for the first-time forced marriage was interpreted by the ICC as an independent crime against humanity satisfying the legal requirements of 'other crimes' as provided for in Article 7 (k) of the Rome Statute of the International Criminal Court (Rome Statute).[50] A detailed discussion of these issues is beyond the scope of this paper, whose main focus is on the role of traditional justice mechanisms in situations where the accused has committed core international crimes, like Ongwen. This section examines the approach by TC IX to the request by the Defence to incorporate the Acholi

47 C. Clapham, 'Gacaca: A successful experiment in restorative justice?', *E-International Relations* (30 July 2012), available online at www.e-ir.info/pdf/24700 (accessed 28 August 2023), p. 1.

48 *Ibid*, p. 2.

49 Human Rights Watch Report, *supra* note 40.

50 K. Stavrou and A. Sauermoser, 'The Prosecutor V Dominic Ongwen: A Judgment Of Many Firsts', *Human Rights Pulse* (11 May 2021), available online at www.humanrightspulse.com/mastercontentblog/the-prosecutor-v-dominic-ongwen-a-judgment-of-many-firsts (accessed 18 March 2023).

traditional justice mechanisms at the sentencing stage as confirmed by the Appeals Chamber.

3.1 *Confirmation of Conviction and Sentence by the Appeals Chamber*

Ongwen was sentenced to 25 years in prison in May 2021, pending the outcome of his appeal. The sentence was passed in accordance with the provisions of Articles 76–78 of the Rome Statute and Rules 145 and 146 of the Rules of Procedure and Evidence.[51] The Appeals Chamber in its decision rendered on 15 December 2022, upheld the decisions of TC IX on Ongwen's conviction and sentence, which means that the conviction and sentencing judgment by TC IX is now final.[52]

There were twelve grounds of appeal, and only the first three will be referred to here. On the first ground, the Defence submitted that Ongwen's rights to a fair trial were violated as TC IX issued the Sentencing Decision before furnishing him with the Conviction Decision translated into Acholi.[53] This was rejected by the Appeals Chamber on the basis that the Trial Chamber had furnished Ongwen with an Acholi interpretation of the verdict and an extensive summary of main findings and underlying reasons, and the defence had been put on notice of potential aggravating factors and they were able to make submissions and introduce evidence with respect to potential mitigating and aggravating circumstances.[54]

On the second ground, the Defence submitted that TC IX had erred in admitting victims'' 'testimonial evidence' submitted by the victims' legal representatives, and using this evidence in the Sentencing Decision.[55] This was rejected by the Appeals Chamber on the basis that TC IX had clarified that it was appropriate to make a direct reference to the victims' legal representatives' submissions as an expression of the victims' will and opinion,[56] and that the Defence did not demonstrate that TC IX had erred in referring to the victims'

---

51 ICC *Ongwen* Sentencing judgment, *supra* note 4, 'Disposition'.

52 International Criminal Court 'Ongwen case: ICC Appeals Chamber confirms the conviction and sentencing decisions', Press Release, *International Criminal Court* (15 December 2022), available at www.icc-cpi.int/news/ongwen-case-icc-appeals-chamber-confirms-conviction-and-sentencing-decisions (accessed 28 August 2023).

53 ICC, Situation in Uganda, *Prosecutor* v *Dominic Ongwen, case* no ICC-02/04-01/15-A- 'Public Redacted Judgment on the appeal of Mr Ongwen against the decision of Trial Chamber IX of 4 February 2021 entitled "Trial Judgment"' (hereinafter ICC *Ongwen* Appeal Judgment), at paras 39–42.

54 *Ibid*, paras 63–65.

55 *Ibid*, paras 75–76.

legal representatives' submissions in the Sentencing Decision.[57] The third ground of appeal will be discussed below.

3.2 *Incorporation of Traditional Justice Mechanisms*

The third ground of appeal submitted by Ongwen's Defence team before the Appeals Chamber was that TC IX erred when it rejected and failed to objectively consider the Acholi Traditional Justice System, in particular the Acholi reconciliation ritual of *mato oput*.[58] This was rejected on the basis, *inter alia*, that TC IX had correctly ruled that it was precluded from incorporating a penalty not provided for in the legal framework of the Rome Statute.[59] The Appeals Chamber also rejected the submission by the Defence that TC IX held a biased view of the Acholi traditional justice system because of its reliance on the testimony of non-Acholi persons and the refusal to hear witnesses, who, according to the Defence, were 'well placed to inform conclusions' on that justice system.[60] The Appeals Chamber also found no merit in the contention by the Defence that TC IX disregarded its submissions on social rehabilitation and reintegration and failed to appreciate correctly the 'relevant cultural beliefs and practices' of Mr Ongwen as a personal circumstance.[61]

During sentencing proceedings before TC IX, Ongwen's Defence team requested the Court to consider incorporating traditional justice mechanisms, in particular the *mato oput*. The majority of Ongwen's victims were from the Acholi clan, and Ongwen himself belongs to this clan. It is not in dispute that Ongwen was abducted by the LRA when he was still a child. In 1987 when Dominic Ongwen was a child of about 9 years, he was abducted by the LRA and turned into a child soldier. There is not much information about him that has been verified, and he lied about his home village to his captors, presumably to protect his family.[62] There is even speculation to the effect that Dominic Ongwen is not his real name and that he gave a false name to his captors as he had been earlier instructed by his parents to do in the event that he were to be abducted; also to protect his family.[63] The Trial Chamber noted that amongst the evidence given regarding his age, the most reliable was evidence from his uncle Johnson Odong, who testified that Ongwen was born in Corom,

56 *Ibid*, para. 84.
57 *Ibid*, paras 85 and 87.
58 *Ibid*, paras 88–90.
59 *Ibid*, paras 96–105.
60 *Ibid*, para. 124.
61 *Ibid*, para. 125.
62 Mas and Zilionyte, *supra* note 6.
63 Issa, *supra* note 6, p. 70.

Northern Uganda in May 1978, and he was abducted in 1987 when he was in his third year of primary school.[64]

Some communities in Northern Uganda advocate for recourse to traditional justice mechanisms in dealing with former child soldiers, because of the circumstances leading to these children's involvement in the conflict.[65] As a child soldier Ongwen endured abuses similar to the abuses he, in his later years as an adult commander within the ranks of the LRA, would later inflict upon his victims. In her Opening Statement in December 2016, the then Prosecutor Fatou Bensouda said that Ongwen,

> ... must have undergone through the trauma of separation from his family, brutalization by his captors, and initiation into the violence of the LRA way of life. He has been presented as a victim rather than a perpetrator ...[66]

During the trial, Prosecution expert witnesses Dr Catherine Abbo (P-0445) noted in her report that,

> From the time of his abduction, a very critical time for rewiring the brain to coming out of the bush, his wiring took a different turn as a result of the traumatic experiences and an unfavorable environment he lived in for over 25 years ... It is however clear the unfavourable environment over which he had no control as an abducted child growing into an adult negated his capacity to refrain from doing wrong because he was not presented with an alternative way of life in the bush, despite knowing that what he was doing was wrong.[67]

Commenting on the possibility of applying *mato oput* to the case of Ongwen Lubaale said,

64 ICC *Ongwen* Trial Judgment, *supra* note 1, para. 29.

65 Lubaale, *supra* note 8, p. 191; C. Blattman and J. Annan, 'Child Combatants in Northern Uganda: Reintegration Myths and Realities', in R. Muggah (ed.), *Security and Post-Conflict Reconstruction: Dealing with Fighters in the Aftermath of War* (Routledge, Abingdon, 2008), pp. 103–126.

66 Situation in Uganda: *The Prosecutor v Dominic Ongwen*, Public Redacted Version of 'Corrected Version' of Defence Closing Brief (hereinafter ICC *Ongwen* Defence Closing Brief)filed on 24 February 2020 ICC-02/04-01/15-1722-Corr-Red, available online at www.icc-cpi.int/sites/default/files/CourtRecords/CR2020_00998.PDF, para 17.

67 ICC *Ongwen* Appeal Judgment, *supra* note 53, para. 227.

> With Ongwen allegedly abducted by the LRA at a tender age of ten … the possibility of dealing with him in terms of Mato Oput cannot be ruled out. With his alleged commission of some atrocities after his attainment of adulthood at the age of 18 … the role of TJM s can be questioned based on the fact that the Juba Peace Agreement advocates the need for high-level perpetrators to be dealt with through criminal prosecution.[68]

Although the Juba agreement was a preliminary agreement and the final agreement was never signed as mentioned above, the fact that it explicitly referred to accountability for gross human rights violations highlights that from the beginning it was inconceivable that atrocities committed during the conflict in Northern Uganda would go unpunished.

> The Defence had argued during closing arguments at trial that should Ongwen be convicted, punishment should be suspended and that the Court should […] order Mr Ongwen to undergo the Mato Oput Process of Accountability and Reconciliation as the final sentence for the crimes for which he is convicted.[69]

The Defence also submitted letters, reports, and statements from people with intimate knowledge of the Acholi traditional justice mechanism.[70] During the sentencing proceedings the Defence however abandoned this line of argument. Considering the gravity of the crimes for which Ongwen was convicted, it would have been a miscarriage of justice for the Defence to expect the Court to wholly suspend Ongwen's sentence. During sentencing the Defence instead proposed that the,

> retributive factor of sentencing suggests that the Chamber issue Mr Ongwen a shorter sentence and allow Mr Ongwen to undergo all of the appropriate rituals in northern Uganda, including Mato Oput.[71]

The Prosecution reiterated that the *mato oput* process required the accused to show remorse for his actions, and Ongwen had not done this.[72] The legal representatives for the victims, Manoba and Sehmi, have explained that the usage of mato *oput* as a traditional mechanism of justice in Northern Uganda

68 Lubaale, *supra* note 8, p. 191.
69 ICC *Ongwen* Sentencing judgment, *supra* note 4, para.17.
70 *Ibid*, para. 15.
71 *Ibid*, para. 18.
72 *Ibid*, para. 20.

has declined with the passage of time.[73] This does not however mean that this mechanism has completely fallen into disuse.

Central to the *mato oput* traditional justice mechanism is the admission of wrongdoing by the perpetrator and showing remorse for the wrongful acts. Unfortunately, throughout the trial Ongwen showed no remorse. The use of *mato oput* in Ongwen's case, even if TC IX had granted the request by the Defence, would presumably not have served the intended purpose. This is because the *mato oput* process can only be said to be complete and legitimate if the perpetrator shows remorse, which in turn allows the victims to forgive him for the wrongful acts. As explained by Latigo, the *mato oput* tradition,

> is predicated on full acceptance of one's responsibility for the crime that has been committed or the breaking of a taboo. In its practice, redemption is possible, but only through this voluntary admission of wrongdoing, the acceptance of responsibility.[74]

The sentence handed to Ongwen and confirmed on appeal is a fairly long one. It cannot be said with absolute certainty that Ongwen will maintain his position of showing no remorse even during the period of serving his sentence. The Prosecution submitted that it had no objection to traditional justice mechanisms if that is what the victims wanted, but that this should only be done after Ongwen had served his sentence or during his sentence, if the necessary arrangements could be made.[75] This proposal by the Prosecution would have been a good compromise, had Ongwen been a good candidate for the *mato oput* tradition by showing remorse, and had the victims been willing to partake of the rituals prescribed by *mato oput*. However, not all victims expressed the view that Ongwen should be forgiven.

The victims' legal representatives said in their joint submissions on sentencing that '… victims indicated that if Mr Ongwen was remorseful, he would have sought forgiveness and would not be harbouring intentions to appeal the verdict'[76] and that,

---

73 J.A. Manoba and A. Sehmi, 'What the Dominic Ongwen trial could mean for traditional justice mechanisms in the ICC, *LSE Blogs* (26 July 2021), available online at blogs.lse.ac.uk/africaatlse/2021/07/26/dominic-ongwen-trial-traditional-justice-mechanisms-uganda-international-criminal-court-icc/ (accessed 28 August 2023).

74 Latigo, *supra* note 24, pp. 107–108.

75 ICC *Ongwen* Sentencing, para. 19.

76 ICC, Situation in Uganda, *Prosecutor v Dominic Ongwen*, case no ICC-02/04-01/15, Victims' Joint Submission on Sentencing, available at www.icc-cpi.int/sites/default/files/CourtRecords/CR2021_03241.PDF (accessed 28 August 2023), para. 100.

> A victim stated that he could not forgive or reconcile with Dominic Ongwen as many members of the LRA were given the chance to return to the community, but Mr Ongwen did not take amnesty when it was offered.[77]

A small minority of the victims expressed the view that Ongwen should serve a light sentence and be forgiven, but that such forgiveness would be conditional upon him compensating the families of the victims, and if he admitted guilt and apologized to the victims.[78] Another small minority was of the view that the fact that the victims were not seeking death sentence but life imprisonment was in itself a form of forgiveness.[79] In addition, the victims' legal representatives also pointed out that the proposal by Ongwen's Defence did not correspond to the views of the victims.[80]

As Ongwen was not remorseful and the majority of his victims were not ready and/or willing to forgive him, incorporating traditional justice mechanisms at the sentencing stage as had been requested by the Defence would presumably have been a futile exercise. However, this paper argues that TC IX missed an opportunity to clarify the issue as to the role of traditional justice mechanisms before the ICC. A pronouncement on this issue by the Chamber would have contributed to the jurisprudence of the Court in this regard, and serve as a guide in future cases, as this was the first time that a request to incorporate traditional justice mechanisms was made.

The Chamber explained that it was not insensitive to established cultural and traditional practices of the Acholi people; and ruled that the Defence's request for the incorporation of traditional justice mechanisms could not be granted because article 23 of the Rome statute explicitly states that sentencing of a convicted person should only be done in accordance with the provisions of the Rome Statute; and Article 77 of the Rome Statute specifies the penalties to be imposed.[81] The Chamber also relied on the Appeals Chamber Decision in the *Bemba* case where it was held that the Trial Chamber can only have recourse to the penalties provided for in the Rome Statute.[82] On the basis of

77 *Ibid*, para. 101.
78 *Ibid*, para. 106.
79 *Ibid*, para. 108.
80 *Ibid*, para. 109.
81 *Ibid*, para. 26.
82 ICC, Situation in the Central African Republic, *Prosecutor v Jean-Pierre Bemba et al, case* no ICC-01,05-01/13, Public Redacted Judgment on the appeals of the Prosecutor, Mr Jean-Pierre Bemba Gombo, Mr Fidele Babala Wandu and Mr Narcisse Arido against the decision of Trial Chamber VII entitled "Decision on Sentence pursuant to article 76 of the Statute", para. 77.

the principle of legality, TC IX then held that it could not grant the request by the defence to incorporate traditional justice mechanisms.'[83]

In the absence of a specific provision in the Rome Statute about the incorporation of traditional justice mechanisms, the Chamber's hands were admittedly tied, as was confirmed by the Appeals Chamber. The ICC is a creation of statute, the Rome Statute, and this calls for the judges of the Court to be guided by the provisions of the Statute in their work. The fact that the Rome Statute makes no mention of traditional justice mechanisms however arguably points to the Eurocentric nature of international law.

There have been claims by scholars who are adherents of the Third World Approaches to International Law (TWAIL) that international law considers values or practices seriously only when they are coming from the global north. TWAIL,

> ... offers a central challenge to international law's Eurocentricity. Broadly, TWAIL argues that international law is the handmaiden of colonialism and imperialism, which is built on racial hierarchies and double standards.[84]

The apparent disregard for values and practices from the Global South is arguably reminiscent of the 'dynamic of difference' and 'standard of civilisation' that was applied during the 19th Century colonial confrontation as explained by Anghie, to justify the colonial encounter.[85] Gevers has noted that despite the fact that the 'standard of civilization' is now obsolete in international law, a number of scholars have pointed to the application of double standards in international criminal law, with different standards seemingly applying to the former colonisers and the former colonies respectively.[86]

The Court's approach towards the request by the Defence, i.e., its failure to comprehensively consider the potential of traditional justice mechanisms before the ICC, arguably lends credence to this double standard claim. It is not in dispute that traditional justice mechanisms such as the *mato oput* constitute part of the lived realities of the African people. As a Court which is expected

---

83 ICC *Ongwen Sentencing*, *supra* note 4, para. 26.

84 S. Xavier, 'Locating and Situating Justice Pal: TWAIL, International Criminal Tribunals, and Judicial Powers', 12(2) *Asian Journal of International Law* (2022) 292–318, doi: 10.1017/S2044251322000145.

85 *See, generally*, A. Anghie, Imperialism, *Sovereignty and the Making of International Law* (Cambridge University Press, Cambridge, 2007). A detailed discussion of the 'dynamic of difference' and 'standard of civilisation' is beyond the scope of this paper.

86 *Ibid.*

to be a truly universal and effective mechanisms of justice and accountability, the ICC ought to seriously consider the lived realities of the African people including those people in Northern Uganda. It has been reported that before the Ongwen trial, an attempt was made to reintegrate Former Abducted Persons (FAPs) through the Acholi traditional Justice mechanisms in 2005.[87] Tom notes that this process was not entirely successful because the FAPs were not completely forgiven by the communities, but that despite,

> the limitations of the Acholi traditional approach to justice in relation to the current circumstances, it still plays a significant role in the reintegration of the returnees. In this case, the traditional and western approaches to justice should not be viewed as being incompatible to each other, but as complementing each other.[88]

Manoba and Sehmi argue that the *mato oput* could not be applied in the *Ongwen* case because, inter alia, not all victims belong to the Acholi clan; and the crimes of which Ongwen was convicted including sexual and gender based violence, have not been resolved through the *mato oput* system before and this limits its applicability.[89] They however contend that the ICC should not outrightly dismiss the possibility of applying traditional justice mechanisms at specific stages of the trial in future cases that may come before the ICC, such as the reparations stage.[90]

This is a sound recommendation, as the concept of reparations is a broad one which goes beyond compensation and includes satisfaction as a form of reparation. Satisfaction includes truth telling and public apologies.[91] Both TC IX and the Appeals Chamber regrettably missed an opportunity to holistically consider the potential of traditional justice mechanisms to complement the prosecution procedure before the ICC. A holistic approach would have been beneficial to possible future cases as this was the first case before the ICC in which the request for the incorporation of traditional justice mechanisms was made. The importance of the ICC giving more context on this issue is

87 P. Tom, 'The Acholi Traditional Approach to Justice and the War in Northern Uganda', *Beyond Intractability* (August 2006), available online at www.beyondintractability.org/casestudy/tom-acholi (accessed 28 August 2023).

88 *Ibid.*

89 Manoba and Sehmi, *supra* note 73.

90 *Ibid.*

91 United Nations Office of the High Commissioner for Human Rights, *Reparations: OHCHR*, available online at www.ohchr.org/en/transitional-justice/reparations (accessed 28 August 2023).

heightened by the divergent views that have been expressed by authors and commentators as to whether traditional justice mechanisms are suitable in cases where core international crimes have been committed, as will be highlighted below.

4 The Place of Traditional Justice Mechanisms in International Crimes Trials

The question to be asked in light of TC IX's approach to the request by the Defence to incorporate traditional justice mechanisms is: Do traditional justice mechanisms have a place in cases where an accused person committed core international crimes, as was the case with Ongwen? This paper argues that traditional justice mechanisms can play a significant role even in cases of gross human rights violations.

The examples of traditional justice mechanisms given above highlight that traditional justice practices are part and parcel of African societies' dispute resolution methods. Scholars including Longman,[92] and Igreja, Dias-Lambranca and Richters,[93] have highlighted a number of advantages associated with traditional justice mechanisms. These include social integration and the fostering of harmony and reconstruction of the society following a period of conflict. Traditional justice mechanisms are also deemed to be appropriate and relevant before international criminal tribunals and courts where local communities are involved in the proceedings.[94] Latigo has explained that traditional justice mechanisms are significant because they strengthen existing structures and help to foster nation-building and reconciliation; they promote unity by encouraging the participation of community members, and that perpetrators usually do not avoid the process.[95]

Despite the opportunities presented by traditional justice mechanisms, a number of criticisms have also been levelled against them. These include the perception that traditional justice mechanisms are archaic, disregard human rights and that they are male-dominated and this makes them unsuitable to

92 T. Longman, 'An Assessment of Rwanda's Gacaca Courts', 21(3) *Peace Review* (2009) 304–312, doi: 10.1080/10402650903099369.

93 V. Igreja, B. Dias-Lambraca and A. Richters, 'Gamba Spirits, Gender Relations, and Healing in Post-Civil War Gorongosa, Mozambique', 14(2) *Journal of the Royal Anthropology Institute* (2008) 353–371.

94 Lubaale, *supra* note 8, p. 181.

95 Latigo, supra note 24, pp. 114–115.

address the needs and concerns of women.[96] It has also been argued that traditional justice mechanisms are culture specific and rigid and are unlikely to be embraced by those who do not relate with the culture or traditions where they originate from.[97] Traditional justice mechanisms have also been criticised for not being uniform and for being unsuitable to deal with crimes which involve people from different ethnicities.[98] Latigo has asserted with respect to *mato oput* that,

> A fundamental weakness of the application of mato oput as a remedy is that, conceptually, it wrongly projects the LRA insurgency as a local Acholi affair. In reality this war had inherent national and international dimensions.[99]

Traditional justice mechanisms are centred around the social fabric in local communities, which has itself been negatively affected by the effects of war such as internal displacement, as was the case in Northern Uganda. This casts doubt on the effectiveness of traditional justice mechanisms such as the *mato oput* and has led to the decline in their usage.[100] There is also a misconception that everyone who agrees or commits to partake in traditional justice practices is willing to forgive and according to Latigo,

> The assumption that underlies the traditional justice process is that the aggrieved party(ies) and the community will be willing to forgive. But *forgiveness* is an extremely delicate and personal thing which *can be influenced but not enforced.*[101]

Lubaale has convincingly argued that whilst the concerns regarding traditional justice mechanisms are valid, traditional justice mechanisms are not inflexible, they are subject to change to suit the evolving dynamics in societies. She points to the inclusion of multiple approaches to justice including traditional justice mechanisms envisaged in the Juba Peace Agreement, as evidence of the

---

96 Lubaale, *supra* note 8, p.192; A. Branch, 'The Violence of Peace: Ethnojustice in Northern Uganda', 45(3) *Development and Change* (2014) 608–630, at 623–625, doi: 10.1111/dech.12094.

97 Tiberindwa, *supra* note 28, p. 38.

98 *Ibid.*

99 Latigo, *supra* note 24, p. 114.

100 Tiberindwa, *supra* note 28, p. 39.

101 Latigo, *supra* note 24, p. 114.

flexibility of traditional justice mechanisms.[102] The criticism that traditional justice mechanisms such as *mato oput* are archaic and rigid are arguably Eurocentric and according to Tiberindwa,

> the assumption of rigidity appears to be based on a flawed 'Eurocentric' paradigm that assumes some notions of justice as necessarily universal when they actually remain a western construct. For instance, in Uganda individuals from different cultural backgrounds are subject to state led judicial processes originating from the British and Roman legal traditions and the Judeo-Christian heritage. Whereas these kinds of justice measures are made applicable to individuals from different cultural backgrounds, usually without the necessary modifications, the application of justice mechanisms drawn from African traditions is resisted on the purport of cultural specificity and rigidity.[103]

With respect to the criticism that traditional justice mechanisms are male dominated and therefore inadequate to address women's rights and concerns, Tiberindwa has suggested that this shortcoming can be mitigated by raising awareness and advocating for the inclusion of women in traditional councils of elders.[104] Tiberindwa notes that Article 32 and Article 35 of the Constitution of Uganda provides for affirmative action to correct the traditional, customary and historically prevalent gender imbalances.

This author is of the view that traditional justice mechanisms have a place in international criminal justice where core international crimes have been committed, alongside the retributive system of justice. This is because due to the gravity of core international crimes, such as the crimes in respect of which Ongwen has been convicted and sentenced, it is not possible for traditional justice mechanisms to be applied in the absence of prosecution. However, traditional justice mechanisms can be implemented simultaneously with the retributive system in proceedings before international criminal tribunals and courts. Lubaale has suggested two options in which this can be made possible. The first option would be to incorporate traditional justice mechanisms through the regulatory regimes of the Rome Statute including the Rules of Evidence and Procedure. This would entail an amendment of the Rome Statute.[105] The second option would be to apply traditional justice mechanisms

102 Lubaale, *supra* note 8, p. 192. For a similar view on the flexibility of traditional justice mechanisms see also Tiberindwa, *supra* note 28, p. 39.

103 Tiberindwa, *ibid*, p. 40.

104 *Ibid*, p. 41; Constitution of the Republic of Uganda 1995, Articles 32 and 33.

105 Lubaale, *supra* note 8, p. 196.

on a case-by-case basis, at the discretion of the court. This author agrees with Lubaale's view that this could be the better option as it does not involve the cumbersome process of having to amend the Rome Statute.[106]

Transitional justice has been described as,

> … the full range of processes and mechanisms associated with a society's attempt to come to terms with a legacy of large-scale past conflict, repressions, violations and abuses, in order to ensure accountability, serve justice and achieve reconciliation.[107]

The wide range of processes encompass both judicial and non-judicial mechanisms which include but are not limited to truth-seeking, reparations, and prosecution initiatives.[108] This means that both international criminal prosecutions before the ICC and traditional justice mechanisms fall under the same umbrella of the term transitional justice. The application of traditional justice mechanisms by African societies therefore does not imply the absence of accountability. Rather, traditional justice mechanisms complement the process of accountability through prosecution initiatives.

5 Concluding Remarks

This paper has examined the role that traditional justice can play in international trials, as seen through the lens of TC IX in the case of *The Prosecutor v Dominic Ongwen*. The paper gave a brief overview of the application of the *mato oput* and *nyono tong gweno* traditional justice mechanisms practiced by the Acholi clan in Northern Uganda, and the establishment of the *gacaca* courts in Rwanda. It examined TC IX's approach to the request by Ongwen's Defence team to incorporate traditional justice mechanisms at the sentencing stage, which was reaffirmed by the Appeals Chamber. The paper argued that although both TC IX and the Appeals Chamber indicated that the Court does not look down upon traditional customs and practices, both Chambers arguably missed an opportunity to holistically explore the possible ways in which traditional justice mechanisms can be incorporated into proceedings before the ICC, and how the Court can in future consider incorporating traditional justice

106 *Ibid.*

107 United Nations office of the High Commissioner for Human Rights, *supra* note 91.

108 *Ibid*; African Union Transitional Justice Policy Framework (adopted February 2019), available online at au.int/sites/default/files/documents/36541-doc-au_tj_policy_eng_web.pdf (accessed 28 August 2023).

mechanisms. It was also explained that as the Rome Statute does not explicitly provide for traditional justice mechanisms, the Chamber was restricted in its approach. This does not however imply that the Chamber was also restricted from bringing clarity to the matter.

To address these allegations of the Eurocentric nature of international criminal law and that of double standards at the ICC specifically, the Court ought to holistically consider the issues that it is faced with, particularly from the global south. As asserted by Manoba and Sehmi, traditional justice mechanisms can possibly be incorporated in international trials at specific stages, but each case ought to be considered on its own merits. The inclusion of traditional justice mechanisms has the potential to strengthen rather than weaken the effectiveness of international criminal justice.[109]

109 Lubaale, *supra* note 8, p. 197.

CHAPTER 5

Proportionality and Moral Blameworthiness in *Ongwen*'s ICC Sentencing Decision

Demetra Fr. Sorvatzioti

Abstract

The ICC's legal framework combines continental and common law features. The sentencing regime provides for a separate hearing process unknown to the continentals. The principle of proportionality governs sentencing determination. Proportionality is met by analysing gravity and moral blameworthiness. In *Ongwen*, the ICC should address his moral blameworthiness by considering his unique dual status as a former abducted child soldier and perpetrator, the expert evidence regarding the LRA and the Acholi culture and history. The Court sentenced Ongwen in a rather formal traditional continental way. However, conviction is not the ICC's ultimatum, and sentencing should not be a pure side effect of conviction. When the ICC tries cases of non-western peoples, it is essential to express its understanding and respect for diversity. By addressing cultural, social, and historical aspects of the case and the offender as part of the sentencing reasoning, the ICC performs the balancing process needed for proportionality.

Keywords

child soldier – gravity – moral blameworthiness – *Ongwen* – sentencing proportionality – social context – victim-perpetrator

> Words and figures cannot adequately portray the physical and psychological harm inflicted on vulnerable children who were brutalized and who lived in constant fear. The loss and grief to their inconsolable families is immeasurable. Their childhood stolen, deprived of education and all

 | DOI: 10.1163/9789004743380_006

human rights, the suffering of the young victims and their families left permanent scars.

BENJAMIN B. FERENCZ[1]

1 Introduction

At age 9, Dominic Ongwen was abducted by the Lord's Resistance Army (LRA). For the next 27 years, he lived in the bush with the LRA. In 2005, at the urging of Uganda's President Museveni, the International Criminal Court (ICC) issued five arrest warrants against Joseph Kony, the LRA founder and Commander in Chief, Vincent Otti, Raks Lukwiya, Okot Odhiambo and Dominic Ongwen, the most junior of the five wanted men. Over the following years, Kony and Otti were never arrested. Odhiabo and Lukwiya died. Ongwen surrendered himself on 16 January 2015. Ongwen, the only LRA person in ICC custody, has been incarcerated since that time.[2]

Ongwen was charged with an indictment containing 70 allegations of war crimes and crimes against humanity.[3] His trial opened on 6 December 2016. During the trial, his defence argued duress and mental incapacitation according to Article 31(1a and d). The Court rejected both defences and convicted him of 61 counts.[4] He was sentenced to 25 years imprisonment.[5] The Appeal Court confirmed this decision by majority.[6] Judge Luz del Carmen Ibáñez Carranza provided an articulate dissenting opinion which is in line with the arguments here.[7]

1 *Ferencz closes Lubanga Case for ICC Prosecution* (August 2011), available online at https://benferencz.org/articles/2010-present/ferencz-closes-lubanga-case-for-icc-prosecution/. *See also* the Schauer report, regarding the multiple phycological disorders child soldiers and ex-combatants suffer in countries with war and violence, *The Prosecutor v Lubanga Dyilo*, ICC-01/04-01/06, 10 July 2012 (Decision on Sentence pursuant to Article 76 of the Statute), paras 39–49.

2 ICC-02/04-01/05, *The Prosecutor v. Joseph Kony and Vincent Otti*, available online at https://www.icc-cpi.int/uganda/kony.

3 ICC-CPI-20160323-PR1202, Press Release (23 March 2016), ICC Pre-Trial Chamber II confirms the charges against Dominic Ongwen and commits him to trial.

4 ICC-02/04-01/15, 4 February 2021, *The Prosecutor v. Dominic Ongwen* (Trial Judgement).

5 ICC-02/04-01/15, 6 May 2021, *The Prosecutor v. Dominic Ongwen* (Sentence).

6 ICC-02/04-01/15-2023, 15 December 2022, Judgment on the appeal of Mr Dominic Ongwen against the decision of Trial Chamber IX of 6 May 2021 entitled 'Sentence'.

7 ICC-02/04-01/15-2023-Anx1, Partly dissenting opinion of Judge Luz del Carmen Ibáñez Carranza, 15 December 2022.

The Trial Court considered the mitigating and aggravating factors listed in the Statute and Rules but in a rather perfunctory manner. Aggravating factors marched in a parade (cruelty, multiplicity of victims, victims particularly defenceless, discrimination on political grounds and discrimination against women) with zero analysis of the prosecutorial burden of proof.[8,9] However, in the 'applicable law' section, the Court said that aggravating factors should be proved beyond a reasonable doubt.[10] This became the beginning and the end of the entire analysis.

When the Court considered the defences of duress and mental capacity for sentencing purposes, it rejected them with reference to the conviction reasoning. Sentencing, especially when long periods of imprisonment are in play, requires more. The drafters and signatories of the Rome Statute accepted that, notwithstanding the gravity of the Rome Statute offences, a range of imprisonment penalties would be available to a sentencing court. This should be interpreted as a reflection of proportionality. While gravity is the central feature of any sentencing regime based on proportionality, a significant element should be moral blameworthiness. Here, the Trial Chamber and the majority of the Appeal Court failed to evaluate how Ongwen's life and experiences affected his moral blameworthiness. The Court's narrow-minded view, which reflects a continental approach, ignored the moral blameworthiness evidence without confronting why it is relevant. Relevance is an important issue in evidence law and in the sentencing process.

There is an important controversy between the majority and the minority of the Appeal Court. While four judges did not understand the concept of moral blameworthiness in relation to the social context of Ongwen, Judge Ibáñez Carranza accurately explained moral blameworthiness via the concept of moral culpability. Regrettably, the majority decision showed a vague understanding of sentencing analysis and ignored the prosecutorial burden of proof. In antithesis, the minority decision, in a modest and articulate way, *spoke the truth*.

This paper suggests that the ICC followed a continental approach lacking an analysis of both proportionality and the burden of proof on sentencing factors. The spine of the discussion is the role of Ongwen's moral blameworthiness[11] and how the ICC misapplied the principle of proportionality. Behind Ongwen's

8 Similar lack of analysis is observed in the trial judgment.

9 *Supra* note 4, para. 131.

10 *Ibid.*, para. 53.

11 Moral blameworthiness is also known as culpability or moral culpability or moral responsibility and is related to sentencing factors.

individual circumstances, was the Ugandan North Acholi social and political context, which was germane to Ongwen's moral responsibility. Ongwen's situation was a socio-political and international criminal law phenomenon. A mere summary by the Court regarding Ongwen's captivity was inadequate to explain the Court's method for balancing proportionality and determining sentencing. Part two examines how the Court defined extreme gravity for sentencing. Part three discusses proportionality and whether the Court analysed it or simply repeated the term several times. A short discussion on sentencing goals with an emphasis on the role of expressive punishment and the case of former child soldiers is offered. Part four explains why Rule 145.2(a)(1) does not impose an *epiclesis* by the Court of the raised defences but a reasoned analysis of how their elements should impact sentencing considerations. Notwithstanding the gravity of the crimes, the Rule does not bend. To understand sentencing analysis for a unique population, part five offers a comparison to the Canadian sentencing jurisprudence regarding aboriginal offenders and discusses how Ongwen's unique status could be seen through the Canadian moral blameworthiness lens. Part six identifies a Western approach to the Acholi peoples' remorse and identifies the twisting process of the Court regarding Ongwen's character. Ultimately, the paper asks whether the sentencing determination reveals a common law or continental approach. While both approaches need to be attentive to the reasoning, the legal tradition familiar to the judges might have influenced their analysis and the judicial thinking process. This is discussed in part seven. The epilogue finds *Ongwen* a disappointing opportunity for an ICC sentencing precedent.

2 Gravity in *Ongwen's* Sentence

The ICC's jurisdiction deals with zenith gravity crimes,[12] where atrocities are sentenced with no mandatory minimums or mandatory life sentences[13] and mitigating and aggravating factors are determined by the Court.[14]

Although gravity plays a significant role in sentencing determination, the vagueness of the ad hoc criminal tribunals and the ICC case law on sentencing reveals ambiguity, while gravity seems to overlap with aggravating factors.[15]

12 M.M. DeGuzman, *Shocking the Conscience of Humanity* (Oxford University Press, Oxford, 2020), p. 35.

13 Article 77(1).

14 Rule 145(2)(a)(b).

15 DeGuzman, *supra* note 12, pp. 170, 174–179, 183. *See also* S. SáCouto, and K. Cleary, 'The gravity threshold of the International Criminal Court', 23 *American University International*

In *Ongwen,* the sentencing Court raised gravity to the "extreme" level without analysis.

It is unclear whether gravity was a jurisdictional issue,[16] or an additional feature for sentencing reasons. For example, the Chamber said, 'the gravity of the crime of torture is in the abstract very high'.[17] For enslavement, 'this incrimination protects the individual's personal liberty, making the crime of enslavement *in abstracto* a crime of considerable gravity'.[18] For rape, it referred to the 'inherent gravity' of rape and marked its' gravity as very high.[19] When the Court looked at the violation of the right to life, liberty, sexual integrity, personal property, the right not to be subjected to cruel or degrading treatment and the right to consensually form a family, it noted that 'the extreme gravity of their violations cannot go unnoticed and unaccounted for'.[20] However, gravity has one jurisdictional aspect and a sentencing impact. The grave importance of a right's violation is not synonymous with the gravity or the extreme gravity of a crime. The latter is examined only via aggravating factors.[21]

The Court stated that it was aware of Ongwen's crimes' extreme gravity, 'especially when considered jointly'.[22] Rule 145(3) and Article 77(1)(b) provide possible life imprisonment when justified by the extreme gravity of the crime *and* the individual circumstances of the convicted person. Here the Court added the gravity of each crime and said: this is a life sentence case, but the individual circumstances permit mitigation. This mathematic syllogism is legally erroneous. Only adding extreme gravity to the offender's circumstances can produce a life sentence, not the crimes' gravity alone. *Ongwen* is not a life sentence case. Kony's might be. Ongwen cannot go beyond thirty years of imprisonment. His unique status should count to reduce a 30-year sentence, not a life.

One aspect of the case, which was viewed paradoxically by the Court only against Ongwen, was the treatment of the kidnapped children by the LRA. The decision provides an identical description of the suffering, Ongwen gave for his life after his abduction.[23] When the Court referred to the 'extreme harsh

---

Law Review (2007) 807–854, regarding 'the amorphous nature of the factors denoting gravity' in sentencing case law of the ad hoc criminal tribunals, p. 842.

16 Article 17.

17 ICC-02/04-01/15, 6 May 2021, *supra* note 4, para. 157.

18 *Ibid.*, para. 162.

19 *Ibid.*, para. 344.

20 *Ibid.*, para. 393.

21 Rule 145(3).

22 *Ibid.*, para. 387.

23 *Ibid.*, para. 360.

treatment of children', it looked at *Ntaganda*. Ntaganda was not a former child soldier. The Court did not differentiate from Ongwen and did not view the child soldiers' treatment as a moral culpability issue in favour of Ongwen, only against him.[24] The Court, for Ongwen, stated that 'it is clear that he intended such treatment of children abducted and integrated into Sinia'.[25] No explanation was offered either for the word *clear* or for Ongwen's purpose of torturing children deliberately despite his well-evidenced indoctrination since he was nine. As for Ongwen's intent, the Court considered his 'degree of participation and degree of intent very high in respect of all of the crimes discussed'.[26] However, it is unclear what the phrase 'very high' intent means in legal terms, even for sentencing.

3 Proportionality in *Ongwen*

Today, proportionality plays a role, often a central one, in most domestic sentencing systems. Going back to the 1960s, two major theoretical strands explained the importance of proportionality. One is known generally as *just deserts*, the primary advocate of which has been Andrew Von Hirsch. Here, proportionality is the engine that ought to drive sentencing. The other is referred to as *limiting retributivism,* where proportionality is the brake, not the engine, on sentencing. That means that other considerations determine the sentencing outcomes, but the scheme cannot extend to produce a disproportionate sentence. This theoretical approach is attributed to the seminal work of Norval Morris. Over time, while both these theories have maintained their original focus on the role of proportionality, they have been modified to include factors that produce similar outcomes.[27]

Given the importance put on proportionality by the *just desert* theorists, it is not surprising that they have given the most consideration to understanding the scope of proportionality. Perhaps the clearest and best-developed example is the book 'Proportionate Sentencing: exploring the Principles' by Von Hirsch and Ashworth.[28] The necessary calculus for determining proportionality is an equation between the seriousness of the offence and the seriousness of the

24 *Ibid.*, para. 361, footnote 655.

25 *Ibid.*, para. 363.

26 *Ibid.*, para. 329. *See also* the phrase 'very high', paras 181, 219, 254, 291, 297, 302, 307, 318, 322.

27 T. Malcolm and A. Manson, 'The Sentencing Theory Debate: Convergence in Outcomes, Divergence in Reasoning', 10(2) *New Criminal Law Review* (2007) 278–310.

28 A. Von Hirsch and A. Ashworth, *Proportionate sentencing: Exploring the principles* (Oxford University Press, Oxford, 2005).

punishment.[29] Of course, a major aspect of seriousness is the assessment of comparative intrinsic gravity between one offence and the others (*cardinal proportionality*), which resulted in what would be essentially a ladder of offences.[30] To determine the distance between the rungs of the ladder and what precise sentence, or range of sentence, do they point, Von Hirsch used what he called *ordinal proportionality*. It involved a process of spacing and anchoring that determined more clearly where each offence fit on the ladder by reference to the past sentencing experience of the particular sentencing system with due regard to restraint in setting the top and bottom limits.

On the other side of the equation, looking at the seriousness of the punishment, an essential element of punishment and sentencing is censure. In other words, for the offender, the victim and the public, the sentence serves to blame the offender for the offence. This means that a proportionate sentence needs to be commensurate with the blameworthiness of the offender.[31] This is why *just deserts* theory distinguished the situation of young offenders or juveniles because they are considered to be, by virtue of their age and lack of maturity, less blameworthy than an adult who commits the same crime. Over time, *just deserts* theorists have incorporated other considerations into the calculus that distinguish between levels of seriousness based on factors like the degree of criminal responsibility attached to the specific offence, not its general category. This would include the role of the offender in the crime and whether the necessary mental element was one of intention or criminal negligence. Other considerations, referred to by Von Hirsch and Ashworth as 'equity factors', have also been included in the calculation.[32] These include factors like mental illness short of insanity. Regardless of the label, what we see is the inclusion within the rubric of blameworthiness of factors that encompass aspects of the offender's circumstances which may lessen the deserved sentence. Essentially, what we have seen is a door opening to consider other aspects which may bear on an offender's blameworthiness (culpability).

Inevitably the above proportionality theory has influenced the discussions on international criminal sentencing goals. However, plurality and ambiguity are found regarding the goals of global institutions.[33] Schabas argues that a human rights approach in sentencing does not permit retribution to guide

29 *Ibid.*, p. 63.

30 For a fuller discussion of ordinal proportionality, see *Ibid.*, pp. 137–143.

31 *Ibid.*, pp. 134–137.

32 *Ibid.*, pp. 165–179.

33 DeGuzman, *supra* note 12, pp. 27–31.

sentencing judges of international criminal tribunals.[34] Ohlin can see only retribution including the death penalty because the offender is a 'community enemy'. Focusing on the gravity of the crimes and the resulting harm, the sentence must be harsh, vindicating the rule of law.[35] However, D'Ascoli argues that the harm produced by the committed crimes can never be proportionate to the imposed sentence.[36] In *Ongwen*, the Court seems to have used a retributive approach by linking proportionality and Ongwen's culpability only to the harm caused.[37] Despite the Court's approach, a proportionality analysis according to Article 81(2)(a) and Rule 145(1) is mandatory.[38]

When looking carefully at Ongwen's case, it is rather difficult to appreciate the utility of the deterrent message of his sentence for the former child soldiers' population. Mark Drumbl argues that no evidence shows the positive results of deterrence, especially when violence is the only 'viable survival strategy' for people. Moreover, the 'normalization of violence', produces a 'deception' hiding the political, historical, social, economic, and colonial factors that led to violence and atrocities.[39] Drumbl promotes the expressive didactic role of punishment, which unlocks the ratio behind punishment, not deterrence. Trial and punishment should mandate 'moral unacceptability' for atrocities to build moral norms.[40] Sentencing should respect certain features of transitional justice applicable in national institutions, as in the case of *Mato Oput* in

---

34 W.A. Schabas, 'Sentencing by International Tribunals: A Human Rights Approach', 7 *Duke Journal of Comparative and International Law* (1996) 461–517. *See also* F. Harhoff, 'Sense and Sensibility in Sentencing-Taking Stock of International Criminal Punishment in Law at War', in O. Engdahl and P. Wrange (eds), *The Law as it Was and the Law as it Should Be*, Volume 22 (Martinus Nijhoff Publishers, Leiden, 2008), pp. 121–140, where Harhoff proposed 'more attention to the reconciliation process', because of the no real impact of general and specific deterrence for war crimes and crimes against humanity, pp. 139–140. As per the contribution of the ICC to deterrence 'on average, it has stronger positive effects on governments than on rebels', H. Jo and B.A. Simmons, 'Can the International Criminal Court Deter Atrocity?', 70(3) *International Organization* (2016) 443–475, p. 444.

35 J.D. Ohlin, 'Proportional Sentences at the ICTY', in B. Swart, G. Sluiter, A. Zahar (eds), *'The Legacy of the International Criminal Tribunal for the Former Yugoslavia'* (Oxford University Press, Oxford, 2011), pp. 322–342, at p. 329.

36 S. D'Ascoli, *'Sentencing in International Criminal Law: The UN ad hoc Tribunals and Future Perspectives for the ICC'* (Hart Publishing, Oxford, 2011), pp. 292–293.

37 M. DeGuzman, 'Proportionate sentencing at the ICC', in C. Stahn (ed.) *The Law and the Practice of the International Criminal Court* (Oxford University Press, Oxford, 2015), pp. 932–962, at p. 936. *See also* the proportionality theories' analysis, *Ibid.*, at pp. 935–943.

38 *See also* DeGuzman, *supra* note 12, p. 182, and B. Hola, 'Sentencing of International Crimes at the ICTY and ICTR', 4 *Amsterdam Law Forum* (2012) 3–24, at p. 9.

39 M. Drumbl, *Atrocity, Punishment and International Law* (Cambridge University Press, Cambridge, 2007), p. 172.

40 *Ibid.*, p. 174.

Uganda.[41] De Guzman agrees with Drumbl that norm expression should be the guide and aim of punishment and favours the imposition of less harsh sentences (minimum retributivism), which in their reasoning, will explicitly reflect deterrence and norm expression for global crime prevention.[42]

The ICC commenced its sentencing case law with *Lubanga*,[43] and said that Rules 145(l)(a) and (b) require the sentence to reflect the culpability of the offender. Therefore, the Court must ensure that the sentence is in proportion to the crime according to Article 81(2)(a).[44] It needs to balance mitigating and aggravating factors along with the offender's circumstances while. additional factors and circumstances to be considered are provided by Rules 145(1)(c) and (2). However, when the Court determines the Article 76(1) *appropriate* sentence, none of the provisions limits the factors to be considered by the Court.[45] The Prosecution must prove aggravating factors beyond a reasonable doubt while mitigating factors must be proved on the balance of probabilities by the Defence.[46]

A proportionality analysis should thoroughly consider the facts of the committed crimes, the offender's personal facts, and the social facts of the case. Being a child soldier is a social and international criminal law phenomenon, not a personal issue or an 'unfortunate personal situation'.[47] The *Ongwen* Court should also have looked at the cycle of violence during the LRA's wartime, and the relevant social facts. The Court referred to proportionality as a sentencing principle,[48] but when it determined the sentence, it rather conflated 'Ongwen's personal background with his culpable conduct and the suffering of the

---

41 *Ibid.*, pp. 173–176. For an analysis on expressivist punishment theory, *see* J. Glasgow, 'The Expressivist Theory of Punishment Defended', 34(6) *Law and Philosophy* (2015) 601–631. For transitional justice, which represents a 'conception of justice associated with periods of political change, characterized by legal responses to confront the wrongdoings of repressive predecessor regimes' *see* N. Roht-Arriaza, 'The new landscape of transitional justice', in N. Roht-Arriaza and J. Mariezcurrena (eds.), *Transitional Justice in the Twenty-First Century: Beyond Truth versus Justice* (Cambridge University Press, Cambridge, 2006), pp. 1–16, at p. 1. Regarding transitional and restorative justice *see* B.E. Mayans-Hermida and B. Holá, 'Punishing Atrocity Crimes in Transitional Contexts: Advancing Discussions on Adequacy of Alternative Criminal Sanctions Using the Case of Colombia', 43(1) *Oxford Journal of Legal Studies* (2023) 1–31.

42 DeGuzman, *supra* note 37, p. 185–186.

43 ICC-01/04-01/06, 10 July 2012, *supra* note 1, para. 36.

44 *Ibid.*, paras 25–26.

45 *Ibid.*, para. 29.

46 *Ibid.*, paras 32–34.

47 ICC-02/04-01/15-1819-Anx, 6 May 2021, Partly Dissenting Opinion of Judge Raul C. Pangalangan, para. 15.

48 ICC-2/04-01/15, 6 May 2021, *supra* note 5, para. 52.

victims'.[49] As *Lubanga* clarified, the proportionality principle is misapplied if the Court does not provide an analysis of the distinction between a) factors relevant to the gravity of the crime and b) factors relevant to the offender's degree of responsibility.[50]

4 Raised Defences as Mitigating Factors

> The holy spirit reported to the chairman [Kony] who selected the soldiers who could be 'on stand' .... All the spirits are with Kony but if you are going to the battle,you feel that something is with you. In the battlefield, they will be doing their duty and take care of you: everyone will feel very strong.[51]

In Ongwen's conviction trial, the Court rejected the raised affirmative defences of duress and mental incapacity. The defence had argued that his childhood in the bush as an LRA soldier, the LRA martial structure and Kony's personality, along with his rather metaphysical control over the LRA soldiers, had a tremendous negative impact on both Ongwen's mental health and his ability to form independent decision making. The conviction decision illustrates a rather superior Western approach that perceives arguments related to spiritualistic control and fears in the jungle as scientifically untested by Western methods. However, the question here is not why expert evidence *A* was more understandable by the Court's culture than expert evidence *B* but which aspects of Ongwen's situation were relevant for sentencing purposes.[52]

According to Rule 145(2)(a)(1), the evidence used unsuccessfully to support affirmative defences at trial may be relevant for sentencing purposes but must be evaluated differently. Here, the sentencing decision lacks depth in analysis, especially concerning the rejection of certain mitigating factors, such as those related to Ongwen's mental state. It feels like Ongwen's trauma, culture, and mental state had an ornamental effect, not an actual impact on his terrible

---

49 *Ibid.*, para. 389.

50 *See also* Morris, *infra* note 82, para. 77.

51 Former commander's interview, K. Titeca, 'The spiritual order of the LRA', in T. Allen and K. Vlassenroot (eds.), *The Lord's Resistance Army: myth and reality* (Zed Books, New York, NY, 2010), p. 64.

52 *See also* A-L. Nistor, A. Merrylees and B. Holá, 'Spellbound at the International Criminal Court: The Intersection of Spiritualism & International Criminal Law', in J. Fraser and B. McGonigle Leyh (eds), *Intersections of Law and Culture at the International Criminal Court* (Edward Elgar Publishing, Cheltenham, 2020), pp. 147–168, at pp. 148–149, 162–164.

life. The Court desperately attempted to show a monstrous savage whose life experience as an abducted indigenous child soldier vanished when he freely, wilfully and happily decided on a career through the LRA hierarchy. In doing so, the Court disregarded expert witnesses who analysed Ongwen's traumatic experiences and their inevitable impact on his captured life.

The circumstances not considered by the Court on sentencing were related to the Uganda-Acholi war and Ongwen's life within a wild rebel group controlled by spirits, mysticism, extreme violence, and fear. He spent 27 years in the bush in continuous war. The Court failed to logically explain how, in its view, Ongwen managed to transform himself into a well-informed rebel military leader and adult man[53] stained only with a *touch* of childhood unhappiness.

The prosecution characterised Ongwen's child and adolescent life as 'extremely difficult', and requested a one-third reduction of the sentence to be imposed on Ongwen, suggesting 20 years minimum imprisonment for a total joint sentence. Surprisingly, the Court decided that the prosecution's proposal simply identified a lower sentence than 30 years imprisonment and did not 'propose a specific joint sentence'.[54] The Court vaguely stated that the mitigating circumstances of Ongwen's childhood, personal background, family circumstances, and 'alleged good character' were 'duly taken into account'.[55]

The Defence requested a short sentence for retributive factors with permission for Ongwen to 'undergo all the appropriate rituals in northern Uganda, including *Mato Oput*'.[56] The Court decided that the principle of legality precluded the Court from introducing, a traditional justice process.[57]

The Court discussed the determination of each crime's sentence, referring to Article 81(2)(a) and Rule 145(1), that provide the principle of proportionality.[58] With respect to Ongwen's abduction, it said that between 1987–2002 Ongwen's life was 'extremely difficult' but he adapted into the LRA and its 'violent methods'. The Court did not emphasise the violence Ongwen suffered and experienced but, instead, focussed on the supposed and unproven wilful adoption of violence by Ongwen. To prove his adoption of violence, the decision stated that in 1996, when Ongwen was 16 years old, he abducted a victim, raped

53 ICC-02/04-01/15, 6 May 2021, *supra* note 4, para. 393.
54 *Ibid.*, para. 9.
55 *Ibid.*, para. 63.
56 *Ibid.*, para. 18.
57 *Ibid.*, para. 26.
58 ICC-02/04-01/15, 6 May 2021, *supra* note 4, para. 51 with reference to ICC-01/04-01/06-3122, 1 December 2014 (*The Prosecutor v. Thomas Lubanga Dyilo*, Judgment on the appeals of the Prosecutor and Mr Thomas Lubanga Dyilo against the 'Decision on Sentence pursuant to Article 76 of the Statute').

her, and made her his wife.[59] Impressively, the Court decided to use this fact to prove Ongwen's wilful adoption of violence even though Ongwen was not criminally responsible at the time. Ample evidence proved that Kony assigned girls and women to his soldiers. Still, the Court decided that the 16-year-old boy had formed a violent interest in rape and forced marriage, ignored Kony's orders and had adopted the LRA violence thoughtfully and voluntarily.

As per Ongwen's alleged childhood trauma, the Court noted that, soon after his abduction, the nine-year-old Ongwen 'was forced to slaughter some people, hang their intestines on a tree and eat beans mixed with their blood', that he said 'he collapsed and became unconscious as a result, and that to this day, he cannot forget this image'.[60] However, Ongwen, at the sentencing hearing, described this incident as follows:

> [t]hey told us if you want to live kill these people … I was beaten with a wire lock. They ordered us to slaughter these people with a knife, remove their intestines and hang their intestines on the tree. Part of their intestines we were ordered to hang on our necks, and we were told to say this was electric wire. We did all that. … they put our plate of beans under the people who were dripping, the bodies that were dripping with blood and the blood was dripping on these plates. They asked us to eat, but I refused. But they told us, that is what we want you to do. So we were forced to eat beans mixed with human blood. … The Acholi culture does not eat humans. When I finished eating, I collapsed, and I became unconscious. I vomited. *That is what happened in my first attempt to escape.*[61]
>
> emphasis added

It is not clear why the Court summarised Ongwen's horrific experience with a blind eye to analyse Ongwen's childhood trauma and his fear.

The Court focused on Ongwen's supposed resilience and adopted Dr Catherine Abbo's evidence that he had a similar street gang socialisation, and his alleged 'favourable early childhood experiences' 'contributed to his resilience' despite the daily traumatic experiences' impact on his brain.[62] Impressively, the Court did not positively refer to expert witnesses' reports and evidence in favour of Ongwen but stated that Ongwen's trauma had no lasting consequences related to mental disorder or disease (which was not

59 *Ibid.*, para. 84.
60 *Ibid.*, para. 73.
61 ICC-02/04-01/15-T-261, 15 April 2021, p. 6 (lines 14–25), p. 7 (lines 1–2, 4–5, 9).
62 ICC-02/04-01/15, 6 May 2021, *supra* note 5, para. 81.

a sentencing question).[63] Ongwen belonged to a 'small minority' who made choices for a 'steep and purposeful rise in the LRA hierarchy'.[64] The sentencing decision repeated the conviction decision that Ongwen was not forced to commit crimes, and despite the opportunities, he did not escape like others.[65]

As per the mental incapacity defence in relation to sentencing, the Court repeated the argument of the conviction decision: 'The possibility of mental disease or defect was discussed at trial and ultimately excluded in the Trial Judgment on the basis of a detailed analysis of evidence, including expert evidence'.[66] However, this does not constitute an analysis of its potential impact on sentencing. Mere reference to Ongwen's mental state at the material time of the committed crimes, a conviction prerequisite, does not resemble a sentencing analysis. Strengthening its view on Ongwen's healthy mental state, the Court marked its high impression when he 'spoke lucidly for one hour and 45 minutes, without a break, sustaining a structured and coherent declaration, while speaking largely freely'.[67] However, Ongwen's speech could never negate the Court's failure to analytically re-consider the mental defence for sentencing reasons.

With respect to Kony's spiritual powers and control and the horrific punishments or death he imposed on his subordinates, the Court repeated its conviction decision on duress rejection, saying there was no room for using that evidence for mitigation.[68] The Court disregarded the report and methodology of Professor Titeca about the LRA's 'cosmological space' and stated:[69] 'the report does not contain any critical assessment of the statements received in particular from Dominic Ongwen, which appear to have been taken at face value'.[70] However, Titeca had clarified that he was not examining whether the LRA soldiers had actual help from spirits during fights but whether they believed they did and how this belief affected them.[71] It was crystal clear

63 *Ibid.*, para. 83.

64 *Ibid.*, para. 85.

65 *Ibid.*, para. 86.

66 *Ibid.*, para. 93.

67 *Ibid.*, para. 104.

68 *Ibid.*, paras 110–111.

69 ICC-02/04-01/15-T-197, 9 November 2018, UGA-D26-P-0060, The Prosecution asked Titeca whether his report described factual experiences or cultural truth and he replied: 'I am not interested in truth per se' (p. 65, line 6). 'I am interested in understanding belief systems as they function' (p. 65, line 9). 'What is secondary is whether this is factually true or not' (p. 65, lines 10–11). 'What is important is the effect it creates' (p. 66, line 12), 'What ethnography as a field tries to do is, again, an emic understanding' (p. 75, line 22).

70 ICC-02/04-01/15, 6 May 2021, *supra* note 5, para. 114.

71 ICC-02/04-01/15-T-197, 9 November 2018, *supra* note 69, p. 17 (lines 15–25), p. 18 (lines 1–6).

that Titeca evaluated the effect of the spiritual order on the LRA combatants. From an epistemological view, there was no room for critical assessments of the collected qualitative data. It was peculiar that the Court negated Titeca's research. Before the Court, Titeca said that 'absolute obedience to the many, and frequently changing spiritual rules' was 'the only way to survive life in the bush'.[72] He confirmed that the more time someone was in the LRA's spiritual environment, the more influence the spirits had on him.[73] Surprisingly, the Prosecutor commented that 'in fact, none of those things are correct in terms of the laws of science'.[74]

Looking at the Court's treatment of Professor Titeca's expert evidence as it related to moral blameworthiness, it is hard to understand why the Court was so dismissive. Perhaps this was an example of an inherent Western inability to appreciate the *other*, non-western 'cosmological space' of the LRA, which was related to Ongwen's moral responsibility. The Court either had no intention or was unable to evaluate the importance of Titeca's expert analysis of LRA's spiritual order, the soldier's blind belief in Kony's power to read their minds, in conjunction with the entire Acholi culture and spiritualism. The Court also rejected evidence submitted by other witnesses who analysed the LRA environment (Erich Awich Ochen, Pollar Awich), and referred again to its rejection in the conviction decision of the duress defence.[75]

According to Article 69(4) and Rule 63(2), the ICC legal framework has incorporated the truth-seeking continental principle, which is not limited to the identification of the crimes. The ICC judge's mandate is to examine and evaluate everything related to the case, the crime and the offender, even when in his favour. Because of the unique LRA regime, the Court needed to hear expert evidence, such as Titeca's, to understand the LRA's operation. Simply hearing this evidence and impressively ignoring whatever favoured Ongwen, does not resemble a thorough truth-seeking process by the ICC. Hence, the trial Court's rejection, especially of Titeca's expert evidence, is hugely problematic.

> [w]ithin the Lord's Resistance Army Joseph Kony, he's the messenger, he's the law, and he is the one who's in contact with these spirits, he is the one who is talking to them

72 Titeca, *supra* note 51, p. 62.

73 ICC-02/04-01/15-T-197, 9 November 2018, *supra* note 69, Titeca explained that for those who came out of the bush either 'the spirit has left them' or 'they no longer believe in the spirit and the spirit has left Kony' (p. 102, lines 11–15). However, spiritual beliefs 'remained present among individual fighters' (p. 103, lines 9–12).

74 *Ibid.*, p. 78 (line 14).

75 ICC-02/04-01/15, 6 May 2021, *supra* note 4, paras 115–116.

and he is the one who is the messenger on them, so when for example, when combatants, or former combatants, say then the spirit said X, Y, Z, in reality this is the leader Joseph Kony who said these things.

While, again, some of these combatants, they had very strong – how would I say-, supra-natural experiences, meaning that they themselves had dreams which had predictive powers, they could see the future, they have spoken with animals,they could see strange creatures, and so on.

Even after having left the Lord's Resistance Army they continue believing in these spirits.[76]

5 Proportionality and Moral Blameworthiness in Canada

Victims, after all, may be imperfect.
Perpetrators may be tragic.
MARK A. DRUMBL[77]

Because the ICC is a sui generis court with a mandate that includes only the world's gravest offences, it is usually a mistake to compare its sentencing framework to domestic systems in which the sentencing scheme must provide a coherent rationale for all offences from the lowest order to the gravest, usually murder and treason. However, sometimes specific circumstances can provide an analogy that permits looking to a domestic system for guidance. This is the case with how Canadian law has refined its conception of blameworthiness when sentencing aboriginal offenders.

Like the Statute of Rome, the statutory framework for sentencing in the Canadian Criminal Code makes it clear that proportionality is the fundamental principle of sentencing. Section 718(1) states that a 'sentence must be proportionate to the gravity of the offence and the degree of responsibility of the offender'. The Supreme Court of Canada has gone further and refined the term 'responsibility of the offender' with the nuanced dimension of 'moral

76 ICC-02/04-01/15-T-197, 9 November 2018, *supra* note 69, p. 19 (lines 5–16).

77 M.A. Drumbl, 'Victims who victimise', 4(2) *London Review of International Law* (2016) 217–246, p. 218. Drumbl suggests sentencing mitigation when the *antipodes* of *pure* victim and *ugly* perpetrator meet in a person creating an imperfect victim (with reference to Ongwen). *See also* E.K. Baines, 'Complex political perpetrators: reflections on Dominic Ongwen', 47(2) *The Journal of Modern African Studies* (2009) 163–191, pp. 177–181, regarding child soldiers as victims, agents and perpetrators focusing on Ongwen, and the importance Justice to understand the suffered violence and its reproduction.

blameworthiness' which might relate to the offender's social history and life experience.

Starting in the late 19th century, the Canadian government began a campaign of oppression and suppression of its native peoples that has been described by Chief Justice McLachlin as an attempt of cultural genocide.[78] It included, along with other acts, the placement of native children in residential schools and their forced removal for adoption by *white* parents.[79] The discrimination extended into the Canadian criminal justice system resulting in a high degree of over-representation of indigenous people in Canadian prisons.[80] Now, in the 21st century, Canada is struggling with how to redress more than a century of ugly and ill-treatment of its indigenous populations. The courts are also struggling with how to sentence Aboriginal offenders who themselves or their ancestors were victims of this state-sponsored campaign of suppression. Eventually, to provide a new lens for the sentencing system, the courts have refined the concept of moral blameworthiness to address the situation of aboriginal offenders in order to recognize their true social and historical context.

With respect to the sentencing of indigenous offenders, the Supreme Court of Canada has said:

> First, *systemic and background factors may bear on the culpability of the offender, to the extent that they shed light on his or her level of moral blameworthiness.* ... Canadian criminal law is based on the premise that criminal liability only follows from voluntary conduct. *Many Aboriginal offenders find themselves in situations of social and economic deprivation with a lack of opportunities and limited options for positive development. While this rarely -if ever- attains a level where one could properly say that their actions were not voluntary and therefore not deserving of criminal*

78 *Canada's Chief Justice Calls Treatment of First Nations an Attempt at 'Cultural Genocide'* (2015), available online at www.cbc.ca/radio/asithappens/as-it-happens-friday-edition-1.3093097/canada-s-chief-justice-calls-treatment-of-first-nations-an-attempt-at-cultural-genocide-1.3095692#:~:text=And%20she%20used%20a%20phrase,Aga%20Khan%20Museum%20in%20Toronto (accessed 12 July 2023).

79 For a full account of these horrors, *see* the Report of the Truth and Reconciliation Commission of Canada, *Honouring the Truth, Reconciling for the Future* (2015), available online at irsi.ubc.ca/sites/default/files/inline-files/Executive_Summary_English_Web.pdf (accessed 12 July 2023).

80 *See* Supreme Court of Canada, *R. v Gladue*, [1999] 1 SCR 688, paras 61–65; Supreme Court of Canada, *R. v. Ipeelee*, [2012] SCC 13, paras 56–63.

> *sanction, the reality is that their constrained circumstances may diminish their moral culpability.*[81]
>
> emphasis added

More recently, the Ontario Court of Appeal in *R. v. Morris*[82] was required to consider whether a similar concept of moral blameworthiness applied to anti-Black racism and the sentencing of a young black offender. At the sentencing hearing, substantial evidence was adduced of discrimination and anti-Black racism in the City of Toronto. This included social context evidence by experts as well as evidence of the offender's previous experiences with the police, the educational system and social service institutions. The trial judge imposed a lenient sentence of one-day imprisonment plus 18 months' probation. The prosecution appealed, arguing that the judge erred essentially because he was overwhelmed by the racism evidence and proposed three years imprisonment as the fit sentence.

The Appeal Court rightly confirmed that the trial judge had erred in using the background evidence to diminish the gravity of the offence. However, it confirmed the mitigating relevance of the evidence regarding the offender's life and experiences, including his interactions with police and other institutions, as it related to the dimension of his moral blameworthiness. Unanimously, the five-member court concluded:[83]

> Social context evidence relating to the offender's life experiences may be used where relevant to mitigate the offender's degree of responsibility for the offence and/or to assist in the blending of the principles and objectives of sentencing to achieve a sentence which best serves the purposes of sentencing as described in s. 718.

Specifically, with respect to the offender's background, the Court concluded:[84]

> There can be no doubt that evidence on sentencing, describing the existence and effect of anti-Black racism in the offender's community and the impact of that racism on the offender's circumstances and life choices

---

81 R. v. Ipeelee, *Ibid.*, para. 73. *See also* Supreme Court of Canada R. *v.* Anderson, [2014] 2 S.C.R. 167, the sentencing syllogism regarding proportionality and moral blameworthiness, para. 21.

82 Ontario Court of Appeal R. v. Morris, [2021] ONCA 680. The accused had been convicted of offences arising from possessing a loaded handgun.

83 *Ibid.*, para. 13.

84 *Ibid.*, para. 91.

> is part of the offender's background and circumstances. The evidence is not only admissible, it is, in many cases, essential to the obtaining of an accurate picture of the offender as a person and a part of society.

The Court said that a 'sentencing process which frankly acknowledges and addresses the realities of the offender's life takes one important step toward the goal of equal justice for all'.[85]

Looking now at the ICC, in *Lubanga,*[86] the accused was convicted of conscripting child soldiers under the age of 15. The Court said:

> Mr Lubanga is clearly an intelligent and well-educated individual, who would have understood the seriousness of the crimes of which he has been found guilty. This marked level of awareness on his part is a relevant factor in determining the appropriate sentence.[87]

In the Court's view, Lubanga's degree in Psychology increased his culpability since he would have been aware of the consequences of his actions. Although the Court did not mention *moral blameworthiness*, this is the concept it used.

Looking at *Morris,* the Court emphasised that whether a disadvantaged environment influences the offender or limits his choices is related to his moral blameworthiness for his acts, not to the seriousness of his offences.[88]

Looking at *Ongwen*, the Court gave a nod to his difficult early years, but ignored, both explicitly and implicitly, his life of 27 years in the bush dominated by an ethos of war, cruelty, forced compulsion, indoctrination, spirituality and lack of education. Surely, this should go to the mitigating dimension of moral blameworthiness. Although the evidence of duress and mental state should have been re-addressed through the sentencing lens,[89] the Court here, simply re-rejected the evidence of the raised defences, not re-addressed it.

Especially for Kony's control, the Court invented an objective standard, without focusing on Ongwen, and said: 'LRA members with some experience in the organization did not generally believe that Joseph Kony possessed spiritual powers.[90] Moral blameworthiness is attached only to the specific perpetrator

85 *Ibid.*, para. 106.
86 ICC-01/04-01/06, 10 July 2012, *supra* note 1, paras 54–56.
87 *Ibid.*, para. 56.
88 *Ibid.*, paras 49, 94, 104, 154.
89 Allan Manson, introducing the moral blameworthiness concept, argues that whenever duress may not meet a full defence standard, it may mitigate the sentence; A. Manson, *The Law of Sentencing* (Irwin Law, Toronto, ON, 2001), p. 140.
90 ICC-02/04-01/15, 6 May 2021, *supra* note 5, para. 112.

at trial. There is no room for a reasonable person's standard portrayed by other people's perceptions and attitudes. Moreover, there is no explicit explanation of how the Court reached the conclusion that Ongwen, on the balance of probabilities (mitigation's burden of proof), was not influenced by Kony. As well, there is no discussion of the fear factor despite the expert evidence adduced.[91] The *Morris* Court appreciated that constant fear was a reality in Morris' life.[92] The *Ongwen* Court speculated that Ongwen did not suffer fear because some testified, they did not. Evidence proved this was not true in real time.[93] The *Morris* Court stated:

> It was open to the trial judge to find that the evidence of anti-Black racism was connected to, or played a role in, Mr. Morris's strong fear for his personal safety in the community. That state of mind offered a mitigating explanation for Mr. Morris's possession of the loaded, concealed handgun. Looked at in this way, evidence of anti-Black racism, which played a role in generating the fear that helps explain why Mr Morris had a loaded gun, is akin, for the purposes of sentencing, to evidence that Mr. Morris had been terrorized by somebody in the community and had armed himself because he genuinely feared that person.[94]

In *Morris*, one can see how life experience and social context evidence may be used by the Court to mitigate: (a) the degree of offender's responsibility and (b) to assist the blending process of sentencing principles and objectives for achieving the sentence which serves the sentencing purposes.[95]

In *Ongwen*, life experiences, fear and trauma were viewed only when related to LRA's victims, never to Ongwen, who had suffered the same by the LRA. The Court ignored the LRA's social context, which ought to play a mitigating role.

Comparing *Lubanga* or *Ntaganda* to *Ongwen*, the context, the social facts and the individual circumstance are in antipodes. Ongwen's exposure to cruel physical and emotional abuse, the absence of a stable and peaceful environment, education and normal social connections in the community were

---

91 Tim Allen testified before the trial Court about the LRAs fear factor, Kony's knowledge of others' thoughts and the LRA people's fear of Kony, UGA-OTP-P-0422 T-28, ICC-02/04-01/15, 16-01-2017, p. 31 (lines 11–25), p. 32 (lines 1–6). *See also* Titeca, *supra* note 73.

92 *Morris*, *supra* note 82, para. 49 with reference to Morris' social history report.

93 Allen and Titeca, *supra* note 91.

94 *Morris*, *supra* note 82, para. 100.

95 *Ibid.*, para. 13.

circumstances that indicated the possibility of a lower sentence.[96] This was the exact view of Professors Baines, Clarke and Drumbl when they suggested a lower than 25 years sentence because of Ongwen's 'moral development'.[97]

President Museveni's backstage role regarding who from the LRA should be accused is well known to all of those who have examined and studied the Uganda Situation. Ongwen was one of the five wanted men. He was the youngest, illiterate, the only former child soldier, and seriously speaking, not a significant figure for the LRA and the entire Ugandan political arena. But the ICC had only Ongwen for the entire Uganda Situation.[98] Either it was arduous for the Court to appreciate the many sufferings of Ongwen, or the continental inexperience in sentencing analysis confused the Court. The majority decision does not explain why Ongwen' decision-making was not related to fear, bad surroundings, war, mysticism, and lack of education. Nor does it explain how the Court reached a reasoned conclusion that the former child soldier became a rebel army career man through free will and informed choice. The absence of explanation shows the Court's failure to properly address aspects relevant to Ongwen's moral blameworthiness for mitigation reasons. The Court also enmeshed factors relevant to the crime's gravity with factors relevant to the offender's degree of responsibility. The entire process indicates a proportionality misapplication.

Remarkably, Judge Ibáñez Carranza's dissenting opinion of the sentencing appeal decision shows the real implications of Ongwen's child soldier life on his personality. Judge Ibáñez Carranza conducted a thorough legal analysis along with a factual analysis based on expert evidence.[99] She evaluated the submitted evidence and emphasised that a fair sentence is a fair trial issue. Her approach showed a broader understanding of moral culpability based on

96 *See also* Ontario Court of Appeal, R. v. Borde, [2003] 168 O.A.C. 317: 'systemic and background factors may have played a role in the commission of the offence and the values of the community from which the offender comes', para. 32, and Ontario Court of Appeal, R. v. Hamilton, [2004], 189 O.A.C. 90 about 'the underlying causes' of crimes when are 'very real and are to a large extent the product of circumstances that are either beyond' the accused 'control, or for which (he)cannot be faulted', para. 137.

97 ICC-02/04-01/15-1906, 23 December 2021, Submission of Amicus Curiae observations on the merits of the legal questions presented in the "Order inviting expressions of interest as amici curiae in judicial proceedings (pursuant to rule 103 of the Rules of Procedure and Evidence) of 25 October 2021 (ICC02/04-01/15A).

98 *See also* L.G. Minkova, 'Expressing what? The stigmatization of the defendant and the ICC's institutional interests in the Ongwen case', 34(1) *Leiden Journal of international Law* (2021) 223–245, pp 235–241.

99 ICC-02/04-01/15-2023-Anx1, *supra* note 7, paras 136–147.

scientific evidence and the law. It was a pragmatic approach which understood Ongwen's moral blameworthiness.

> In particular, in this case, it is of *crucial importance to consider the impact* that Mr Ongwen's abduction, conscription, violent indoctrination, being forced to carry out and participate in criminal acts when he was still a defenceless child of about nine years of age, *and his upbringing* in the coercive environment of the LRA had on his personality, the development of his brain and moral values, and future opportunities. *A determination of the appropriate sentence* requires thus both a holistic and intersectional analysis that takes into consideration both *the blameworthiness of the convicted person and his or her individual circumstances. Mr Ongwen's condition as a victim did not cease when he turned 18 years old.*[100]
>
> emphasis added

6 Sentencing Ongwen's 'Remorse' and 'Good Character'

Ongwen's Defence requested the Court to recognise the mitigating factors of remorse,[101] and good character.[102] These factors are clearly related to Ongwen's moral responsibility and therefore, the Court's perception was crucial for determining a proportional sentence.

The remorse discussion in the sentencing decision reveals the Court's lack of understanding of the Acholi culture and Ongwen's testimony before the Court. The Rome Statute identifies remorse as a mitigating factor without setting any standard, let alone a Westernised, dogmatic Christian ideal. It is the ICC's global role and duty to appreciate remorse according to the culture of the accused, not the accused's responsibility to show remorseful behaviour according to Western court's perception. The truth is that Ongwen surrendered himself to the ICC and stated he felt bad for what happened to the victims, mentioning that he was also a victim.

Ongwen before the Court said:

> If you are mindful about the sufferings that I have gone through, then you should not take this judgement, this sentencing with a lot of anger. I

100 *Ibid.*, pp. 3–4.

101 ICC-02/04-1/15, 6 May 2021, *supra* note 5, para. 42.

102 *Ibid.*, para. 121.

> request you, I appeal to you that you should also be mindful of the sufferings I went through.
> I know that you have heard a lot of evidence before this Court, but of what happened I am also remorseful. I feel bad for the things that have happened. The things that happened on me, on my family were also grievous things. But there is no difference. I was – I'm a person, my parents were also humans. Those other victims that those things happened to them are also humans. So we all went through the same grievous harm. So if indeed you mind about my suffering that I went through, then please look at it because I also want to become free and lead a free life.[103]

The Court decided:

> Dominic Ongwen has not expressed any such remorse. The absence of remorse became very clear during his personal statement at the sentencing hearing, where, in a display of self-pity, he acknowledged the suffering of (presumably) the victims of his crimes only to claim that his own suffering was equal.[104] [...]
> The Chamber cannot overlook the absence, in Dominic Ongwen's submissions during the hearing on sentence, of any expression of empathy for the numerous victims of his crimes-and even less of any genuine remorse – supplanted by a lucid, constant focus on himself and his own suffering eclipsing that of anyone else.[105]

From a sentencing point of view, reaching the trial Court's conclusion is quite onerous. However, the references of Chief Judge Schmitt to the German system might show an indication of the continental yardstick the Court used to measure remorse in African-Acholi culture.[106] Nevertheless, the ICC serves fairness and justice via a specific legal framework. The judges' national trial experience is helpful but cannot be predominant in ICC decisions. Otherwise, a national legal tradition will hinder the ICC's international and intercultural legal and social mandate. Regrettably, in *Ongwen*, the ICC proved not to have the experience or the willingness to appreciate intercultural remorse, given that Acholi people do not ask for forgiveness the way the Westerners do.

---

103 ICC-02/04-01/15-T-261, 15-04-2021, p. 26 (lines 4–13).
104 *Ibid.*, para. 42.
105 *Ibid.*, para. 394.
106 *See, for example,* ICC-02/04-01/15-T-162-Red-ENG WT 19-03-2018, p. 37 (line 25), p. 54 (line 20); ICC-02/04-01/15-T-163-Red-ENG WT 20-03-2018, p. 4 (line 1), p. 21 (line 4), p. 89 (line 25); ICC-02/04-01/15-T-166-ENG CT WT 26-03-2018, p. 9 (line 24).

As per the mitigating factor related to Ongwen's good character and especially that he saved the lives of many in the LRA, the Court said:

> [w]hen Dominic Ongwen saved lives of other members of the LRA, including by standing up to Joseph Kony, indicate to the Chamber, once more, that Dominic Ongwen was fully able to appreciate the value of human life [...]. Further, they suggest that the circumstances of his upbringing, and stay, within the LRA constituted no obstacle to him forming his own views, and acting accordingly, in spite of the positions of other members of the group, including individuals higher than him in the LRA hierarchy and Joseph Kony himself. These episodes [...] in which Dominic Ongwen helped people in the bush because he 'cared about people' cannot but demonstrate further that at no time he lost his ability to distinguish between right and wrong and to act independently.[107]

The Court here conflated the mitigating factors at sentencing with the mental state defence at trial. It seems as if the ICC twisted the Defence arguments to prove something other than what they were submitted for. This is a rather speculative outcome not proven by the evidence, familiar to continentals who are mainly investigating the truth, not evaluating the evidence.[108] But twisting the sayings, not finding the truth, divulges vengeful shadows among the letters of the alphabet.

7 The ICC's Continental Style of Sentencing in *Ongwen*

The Rome Statute provides a separate hearing process for sentencing.[109] This process is foreign to classic continental systems. Continental legal tradition provides separate reasoning for sentencing, but not a separate sentencing trial after conviction. Even if the common law court decides to proceed with a decision on sentencing immediately after conviction, the procedure still requires two separate decisions following two separate processes.[110]

---

107 ICC-02/04-1/15, 6 May 2021, *supra* note 5, para. 129.

108 D. Sorvatzioti and A. Manson, 'Burden of Proof and L'intime conviction: Is the Continental Criminal Trial Moving to the Common Law?', 23(1) *Canadian Criminal Law Review* (2018) 107–129, p. 114.

109 Article 76(2).

110 The judges of the *ad hoc* tribunals abolished the previously adopted separate sentencing trial because they perceived it as a common law jury trial feature; W.A. Schabas, *The International Criminal Court: A commentary on the Rome Statute* (Oxford University Press, Oxford, 2016), pp. 1147–1148.

Sentencing in common law represents a separate branch of law and is not synonymous with Penology. Penology studies punishment theories, the scope and the types of sentences and evaluates their application.[111] Sentencing is not synonymous with punishment. Punishment is the response to a crime by an imposition of a sentence by a court. Sentencing is the judicial process that precedes punishment. It determines and decides a just punishment(sentence) for a particular offender who committed a particular crime. Allan Manson argues that to not confuse sentencing with punishment and to comprehend its role, three prominent aspects need to be distinguished: the importance of sentencing in the criminal justice system, its historical perspectives and its philosophical and political sources.[112]

For the continentals, a single court hearing is provided by the criminal procedure for both conviction and sentencing. It includes evidence regarding both conviction and sentencing before the parties' closing arguments, even though the accused may have pleaded not guilty.

Both common law and continental judiciary and practitioners might consider the process of each other system peculiar. The continental process seems prejudicial and unfair from a common law perspective, given that character and predisposition evidence is adduced before the conviction decision.[113] For the continentals, no matter if the accused pleads guilty or not, the trial will take place because a guilty plea does not have the effect of confirming conviction as at common law. However, in the absence of evidence rules in the continental system, any evidence submission, prejudicial or not, is compatible with the principle of free evaluation of evidence and the Court's truth-seeking mandate without typically affecting the fairness of the trial.[114]

Now, modern common law systems, as the Canadian, that have developed sentencing law have been able to focus and refine discussions related to a more individualised punishment and the role and objectives a sentence should serve. This is the reason behind the nuanced approach of the moral blameworthiness concept seen in Canadian sentencing case law.

Judges who are not experienced in their respective national systems with a separate sentencing hearing perceive sentencing as punishment imposition, a mere side effect of conviction. They are not aware of the functionality of the common law sentencing trial. The reason is that the continental criminal

111 D. Scott, *Penology* (Sage, Thousand Oaks, CA, 2008) p. 7.

112 Manson, *supra* note 89, pp. 1–4.

113 D. Sorvatzioti, 'Why Sentencing Needs a Separate Trial in the Continental System' in C. Papacharalambous (ed.), *The Aims of Punishment* (Nomos, Baden-Baden, 2020), pp. 145–166, at pp. 160–161.

114 Sorvatzioti and Manson, *supra* note 108, p. 114.

procedure code does not permit a separate sentencing trial. Continental judges do not have tools such as pre-sentence reports, victim impact statements, or separate evidence submissions, including expert evidence. Sentencing determination follows a rather fast-track process where both conviction and sentencing evidence have been presented almost simultaneously.[115] They are neither accustomed to addressing and refining legal issues for sentencing determination nor analysing the burden of proof. Given that the continentals, at least in the European Union, were mandated to include the prosecutorial burden of proof beyond a reasonable doubt in their respective systems in 2018, their inexperience with the burden analysis is rather justifiable.[116]

Looking at Ongwen's sentencing decision, there is a reference to what is required by the ICC legal framework but not analysis to transparently reveal the judicial thinking process of the Court. A common law approach is found in *Ntaganda*. The sentencing Court addressed the arguments submitted by the parties on specific legal issues through an explicit discussion of the burden and the standard of proof.[117]

In *Ongwen*, the Court rejected the mitigating factors Ongwen's defences represented with mere reference to its conviction decision and did not analyse, let alone discuss, the burden and the standard of proof for aggravating or mitigating factors. This has been the continental judicial practice for centuries. Only the minority appeal decision gave a thorough analysis. Whether the approach is continental or common law, or a marriage of the two, depends on the reasoning, how the Court discusses evidence issues, the burden of proof and whether there is room in sentencing determination for expert evidence to help define a proportional sentence. Defending the effective survival of the ICC, there is no 'inescapable dyad' regarding the applicable legal tradition (too common law/too continental). I suggest there is a 'right size' approach.[118] The Statute of Rome gives room to introduce a tailormade evolving sentencing case law for the ICC. Paradigms from evolved modern legal orders as Canada, may provide a helpful vehicle for those of the judiciary and lawyers from jurisdictions with less applied experience in refining nuanced concepts of harm, moral blameworthiness and proportionality.

115 Sorvatzioti, *supra* note 113.

116 Directive (EU) 2016/343, Article 6. *See also* A. Chouliaras and M. Skandamis, 'The Intensification of the Preventive Rationale in European Criminal Justice Policies: the Evolution of Dangerousness and its Transformation into Risk', in C. Papacharalambous (ed.), *The Aims of Punishment* (Nomos, Baden-Baden, 2020), pp. 121–144, at pp. 124–128.

117 ICC-01/04-02/06, 7 November 2019, paras 212, 214–215, 224.

118 D. Robinson, 'Inescapable Dyads: Why the International Criminal Court Cannot Win', 28(2) *Leiden Journal of International Law* (2015) 323–347, pp. 324–327.

8 Epilogue

Ongwen's case illustrates the *rotten social background* of abducted indigenous children who become perpetrators.[119] However, there is an asymmetry between justice and desert when sentencing perpetrators of dual status. We can locate the 'unjust' in Ongwen's sentence, but we cannot precisely define the 'deserved'.[120]

There is no indication that the Rome Statute drafters had in mind perpetrators of international crimes being victims of identical crimes. This does not vindicate the ICC to essentially brush off the dual status of *Ongwen*. However, the *proper* explanation might be their inexperience in complex sentencing considerations. But the obliteration of *Lubanga* regarding the fear and permanent scars of child soldiers is problematic.[121] Given the ICC's imperative to find the truth, here it found only the crimes committed. Consequently, the truth-seeking process failed dramatically.

Ongwen's unique case gave the ICC an enormous opportunity to create a hugely influential precedent for the world's courts. It was the first opportunity for the Court to establish the ICC's sentencing norms for former child soldiers who become perpetrators and are different from non-child soldiers. Sadly, the trial Court's sentencing decision, confirmed by the majority of the Appeal Court, is not ground-breaking but instead provides a westernised continental narrow view, a mechanical check-list sentencing analysis.

Acknowledgements

I want to thank my dearest Allan Manson for our sentencing law discussions, Mark Drumbl for the conversations we had regarding child soldiers and *Ongwen*, Adina Nistor for the discussions regarding Ongwen's trial and the ICC's approach, and the anonymous reviewer who made thoughtful comments for a better paper.

---

119 *See also* R.L. Aguiling Pangalangan, 'Dominic Ongwen and the Rotten Social Background Defense: The Criminal Culpability of Child Soldiers Turned War Criminals', 33 *American University International Law Review* (2018) 605–635, pp. 626–632.

120 Thorburn and Manson, *supra* note 27, citing Anthony Bottoms when discussing justice and desert, p. 285.

121 The Court in *Lubanga* explicitly discussed the tremendous permanent effects conscription has on children under 15, paras 37–44, ICC-01/04-01/06-2901, 10 July 2012. Regarding consistency, as one of the fundamental principles of justice, *see* Hola, *supra* note 38, p. 3. *See also* Amicus Curiae, *supra* note 97, where consistency, with reference to *Lubanga,* was emphatically mentioned, paras 13, 41. *See also* Drumbl, *supra* note 77, p. 242.

CHAPTER 6

Fighters, Not Victims: On Victimhood Recognition and Gender Representations in the Enslavement Charges in the *Ongwen* Case

Silvina Sánchez Mera

Abstract

In the *Ongwen* case, according to the OTP women were abducted to be wives and men to be soldiers, women were forced to work and men forced to fight. The OTP brought enslavement charges for some of these crimes. Absent from the charges was the forced fighting of men. This paper discusses the crime of enslavement in the *Ongwen* case. By combining a doctrinal analysis and a feminist approach, I seek to show how gender representations emerge in the application of the law in detriment of men's victimhood. I argue that the application of the law responds to gender representations in war. Men are not perceived to be victims once they become 'soldiers'. Likewise, for women, the effect is their continuous perception as non-fighters and victims of war. This leads to reinforcing those representations, to lack of acknowledgment of victimhood for men and to reducing the experiences of women.

Keywords

enslavement – forced fighting – gender representations – *Ongwen* – victimhood recognition

1 Introduction

On the 4th of February 2021, Dominic Ongwen, former Lord's Resistance Army (LRA) commander, was found guilty of an extensive list of crimes at the International Criminal Court (ICC).[1] The case can be considered a milestone

1 ICC, *Prosecutor v Dominic Ongwen*, ICC-02/04-01/15, Trial Chamber IX, Judgement, 4 February 2021 (Ongwen Judgement).

 | DOI: 10.1163/9789004743380_007

for the ICC. Ongwen is the first person to be convicted for crimes he was once victim of.[2] He is also the first person to have been convicted of these many charges, 61 out of 70 charges.[3]

While current academic discussions focus on Ongwen himself and his victim-perpetrator status,[4] the 'spiritual' influence of the LRA and his leader Joseph Kony,[5] and the systematic sexual abuse on women and girls,[6] this article focuses on some aspects of the application of the Rome Statute by the Office of the Prosecutor (OTP) and the Chambers in the *Ongwen* case. The focus is not on Ongwen as a person—neither as a former child soldier nor as a perpetrator of the present crimes. Instead, this article looks at how the OTP and the Chambers have addressed the crime of enslavement against civilians abducted by the LRA, the gender representations that emerge (and are reinforced) therein and the consequences for victimhood recognition.

This paper focuses on the charges (and conviction) of enslavement as a crime against humanity as brought by the OTP. The OTP charged enslavement

2 He is a former child soldier, who was integrated into the LRA when he was abducted on his way to school when he was between 10–14 years old. He then survived and rose into the ranks of the LRA becoming a Commander of one of the four brigades, the Sinia Brigade. *See ibid.*

3 ICC, *Prosecutor v Dominic Ongwen*, ICC-02/04-01/15, Trial Chamber IX, Sentence, 6 May 2021 (Ongwen Sentence).

4 F. Strandberg Hassellind, 'The International Criminal Trial as a Site for Contesting Historical and Political Narratives: The Case of Dominic Ongwen', 30(5) *Social & Legal Studies* (2021) 790–809; M. Kersten, 'The Life and Trials of Dominic Ongwen: A JiC Symposium', *Justice in Conflict* (1 February 2021), available online at https://justiceinconflict.org/2021/02/01/the-life-and-trials-of-dominic-ongwen-a-jic-symposium/ (accessed 10 October 2022); C.F. Moran, 'To Be Responsible for Ourselves: Dominic Ongwen and Defences Before the International Criminal Court', *Opinio Juris* (19 December 2016) available online at http://opiniojuris.org/2016/12/19/to-be-responsible-for-ourselves-dominic-ongwen-and-defences-before-the-international-criminal-court/(accessed 10 October 2022).

5 A.-L. Nistor, A. Merrylees and B. Holá, 'Spellbound at the ICC: The Intersection of Spirituality and International Criminal Law', in J. Fraser and B. McGonigle Leyh (eds), *Intersections of Law and Culture at the International Criminal Court* (Edward Elgar, Cheltenham, 2020), pp. 147–168; K. Kiyimba, 'An Analysis of the Epistemic Link between the Catholic Religion and Violence in Uganda's History', 30(1) *Journal for the Study of Religion* (2017) 26–51.

6 S. Kramer, 'Forced Marriage and the Absence of Gang Rape: Explaining Sexual Violence by the Lord's Resistance Army in Northern Uganda', 23(1) *Journal of Politics and Society* (2012) 11–49; J. Annan, C. Blattman, D. Mazurana and K. Carlson, 'Women and Girls at War: Wives, Mothers, and Fighters in the Lord's Resistance Army', *HiCN Working Papers* 63 (Households in Conflict Network, Berlin, 2009); R. Grey, *Prosecuting Sexual and Gender-Based Crimes at the International Criminal Court: Practice, Progress and Potential* (Cambridge University Press, Cambridge, 2019); E. Baines, 'Forced Marriage as a Political Project: Sexual Rules and Relations in the Lord's Resistance Army' 51(3) *Journal of Peace Research* (2014) 405–417.

for the forced labour that civilians were subjected to from the moment of their abduction until they arrived on the LRA camp, and for the forced labour women and girls suffered while in the camp, and that related to domestic chores, under gender-based crimes. There is no charge of enslavement for the forced military training and fighting men were subjected to do.

I argue that the application of the Rome Statute by the OTP and the Trial Chamber, regarding the enslavement charges, responds to gender representations in war, representations that are reinforced by their repetition, affecting victimhood recognition. Combining a doctrinal analysis and a feminist approach, I seek to show how gender representations emerge in the application of the law in detriment of men's victimhood. Men are not perceived to be victims once they become 'soldiers'. Likewise, for women, the effect is their continuous perception as non-fighters and victims of war. This leads to reinforcing those representations, to lack of acknowledgment of victimhood for men and reducing the experiences of women.

Crimes against women (and girls) were at the centre of the OTP's focus. Especial attention was given to, as labelled by the OTP, 'gender-based crimes'. This prompt academics to state that the case 'has become one of the most innovative cases on gender-based crimes in the ICC to date'.[7] Whereas this is a positive aspect, the over focus on women and girls as victims has helped reinforce gender representations. I do not want to dismiss the fact that women (and girls) are disproportionately affected by armed conflict and that their victimisation comes largely at the hands of men. My intention here is to draw attention to some of the consequences, on men, of over-focusing on women as victims.

The paper is structured into six sections. Section 2 starts with an overview of the *Ongwen* case at the ICC and a description of the different charges on enslavement as a crime against humanity as brought by the OTP. It notes the differences between the charges that will be the object of analysis. Section 3 turns to the situation of male abductees in the LRA and shows that their fate in the LRA meet the elements of enslavement as crime against humanity, even though these were not charged. Section 4 looks at international jurisprudence and the criminalisation of forced fighting as different offenses of crimes against humanity and war crimes. The aim of this section is to show that forcing someone to fight has been successfully prosecuted as an international crime, including enslavement. Section 5 discusses gender representations in

7 Grey, *supra* note 6, p. 171.

war, specifically 'women are victims, men are soldiers' and shows how the enslavement charges respond and reinforce this representation. The paper concludes that the ICC is sustaining an unequal approach that reinforces representations regarding men and women in war.

2 The Lord's Resistance Army at the International Criminal Court: The *Ongwen* Case

Uganda was the first State party to (self) refer a situation to the ICC.[8] The country had been the scene of long-lasting armed conflict between the Lord's Resistance Army, an ethnic-religious based group, and the government that started in 1987. The LRA had conducted a guerrilla type warfare against anyone perceived to be a government supporter.[9] Led by Joseph Kony, the LRA became associated with forced recruitment and abductions. By the 1990s, Internally Displaced People's Camps (IDP) would be raided for 'recruits' and goods. In order to grow their ranks and thus sustain the military campaign, the LRA systematically abducted people, with focus on young and bodily able people irrespective of gender.[10] All abductees were military trained and participated in military campaigns. On top of this, women and girls were 'distributed' to commander's households to serve as sexual slaves or 'wives' or 'ting tings'.[11]

8 ICC, President of Uganda refers situation concerning the Lord's Resistance Army (LRA) to the ICC, *ICC* (24 January 2004), available online at https://www.icc-cpi.int/news/icc-president-uganda-refers-situation-concerning-lords-resistance-army-lra-icc (accessed 18 October 2022).

9 For information and analysis on the LRA, *see* T. Allen and K. Vlassenroot (eds), *The Lord's Resistance Army: Myth and Reality* (Zed Books, London, 2010); A. Dolnik and H. Butime, *Understanding the Lord's Resistance Army Insurgency* (World Scientific, Singapore, 2017); R. Doom and K. Vlassenroot, 'Kony's Message: A New Koine?The Lord's Resistance Army in Northern Uganda', 98(390) *African Affairs* (1999) 5–36; K. Titeca and T. Costeur, 'An LRA for Everyone: How Different Actors Frame The Lord's Resistance Army', 114(454) *African Affairs* (2015) 92–114; J. Otieno Wasonga, *The International Criminal Court and the Lord's Resistance Army: Enduring Dilemmas of Transitional Justice* (Taylor & Francis, Oxford, 2019).

10 P.N. Pham, E. Stover and P. Vinck, *Abducted: The Lord's Resistance Army and Forced Conscription in Northern Uganda: June 2007* (Berkeley-Tulane Initiative for Vulnerable Populations, Berkeley, CA, 2007); C. Blattman and J. Annan, 'On the Nature and Causes of LRA Abduction: What the Abductees Say', in T. Allen and K. Vlassenroot (eds), *The Lord's Resistance Army: Myth and Reality* (Zed Books, London, 2010) 132–155.

11 Pre-pubescent girls who would do household chores or babysit babies.

Following the State self-referral, an investigation opened in 2004.[12] The Office of the Prosecutor focused on crimes committed by the LRA and their leadership: Joseph Kony and the Commanders of each of the four brigades the LRA was comprised of. To this date, the only suspect that surrendered to the court was Dominic Ongwen.[13] Like most members of the LRA, Dominic Ongwen was forcefully integrated into the armed group. He is a former child soldier, having been abducted around the age of 10,[14] who rose the ranks and became Commander of the Sinia Brigade.

By the time of Ongwen's surrender, in 2015, the OTP indicted him with 70 counts that included both war crimes and crimes against humanity from the period of 1 July 2002 to 31 December 2005.[15] These crimes included enslavement as a crime against humanity against intra-party members, making it a first for the ICC. All the 70 charges were confirmed in March 2016 by the Pre-Trial Chamber[16] with the trial starting soon after. On the 4th of February 2021, the ICC Trial Chamber IX rendered its judgement finding Ongwen guilty of 61 crimes committed from 1 July 2002 and 31 December 2005.[17] Ongwen was sentenced to 25 years of imprisonment.[18] His sentence was confirmed on appeal.[19]

12 ICC, 'Prosecutor of the International Criminal Court Opens an Investigation into Northern Uganda', *ICC* (24 July 2004), available online at http://www.icc-cpi.int/news/icc-prosecutor-international-criminal-court-opens-investigation-nothern-uganda (accessed 18 October 2022).

13 Joseph Kony and Vincent Otti remain at large. The ICC terminated the cases against Raska Lukwiya, Okot Odhiambo following their deaths. The Prosecutor v. Joseph Kony et al, Notification Confirming the Death of Raska Lukwiya, ICC-02/04-01/05-270, 02 November 2006; 'ICC Terminates Proceedings against Okot Odhiambo Following Forensic Confirmation of His Passing', *ICC* (10 September 2015), available online at http://www.icc-cpi.int/news/icc-terminates-proceedings-against-okot-odhiambo-following-forensic-confirmation-his-passing (accessed 10 May 2023).

14 Estimations on his exact age at the time of abduction are between 10 and 14.

15 ICC, *Prosecutor v Dominic Ongwen*, ICC-02/04-01/15, Document Containing the Charges (Office of the Prosecutor), 22 December 2015 (Ongwen, Document Containing the Charges).

16 ICC, *Prosecutor v. Dominic Ongwen*, ICC-02/04-01/15-422-Red, Pre-Trial Chamber II Decision on the confirmation of charges against Dominic Ongwen, 23 March 2016 (Ongwen, Confirmation of Charges).

17 For a complete procedural history *See* Ongwen Judgement, *supra* note 1, p. 13.

18 Ongwen Sentence, *supra* note 3.

19 ICC, *Prosecutor v Dominic Ongwen*, ICC-02/04-01/15-2023, Appeal Chamber, Appeals Judgement, 15 December 2022.

2.1 *The Enslavement Charges in the* Ongwen *Case*

Given the extensive list of crimes Ongwen was charged with, the Office of the Prosecutor grouped them into 3 'blocks', the Trial Chamber followed the same approach in the judgement.[20] A first block included all crimes committed during LRA attacks to four different Internally Displaced People's camps. A second block encompassed crimes directly perpetrated by Dominic Ongwen, specifically, gender-based crimes committed against seven women. The last block of charges was denominated 'sexual and gender-based crimes and conscription and use on hostilities of children below the age of 15',[21] and included crimes perpetrated against women and children integrated into the LRA.[22] Counts of enslavement, as a crime against humanity,[23] were included in all 3 blocks.[24] However, of relevance for the purpose of this article are the enslavement charges in blocks 1 and 3, as these crimes are viewed as crimes committed 'by the LRA'. This section describes the factual charges of these crimes object of analysis in this article, as brought by the OTP and followed by the Trial Chamber.

As per the contextual elements of crimes against humanity, the Trial Chamber was satisfied these were met. The Chamber held that 'the LRA killed, injured and enslaved a large number of civilians in numerous attacks on individual civilians, IDP's camps and other civilian locations', and that this constituted an attack against the civilian population.[25] These attacks were not only of a systematic nature as they followed coordinated efforts to target the civilian population of Northern Uganda, but also in furtherance of the LRA policy of growing their ranks through abductions.[26]

With respect to block 1, four counts of enslavement as crimes against humanity were included. One count for each of the four attacks to the IDP's

20 Ongwen Judgement, *supra* note 1.
21 *Ibid*; Ongwen, Confirmation of charges, *supra* note 16.
22 Dominic Ongwen was charged under different modes of liability, such as indirect perpetration and ordering these crimes. *See* Ongwen, Document Containing the Charges, *supra* note 15; Ongwen Judgement, *supra* note 1.
23 Under the Rome Statute, enslavement is an underlying offense of crimes against humanity, thus enslavement can only be charged under crimes against humanity, not war crimes. An exception is the crime of sexual slavery which is characterised as both a crime against humanity and a war crime.
24 Ongwen Judgement, *supra* note 1; Ongwen, Document Containing the Charges, *supra* note 15; Ongwen, Confirmation of Charges, *supra* note 16.
25 Ongwen, Judgement, *supra* note 1, para. 2798.
26 *Ibid.*, paras 2799–2804.

camps.[27] The OTP submitted that 'on or about' the date of attack[28] the LRA would abduct the residents and forced them to carry looted goods and wounded fighters back to the LRA camp. For example, in relation to the attack of Pajule camp the OTP stated:

> LRA fighters deprived civilians of their liberty by abducting them and placing them under military guard to prevent their escape. LRA fighters abducted hundreds of civilians and made them carry items and other equipment that they had looted from the camp. In doing so, attackers exercised any or all of the powers attaching to the right of ownership over the abductees including by depriving them of their liberty and exacting forced labour, reducing them to a servile status.[29]

The Trial Chamber found Ongwen guilty of these crimes. The Chamber held that abductees were subjected to forced labour, by being made to carry looted

27 The camps attacked were Pajule (count 8), Odek (count 20), Lukodi (count 33) and Abok (count 46). *See* Ongwen Confirmation of Charges, *supra* note 16; Ongwen Judgement, *supra* note 1.

28 'on or about 10 October 2003, at or near Pajule IDP camp' (count 8), on or about 29 April 2004, at or near Odek IDP camp' (count 20), 'on or about 19 May 2004 at or near Lukodi IDP Camp' (count 37), 'on or about 8 June 2004, at or near Abok IDP camp' (count 49). Ongwen, Document Containing the Charges, *supra* note 15.

29 Ongwen, Document Containing the Charges, *supra* note 15 para. 23. Similarly, in relation to the attack of Odek Camp the OTP stated 'LRA fighters deprived civilians of their liberty by abducting them and placing them under military guard to prevent their escape. Civilian men, women and children were abducted and forced to carry away the looted food from Odek IDP camp. Children were tied together with ropes and dragged away from their homes. In doing so, attackers exercised any or all of the powers attaching to the right of ownership over the abductees including by depriving them of their liberty and exacting forced labour, reducing them to a servile status.'; with relation to the attack of Lukodi camp it noted 'LRA fighters deprived civilians of their liberty by abducting them and placing them under military guard to prevent their escape. Men, women and children were abducted, many of whom were forced to carry away looted goods from Lukodi IDP camp. In doing so, attackers exercised any or all of the powers attaching to the right of ownership over the abductees including by depriving them of their liberty and exacting forced labour, reducing them to a servile status.'; lastly with respect to the attack of Abok the OTP said 'LRA fighters deprived civilians of their liberty by abducting them and placing them under military guard to prevent their escape. Before attacking the camp, LRA fighters abducted a number of camp residents. During the attack, attackers abducted approximately 26 men, women and children and forced them to carry looted goods away from the camp under threat of death. The attackers exercised any or all of the powers attaching to the right of ownership over these abductees including by depriving them of their liberty and exacting forced labour, reducing them to a servile status.' Ongwen, Document Containing the Charges *supra* note 15, paras 36, 48 and 62.

items, and that measures to prevent their scape were in place, such as military guards and threats of beating and death if they tried to escape.[30] Therefore, it concluded that 'LRA fighters exercised powers attaching to the right of ownership over the abductees by imposing on them a deprivation of liberty similar to those explicitly stated in Article 7(2)(c) of the Statute'.[31]

In relation to block 3, crimes grouped under 'sexual and gender-based crimes and conscription and use on hostilities of children below the age of 15', one count of enslavement as crime against humanity committed against women was brought up by the OTP (count 68).[32] Unlike the charges in block 1, the ones in block 3 were not necessarily related to IDP's camps attacks, and included women and girls integrated into the LRA (whether abducted during the attack to IDP's camps or in other circumstances).

The OTP submitted that '[f]rom at least 1 July 2002 until 31 December 2005, in northern Uganda, Dominic Ongwen, Joseph Kony, and Sinia brigade leadership (the "SGBC co-perpetrators") pursued a common plan to abduct girls and women to serve as domestic servants.'[33] The OTP stated that powers attaching to the right of ownership were exercised by LRA commanders. That women (and girls) were forced to perform different tasks, and that they had no choice but to comply.[34] These women and girls were deprived of their liberty, forced to work, and physically and psychologically abused if they refused to do so. The OTP noted:

> LRA commanders and fighters, exercised any or all of the powers attaching to the right of ownership over these women and girls. They deprived them of their liberty and exacted forced labour, reducing them to a servile status. The victims had no choice but to submit to rape, enslavement, sexual slavery and become forced wives. Non-compliance with demands for sex and the performance of domestic tasks resulted in severe beatings and other forms of abuse.[35]

30 Ongwen Judgement, *supra* note 1, paras 2839–2840, 2895–2896, 2948–2949, 2994–2995.

31 *Ibid.*, para. 2840. *Similarly*, paras 2896, 2949, 2995.

32 The OTP also brought up sexual slavery charges, which is slavery. However, because of the division the OTP made, this paper only focuses on the charges of enslavement as brought by the OTP.

33 Ongwen, Document Containing the Charges, *supra* note para. 129.

34 *Ibid.*, para. 131. *See also* paras 129–130.

35 Ongwen, Document Containing the Charges, *supra* note 15, para. 131. *See also* paras 129–130.

The Chamber agreed with the OTP and noted that abducted women and girls were 'severely beaten for attempting escape or if they failed to perform the work demanded of them.'[36] That '[t]he women and girls were coerced, due to the physical force used by the Sinia brigade members and due to the threat of punishment for disobedience and their dependence on the Sinia brigade members for survival.'[37] This enslavement charge relates then to force labour of women (and girls) as domestic servants while in the LRA. This enslavement charge was categorised, by the OTP, as a gender-based crime.[38]

The different enslavement charges respond to the OTP's narrative and focus of the case: the mistreatment of the civilian population in Northen Uganda at the hands of the LRA and, in particular, the fate of women. At the centre of all the enslavement charges is the acknowledgement of the forced labour abductees performed under coercive circumstances. However, as the following sections will show, not all abductees were acknowledged as victims despite their forced labour.

3 The Fate of Male Abductees in the LRA: Does Forced Fighting Meet the Criteria for Enslavement?

The enslavement charges in the *Ongwen* case do not include the forced military training and forced fighting of men (and women) in the LRA. Here I argue that the situation of male abductees in the LRA, particularly as per the OTP's narrative—their abduction to become fighters- could constitute enslavement under Article 7.1.c of the Rome Statute.

The Rome Statute defines enslavement as 'the exercise of any or all of the powers attaching to the right of ownership over a person and includes the exercise of such power in the course of trafficking in persons, in particular women and children'.[39] In turn, the Element of Crimes indicate that for enslavement to take place the 'perpetrator exercised any or all of the powers attaching to the right of ownership over one or more persons, such as by purchasing, selling, lending or bartering such a person or persons, or by imposing on them a similar deprivation of liberty'.[40] 'Similar deprivation of

36 Ongwen Judgement, *supra* note 1, para. 3073.

37 *Ibid,* para. 3080.

38 Count 68, *See* Ongwen Document Containing the Charges, *supra* note 15; Ongwen Confirmation of Charges, *supra* note 16; and Ongwen Judgement, *supra* note 1.

39 Rome Statute of the International Criminal Court (adopted 17 July 1998, entered into forced 1 July 2002), Article 7.2.c.

40 Article 7.1.c Elements of Crimes, International Criminal Court.

liberty' may include forced labour or reducing the person to servile status.[41] Forced or compulsory labour has been defined by ILO Convention No 29 as 'all work or service which is extracted from any person under the menace of any penalty and for which the said person has not offered himself voluntarily.'[42] Forced labour can be then an indicia for enslavement, but it is not a crime per se.

The ICC has interpreted the elements of the crime of enslavement in previous cases. In the *Katanga* case, the Trial Chamber held that 'the powers attaching the right of ownership' could take different forms but would deprive the victim of 'any form of autonomy'.[43] In *Ongwen*, when analysing the elements of enslavement, the Trial Chamber followed the jurisprudence of the International Criminal Tribunal for the former Yugoslavia (ICTY) in *Kunarac*, providing a non-exhaustive list of factors that can indicate slavery.[44] The Chamber noted that the indicia or factors that can show the exercise of ownership over a person could include: (i) control or restrictions of someone's movement and, more generally, measures taken to prevent or deter escape; (ii) control of physical environment; (iii) psychological control or pressure;

41 The footnote in Article 7.1.c of the Element of Crimes note: It is understood that such deprivation of liberty may, in some circumstances, include exacting forced labour or otherwise reducing a person to a servile status as defined in the Supplementary Convention on the Abolition of Slavery, the Slave Trade, and Institutions and Practices Similar to Slavery of 1956.

42 ILO Convention No. 29 Article 2 para. 1. However, not all forms of compulsory labour are prohibited during armed conflicts, some are allowed as long as the persons are remunerated. For example, in international armed conflicts Article 40 of the IVGC establishes that 'Protected persons may be compelled to work only to the same extent as nationals of the Party to the conflict in whose territory they are. If protected persons are of enemy nationality, they may only be compelled to do work which is normally necessary to ensure the feeding, sheltering, clothing, transport and health of human beings and which is not directly related to the conduct of military operations. In the cases mentioned in the two preceding paragraphs, protected persons compelled to work shall have the benefit of the same working conditions and of the same safeguards as national workers, in particular as regards wages, hours of labour, clothing and equipment, previous training and compensation for occupational accidents and diseases.' In turn, Article 5.1.e of APII indicates that people detained 'shall, if made to work, have the benefit of working conditions and safeguards similar to those enjoyed by the local civilian population.'

43 ICC, *Prosecutor v Germain Katanga*, ICC-01/04-01/07, Trial Chamber II, Judgement, 7 March 2014. para. 975.

44 ICTY, *Prosecutor v Kunarac et al.*), IT-96-23 and 23/1, Trial Chamber II, Judgement, 22 February 2001, para. 543; ICTY, *Prosecutor v Kunarac et al.*, IT-96-23 and 23/1-A, Appeals Chamber, Appeal Judgement, 12 June 2002 para. 119. *See also* SCSL, *Prosecutor v Issa Hassan Sessay et al.*, Case No. SCSL-04-15-T, Trial Chamber I, Judgement, 2 March 2009, paras 160, 199 (RUF Judgement).

(iv) force, threat of force or coercion; (v) duration of the exercise of powers attaching to the right of ownership; (vi) assertion of exclusivity; (vii) subjection to cruel treatment and abuse; (viii) control of sexuality; (ix) forced labour or subjecting the person to servile status; and (x) the person's vulnerability and the socio-economic conditions in which the power is exerted.[45]

Additionally, the ICC held that deprivation of liberty 'may cover situations in which the victims may not have been physically confined but were otherwise unable to leave as they would have nowhere else to go and feared for their lives'.[46] The Trial Chamber examined these aspects regarding the victims of enslavement in all charges brought by the OTP. Of interest here is the examination pertaining to the charge of enslavement in block 3, that had only women (and girls) as the victim group. This charge deals with the fate of abducted women during their stay at the LRA. Enslavement was found to have happened in the *Ongwen* case due to the subjection of forced labour under coercive circumstances. I argue that abducted men integrated into the LRA lived under the same coercive conditions.

The judgement described extensively the LRA as an organisation, the structure of command and the ways to 'ensure capability in military operations'.[47] Emphasis was given to the LRA's modus operandi. The Trial Chamber noted that '[t]he LRA also became associated with forced recruitment or abductions.'[48] This applied to women and men; and was the way in which the LRA would maintain and increase their ranks. Most of its members were abductees.[49] The Chamber also pointed out that abductions were targeted at civilians capable of fighting. Once abducted, the civilians would undergo military training. Several measures were taken to deter and prevent escape, these included initiation rituals, beatings, forcing to kill and threats of death if they tried to escape.[50] The Chamber noted that the LRA maintained obedience

---

45 Ongwen Judgement, *supra* note 1, para. 2712. Similarly, in Ntaganda the Pre-Trial Chamber held that ownership can be show by a combination of factors such as 'the detention or captivity in which the victim was held and its duration, the limitations to the victim's free movement, measures taken to prevent or deter escape, the use of force, threat of force or coercion, and the personal circumstances of the victim, including his/her vulnerability'. ICC, *Prosecutor v. Bosco Ntaganda*, No. ICC-01/04-02/06-309, Pre-Trial Chamber II, Decision Pursuant to Article 61(7)(a) and (b) of the Rome Statute on the Charges of the Prosecutor Against Bosco Ntaganda, 9 June 2014, para. 275.

46 Ongwen Judgement, *supra* note 1, para. 2713. The ICC followed previous jurisprudence of the ICTY and the Special Court of Sierra Leone, *see* Kunarac et al. Trial Judgement, *supra* note 44 para.750; RUF Judgement, *supra* note 44, para. 161.

47 Ongwen Judgement, *supra* note 1, para. 121 *et seq.*

48 Ongwen Judgement, *supra* note 1, para. 7.

49 Pham et al., *supra* note 10, Blattman and Annan, *supra* note 10.

50 Ongwen Judgement, *supra* note 1, para. 129.

through strict rules, and if broken, abductees were subjected to punishment that ranged from beatings to executions.[51] Further, the Chamber highlighted that LRA members lived in conditions of constant fear:

> Sinia members, and LRA members generally, were threatened with death if they attempted escape. On certain occasions, execution of re-captured escapees in fact took place. Dominic Ongwen personally issued threats to LRA members that they would be killed if they attempted to escape and ordered killings of abductees in front of LRA members to illustrate this threat. Members were also threatened that their home areas would be attacked by the LRA if they escaped. A further measure taken to discourage escaping was giving soldiers false or negative information about life outside of the LRA ...[52]

What this demonstrates then, is the coercive environment abductees, irrespective of gender, lived in while in the LRA.

With respect to the indicia that shows the exercise of the powers attaching to ownership, several can be identified in relation to the abducted men (and boys). A number of different measures to prevent escape were taken (beating, killings, threats); psychological pressure, coercion and threats, cruel treatment, and forced labour were present. The latter as these abductees were forced to fight. The Special Court for Sierra Leone (SCSL) held in the *Revolutionary United Front* (RUF) and *Taylor* cases that to establish forced labour as enslavement, the pertinent consideration is whether 'the relevant persons had no choice as to whether they would work'.[53] In the *Ongwen* case, the Trial Chamber noted that 'a considerable number of witnesses, in particular lower ranking insiders, testified categorically that in the LRA, no one could refuse orders.'[54] For example, witness P-0252 was asked whether he could refuse to participate in an attack, stating that 'You cannot refuse. There is no way out when you are told to go'.[55] Abducted men turned soldiers could not refuse fighting, their labour (fighting) was forced.

---

51 *Ibid.*, para. 131.

52 *Ibid.*, para. 132. The Chamber also stated: 'This, even if just a personal perception on the part of the witness, illustrates the constant state of fear and apprehension created by the conditions in which LRA members lived.' para. 1012.

53 SCSL, *Prosecutor v Charles Taylor*, SCSL-03-01-T, Trial Chamber II, Judgement, 18 May 2012 paras 1679–1981, 1694–1695), para. 448 (Taylor Judgement); RUF Judgement, *supra* note 44, para. 202, citing Krnojelac Trial Judgement, para. 359. *See also Prosecutor v. Krnojelac*, Judgement (Appeals Chamber), IT-97-25-A, 17 September 2003, paras 194–195.

54 Ongwen Judgement, *supra* note 1, para. 951.

55 *Ibid.*, para. 954.

Therefore, it could be said that the circumstances in which civilian abductees integrated as fighters into the LRA met the elements of enslavement under Article 7.1.c of the Rome Statute. However, as noted in the previous section, no charges that had male abductees integrated into the LRA and forced to fight were brought up by the OTP, similarly women's fighting roles were not included in the enslavement charges.

4 Forcing Someone to Fight Can Be an International Crime: On International Law and Jurisprudence

As noted, absent from the enslavement charges in the *Ongwen* case is the fact that abductees were forced to fight and forcibly military trained. The ICC has yet to prosecute forced fighting as an international crime. Other international tribunals, however, have successfully prosecuted forced fighting under different offenses. This section traces international jurisprudence on the matter to show that forced fighting has been recognised as a crime and can fall under different categories of international crimes.

Whether forced fighting is considered a crime would depend on the circumstances of the forced labour. Not only is not a crime for State to compel their own nationals to serve in the armed forces, but it is not considered 'forced' labour.[56] The reasoning behind the exception is to prioritise matters of national defence and sovereignty.[57] In other circumstances, forcing someone to fight constitutes an autonomous crime. For example, Articles 8.2.a.v and 8.2.b.xv of the Rome Statute criminalise compelling a prisoner of war or civilian to serve in the forces of the hostile power or compelling nationals of the hostile party to take part in war operations against their country as a war crime.

The Rome Statute draws on the Geneva Conventions III and IV that include provisions that protect both civilians and combatants from being compelled to serve in the hostile forces.[58] In both Conventions, these provisions are

---

56 ILO Convention 29 establishes as an exception of forced labour 'any work or service exacted in virtue of compulsory military service laws for work of a purely military character', ILO Convention 29, *supra* note 38, Article 2.a. Likewise the International Convention on Civil and Political Rights provides in Article 8 a prohibition of forced labour, establishing that 'the term "forced or compulsory labour" shall not include any service of a military character'. International Covenant on Civil and Political Rights, Article 8.3.ii.

57 J. Allain, *Slavery in International Law: Of Human Exploitation and Trafficking* (Brill, Leiden, 2012).

58 Geneva Convention Relative to the Treatment of Prisoners of War (Geneva Convention III), Article 130; Geneva Convention Relative to the Protection of Civilian Persons in Time of (Geneva Convention IV), Article 147.

considered a grave breach. The 2020 Commentary on the Geneva Convention III notes that the prohibition of compelling a prisoner of war (POW) to serve in the hostile power is 'indirectly linked to Article 50'.[59] The latter includes an exhaustive list of labour prisoners of war can be employed to do, neither of which is of military character. Of importance here is the fact that coercing a POW to, for example, fight is considered a prohibited labour, and a war crime. Likewise, the same could be said about civilians that belong to the other party to the conflict and are coerce into serving the enemy forces.

The underlying rationale of the provisions is that a State cannot force someone to fight for their country's enemy state and against their own.[60] It is a matter or respecting allegiances.[61] However, these actions, compelling a prisoner of war or a civilian to serve in the hostile forces, are crimes only in an international armed conflict. There are no similar provisions for non-international armed conflicts.

In non-international armed conflicts where the belligerent parties are either a State against an armed group or the fighting takes place between armed groups, forcing someone to fight for an armed group against their State or against another armed group is not an autonomous crime. This is the situation in the *Ongwen* case, in which the fighting took place between the LRA and the Ugandan Government. In this non-international armed conflict, civilians were abducted and forcefully integrated into the LRA.

A look at international jurisprudence shows a myriad of responses to forcing civilians to fight or undergo activities that could be considered participation in hostilities (albeit not direct fighting). Forcing someone to fight has been prosecuted as crimes against humanity as well as war crimes. The difference between the two lies on the contextual elements of the crimes. Crimes against humanity require a systematic or widespread attack against the civilian population in furtherance of a State or organisational policy, whereas war crimes require the existence of an armed conflict and a nexus of the conduct to such conflict.[62]

The first international tribunal to address forced participation in the war effort was the International Military Tribunal of Nuremberg. The Nuremberg Tribunal found the accused guilty of deportation for forced labour as crimes

---

59 Convention (III) relative to the Treatment of Prisoners of War. Geneva, 12 August 1949. Commentary of 2020, Article 130, paras 5271–5276.

60 O. Triffterer and K. Ambos (eds), *Rome Statute of the International Criminal Court: A Commentary* (3rd Revised edition (Beck/Hart, Munich, 2016).

61 M Cherif Bassiouni, *Crimes against Humanity: Historical Evolution and Contemporary Application* (Cambridge University Press, Cambridge, 2011).

62 Rome Statute Articles 7 and 8; ICTY Statute.

against humanity and forced labour as a war crime[63] for forcing civilians to join German Legions and Organisations, which had a military nature and contributed to the war effort. The Tribunal stated '[a]ll the civilians so conscripted were forced to work for the German war effort. Civilians were required to register and many of those who registered were forced to join the Todt Organization and the Speer Legion, both of which were semi-military organizations involving some military training.'[64] Civilians were forced to fight.

Similarly, the ICTY had also successfully prosecuted forcing civilians to contribute to the military effort as a war crime and a crime against humanity. During the conflict in the Former Yugoslavia, cities were raided, and civilians were detained in camps. Several of these detainees were then forced to dig trenches for their captors, often under fire.[65] This activity directly contributed to the war effort and thus would fall under participation in hostilities.

Broadly, two set of crimes were charged and prosecuted over the forced trench digging: inhumane treatment as a violation of Common Article 3 of the Geneva Conventions (war crime) and persecution as a crime against humanity.[66] The tribunal considered that forcing civilians to do hazardous labour that involved active participation in hostilities was a war crime. Further, because these acts were directed at subjugating the Bosnian Muslim population, they also amounted to persecution as a crime against humanity.

So far, the only tribunal that has prosecuted forcing civilians to fight as enslavement as a crime against humanity has been the Special Court of Sierra Leone. The establishment of the SCSL was aimed at dealing with the crimes of a decade long civil war in the country. As a hybrid court, the jurisdiction of the

---

63 Article 6.b and c of the Nuremberg Charter reads '(b) WAR CRIMES: namely, violations of the laws or customs of war. Such violations shall include, but not be limited to, murder, ill-treatment or *deportation to slave labour* or for any other purpose of civilian population of or in occupied territory, murder or ill-treatment of prisoners of war or persons on the seas, killing of hostages, plunder of public or private property, wanton destruction of cities, towns, or villages, or devastation not justified by military necessity; (c) CRIMES AGAINST HUMANITY: namely, murder, extermination, *enslavement*, *deportation,* and other inhumane acts com- mitted against any civilian population, before or during the war, or persecutions on political, racial, or religious grounds in execution of or in connection with any crime within the, jurisdiction of the Tribunal, whether or not in violation of domestic law of the country where perpetrated.'(emphasis added).

64 International Military Tribunal for Nuremberg, Judgement and Sentence, 1 October 1946 (Nuremberg Judgement), p. 62.

65 ICTY, *Prosecutor v. Kordic and Cerkez*, Case No. IT-95-14/2-T, Trial Chamber, Judgement, 26 February 2001, para. 10 (Kordic and Cerkez, Judgement).

66 ICTY, *Prosecutor vs Blaskic*, Case No. IT-95-14, Trial Chamber, Judgement, March 3, 2000; Kordic and Cerkez, Judgement, *supra* note 65; ICTY, *Prosecutor v. Aleksovski*, Case No.: IT-95-14/1-T Trial Chamber, Judgement, 25 June 1999.

SCSL not only included international crimes, but also domestic ones relevant to the conflict.[67] The SCSL dealt with crimes committed by all parties to the conflict. The main armed group fighting the government was the RUF.

One of the characteristics of the RUF was the mistreatment of the civilian population. Amongst the harmful acts, civilians were abducted and forced to work. Some were sent to diamond mines, others were trained and sent to fight.[68] The SCSL found that on arrival to the camp, the rebels (RUF members) 'would register the names of the recruits and place them in platoons'. They would then undergo military training raging from physical exercise to guerrilla tactic and use of different weapons.[69] Once they 'graduated' they were sent to front lines to engage in combat.[70] The Court, when referring to the attack to Freetown, stated 'many among their ranks (RUF) were civilians who were forcibly recruited and trained'.[71] These civilians actively participating in combat committed crimes as well. Both situations, the forced military training and forced mining, were charged and successfully prosecuted as the crime against humanity of enslavement.

International jurisprudence shows that forcing someone to fight can be prosecuted as international crimes provided the elements of those crimes are met. Forcing someone to fight was considered forced labour and prosecuted as war crimes and crimes against humanity under different offenses that included deportation, inhumane treatment, persecution and enslavement. The *Ongwen* case significantly resembles the *RUF* case at the SCSL. Both conflicts were of non-international character, and in both the armed group abducted civilians to forced them to fight, and in both cases the prosecutors dealt with intra-party crimes. Yet, in the *Ongwen* case, male abductees were not recognised as victims of crimes.

5 On Gender Representations and the Enslavement Charges in the *Ongwen* Case

The previous section has shown that forcing someone to fight has been successfully prosecuted under different (international) crimes by some

67 However, no one was indicted for domestic crimes at the SCSL.

68 RUF Judgement, *supra* note 44, paras 1260, 1382, 1414, 1434, 1487. *See also* Taylor Judgement, supra note 53, paras 1679–1981, 1694–1695.

69 RUF Judgement, *supra* note 44 para. 1262; *See also* Taylor Judgement, *supra* note 53.

70 RUF Judgement, *supra* note 44, para. 1265.

71 *Ibid.*, para. 1513.

international tribunals, including enslavement as a crime against humanity. I have also argued that the treatment, military training, fighting and circumstances in which male abductees lived in the LRA met the criteria for enslavement as a crime against humanity. Nevertheless, the enslavement charges did not include them nor any other charge was brough to cover the situation of male abductees in the LRA.

While there are always considerations of prosecutorial discretion in the charging and prosecution of crimes, I argue however that the way in which the enslavement charges were brought by the OTP reflect gender representations in war, in particular the representation that 'women are victims and men are soldiers' that are then reinforced by the Trial Chamber. This affects the application of the Rome Statute in detriment of men, who are overlooked as victims once they become 'soldiers', while women's representation as victims displaces their fighting roles. The fact that a person is individualised as a fighter, strips away victimhood and instead turns the person into the criminal, leaving no space for nuance. Three characteristics of the charges, as brought by the OTP, support this view: the victims, the temporal scope of the enslavement charges in block 1 and the type of work considered forced labour.

With respect to the victims, one of the main differences between the enslavement charges in block 1 and the enslavement charge in block 3 is the victim group. The enslavement charges in block 1 have 'women, men and children' as victims. This means everyone targeted by the LRA during the attacks to the IDP camps. Conversely, the enslavement charge in block 3 only has women (and girls) as its victims. Thus, while everyone is considered a victim of enslavement in block 1, only women are considered victims of enslavement in block 3.

The other important distinction between the enslavement charges in block 1 and the enslavement charge in block 3 is the temporal scope of the crimes, as considered by the OTP. The charges in block 1 have a *constrained* period of time and recognise the situation of the abductees *up until their arrival* to the LRA camp. For example, in relation to the attack on Pajule, the OTP submitted that 'Dominic Ongwen is charged with enslavement as a crime against humanity, pursuant to Article 7(1)(c) of the Statute, *on or about 10 October 2003, at or near Pajule IDP camp*' (emphasis added).[72] The same occurs with the other three

72 Ongwen, Document Containing the Charges, *supra* note 15; Ongwen Judgement, *supra* note 1, para. 2838.

counts of enslavement in block 1.[73] Consequently, according to these charges, people were enslaved for about a day.

The temporal scope of the count of enslavement in block 3 is very different. For this count the OTP stated 'Ongwen is charged with enslavement as a crime against humanity, pursuant to Article 7(1)(c) of the Statute, *from at least 1 July 2002 until 31 December 2005*' (emphasis added).[74] This latter temporal scope responds to the temporal jurisdiction of the case at the ICC. This means that enslavement, for the charge in block 3, is a continuum. In other words, enslavement charges in block 1 recognised the fate of all abductees up until their arrival to the LRA camp, while the charge in block 3 recognised the fate of women *during their stay in* the LRA, thus once integrated into the LRA.

According to the OTP (and the Trial Chamber), the LRA abducted residents from the IDP's camps and, as noted previously, forced them to carry loot and wounded fighters to the LRA camp. Once at the LRA camp, some were released, but the young ones and bodily able were not.[75] They were forcefully integrated into the LRA. Following the OTP's narrative of the case, men integrated into the LRA were turned into fighters and women were distributed as wives.[76]

What is interesting is that slavery is a continuous crime.[77] This means that the enslavement does not cease because, for example, the nature of the work changes. Enslavement ceases when the victim is released, escapes or dies. Consequently, those abductees from the IDP's camps that were forcibly integrated into the LRA would have remained 'enslaved'. However, this aspect was only acknowledged for women, not men. There are no enslavement charges committed against men while staying in the LRA, they all relate to women (and girls).

In both cases (enslavement in block 1 and 3), the nature of labour these civilians were forced to performed and that was recognised as 'forced labour' by

---

73 'Under Count 20, Dominic Ongwen is charged with enslavement as a crime against humanity, pursuant to Article 7(1)(c) of the Statute, on or about 29 April 2004, at or near Odek IDP camp.'; 'Under Count 33, Dominic Ongwen is charged with enslavement as a crime against humanity, pursuant to Article 7(1)(c) of the Statute, on or about 19 May 2004, at or near Lukodi IDP camp.'; 'Under Count 46, Dominic Ongwen is charged with enslavement as a crime against humanity, pursuant to Article 7(1)(c) of the Statute, on or about 8 June 2004, at or near Abok IDP camp' Ongwen, Judgement, *supra* note 1, paras 2894, 2947, 2993. *See also* Ongwen, Document Containing the Charges, *supra* note 15; Ongwen, Confirmation of Charges *supra* note 16.

74 Ongwen Judgement, *supra* note1, para. 3085. *See also*, Ongwen, Document Containing the charges, *supra* note 15; Ongwen, Confirmation of Charges, *supra* note 16.

75 Ongwen Judgement, *supra* note 1, para. 176.

76 *Ibid.*, paras 129, 212, 214.

77 Triffterer and Ambos, *supra* note 60. *See also* Taylor Judgement, *supra* note 53, para. 118.

the OTP and the Trial Chamber, was of non-military character. For the victims in the block 1, the forced labour included carrying looted items and wounded soldiers. For the women integrated into the LRA the forced labour included domestic chores, such as fetching water, cooking, carrying items, doing laundry, and babysitting. The acknowledgement by the ICC that forced domestic labour constitutes enslavement and stressing its gendered dimensions are issues to be praised and can be considered one of the 'lights' in the *Ongwen* case. This type of activity is traditionally viewed as a 'women' activity. Thus, by highlighting the gender dimension the OTP and the Chambers are recognising how war can impact women differently. Nevertheless, it can also help reinforce representation of women as victims by completely disregarding women's fighting roles in the LRA.

In the *Ongwen* case, 'fighting' is not being viewed as 'labour' but instead operates to exclude potential victimhood status or to reinforce representations, specifically regarding women's passivity and men as soldiers. Women have been traditionally viewed and represented as objects of protection who lack agency.[78] This leads to a minimisation of their roles as fighters[79] or dismissing them completely. Although this traditional understanding, that women do not fight, has been challenged by feminist research and women's roles as fighters documented,[80] this gender representation still permeates analysis and practice.

---

78 J. Gardam, 'Women and the Law of Armed Conflict: Why the Silence?', 46 *The International and Comparative Law Quarterly* (1997) 55–80; J. Gardam, 'An Alien's Encounter with the Law of Armed Conflict', in N. Naffine and R.J. Owens (eds), *Sexing the subject of law* (LBC Information Services, Kew, 1997), pp. 233–250; A. Orford, *Reading Humanitarian Intervention: Human Rights and the Use of Force in International Law* (Cambridge University Press, Cambridge, 2003); H.M. Kinsella, 'Gendering Grotius: Sex and Sex Difference in the Laws of War', 34 *Political Theory* (2006) 161–191; H.M. Kinsella, *The Image before the Weapon: A Critical History of the Distinction between Combatant and Civilian* (Cornell University Press, Ithaca, NY, 2011); R.C. Carpenter, *'Innocent Women and Children': Gender, Norms and the Protection of Civilians* (Taylor & Francis, Oxford, 2006).

79 The Chamber stated 'There is ample evidence of the LRA abducting persons in Northern Uganda, and of the integration of the abductees into the LRA as fighters. Although there is evidence of female LRA members participating in military training and operations, including combat, the evidence discussed below indicates that the role of fighter was primarily intended for male abductees.' Ongwen Judgement, *supra* note 1, para. 894.

80 D. Mazurana, 'Women, Girls, and Non-State Armed Opposition Groups' in Carol Cohn and Cynthia H Enloe (eds), *Women and Wars: Contested Histories, Uncertain Futures* (Wiley, New York, NY, 2012), pp. 146–168; C.O.N. Moser, *Victims, Perpetrators or Actors?: Gender, Armed Conflict and Political Violence* (Zed Books, London, 2001); M. Alison, 'Women as Agents of Political Violence: Gendering Security', 35 *Security Dialogue* (2004) 447–463; M. Alison, 'Cogs in the Wheel? Women in the Liberation Tigers of Tamil Eelam', 6 *Civil Wars* (2003) 37–54; E.J. Friedman and I.A. Luciak, 'After the Revolution: Gender and Democracy

During trial, several witnesses accounted for women participation in fighting.[81] Further, as Dolnik and Butime state '[b]y allowing women to participate in combat operations, the group is in a position to harness all its human resources.'[82] All new abductees in the LRA would go through training irrespective of gender.[83] This indicates that, despite a perception of women as non-fighters, and their continuous reference as 'wives', their roles were fluid and they did contribute to the war effort as well. Yet, the OTP and the Chamber stressed that women were abducted to 'force them to serve in Sinia brigade as so-called 'wives' of members of Sinia brigade, and as domestic servants.'[84] By dismissing women's fighting roles, their victimhood is asserted. Likewise, by emphasising men's fighting roles their victimhood is negated.

Lastly, the OTP categorised the enslavement charges in block 3 as gender crimes. The Rome Statute was the first international criminal law convention to define 'gender'.[85] The Statute provides that 'the term "gender" refers to the two sexes, male and female, within the context of society. The term "gender" does

---

in El Salvador, Nicaragua, and Guatemala', 66 *The Journal of Politics* (2004) 1328–1330; E.J. Wood, 'Armed Groups and Sexual Violence: When Is Wartime Rape Rare?', 37 *Politics & Society* (2009) 131–161.

81 Ongwen Judgement, *supra* note 1, paras 166, 266, 270, 417. There is even an account of a female fighter raping a female, which was not brought up as rape by the OTP. 'During the attack in the camp, a female LRA attacker raped, a civilian resident of the camp, with a comb and a stick used for cooking, while the victim's husband was forced to watch. The rape was committed with such force that started to bleed.' Ongwen Judgement, *supra* note 1, para. 166.

82 A. Dolnik and H. Butime, *Understanding the Lord's Resistance Army Insurgency* (World Scientific, Singapore, 2017), p. 209.

83 'They received us in the barracks, they cleaned and washed our wounds, until our wounds where healed they kept us well. They then started recruiting us into the armed forces by training us ... Then they gave us guns ... (Informant 10)'. M. Gustavsson, J. Oruut and B. Rubenson, 'Girl Soldiers with Lord's Resistance Army in Uganda Fighting for Survival: Experiences of Young Women Abducted by LRA', 15 *Children's Geographies* (2017) 690–702, p. 695. 'After training in military tactics and use of weaponry, girls participate in front-line combat, with some holding command positions within the LRA.' S. McKay, 'Girls as "Weapons of Terror" in Northern Uganda and Sierra Leonean Rebel Fighting Forces', 28 *Studies in Conflict & Terrorism* (2005) 385–397, p. 390.

84 Ongwen Judgement, *supra* note 1, para. 212.

85 For a discussion on this topic *See*: Grey, *supra* note 6; V. Oosterveld, 'The Definition of Gender in the Rome Statute of the International Criminal Court: A Step Forward or Back for International Criminal Justice', 18 *Harvard Human Rights Journal* (2005) 55–84; V. Oosterveld, 'Constructive Ambiguity and the Meaning of "Gender" for the International Criminal Court', 16 *International Feminist Journal of Politics* (2014) 563–580; I. Rosenthal, V. Oosterveld and S. SáCouto (eds), 'What Is "Gender" in International Criminal Law?' in *Gender and International Criminal Law* (Oxford University Press, Oxford, 2022), chapter 1.

not indicate any meaning different from the above.'[86] In 2014 the OTP published its Policy on Gender in which it interprets and understands the definition of gender. In the Policy, the OTP 'acknowledges the social construction of gender, and the accompanying roles, behaviours, activities, and attributes assigned to women and men, and to girls and boys.'[87] The Policy also defines gender-based crimes as 'those committed against persons, whether male or female, because of their sex and/or socially constructed gender roles'.[88] If, according to the OTP, women were abducted to become 'wives' and domestic servants and men were abducted to become soldiers, then not only the crimes committed against women are gender-based crimes, but also those committed against men, as both of these respond to traditional understanding of gender roles. Yet, the fate of men in the LRA was not considered criminal by the OTP nor the Trial Chamber.[89] Gender-based crimes in the *Ongwen* case are synonymous with crimes against women. This reinforces women's representations as victims and men's representation as perpetrators.

6 Conclusion

At the ICC, forcing someone to fight is yet to be considered enslavement, or any other international crime. Arguable, the *Ongwen* case was, in this regard, a lost opportunity. Dominic Ongwen was charged with (and found guilty of) several counts on enslavement as crime against humanity. The factual charges differ between the ones in block 1 and the one in block 3. The four counts of enslavement in block 1 include the period in which abductees, men, women, and children, were made to carry items and wounded soldiers from the IDP camp to the LRA camp. The one in block 3 includes the domestic labour women were forced to do while staying in the LRA. The exclusion of men as victims of enslavement (in block 3) is due to men being represented only as fighters, and therefore as perpetrators. In turn, women's fighting roles have been dismissed and they are only represented as victims.

The enslavement charges in the *Ongwen* case, show how gender representations in war impact victimhood recognition at the ICC. Men are not

86 Rome Statute, Article 7.3.

87 ICC, Policy Paper on Sexual and Gender-based Crimes, June 2014, p. 3.

88 *Ibid.*

89 Except for the conscription, enlistment, and use of children below the age of 15 to actively participate in hostilities, a crime that was charged and of which Ongwen was found guilty of. However, this crime only protects younger children.

considered victims once they become fighters, women in turn are considered victims at the expense of their fighting roles. The LRA increased their ranks through abductions. All abductees in the LRA were subjected to mistreatment, threats of death if they tried to escape and physical punishment when disobeying orders. The environment in which they were in was coercive. They were all forced to work, including military training, and fighting. Despite that enslavement is a continuous crime, that forcing a civilian to fight can be an international crime, as supported by international jurisprudence, and that the elements of enslavement were met with relation to men in the *Ongwen* case; men's fate in the LRA was not object of the enslavement charges. The charges that had men as victims were limited in time, up until the moment they were forced to become fighters. For women, enslavement appears as a continuum but only had some aspect of the forced labour women endured recognised. Their fighting roles were not included in the charges.

The OTP held that men were abducted to become fighters and women to become 'wives'. But the OTP only made the latter a gender-based crime, ignoring men's gendered dimension. Grey has stated that 'the inclusion of gender-based crimes in the ICC's legal framework did not guarantee that these crimes would be effectively investigated and prosecuted in practice.'[90] Heathcote et al have warned that international criminal law structural bias 'places individuals and harms into specific gendered categories'.[91] This can be seen in the *Ongwen* case with respect to the enslavement charges. The ICC's approach to the crime of enslavement in this case sustains an unequal protection that leads to the reinforcement of gender representations, in particular the role of men and women in war.

---

90 Grey, *supra* note 6, p. 3.

91 G. Heathcote, S. Bertotti, E. Jones and S.A. Labenski, *The Law of War and Peace: A Gender Analysis Volume 1* (Zed Books, London, 2021), p. 185.

CHAPTER 7

Constructing a Sensory Alternative to the *Ongwen* Judgment

Raghavi Viswanath and Fangyi Li

Abstract

Much ink has been spilt criticising the ICC's *Ongwen* trial judgment for its failure to grasp the cultural context in which the accused Ongwen and the Acholi community were embedded. Some scholars blame this on the poor quality of translation services, others attribute it to the 'binarism' of judgments. We offer another explanation for the *Ongwen* judgment's deficiencies: its purely textual format. The judgment shows that the continued preference for textual judgments in international criminal law sterilises victims' experiences, decontextualises evidence, and muffles objectivity. This ties into the historical preference for text over senses, a colonially engineered decision aimed at suppressing non-Western epistemologies. In this paper, we call for the international criminal law judgment to embrace 'the opportunities of the wider sensory field'. Drawing on the pervasive sensory dimensions of international criminal law, we argue that a sensory reimagination of judgments would better serve international criminal law's affective potential by empowering survivors and achieving a more reparative and reconstructive justice.

Keywords

international criminal justice – judgments – *Ongwen* – senses and affect – textual medium

1 Introduction

On 4 February 2021, Trial Chamber IX of the International Criminal Court (hereinafter ICC) declared Lord's Resistance Army (hereinafter LRA) Brigade Commander Dominic Ongwen guilty of 61 counts of war crimes and crimes

 | DOI: 10.1163/9789004743380_008

against humanity committed in Uganda from 1 July 2002 to 31 December 2005.[1] The *Ongwen* case implicated thorny questions including the ICC's jurisdiction over minors committing war crimes and duress as a defence to international criminal liability. Scholars and practitioners have since launched multiple critiques of the failure of the judgment to adopt a culturally-sensitive approach in analysing the elements of war crimes and in establishing jurisdiction.[2] The Court's narrow reading of otherwise elastic terms like 'kadoge'/'kadogi' (Acholi terms typically used to refer to anyone 'younger than oneself') to draw equivalence with the legal bracket of childhood as under the Rome Statute has been a constant subject of this critique.[3]

Some scholars attribute the Court's failure to the poor quality of translation services.[4] Others attribute it to the 'binarism' of judgments, as instruments which have no bandwidth for ambiguities or internal contestations.[5] Judges are therefore left with no choice but to construct linear narratives by cherry-picking from amongst bundles of testimonies.

In this paper, we offer a different, more fundamental explanation for the *Ongwen* judgment's deficiencies: the *purely* textual format of the judgment. One look at the court records for the *Ongwen* case shows that there are no full public audio/video recordings of the witness testimonies (which formed the basis of the trial judgment). When seen in conjunction with the final judgment (which is purely textual and cites only written material),[6] the legacy of the case remains purely textual.

We argue that a textual judgment afflicts significant epistemic and material injuries on the victims for whom it is delivered. Our argument rests on two

1 ICC, *Prosecutor* v. *Dominic Ongwen*, ICC-02/04-01/15-1762-Red, Trial Chamber IX, Judgment, 4 February 2021 (hereinafter Judgment).

2 P. Chifflet and I. Freckelton, 'The Mental Incapacity Defence in International Criminal Law: Ramifications from the *Ongwen* Trial Judgment', 22(4) *International Criminal Law Review* (2022) 751–779; J.I. Bishay, 'Cultural Expertise and International Criminal Law', in L. Holden (ed.), *Cultural Expertise, Law, and Rights* (Routledge, London, 2023), pp. 177–187; A. Nistor, *Ongwen blog symposium: Culture as evidence and the construction of (un)certainty in the Dominic Ongwen trial* (2021), available online at www.armedgroups-internationallaw.org/2021/04/15/ongwen-blog-symposium-culture-as-evidence-and-the-construction-of-uncertainty-in-the-dominc-ongwen-trial/ (accessed 10 March 2023).

3 Nistor, *ibid.*

4 L.S. Van-Lin, 'When We Don't Speak the Same Language: The Challenges of Multilingual Justice at the ICC', in E.A. Ankumah (ed.), *The International Criminal Court in Africa: One Decade On* (Intersentia, Cambridge, 2016), pp. 275–298.

5 S. D'hondt, J.-P. Peréz-León-Acevedo, F. Ferraz de Almeida and E. Barrett, 'Trajectories of spirituality: Producing and assessing cultural evidence at the International Criminal Court', *Language in Society* (forthcoming).

6 Judgment.

limbs. Firstly, it is based on the deficiencies of the textual medium, such as its proclivity for singular and depersonalised narratives that are isolated from socio-cultural contexts. Secondly and relatedly, we show that despite these deficiencies, text is preferred over sensory and affective mediums because it prevents challenges to the epistemic and social monopoly of law and its community of arbiters. Here, sensory experiences speak to causal results of external stimuli and affective experiences speak to internal, emotional changes.[7] In this paper, we read affect as the necessary by-product of senses, and consider the value of affect in this attendant form alone. Although engaging with international criminal law remains a predominantly sensory and affective exercise, the tool of the judgment—which is the final and lasting legacy of each case—erases this aspect of the victims' lived experiences by sticking to the textual medium.

This paper joins the long-standing pedigree of socio-legal scholars such as Mulcahy who have lamented lawyers' obsession with text and have asked different questions about how legal phenomenon are experienced, constructed, conditioned, or challenged through senses.[8] At the same time, it joins scholarship that spotlights the reparative value of senses and affect for international criminal law. As Thorne argues, unlike text, senses and affect are by nature dynamic, emotional, immediate, emancipatory, and hold immense potential for negotiation, challenge, and memory-making.[9] We spotlight these values and call for the making of a jurisprudence of *senses*. In particular, we turn our attention to the tool of the judgment, which is universally understood as the pinnacle of the case, to attend to the 'full panoply of sensory dynamics'.[10]

Using the *Ongwen* trial judgment as a case study, Section 2 of this paper spotlights multiple instances where text afflicts injustice—epistemic, legal, and procedural. In so doing, it also queries why text is preferred as the medium of the judgment at the expense of senses and affect. In other words, it gives historical and social reasons for international criminal law and particularly judgments' aversion to senses and affect. The *Ongwen* case, as we explain below, is suited for this study given that it emerges from a conflict seeped in sensory experiences and from mass sexual crimes that rely heavily on sensory

7 A. Philippopoulos-Mihalopoulos, 'Atmospheres of law: Senses, Affects, Lawscapes', 7 *Emotion, Space and Society* (2013) 35–44.

8 L. Mulcahy, E. Rowden and K. Orr, 'Making Sense of Law: Pungency, Feel and Rhythm', 14(2) *Law, Culture and the Humanities* (2018) 199–201.

9 B. Thorne, 'Atrocity archive: Sensory expression of past-present-future', 15(2) *Law and Humanities* (2021) 272–278.

10 L. Mulcahy, 'Eyes of the Law: A Visual Turn in Socio-Legal Studies?', 44 *Journal of Law and Society* (2017) 111–128.

subjugations. The trial judgment is especially relevant because of the density of sensory material it considers and the value that the sensory experiences carry for the Acholi community. In fact, one witness in the case even remarked that 'if the world should know what happened [in Uganda], then this photo would be a very clear message',[11] making a reference to how photographs and videos from the conflict told a much clearer story of the extent of loss suffered by the Acholi community.

With this background, Section 3 launches into a historical examination of international criminal law's engagement with senses and affect—both inside and outside the courtroom. Upon reflecting on the pervasive presence of senses and affect in international criminal law and the reasons why this presence is systematically censored in the judgment, Section 4 discusses how the stakeholders of international criminal law are better served by activating the sensory and affective potential of judgments, drawing on examples from the *Ongwen* case. This section demonstrates how the current toolboxes of the ICC can be channelled to equip judgments to provide direct outlets for the voices/ faces of the unheard local communities and create meaningful relationships with the international criminal justice project's multiple stakeholders.

2 Limitations of Textual Judgments

As Goodrich notes, the legal tradition—both religious and secular - has been predominantly etched in text.[12] Legal interpretation has been mainly concerned with finding textually correct meanings of legal words and phrases. This textual correctness has been transported to most parts of the world as a result of the linguicism that is endemic in domestic and international legal systems.[13] Some argue that the dominance of text came to be because text was perceived as stable and impervious to quick change.[14] To others, text guaranteed accessibility and clarity.[15]

11 ICC, *Ongwen case: "In the courtroom" programme, 1 May–17 July 2017*, available online at www.youtube.com/watch?v=wJcUeBYbjcU (accessed 20 August 2023).

12 P. Goodrich, 'Traditions of interpretation and the status of the legal text', 6(1) *Journal of the Society of Legal Scholars* (1986) 53–69.

13 O. Ammann, 'Language Bias in International Legal Scholarship: Symptoms, Explanations, Implications and Remedies', 33(3) *European Journal of International Law* (2022) 821–850.

14 F.K. von Savigny, *System des heutigen römischen Rechts* (Bei Veit und Comp, Berlin, 1841), p. 220.

15 O. Ammann, 'The Interpretative Methods of International Law: What Are They, and Why Use Them?', in *Domestic Courts and the Interpretation of International Law* (Brill Nijhoff, Leiden, 2020), pp. 191–222.

These virtues are valued the most in the tool of the written judgment, which, as Judge Bertram Schmitt observed in his oral pronouncement of the summary of the *Ongwen* judgment, is the 'only authoritative document' articulating the Court's position.[16] The judgment is the lasting legacy of the case, the most decisive pronouncement by the Court of what is right and what is wrong. In international criminal tribunals, more than the substantive outcome, judgments serve as carriers of collective memory of violent conflicts and offer descriptions of historical events.[17] As David Scheffer, the former UN Secretary-General's special expert on assistance to the Khmer Rouge trials, remarked, the rendering of the judgment against the former Khmer Rouge leaders by the Extraordinary Chambers in the Courts of Cambodia (hereinafter ECCC) was a 'Nuremberg moment, carrying significant weight for Cambodia, international criminal justice, and the annals of history'.[18] For international institutions, judgments are also ways to firm up their own power and legitimacy as well as that of the international society on whose behalf they consider themselves to be speaking.[19] Text—and its attendant clarity and accessibility—is in service of this objective.

However, the *Ongwen* case usefully illustrates that text, especially within the international criminal law setting, afflicts more harm than one would have imagined. If so, it bears querying why international criminal law prioritises text over senses and affect. What is in it for international criminal law and those who make and unmake it?

First, a textual judgment has the effect of depersonalising key stakeholders in the international criminal law story. Feminist scholars such as Williams and Minow note how the emancipatory potential of voice cannot be slighted.[20] Even if international legal tribunals suffer from problems of Eurocentrism,[21]

---

16 ICC, *Ongwen case: Summary of the verdict, 4 February* 2023, available online at www.youtube.com/watch?v=A858kVSh20c, minute 1:58 to 2:05 (accessed 20 August 2023).

17 M. Hirsch, 'The Role of International Tribunals in the Construction of Collective Memories', 16–43 *Hebrew University of Jerusalem Legal Research Paper* (2016) 1–12, p. 3.

18 'Khmer rouge leaders found guilty of genocide in landmark ruling', *AFP* (16 November 2018).

19 S. Nimage, 'An International Conscience Collective? A Durkheimian Analysis of International Criminal Law' 7 *International Criminal Law Review* (2007) 561–619, pp. 605–607.

20 P. Williams, *The Alchemy of Race and Rights* (Harvard University Press, Cambridge, MA, 1991), p. 153; M. Minow, *Making All the Difference: Inclusion, Exclusion, and American Law* (Cornell University Press, Ithaka, NY, 1991).

21 N. Tzouvala, 'The Specter of Eurocentrism in International Legal History', 31(2) *Yale Journal of Law and the Humanities* (2021) 413–432.

enjoying personhood and voice in these institutions is imperative for the communities whose life stories these institutions are adjudicating to be able to claim ownership over them.

As Kalpouzos suggests, the losing of voice at adjudicative tribunals afflicts double victimisation - where communities are first divested of their agency by violent conflicts and then have to go through this loss of voice again when they attempt to seek legal recourse.[22] This is what we see in the *Ongwen* case as well, where the text of the judgment reduces victims to mere pseudonyms. Case in point is witness P-0280. P-0280, a former child soldier abducted from the Abok IDP camp in 2016 when he was around 15 years old, testified in his own voice about how he was treated upon abduction and why the LRA chose to abduct younger men.[23] However, his voice found no microphone or audience in the written judgment.

As the psychoanalyst Ferenczi showed, silencing through loss of voice is an inherent characteristic of sexual abuse. In such a case, when a victim does decide to testify in their own voice, treating them as voiceless in a court can have a traumatising effect, mirroring their silencing by the perpetrator.[24] In the *Ongwen* case, this is what was done to witness P-0352, a victim of sexual crimes who was assigned to Ongwen's household and forced to marry an LRA soldier, who testified to Ongwen's sexual crimes.[25] Her testimony was crucial in establishing the crimes committed by the LRA and the accused Dominic Ongwen. But the judgment only offered judge-renditions of her profound testimony, stripped of her lived experience and bravery.[26]

In cases like *Ongwen* which are marked by rampant sexual crimes, testimonies lean heavily on sensory details. As van der Kolk notes, 'the imprints of traumatic experiences are organised not as coherent logical narrative but as fragmented sensory and emotional traces'.[27] Several neurobiological and psychological studies have also found testimonies of sexual abuse survivors to be non-linear and consisting of primary sensory information (sights, smells,

22 I. Kalpouzos, 'International Criminal Law and the Violence against Migrants', 21(3) *German Law Journal* (2020) 571–597. H. Arendt makes a similar argument in *The Origins of Totalitarianism,* New Edition with Added Prefaces (Harcourt Brace, Lomdon, 1951/1979).

23 Judgment, paras 501–505; ICC, *supra* note 11 (1:40–2:35).

24 M.R. Khan, 'Between spoken word and written language: Playing', 29 *Etudes Psychotherapiques* (1977) 163–164.

25 Judgment, paras 404–405; ICC, *supra* note 11 (3:01–4:19).

26 Judgment, paras 404–405, 2151–2152, 2184–2186.

27 B.A. van der Kolk, 'Trauma and memory', 52(S1) *Psychiatry and Clinical Neurosciences* (1998) S52–S64.

sounds) linked to physiological fear symptoms.[28] There are several examples of this in the *Ongwen* trial itself. P-0396, one of the abducted wives in the LRA household, testified about her experiences with facial blurs.[29] She described her husband as 'as tall and light-skinned, with long hair, and said, notably, that he could not straighten his arms 'because they were a bit bent'.[30] She also spoke of how the abductees were each 'given a human being to remove the liver, heart and swallow it in order to become strong'.[31] Another sexual abuse survivor P-0101, when describing the events of her abduction by Ongwen, vividly recalled her school uniform, 'a pink skirt and white blouse with red stripes on the arms'.[32] She also remembered that Ongwen smeared water and shea nut oil on her in 'order to mark her as his'.[33] While a reading of such details offers possibilities to visualise the perpetrators described, the centrality and gravity of the sensory details contained gets buried in the printed text. In fact, text treats these sensory details as irrelevant and incoherent, rather than crucial evidence of the victims' trauma. In written form, silences or incoherence or randomness can be incorrectly translated as a lack in the speaker to relate the actual traumatic event.

Mandel recognises that voice—even through acute silences and epistemological gaps—is better equipped to capture the traumatic impact of certain experiences on the speakers' psyche.[34] In this way, voice is able to overcome the limitations of language when trying to convey the horror of trauma.[35] That said, although there is reason to believe that voice is better equipped to convey trauma, it could also have retraumatising effects. As studies reveal, even a 'particular accent or intonation, the pitch of a voice, or the sound of a language can trigger intrusions and flashbacks by which the traumatic event is relived'.[36]

In the case of the judgment, this trauma would be more accurately conveyed if the judgment were to plug in audio-excerpts from witnesses' testimonies in their own voice, with the blurs. Notably, ours is not a call to remove the

---

28 C.R. Brewin, 'The Nature and Significance of Memory Disturbance in Posttraumatic Stress Disorder', 7(1) *Annual Review of Clinical Psychology* (2011) 203–227.
29 Judgment, paras 418–427.
30 Judgment, para. 420.
31 Judgment, para. 423.
32 Judgment, para. 2013.
33 *Ibid.*
34 *Ibid.*
35 N. Mandel, *Against the Unspeakable: complicity, the Holocaust and slavery* (University of Virginia Press, Charlottesville, VA, 2006).
36 B. Busch and T. McNamara, 'Language and Trauma: An Introduction', 41(3) *Applied Linguistics* (2020) 323–333.

protections offered to witnesses by any means. It is only a call to acknowledge witness identities in the way that they intend, without reducing them to mere written figments. By the Trial Chamber's own admission, 'these victims have a right not to be forgotten. They have the right to be mentioned explicitly'.[37] As much as we recognise the Court's duty towards safeguarding the safety of the witnesses, a mere written account of their testimony in a judge's words is insufficient.

However, as we probe the reasons for the preference of text as the chosen medium for judgments, it becomes overtly clear, as scholars like Mulcahy explain, that this preference is neither unique to international criminal law, nor is it new. All forms of law and its many dispensers have traditionally strived to ensure that their epistemic control remains unchallenged.[38] This is what has motivated both the preference for text and the systematic erasure of sensory epistemologies—particularly epistemologies of those who are not lawmakers or judges. A historical study reveals that as colonialism became more widespread, the preference for written text was widely enforced to justify the disqualification of colonised peoples from law-making spaces, citing their illiteracy and incompetence.[39]

A similar imbalance in epistemic authority has been built into international criminal law.[40] Even now, decades after the formal demise of colonialism in most parts of the world, the Rome Statute and the Rules of Procedure and Evidence retain orthodox and Eurocentric notions of 'literacy' to classify those who seek redress from the Court. Rule 102 of the Rules of Procedure and Evidence of the Court allows illiterate persons to submit communications in audio, video, or other electronic forms. The framing of this rule as a type of 'accommodation' made by the Court strongly indicates the superiority of status enjoyed by literate persons and the lowly place awarded to those who do not meet such thresholds of literacy. On this basis, those who are not well-versed with textual epistemologies are discredited in their capacity as knowers. In other words, international criminal law also leaves no room for visual, sonic, and oral epistemologies.[41]

37 ICC, *Ongwen case: summary of the verdict, 4 February 2021*, available online at www.icc-cpi.int/sites/default/files/itemsDocuments/ongwen-verdict/2021.02.03-Ongwen-judgment-Summary.pdf (accessed 15 April 2023), para. 10.

38 Mulcahy *et al.*, *supra* note 8.

39 *Ibid.*

40 Ammann, *supra* note 13.

41 A. Craft, *Anishinaabe Nibi Inaakonigewin Report: Reflecting the Water Laws research gathering conducted with Anishinaabe elders at Roseau River*, available online at ssrn.com/abstract=3433235 (accessed 3 August 2023).

We argue that the harms of such a hierarchy in literacy are most clearly seen in the written judgment,[42] which as Judge Schmitt observed in his oral pronouncement of the summary of the *Ongwen* judgment, is the 'only authoritative document' articulating the Court's position.[43]

The task of arriving at a judgment confers great power and responsibility in the judges. In Sander's words, 'judges act as positivist historians, imposing consensus on contrasting and conflicting evidence, by selecting one narrative in preference to others, and ultimately by conferring the mantle of fact on the narratives they construct and validate in their judgments'.[44] Judges become the sole gatekeepers of the histories and realities encapsulated in the dispute.[45] Judges—especially in international criminal tribunals - are acutely conscious of this responsibility. Typically, the expectation of judges, as former judge Theodor Meron notes, is their 'will and ability to overcome their preconceived preferences and consider the case at issue dispassionately, objectively, and fairly'.[46] However, the truth is that judges are self-interested individuals. The judgment is an instrument for judges to craft their personal legacies, legacies that they prefer to keep immune from tarnish. The first name that comes to mind in conversations about judges creating personal legacies through judgments is Judge Cassese. With every move, from the International Criminal Tribunal for the Former Yugoslavia to the Special Tribunal for Lebanon, Cassese drove the law forward in ways that were thought to be beyond the remit of judges.[47] In an interview, Cassese admitted that he 'was not only a judge, passive and

42 B. Sander, 'The Method is the Message: Law, Narrative Authority and Historical Contestation in International Criminal Courts', 19(1) *Melbourne Journal of International. Law* (2018) 299–334.

43 ICC, *supra* note 16 (1:58–2:05).

44 B. Sander, 'Introduction', in *Doing Justice to History: Confronting the Past in International Criminal Courts* (Oxford University Press, Oxford, 2021), pp. 1–25; E.H. Reiter, 'Fact, Narrative, and the Judicial Uses of History: Delgamuukw and Beyond', 8 *Indigenous Law Journal* (2010) 55–78.

45 V. Nesiah, 'The Trials of History: Losing Justice in the Monstrous and the Banal', in R. Buchanan and P. Zumbansen (eds.), *Law in Transition: Human Rights, Development and Transitional Justice* (Bloosmbury, London, 2014), pp. 289–308. (highlighting how transitional justice institutions operate as 'official gatekeepers—privileging some histories while obscuring others').

46 T. Meron, *Standing Up for Justice: The Challenges of Trying Atrocity Crimes* (Oxford University Press, Oxford, 2021), p. 177.

47 Listen to this excellent podcast series 'Antonio Cassese: The Stubborn Sparrow' (episodes 0, 1, and 5 are of particular relevance to our point), available online at antonio-cassese-the-stubborn-sparrow-f3145101.simplecast.com/episodes (accessed 25 April 2023).

waiting for the prosecution'.[48] He 'was acting as a president of an international tribunal. That leadership role called on him to push for action also'. This is not merely a statement of expectation, but also one of aspiration. Text—with its inner attribute of finality—acts as the perfect accomplice for these aspirations of judges. It disguises the self-interest of judges, and still allows judges to weld the directions of international criminal law without being seen as internal cogs in the machine.

Second, the exclusive reliance on text in the written judgment ignores the wider interactional context and may end up distorting what the witnesses intended to say. Illustratively, in their article, D'hondt, Perez-Leon-Acevedo, Ferraz de Almeida and Barrett show how judges selectively quote short pieces of witness testimonies without going so far as to contextualise.[49] When discussing the belief within the LRA in the spiritual powers of Joseph Kony, the then-leader of the LRA, the Trial Chamber put forward a theory that the young, newly inducted child soldiers tend to believe in Kony's powers and their belief subsided/disappeared the longer they stayed.[50] In doing so, the Court referenced testimonies of witness P-0231 by gluing his answers to questions posed by different actors together and made it look like 'a monological statement by P-0231 delivered in a continuous stretch of talk'.[51] However, when we see the testimony following the excerpt, it becomes clear that P-0231 lost faith in Kony's powers because of a political rift, which took place after the period during which Ongwen's charged crimes occurred, revealing that the length of stay had nothing to do with his belief.[52]

Similarly, Nistor notes how the term 'kadoge'/'kadogi' (meaning 'child') was quite elastic in the Acholi language. It could be used to describe anyone younger than oneself. But the Trial Chamber cherry-picked some parts of the witness testimonies to pin down the 13–15 years age bracket for 'childhood', without giving credit to its flexible, ever-changing meaning in the Acholi vernacular.[53]

48 H.V. Stuart and M. Simons, *The Prosecutor and the Judge: Benjamin Ferencz and Antonio Cassese - Interviews and Writings Paperback* (Amsterdam University Press, Amsterdam, 2010). *See* excerpt available online at press.uchicago.edu/Misc/Chicago/9789085550235.html (accessed 2 May 2023).

49 D'hondt *et al.*, *supra* note 5.

50 Judgment, para. 2645.

51 D'hondt *et al.*, *supra* note 5; Judgment, para. 2646.

52 ICC, *Prosecutor* v. *Dominic Ongwen*, ICC-02/04-01/15-T-123-Red2-ENG, Trial Chamber IX, Transcript, 2 November 2016, lines 20–23.

53 A. Nistor, A. Merrylees and B. Hola, 'Spellbound at the International Criminal Court: The intersection of spirituality & international criminal law', in J. Fraser and B.M.G. Leyh (eds.), *Intersections of Law and Culture at the International Criminal Court* (Edward Elgar, Cheltenham, 2020), pp. 147–168; Nistor, *supra* note 2.

Nistor's example exposes the Court's inability to escape its Western gaze when engaging with different cultural contexts.[54] The Court's mis-reading of the Acholi terms 'kadoge' and 'kadogi' emerge from its predisposition to Western epistemologies which expect consistency and fixedness in language. This is also visible in the Court's constant use of the qualifier 'so-called' when referring to the wives and husbands in the LRA camps, for instance in its recounting of P-0396's testimony.[55] Interestingly, the witness herself never used the qualifier, instead choosing to speak of the wives and husbands of the household in a matter-of-fact way.[56] Similarly, when referring to her statement that she was forced to cut open an abductee and swallow their organs, the Court almost exoticised the experience without offering any consideration for the trauma it afflicted on her. Case in point is this excerpt from the transcript of her testimony:

> QUESTIONED BY MR AYENA ODONGO:
> Q. [12:38:42] Madam Witness, can you kindly tell Court how big you discovered the human liver to be, the liver of that girl, and then her heart? How big were they?
> A. [12:39:08] I cannot know how big. I cannot know the size.
> Q. [12:39:15] Were you asked to chew or you just were asked to swallow?
> A. [12:39:34] How can you swallow something without chewing?
> PRESIDING JUDGE SCHMITT: [12:39:39] May I shortly, just shortly. Madam Witness, was—were these body parts, were they cut into smaller pieces? Or could you explain it to us in a way that we can picture it, that we have also an idea in our heads what has happened?
> THE WITNESS: [12:40:02] (Interpretation) It was cut into pieces.
> PRESIDING JUDGE SCHMITT: [12:40:06] And who cut it?
> THE WITNESS: [12:40:15] (Interpretation) I do not know who cut it.

As one can see, the judge and the lawyer seem to be constantly questioning the witness about the size of the organs, how she consumed them, and whether

---

54 U. Obo and D. Ekpe, 'Africa and the international criminal court: A case of imperialism by another name', 3(10) *International Journal of Development and Sustainability* (2014) 2025–2036.

55 Judgment, paras 419, 420, 427.

56 ICC, *Prosecutor* v. *Dominic Ongwen*, ICC-02/04-01/15-T-126-Red2-ENG, Trial Chamber IX, Transcript, 8 November 2017; ICC, *Prosecutor* v. *Dominic Ongwen*, ICC-02/04-01/15-T-127-Red2-ENG, Trial Chamber IX, Transcript, 9 November 2017.

they had been cut into pieces.[57] The witness even expresses her own annoyance at the relevance of these questions and her discomfort in answering them. The hostile and clinical nature of the questioning does not have margin for cultural sensitivity. In fact, in her autobiography, Evelyn Amony, a former LRA abductee, speaks at length about how the eating of goat livers was a celebratory practice in the Acholi community.[58] The Court, however, did not acknowledge or bring this cultural knowledge onto its record. This is only one of several instances which reveal the Court's Western gaze.

Several scholars have written about how international criminal law's Western gaze has been cultivated through notions of disgust and savagery.[59] These notions often use *shadows* of senses and affect. As López's remarks, 'given the longstanding characterisation of international crimes as evil, it perpetuates well-documented stereotypes of darker *skin* being associated with wickedness, thereby building on a pernicious narrative of the 'evil Black body'.[60] Fino writes about how prosecutors bolster rhetorics of perpetrators being immoral and savage using sounds, sights, and smells *described by* eyewitnesses.[61] For instance, during the proceedings of Case 002/02 at the ECCC, Witness Him Huy graphically described how the prisoners detained in the Choeung Ek Genocidal Center would be executed to the sound of bleating generators, so that the screams of the prisoners would be inaudible.[62] The *Ongwen* case is littered with such examples. For instance, when ascertaining whether Ongwen genuinely had a mental disorder, the Court relied on expert testimonies which claimed that Ongwen's ability to experience the *smell of* blood or gun powder in anticipation of an attack were signs of his mental instability.[63] P-0286 also testified about how he 'heard people whistling while others were burning the

57 *Ibid.*

58 E. Amony, *I Am Evelyn Amony* (2016), available online at www.unwomen.org/en/news/stories/2016/6/i-am-evelyn-amony-a-memoir-of-war-rape-and-survival (accessed 21 August 2023).

59 S. Xavier and J. Reynolds, '"The Dark Corners of the World": TWAIL and International Criminal Justice', 14 (4) *Journal of International Criminal Justice* (2016) 959–983.

60 R. López, 'Black Guilt, White Guilt at the International Criminal Court', in M. Sirleaf (ed.), *Race and National Security* (Oxford University Press, Oxford, 2023), pp. 211–228.

61 A. Fino, *The Sound, Smell, and Taste of Atrocity Crimes - Witnesses' and Perpetrators' Perspectives in International Courtrooms*, available online at research.rug.nl/en/publications/the-sound-smell-and-taste-of-atrocity-crimes-witnesses-and-perpet (accessed 25 April 2023).

62 ECCC, *Case 002/02*, E1/427.1, Trial Chamber, Transcript of Hearing on the Substance in Case 002/02, 4 May 2016, p. 43.

63 Judgment, para. 2538.

camp'.[64] In paragraph 1897, the Court extensively relied on witness descriptions of the sounds they heard and savage sights they saw during the LRA attack on the Ibok IDP camp.[65]

Facially, such engagement—with smells, sights, and sounds of atrocity crimes—suggests that international criminal law judgments sometimes embrace senses and affect. When we read about loudspeakers muffling sounds of executions in Cambodia or the smell of burnt belongings in Srebrenica, we momentarily forget that we did not hear the loudspeakers or experience these smells ourselves. We also start to think of judgments as sense-scapes[66] offering more than judge renditions of atrocity crimes. However, this engagement is merely illusory as in reality, the judgment is fully dressed in text before it is produced to the reader.

This affinity for text is not coincidental. It is the result of a deliberate censorship of senses by the law. As scholars like Ahmed argue, this is because senses and affect are inherently unpredictable and contingent on others' experiences.[67] Their contingency poses a direct affront to the legal project, which has historically benefited from enforcing and maintaining conditions of inequality.[68] It is to sustain these unequal structures that law desperately regulates which surfaces we touch, which smells we enjoy and which ones we are disgusted by, which colours we find appealing and which ones we reject.[69] The law then uses the separation of already existing senses and affect to create *different* classes of people, to create hierarchies between social classes, and to make itself indispensable in preserving these classifications.[70] Text serves as the tool of choice for the law in this project of differentiation.

Third, the format of the written judgment enforces a singular narrative, showing the door to multiple and even internally conflicting interpretations.[71] In the *Ongwen* judgment of the Trial Chamber, for instance, text is used to present a unified victim experience and a singular understanding of the compassion-less accused Dominic Ongwen, eliciting the empathy of the

---

64 *Ibid.*

65 Judgment, para. 1897, footnote 5012.

66 F. Ross, 'Sense-scapes: senses and emotion in the making of place', 27(1–2) *Anthropology Southern Africa* (2004) 35–42.

67 S. Ahmed, *The Cultural Politics of Emotion* (Edinburgh University Press, Edinburgh, 2006).

68 P. Virilio, *L'insécurité du territoire* (Editions Galilee, Paris, 1993).

69 G. Deleuze and F. Guattari, *A Thousand Plateaus: Capitalism and Schizophrenia* (Bloomsbury, London, 2013).

70 J. Bens, *The Sentimental Court: The Affective Life of International Criminal Justice* (Cambridge University Press, Cambridge, 2022).

71 R.M. Cover, 'Violence and the Word', 95 *Yale Law Journal* (1986) 1601–1630; R.M. Cover, 'Foreword: nomos and narrative', 97(1) *Harvard Law Review* (1983) 4–68.

readers towards the victims while ignoring Ongwen's own victimhood.[72] For one, the judgment actively uses the 'you' voice.[73] Amongst others, in paragraph 1731, the judgment quotes witness P-0410 and notes how he could tell that the civilians were indeed dead. In the judgment's rendition, the witness says 'you keep on moving. You find another corpse. You jump over it and keep moving'.[74] Now, it is true that the 'you' voice is commonly used in Acholi.[75] But it performs a particular function in the judgment—which is that of putting the readers in the shoes of the victim(s) alone and arousing their indignation at the perpetrator's actions alone.

Such singularity is difficult to enforce through sensory experiences. Senses and affect are inherently free from reign.[76] It is impossible to predict how one will register a taste or smell or temperature, based on another's experiences. Given that sense and affect are also relational, their unpredictability is compounded as each emotion creates a ripple of responses amongst people in whose company it is experienced, and this chain carries on.[77]

That is not to say that senses and affect cannot be instrumentalised for political ends. For instance, Tallgren, in her work, cites several examples including the 'Justice Matters' exhibition, a touring exhibition set up inside the ICC premises, in which survivors of sexual violence are shown as ravaged and mutilated, and the officers of the Court are dressed in white and presented as guardians of the virtues of international criminal justice.[78] Despite this potential to be propagandised, the power of such media lies in the fact that they do not live in isolation. To bring this back to the example proffered by Tallgren, that the exhibition was staged at the glass-walled and fenced premises of the Court reveals much about the Court's own leanings, which allow viewers of the exhibition to contextualise its contents.

---

72 R.L. Turok-Squire, 'A Judgment like a Spiderweb: Catching Dominic Ongwen in the language of the International Criminal Court', 3 *Journal of International Criminal Law* (2022) 54–93.

73 *Ibid.*, pp. 66–69.

74 Judgment, para. 1731.

75 Turok-Squire, *supra* note 72; L. Swigart, 'Unseen and Unsung: ICC Language Services and their Impact on Institutional Legitimacy', in F. Baetens (ed.), *Legitimacy of Unseen Actors in International Adjudication* (Cambridge University Press, Cambridge, 2019), pp. 272–296.

76 S. Connor, 'Michel Serres' five senses', in D. Howes (ed.), *Empire of the Senses: The Sensual Culture Reader* (Routledge, London, 2004), pp. 318–334.

77 B. Massumi, *Parables for the Virtual: Movement, Affect, Sensation* (Duke University Press, Durham, NC, 2002).

78 I. Tallgren, 'Come and See? The Power of Images and International Criminal Justice', 17(2) *International Criminal Law Review* (2017) 259–280.

On a more pragmatic level, the exclusive reliance on text strains the Court's resources. Importantly, the requirement to translate and transliterate is attached to the Court's obligation to respect the accused's fair trial rights.[79] For one, accurate interpretations and transliterations are hard to be guaranteed due to the difficulty of capturing the essence of video and oral testimonies in text and the inevitable loss of cultural and emotional nuances during the transliteration process.[80] Transliteration is also an extremely costly affair. Every day, the ICC spends thousands of dollars on transliterating and printing transcripts from the hearings of the day. In fact, in its proposed programme budget for 2023, the ICC Office of the Prosecutor has asked for 1.8 million dollars to support its language services unit, with a touted 31 new staff members being hired to meet the changing language needs of the Court's docket.[81] In so doing, the Court has become more and more dependent on textual mediums and transliterators. What this ignores is that many dialects are purely oral and there are hardly any people who are trained to capture these dialects in written form. This is exemplified in the *Banda* case, where efforts to transliterate evidentiary material into the little known and unwritten language of Zaghawa, the only language that Abdallah Banda was able to speak and understand, delayed the trial for years and created huge costs.[82] At its heart, these costs were the result of the Court's refusal to recognise that Zaghawa was a purely oral vernacular.[83] This struggle has also been acutely felt in the Court's efforts to transcribe Acholi, a vernacular with limited vocabulary where single words take on different meanings depending on context and pronunciation.[84]

---

79 Article 67(1)(a) of the Rome Statute of the International Criminal Court (1998).

80 Y. Xu, 'Cultural Image Translation Strategies from the Perspective of Eco-Translatology', 12 *Creative Education* (2021) 1207–1214.

81 International Criminal Court Assembly of States Parties, *Proposed Programme Budget for 2023 of the International Criminal Court* (ICC-ASP/21/INF.2), para. 597.

82 Van-Lin, *supra* note 4.

83 ICC, *Prosecutor* v. *Adallah Banda Abakaer Nourain and Saleh Mohammed Jerbo Jamus*, ICC-02/05–03/09–131, Office of the Prosecutor, Prosecutions Response to the Trial Chamber's Request for Written Submissions on issues to be addressed during the Status Conference on 19 April 2011, 14 April 2011, para. 7; I. Compes, *Zaghawa-Wagi: Towards documenting the Sudanese dialectal variant of Zaghawa. Endangered Languages Archive*, available online at ifl.phil-fak.uni-koeln.de/en/general-linguistics/projects/current-projects-gl/zaghawa-wagi-towards-documenting-the-sudanese-dialectal-variant-of-zaghawa (accessed 15 April 2023).

84 University of Wisconsin-Madison, 'Acholi: "Literary" Acholi', *University of Wisconsin-Madison Students in African* 671 (University of Wisconsin-Madison, Madison, WI, 2019), available online at wisc.pb.unizin.org/lctlresources/chapter/acholi-literary-acholi/ (accessed 20 April 2023).

3 Senses around International Criminal Law

Despite the law's motives and practices of sensory censorship, the oeuvre of the law has traditionally borne strong sensory and affective dimensions. When one is alive to the ubiquity of what Philippopoulos-Mihalopoulous calls lawscapes,[85] it becomes clear that the law intrudes even our most private experiences—from the water we use to bathe to our sexualities and sexual relationships to our food and internet connections. These private experiences - perceptibly and invisibly—offer both senses and affect in abundance.[86]

This is heightened in the case of international criminal law, which is born out of war and conflict, which as Cordoba aptly remarks, 'senses were the ammunition for'.[87] Historians have written about the intersensorial histories of the World War II—an event which defined the course of international criminal law.[88] Mrozek, for instance, writes about border networks that were created through smells that wafted across the Berlin Wall, communities who were able to smell Soviet armies, and diplomacies that were forged by the sending of Eisenhower food packages.[89] The *Ongwen* case, similarly, was born out of an alarmingly violent civil war in Uganda that heavily relied on mass sexual crimes and the conscription of child soldiers—both steeped in sensory deprivations. The LRA is also known for its heinous practices of cutting off the lips, ears, and noses of thousands of Ugandan civilians—another tactic directly targeting the sensory abilities of the victims.[90]

When these conflicts become the subjects of court proceedings, then their sensory baggage wafts into the hallowed walls of courts too. Here, it is important to clarify where the ambit of international criminal law itself begins. At the outset, as Philippopoulos-Mihalopoulos argues, our understanding of space has been produced by and is mediated by our understanding of law: '[i]deas

---

85 A. Philippopoulos-Mihalopoulos, *In the lawscape* (Routledge, London, 2007).

86 A. Philippopoulos-Mihalopoulos and S.A. FitzGerald, 'From space immaterial: the invisibility of the lawscape', 17 *Griffith Law Review* (2008) 438–454.

87 C. Cordoba, *Sino-Swiss Relations during the Cold War (1949–1989): Between Soft Power & Propaganda* (Routledge, London, 2022).

88 B. Mrozek, *Tagungsbericht: Conflict and the Senses in the Global Cold War: From Propaganda to Sensory Warfare*, available online at www.hsozkult.de/conferencereport/id/fdkn-127425 (accessed 21 April 2023).

89 B. Mrozek, *The scents of others: An olfactory history of the German military division*, available online at www.ifz-muenchen.de/en/research/ea/research/the-scent-of-others-an-olfactory-history-of-german-division?no_cache=1&print=1&type=98&cHash=ca8e51021fd597b32d4cb109e32515c4 (accessed 10 August 2023).

90 Human Rights Watch, 'DR Congo: Lord's Resistance Army Rampage Kills 321', *Human Rights Watch* (2010), available online at www.hrw.org/news/2010/03/28/dr-congo-lords-resistance-army-rampage-kills-321 accessed 21 August 2023).

of space as representation, text, abstraction, system and closure ... all come from a juridical understanding of space'.[91] That said, while space is a juridical construction, it is not a component of applied law as such. Like conflicts are spaces which trigger international criminal law rules, courtrooms are spaces which apply international criminal law. Neither activate the remit of the law itself.

In this context, it appears that the spaces in which international criminal law is applied carry many sensory imprints. For instance, the Nuremberg trial discussed how orchestras were played on the platforms of Auschwitz, to soothe the fears of the Jews arriving to their unknown fates.[92] During the proceedings of Case 002/02 at the ECCC, Witness Him Huy graphically described how the prisoners detained in the Choeung Ek Genocidal Center would be executed when the generators were blaring loudly, so that the screams of the prisoners would be inaudible.[93]

As the sensory presence in the trials magnifies, trials take on a more affective framing. In their work, Tallgren, Ainley, and Humphreys draw persuasive parallels between international criminal law trials and film.[94] They remark how international criminal trials toy at the emotions and outrage of victims, audiences, the accused, the legal officers, and the legal fraternity.[95] The Court is the Holy Grail where heroes are born, narcissists and villains shamed, and victims avenged. One can see how this cinematic affective vocabulary permeates the *Ongwen* trial too. An animated film about the case produced by the ICC's outreach office in 2019 is case in point.[96] The video (screengrabs in Figure 1)—albeit superficially—teases out the two main narratives that framed the case. One of the helpless, caged former child soldier. The video begins with a short soundbite of a former child soldier, recounting the ordeal of his conscription and the complete stripping of his aspirations. The viewer is made to feel sympathy for the child soldier. This empathy is soon brusquely cut off, by a stark reminder of the ruthless monster that this child soldier turns into. The film ends with a (rather awkward) still of a caged bird being tried by

91 A. Philippopoulos-Mihalopoulos, 'And For Law: Why Space cannot be understood without Law', 17 *Law Culture and the Humanities* (2018) 620–639, p. 627.
92 *See* T.H. Sachnowitz's comment here: holocaustmusic.ort.org/places/camps/death-camps/auschwitz/camp-orchestras/ (accessed 2 May 2023).
93 ECCC, *supra* note 62.
94 K. Ainley, S. Humphreys and I. Tallgren, 'International criminal justice on/and film', 6(1) *London Review of International Law* (2008) 3–15.
95 G.J. Bass, *Stay the Hand of Vengeance: The Politics of War Crimes Tribunals* (Princeton University Press, Princeton, NJ, 2000).
96 ICC, *"I want to start my life again" - Using child soliders is a crime*, available online at www.youtube.com/watch?v=wtRx5Pe5eiU (accessed 5 May 2023).

FIGURE 1 Screenshots from www.youtube.com/watch?v=wtRx5Pe5eiU/
COURTESY OF ICC.

the ICC. This film only teases the actual scale of the cinematic narratives that the *Ongwen* case fed off.

To us, it seems that the basis of international criminal law and the spaces where it is applied (the courtroom) are inundated by senses and affect. The question then is, should we allow international criminal law to continue censoring senses and affect?

4 Sensorily Reimagining the *Ongwen* Judgment

As international criminal law comes face to face with its troubled past, the calls for epistemic diversity in the field are becoming louder and louder.[97] Ours too is one such call, specifically directed at the tool of the written judgment. We argue that as the capstone of the case, the judgment ought not to be confined to text. If the case's lasting legacy is known only through words, that too of the judges, then it afflicts great epistemic injustice and symbolic harm to the many stakeholders in international criminal justice. In response, we suggest that the judgment be reimagined sensorily. How, then, does an affective re-imagination of judgment promote the interests of international criminal law stakeholders?

The first community of stakeholders who benefit from this re-do are victims. We argue, as a rich pedigree of scholars before us have done, that embracing art-based or sensory mediums in judgments can facilitate recognition of

97 B. Fagbayibo, *Ballads of Dissent: Music as a Tool for Rethinking International Law in Africa*, available online at twailr.com/ballads-of-dissent-music-as-a-tool-for-rethinking-international-law-in-africa/ (accessed 17 April 2023).

personhood.[98] When in place of a written transcript, one can hear a witness's testimony in their voice; where instead of judge's narrations of visuals, the receiver is able to see the wreckage of the perpetrator's crimes through their own eyes, there is an immediate recognition of the personhood of the victim.

This is best illustrated through the Court's treatment of the testimonies of two former LRA abductees: Evelyn Amony and Florence Ayot.

Amony was one of Joseph Kony's wives.[99] She was abducted by the LRA at the age of 11. Amony testified to the Court about her abduction in 1994, her subsequent escape from the LRA, and participation in the Juba peace talks between Kony and the Ugandan peace delegates. Her testimony also contained several details about how the LRA engaged with ting tings, the relationship between wives and LRA husbands, etc (as one can see in the video from 13:03 to 16:56; screenshot in Figure 2).[100] Amony testified without any facial or voice blurs, speaking in her capacity as a survivor as well as an advocate against sexual crimes. Despite having classified her testimony as credible and reliable, the Court only offered a measly written summary of her statement. More importantly, it referred to her via pseudonym D-0049 despite her brave decision to testify with her real name.

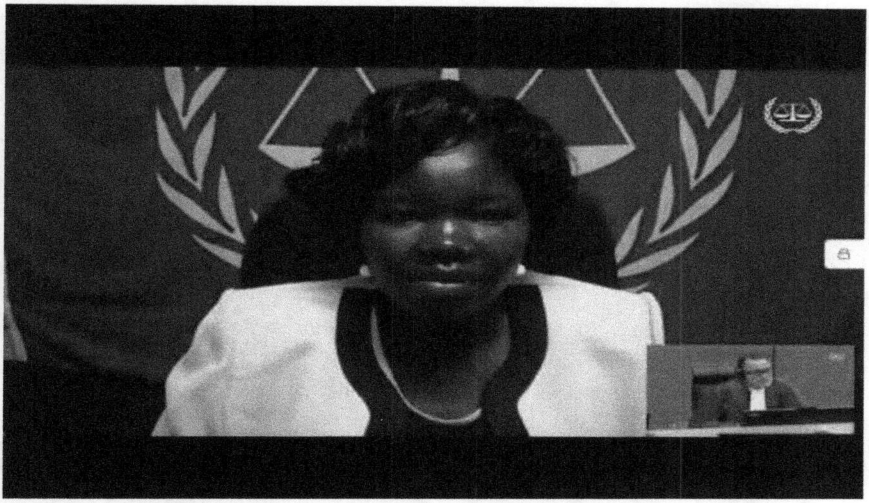

FIGURE 2 Screenshot from www.youtube.com/watch?v=nyqLdNoYh-I
COURTESY OF ICC.

98 M.M. Rahman, '"Humanising" Statelessness through an Artistic Approach', 2(2) *Statelessness & Citizenship Review* (2020) 272–299.
99 Judgment, para. 433.
100 Judgment, para. 2218.

This treatment was not reserved to Prosecution witnesses alone. Case in point is Defence witness Florence Ayot.[101] Ayot was one of Ongwen's wives and made a strong case for why he should be allowed to return to Uganda.[102] She spoke of how difficult Ongwen's incarceration has been for her family. Although the Court engaged more substantively with Ayot's testimony than Amony's, even here the testimony was only made available through text despite Ayot's decision to testify without any facial/voice blurs. A video excerpt (from 16:57 to 22:52 in the above video) more accurately conveys how Ayot herself was battling with her harrowing experience as an LRA abductee even as she lent her voice in Ongwen's support.

Personhood is not relevant for survivors of sexual crimes alone. One of the witnesses Joseph Ywakomoi Oywak (P-0009) testified at length about the LRA's attack on the Pajule IDP camp and the LRA's activities in the region during the period of the charges.[103] Oywak testified in court without facial blurs. His testimony was considered reliable, but was confined to text.[104] What is ironic is that Oywak's testimony relied heavily on photographs that he had preserved from the Pajule camp. Speaking of one such photograph of Vincent Otti with a young child approximately 10 or 11 years of age wearing a Pajule school uniform, Oywak explicitly said 'we acquired these photographs from some children who returned from the LRA camps, we felt it necessary that if the world should know what happened, then this photo would be a very clear message'.[105]

Moreover, our call for a sensory reimagination of judgments threatens to break the epistemic monopoly of judges and instead treats victims as the rightful narrators of their lived experiences. Unlike text, senses and affect are not partitioned by literacy or expertise. Senses are experienced by everyone. As Bermúdez notes, '[e]ach of us experiences our own body in a distinctive way. Part of that distinctiveness is that we each experience our body and our limbs *as our own*'.[106] Of course, this is not to say that senses are immune from social hierarchies.[107] However, they are relatively more egalitarian in their experience than text which is otherwise premised on assumptions of literacy.

---

101 Judgment, para. 398.

102 Judgment, para. 2519.

103 Judgment, para. 441.

104 ICC, *Ongwen case: "In the courtroom" programme (in Acholi), 1 May–17 July 2017*, available online at www.youtube.com/watch?v=XHFB6Yp3odc (accessed 2 August 2023).

105 *Ibid.*

106 J.L. Bermúdez, 'Ownership and the Space of the Body', in *The Bodily Self: Selected Essays* (MIT Press, Cambridge, MA, 2018), pp. 183–201.

107 K. Herrity, B.E. Schmidt and J. Warr (eds.), *Sensory Penalities: Exploring the Senses in Spaces of Punishment and Social Control* (Emerald, Bingley, 2021).

With this mind, a sensory judgment—in our view—would create room for plural knowledges to breathe.[108] In a recent talk organised by the Grotius Centre for Legal Studies, McCallum launched a powerful critique of how international criminal justice does not 'listen' to indigenous identities and traumas.[109] This deafness is evident in the Western models of evidence-taking, the speaking of colonial vernaculars, and the denial of self-identification as survivors/victims at the Court. A sensory judgment may work to remedy this. A sensory judgment effectively transcends limitations imposed by the official working languages of the Court. In the *Ongwen* case, most of the intercepted evidence concerned tape recordings of people speaking in Acholi or Luo, both of which are not working languages of the court.[110] The Chamber readily dismisses most of this evidence citing lack of translation capacity. Sensory evidence, then, allows even for such stakeholders to be heard—if not understood—in their self-determined ways. It allows for non-linear, disorganised, random, and everyday encounters to feature in the international criminal law script.[111] For instance, sexual abuse survivor P-0101, when describing the events of her abduction by Ongwen, vividly recalled the colours of her school uniform, 'a pink skirt and white blouse with red stripes on the arms'.[112] She also remembered that Ongwen smeared water and shea nut oil on her in 'order to mark her as his'.[113] While these details facially seem removed from the sexual crime and are likely to be edited out of the judgment for reasons of irrelevance, a sensory excerpt would allow the Court to better appreciate why a victim is more attached to memories of their everyday life before the assault.[114] In so doing, the judgment can be repurposed to generate discourse which is relational, reparative, diverse, and porous.

Sensory re-imaginations also enrich the *quality* of criminal justice offered to communities. Opening up the judgment to the wider sensory field instantly creates an outlet for the multidimensionality of justice to seep into the fold of international criminal law discourse. Justice is then no longer bound up by the binary outcomes of conviction or acquittal conveyed through a judgment.

---

108 N. wa Thiong'o, *Moving the Centre: The struggle for cultural freedoms* (James Currey, London, 1993).

109 Leiden University, *Justice through Indigenous Lenses* (2022), available online at www.universiteitleiden.nl/en/events/2022/01/justice-through-indigenous-lenses (accessed 23 March 2023).

110 Judgment, para. 650.

111 D. Redmon, 'Video Methods, Green Cultural Criminology, and the Anthropocene: SANCTUARY as a Case Study', 39(4) *Deviant Behavior* (2018) 495–511.

112 Judgment, para. 2013.

113 Judgment, para. 2013.

114 Mandel, *supra* note 35.

In his work on sensory archives, Thorne observes that 'words can be hard to find, particularly those that seek to describe traumatic and complex social events and relationships'.[115] But sensory stimulations are capable of capturing traumatic pasts and generating hope for repair. In his words, the sensory fragments in atrocity legal archives 'can open up understanding about how justice, peace, and social repair might look, sound and feel like to those who have experienced horrendous suffering.' The *Ongwen* trial was flooded with sensory fragments of the impact of Ongwen's crimes—outside the courtroom, the public were exposed to images of the memorial for the 60 people killed in the Lukodi massacre[116] to documentaries about the LRA leaders[117] to visuals of Ongwen's family watching his trial.[118] Even more powerful were the sensory evidence brought into the courtroom - from photographs of children conscripted when wearing their school uniforms, videos of camps after LRA attacks to videos of several internally displaced children and women.[119] Added to this were video excerpts of Ongwen's statement from the trial which reveals both his culpability and his helplessness and anger towards his own position.[120] As Mannivannan notes, the act of retelling itself can be reparative.[121] Whether in voice or in image. Perhaps this could translate into responses aimed at reducing vulnerabilities or repairing harm.[122]

---

115 Thorne, *supra* note 9.

116 J. Jiwa, *Trial of LRA commander Ongwen still divides Northern Uganda*, www.thenewhumanitarian.org/news-feature/2021/6/30/trial-of-LRA-commander-ongwen-still-divides-northern-uganda (accessed 21 August 2023.

117 Save the Children, *Moving on – Surviving the Lord's Resistance Army*, available online at resourcecentre.savethechildren.net/3ba158d/ (accessed 15 September 2022).

118 S. Hayden, 'In Dominic Ongwen's home village, many see a victim more than a perpetrator', *Irish Times* (2023), available online at www.irishtimes.com/news/world/africa/in-dominic-ongwen-s-home-village-many-see-a-victim-more-than-a-perpetrator-1.4476487 (accessed 21 August 2023).

119 ICC, *supra* note 11.

120 ICC, *Ongwen case: In the Courtroom programme, January 2021 ACHOLI*, available online at www.youtube.com/watch?v=IHQHYgRpQOU (accessed 20 August 2023); ICC, *Ongwen case: In the Courtroom programme, January 2021 ENGLISH*, available online at www.youtube.com/watch?v=A1fNyica1FA (accessed 20 August 2023); J. Burke, S. Okiror and S. Lundin, 'Ugandan ex-child soldier guilty of war crimes and crimes against humanity', *The Guardian* (2021), available online at www.theguardian.com/law/2021/feb/04/uganda-ex-child-soldier-dominic-ongwen-guilty-of-war-crimes-against-humanity (accessed 21 August 2023).

121 Q. Manivannan, *Imagining a Care Curriculum*, available online at www.kcl.ac.uk/imagining-a-care-curriculum (accessed 13 March 2023).

122 A.K. Azad, D. Nadkarni and J.G.F. Bunders-Aelen, 'Beyond Resistance, Beyond Assimilation: Reimagining Citizenship through Poetry', 14(3) *Journal of Human Rights Practice* (2022) 986–1004.

The Court and the Office of the Prosecutor also stand to gain from such a re-imagination. Clarke's work on affective justice is a glowing (hypothetical) example of this. The author rearticulates international justice using the vocabulary of emotions, as an assemblage of 'power, history, and contingencies'.[123] She focusses on the relationship between African States and the Court and the controversies marring it. Clarke's work shows that the utility of affect cannot be understated. Affect essentially equips international criminal law to transcend the fixed grammars of law.[124] The politics of international criminal law then does not remain separated from the juridical life of international criminal law. Instead, the two are put in conversation. To borrow an illustration from Clarke's book, the trial of Ruto and Sang embroiled both the Court and the government of Kenya in a match of political mud-slinging, with the government of Kenya investing diplomatic and monetary resources in framing the Court as a 'meddling force that was doing the bidding of Western powers in Africa'.[125] While the Court struggled to find legal responses, ultimately calling off the case as an instance of a 'mistrial',[126] the race to find juridical solutions completely invisibilised the heavy affective rifts that the initiation of the case had caused. Ruto and Sang's election victory stood on postcolonial rhetoric. The ICC—having already intervened in Kenya—had been firmly branded as an exogenous, Western intervention.[127] While much of this is true, the Court's complete lack of engagement with the domestic political rhetoric is what enabled the formation of the Jubilee Alliance (a united front against ICC charges) and ultimately secured Ruto's acquittal and his election victory in Kenya.[128] In essence, this was a domino effect of the Court's initial dismissal of the case as a 'failure' to award justice, a framing that was regarded as blind to the community's expectations of the Court and their own political leaders. A more reflexive acknowledgment of this affective dimension would have

123 K.M. Clarke, *Affective Justice: The International Criminal Court and the Pan-Africanist Pushback* (Duke University Press, Durham, NC, 2019).

124 H. Lovat, 'Affective Justice: The International Criminal Court and the Pan-Africanist Pushback', 31(4) *European Journal of International Law* (2020) 1603–1610.

125 M. Kersten, 'A Missed Trial or a Mistrial? The End of the ICC Cases against Ruto and Sang', *Justice in Conflict* (2016), available online at justiceinconflict.org/2016/04/07/a-missed-trial-or-a-mistrial-the-end-of-the-icc-cases-against-ruto-and-sang/ (accessed 4 April 2023).

126 ICC, *Prosecutor* v. *Ruto and Sang*, ICC-01/09-01/11-2027-Red-Corr, Trial Chamber V, Decision on Defence Applications for Judgments of Acquittal, 5 April 2016.

127 Clarke, *supra* note 123.

128 Kersten, *supra* note 125.

allowed the Court to be seen as an accessible forum of redress for the victims in Kenya.

This also rings true in the context of the prosecution of Ongwen. Like the Kenyan situation, the *Ongwen* case was triggered by a self-referral from the state of Uganda. As Kersten notes, the self-referral was a strategic tool for the authoritarian Museveni government to prevent the ICC from investigating the crimes of the government forces.[129] At the same time, by self-referring, Uganda positioned itself as an ally to the ICC. However, this did not stop Musiveni from joining forces with other African leaders to complain about the Court's unfair targeting of African defendants and indicting its Western biases.[130] On the Court's part, the agenda of resolving the conflict between the LRA and the Ugandan government has been of chief priority since the Court's inception. In fact, the ICC was heavily invested in facilitating the Juba peace talks between the two factions from 2006–2008.[131] The peace talks were initiated after the ICC had issued arrest warrants against the LRA's top brass,[132] in the hopes that the Court's involvement would incentivise both factions to bargain and arrive at an armistice of some sort. It was in this context that the trial of Ongwen took place. The trial therefore presented an opportunity for the Court to play a more instrumental role in the making of the peace process in Uganda. However, the Court chose not to fully consider the history of the Ugandan conflict or the political stakes of the case. Instead, it adopted a more clinical and legalistic approach towards adjudicating the crimes that Ongwen was charged with.

Soon after the start of the trial, the defences of duress and mental disease or defect became the focus of the case. Ongwen's lawyers invoked the defence of duress by arguing that Ongwen was under the control of Joseph Kony (supported by his belief in Kony's spiritual powers) and 'disobeying Kony or leaving the LRA would be punished by death'.[133] The defence lawyers also relied

---

129 M. Kersten, 'Between Disdain and Cooperation—Uganda's Controversial Place in the ICC-Africa Relationship', *Justice in Conflict* (2017), available online at justiceinconflict.org/2017/03/29/between-disdain-and-dependency-ugandas-controversial-place-in-the-icc-africa-relationship/ (accessed 4 August 2023).

130 B. Momanyi, 'Ugandan Leader Lashes Out at ICC', *IWPR* (2023), available online at iwpr.net/global-voices/ugandan-leader-lashes-out-icc (accessed 4 August 2023).

131 M. Kersten, 'The ICC and the Road to Juba', in *Justice in Conflict: The Effects of the International Criminal Court's Interventions on Ending Wars and Building Peace* (Oxford University Press, Oxford, 2016), pp. 64–91.

132 ICC, *Prosecutor* v. *Joseph Kony and Vincent Otti*, ICC-02/04-01/05-57, Pre-Trial Chamber II, Warrant of Arrest for Dominic Ongwen, 9 July 2005.

133 ICC, *Prosecutor* v. *Dominic Ongwen,* ICC-02/04-01/15-1722-Corr-Red, Defence, Public Redacted Version of 'Corrected Version of "Defence Closing Brief", filed on 24 February 2020', 13 March 2020.

on medical experts to show that Ongwen suffered from dissociative disorders, depressive illness, and PTSD ('post-traumatic stress disorder').[134] However, the Court found that this diagnosis of Ongwen's trauma did not meet the conditions for mental defect under the Rome Statute.[135] Ongwen's lawyers also proposed a cumulative insanity-duress defence, which recognises that certain defendants may have enough lucidity to not qualify for the insanity defence but may still need to be absolved of some liability because of their trauma-induced dysfunctions.[136] This proposal also fell on the deaf ears of the Court.

In rejecting Ongwen's pleas for recognition of his own victimhood based on his trauma, the Court lost an opportunity to pay heed to the affective foundations of the case.[137] One may even argue that the Court's framing of the LRA rebels as pathological criminals deters the possibility of the LRA's cooperation with the Court or with the Ugandan government.

We think that a sensory reimagination has the potential to fill these affective gaps. As shown previously, senses and affect always go together. Creating space for senses then automatically makes the Court infrastructure more alive to the affective implications of the justice it dispenses.[138] This likely facilitates a considered understanding of the Court's goals amongst victim communities and makes it seem less like an exogenous, Western outfit. It is our argument that a sensory/affect friendly judgment would also foster trust-building in the ICC.

Here, it is important to credit the ongoing efforts to foster sensory experiences in the international criminal law narrative. Art and International Justice's 2019 visual and experiential exhibitions surrounding the Marshall Islands judgment of the International Court of Judgment was a commendable effort to centre the conversation about affect and international justice.[139] Tallgren's work on visuality on international criminal justice also deserves credit.[140] This only goes to show that a sensory judgment is not all that illusory or utopian

---

134 Judgment, paras 2576–2578.

135 Article 31(1)(a) of the Rome Statute of the International Criminal Court (1998); Judgment, para. 2580.

136 ICC, *supra* note 133.

137 L. Hiromoto and L.F. Sparr, 'Ongwen and Mental Health Defenses at the International Criminal Court', 51(1) *Journal of the American Academy of Psychiatry and the Law* (2023) 61–71.

138 Bens, *supra* note 70.

139 Art and International Justice Initiative, 'Workshop: Art and International Justice: Sounds, Design, Visuals', *Art and International Justice Initiative* (2022), available online at artij.org/en/art-and-international-justice-sounds-design-visuals.html (accessed 9 March 2023).

140 Tallgren, *supra* note 78.

a suggestion. Notably, such retellings have been explored frequently in other fields. Documentary criminology, for instance, employs images, sounds, and textures to reconfigure atmospheres in which criminal encounters take place.[141] Documentary criminology 'calls us to a series of systematic reflections within which we question and clarify that which we intimately live, but which has been lost to our reflective knowledge through habituation and/or institutionalization'.[142] Some such affective retellings have permeated human rights conversations too, albeit only in the fringes. In her stunning piece on music and song in struggles for gender equality, Ghadery notes that departing from text-based doctrine can help us appreciate the multiple non-liberal philosophies which illuminate rights as sites of contestation/recontextualisation.[143] Ghadery caveats against using sensorily loaded mediums as instruments. Instead, she nudges us to think about music as another rights language, one which can be created and curated collectively.[144] Similarly, the works of Azad,[145] Nadkarni,[146] and Rizwan[147] guide us to see how poetry and literature can forge a genuine plurality of interactions, sans any hierarchies or discriminations.

Of course, the chief roadblock to the execution of this idea is the practical execution. In essence, we envision a sensory reimagination of the judgment to resemble this paper itself, where text is interspersed with other sensory sources. It seems that most criminal tribunals are already equipped with the tools to enable such makeovers. In fact, the ICC has now begun publishing livestreams of oral pronouncements of summary judgments. The *Ongwen* trial judgment, as well, was preceded by a short summary read out by Judge Schmitt.[148] This procedure was presumably introduced to create a space where the immediate affective impact of the judgment can be felt and expressed by stakeholders in the case and beyond. Crushingly, however, this opportunity is made available

---

141 Redmon, *supra* note 111; J. Bennett, *Vibrant Matter: A Political Ecology of Things* (Duke University Press, Durham, NC, 2010).

142 Redmon, *supra* note 111; V. Sobchack, 'The Active Eye: A Phenomenology of Cinematic Vision', 12(3) *Quarterly Review of Film and Video* (1990) 21–36.

143 F. Ghadery, 'Beyond international human rights law – music and song in contextualised struggles for gender equality', 13(1) *Transnational Legal Theory* (2022) 31–58.

144 *Ibid.* She also cites Mani in support of this point: R. Mani, 'Women, Art and Post-Conflict Justice', 11(3) *International Criminal Law Review* (2011) 543–560, p. 543.

145 Azad *et al.*, *supra* note 122.

146 D. Nadkarni, 'I Understand You, Across the Chasm that Divides Us: Rethinking Community Through Poetry', 40 *Jaarboek voor Vrouwengeschiedenis* (2021) 137–142.

147 R. Rizwan, 'Local Flows: The Pleasure-centric Turn in Human Rights Advocacy in South Asia', 22(1–2) *Tilburg Law Review* (2017) 31–61, p. 48.

148 ICC, *supra* note 16.

in a way where only the judges, court staff, the Prosecutor, and the accused are personified and recognised. Victims are glaringly missing, though it is their story whose end has just been determined by the Court. As of 2008, the ICC began filming all its cases. The YouTube channel of the Court suggests that full-length livestreaming of hearings of cases began in 2013.[149] At the ECCC, statements of apology were filmed and broadcasted as early as 2009.[150] That apart, as a corollary of their investigative mandates, most criminal tribunals already have well-functioning evidence and analysis units that are specialised in preserving the integrity and textures of evidence, in processing sounds, and in offering protections for aural/filmic witness disclosures. A sensory judgment will only require these pre-existing tools to be refashioned for a different purpose. In some ways, this would also reduce the time and monetary costs associated with transliterating into every language spoken and understood by the parties.

5 Conclusion

In this paper, we examine the *Ongwen* trial judgment using the lens of senses and affect and query the limitations of the exclusive reliance on text in the judgment. Our paper starts with the premise that text is incapable of capturing cultural nuances, that it serves to depersonalise victims, and lends weight to problematic singular narratives about perpetratorship and victimhood. We show that the dominance enjoyed by text in international criminal law is not coincidental or innocuous. Instead, international criminal law has deliberately engineered text to censor other sensory or affective experiences in order to preserve the epistemic and social control enjoyed by law and its adjudicators. This desire is only compounded by the contingent, unpredictable, and egalitarian character of sensory and affective experiences. However, we argue that instead of seeing the rupture in control ushered by senses and affect as a threat, international criminal law should open itself up to sensory possibilities. This is what would do justice to the rich sensorial and affective imprints of international criminal law itself. As a solution, we propose the adoption of a sensory alternative model of judgments. We argue that only through a display of multi-dimensional senses and affect can international criminal law become truly reparative and epistemically diverse. Such a rethinking would also

149 ICC, www.youtube.com/@intlcriminalcourt/videos (accessed 5 March 2023).

150 ECCC, video archive, available online at www.eccc.gov.kh/en/video/archive?page=2 (accessed 5 March 2023).

incentivise victims and other stakeholders to repose trust in the Court as a guardian of their agency. As the lasting legacy of the case, it is only fitting that this reimagination starts with the tool of the judgment. To quote Redmon, 'we are sensual before we are verbal'.[151] This piece is a reminder to appreciate that.

Acknowledgements

The authors would like to thank Naman Singh, an undergraduate student at the Hidayatullah National Law University, Raipur for his excellent research assistance. They would also like to thank the anonymous reviewer, the guest editors Juan-Pablo Peréz-León-Acevedo and Fabio Ferraz de Almeida, Andy Aydın-Aitchison, Michelle Burgis-Kasthala, Benjamin Thorne, Adina Nistor, and everyone who gave feedback at the April 2023 work-in-progress session organised by the Edinburgh Centre for International and Global Law.

151 Redmon, *supra* note 111.

CHAPTER 8

Culture and the Illusion of Self-Evidence: Spiritual Beliefs in the *Ongwen* Trial

Adina-Loredana Nistor

Abstract

By definition, criminal trials are set to determine the guilt or innocence of the accused. In this process, judges are tasked with assessing not only evidence that presents itself in quantifiable forms, but also as personal experiences. In the case of Dominic Ongwen, a former child soldier and commander of the Lord's Resistance Army (LRA), the issue of spiritualism played a significant role, particularly in relation to the affirmative defences of mental incapacity and duress. Assessing such culturally charged evidence, inherently interconnected to local beliefs, through the lens of an international criminal law trial raises a number of challenges. In the construction of the legal truth, such immaterial evidence undergoes a process through which only certain elements, which are deemed relevant in light of specific arguments, are ultimately selected, filtered through the legal framework, contested by the parties and ultimately decided upon by the judges. Spiritual beliefs therefore become patterns, and patterns become certainties. Based on an in-depth analysis of 408 trial transcripts, along with main submissions and decisions, this article sheds light into how framing spiritualism according to the criteria laid out in the Rome Statute has played out in the trial of Dominic Ongwen. It maps the way in which cultural concepts related to spirituality have been introduced into the trial, by which parties and for what purpose. It also looks at how the system of spiritual powers guiding the LRA and its fighters was assessed by the judges and potentially why.

Keywords

anthropology – culture – international trials – justice – spiritual beliefs

 | DOI: 10.1163/9789004743380_009

> When I went with that stone I did exactly what I was told, and indeed the stone flew off my hands and it brought an image of the cross like with a colour – like the colour of a rainbow and it went off like a bomb. I was scared. It was the first time seeing such magic. I can never forget that. Up to now I remember it. When you are just told these things, you don't believe, but many people in Uganda know about this. But there were rules regarding those bombs. No one was allowed to talk about Kony turning stones into bombs or Kony doing magic with those stones. But, for me, who is before this international court, I need to let the world know what took place. God knows I shouldn't tell lies. That was the first miracle I saw in the LRA.
>
> Dominic Ongwen, Sentencing Hearing

1 Introduction[1]

On 15 April 2021 Ugandan defendant Dominic Ongwen made an unsworn statement in front of the judges at the International Criminal Court (ICC) in the Hague. In what the Chamber later characterized as a 'display of self-pity',[2] the former child soldier talked about his brutal(izing) life in the bush. Kidnaped at the age of nine by the Lord's Resistance Army (the LRA) led by Joseph Kony, his life had been, in his own words, 'ruined'.[3] He asked the Court to help rehabilitate him.[4] As a victim of the war in Northern Uganda, he felt that his freedom had been taken away and that he had already been condemned twice: once when he was abducted by the rebels, and again when he 'surrendered' to the Court and 'the world just snatched' him with a rope around his neck.[5]

1 The title of this article was inspired by van Binsbergen's paper in which he discusses how 'culture' can produce the illusion of self-evidence. *See* W.M.J. van Binsbergen, "Cultures do not exist': Exploding self-evidences in the investigation of interculturality', in *Intercultural encounters: African and anthropological lessons towards a philosophy of interculturality* (LIT, Berlin, 2003), pp. 459–522.

2 ICC, *Prosecutor v Dominic Ongwen,* Case No. ICC-02/04-01/15, Trial Chamber IX, Sentencing, 6 May 2021, p. 18.

3 ICC, *Prosecutor v Dominic Ongwen,* Case No. ICC-02/04-01/15, Trial Chamber IX, Sentencing Hearing, 15 April 2021, p. 19.

4 ICC, *supra* note 3, p. 19.

5 ICC, *supra* note 3, p. 19.

Since the start of his trial, this would be the second time that he would address the judges directly. In 2016, when the charges that he stood accused of were read out to him, he stated that he did not understand them because he was 'not the LRA.'[6] He maintained that he should not be held responsible for the crimes of an entire organization. Six years later, during the Sentencing Hearings, he talked for the first time about the indoctrination he was subjected to, about his beliefs in the mystical powers of Joseph Kony. He begged the judges to see that he is 'just human.'[7] He described everything that he endured as 'despair'[8] brought to his life from an early age, a despair so gripping that he felt unlucky to be still alive.[9] After six years of various testimonies and expert reports on the belief system of the LRA, all aimed to determine whether Ongwen was indeed under the spirits' command, the voice of the defendant was finally heard. He recalled his first encounter with the 'miracles' and the supernatural powers of Joseph Kony, issues that, as he stated, he was not previously allowed to talk about.[10] Perhaps even as he took the stand before the judges, removed from the grip of the rebel forces, he did so with reluctance. He believed that Joseph Kony held everyone 'in his hands'[11] and therefore controlled not only Northern Uganda, but the whole world, which by extension, would (also) mean the Court in the Hague. At the time he made his plea to the judges, he had already been found guilty of 61 counts of war crimes and crimes against humanity.[12]

From the outset of the trial, the Defence characterized the conflict in Northern Uganda as 'complex in nature, steeped in metaphysics and spiritualism',[13] words that would be repeated in its Closing Statement.[14] The Defence pleaded for an acquittal or for having Ongwen undergo the Acholi process of *Mato Oput*.[15] On 4 February 2021 Dominic Ongwen was found guilty for most of the charges leveraged against him and on 6 May 2021, he was sentenced to 25 years

6 ICC, *Prosecutor v Dominic Ongwen,* Case No. ICC-02/04-01/15, Trial Chamber IX, Prosecution Opening Statement, 6 December 2016, p. 17.

7 ICC, *supra* note 3, p. 8.

8 *Ibid*, p. 9.

9 *Ibid.*

10 *Ibid*, p. 18.

11 ICC, *supra* note 2, p. 19.

12 ICC, *Prosecutor v Dominic Ongwen*, Case No. ICC-02/04-01/15, Trial Chamber IX, Judgment, 4 February 2021.

13 ICC, *Prosecutor v Dominic Ongwen*, Case No. ICC-02/04-01/15, Trial Chamber IX, Defence Opening Statement, 18 September 2018, p. 4.

14 ICC, *Prosecutor v Dominic Ongwen*, Case No. ICC-02/04-01/15, Trial Chamber IX, Trial Transcript, Defence Closing Statement, 12 March 2020, p. 3.

15 ICC, *Prosecutor v Dominic Ongwen*, Case No. ICC-02/04-01/15, Trial Chamber IX, Defence Closing Brief, 13 March 2020, p. 197.

of imprisonment, five years more than what the Prosecution had suggested. In its opening[16] and Closing Statement, the Prosecution had acknowledged that '15 years before he committed these terrible crimes, Mr Ongwen was himself a victim of the LRA'[17] and that:

> the testimony of other former child soldiers is enough to tell us that he probably suffered greatly. He would have been beaten, forced to beat or even kill others, and subjected to spiritual and political indoctrination. He would have suffered hunger, grief, and fear. In effect, the LRA stole from Mr Ongwen his childhood, his education, and his best chance to lead a normal life surrounded by family and friends.[18]

The Prosecution also added that his 'previous experience as a child soldier does not in any way diminish the gravity of the crimes, nor does it diminish his criminal culpability for those crimes.'[19] The judges ultimately determined that Ongwen was guilty of most of the crimes he stood accused of, and furthermore, that 'much of his relevant conduct resulted instead from his own initiative.'[20] They reasoned that if his past shields him from anything, it is from a sentence of life imprisonment which 'would surely be in order in the present case.'[21] On the issue of spirituality, the Chamber concluded that many of the soldiers who had been in the LRA long enough no longer believed in the powers of Joseph Kony and inferred this must have been the case for Ongwen himself.[22]

Through an in-depth analysis of the *Ongwen* proceedings, which includes all publicly available trial documents in English (one of the working languages of the Court), this paper maps the way in which culture, broadly, and spiritualism in particular, was introduced into the trial and assessed by the parties. A total of 408 trial hearing transcripts, in addition to party submissions and decisions (in particular the trial judgment, the sentence and appeal judgment) were analysed using the qualitative software, Nvivo. Through coding, also known as tagging, I identified which key concepts were explicitly defined by the trial participants as cultural, with a particular focus on concepts related to

16 ICC, *supra* note 6, pp. 35–36.

17 ICC, *Prosecutor v Dominic Ongwen,* Case No. ICC-02/04-01/15, Trial Chamber IX, Sentencing Hearing, 14 April 2021, p. 8.

18 *Ibid.*

19 ICC, *supra* note 17.

20 ICC, *supra* note 12, para 2665, p. 935.

21 ICC, *supra* note 2, para 386, p. 127.

22 *Ibid.*

spiritualism. I linked these concepts to the trial participants that addressed them, and I grouped them under broader themes. A map depicting the prevalence of these cultural concepts and their relationship with the actors in the trial emerged from the coding. This map provides: (i) an overview of which concepts were introduced into the proceedings and at what stage during the trial; (ii) by which actor (Prosecution, Defence, Victims' Representatives, witnesses); (iii) for what purpose were they introduced; (iv) their interaction with the legal framework that governs the trial proceedings; and (v) the way in which they were addressed in the trial decisions (most importantly the judgment and appeal). This paper will therefore highlight the main findings of this qualitative analysis based on an in-depth reading of the court documents pertaining to this trial. In this study, culture is understood as, on the one hand, a 'a system of inherited conceptions expressed in symbolic forms' though which people 'communicate, perpetuate, and develop their knowledge about and attitudes toward life.'[23] Spiritual beliefs are therefore part of this system of conceptions. Culture equally manifests as a series of 'orientations'[24] that individuals draw upon in order to navigate daily life, on the other hand. As a product of specific societal norms, law as an 'objective' tool is not the opposite of 'subjective' culture, but *is* culture as well.[25]

In order to map the way in which culture broadly, and spirituality in particular, played a role in the trial of Dominic Ongwen at the ICC, this paper addresses several key issues. First of all, section two provides an overview of the legal framework under which the issue of spirituality was put forward by the Defence. Section three focuses on how culture and spiritual beliefs were presented in order to meet the legal criteria of duress and mental incapacity. Section four looks at how the judges evaluated this type of evidence and highlights the tensions surrounding what is 'reasonable' to believe in determining whether Ongwen had 'a mind of his own.'[26] Section five provides a few concluding remarks.

23 C. Geertz, *The Interpretation of Cultures*, third edn (Basic Books, New York, NY, 2017), p. 95.

24 Van Binsbergen, *supra* note 1, p. 476; It must be noted that one limitation of this paper is that it is not devoid of the author's own 'cultural orientation', which stems from her own background and training. To a certain extent this has been mitigated by the fact that the author does not seek to define which submissions are cultural, but to highlight what the parties themselves have identified as 'culture.'

25 *See* J. Fraser and B. McGonigle Leyh (eds), *Intersections of Law and Culture at the International Criminal Court* (Edward Elgar, Cheltenham, 2020).

26 ICC, *supra* note 13, p. 4.

2 Legal Framework – the Affirmative Defences of Mental Incapacity and Duress

Arguing duress and mental incapacity, the Defence submitted that Ongwen, who had been subjected to a military and spiritual 'indoctrination that has shocked the conscience of the world',[27] should be acquitted of all charges. The following section will firstly highlight the legal framework under the Rome Statute in relation to the mental elements required for criminal responsibility, with a specific focus on the defences of mental incapacity and duress available at the ICC. It will then show how these affirmative defences were pleaded in relation to the issue of spiritual beliefs.

Article 30 of the Rome Statute[28] provides several criteria that must be satisfied in order for the Court to find an accused criminally responsible. The accused must have 'intent' and 'knowledge' which are accordingly defined as requiring that: (i) the accused must mean to engage in the conduct with which he/she is charged and; (ii) that he/she is aware of the consequences that will occur as a result of his actions. In the context of an international criminal trial, such as Ongwen's, the Prosecutor would be required to prove these mental elements beyond a reasonable doubt, in order to satisfy the Trial Chamber that the defendant was criminally responsible. If these mental elements had been lacking, then Dominic Ongwen could not have been held to be criminally responsible.

However, the Rome Statute further provides for, in Article 31,[29] specific grounds where criminal responsibility can be excluded and contains what can be conceptualized as the 'affirmative defences' for an accused. Article 31 of the Statute is somewhat unique in that it represents the first comprehensive codification of 'affirmative defences' at the international criminal level.

2.1 *Mental Incapacity*

Article 31(1)(a) represents the Defence of 'mental incapacity.' The phrasing of the provision is disjunctive in that the accused must suffer from a mental disease or defect that destroyed (i) his or her capacity to appreciate the unlawfulness or nature of his or her conduct or (ii) his or her capacity to control his or her conduct to conform to the requirements of the law. Notably, 'mental disease or defect' is not further defined in the Statute nor in the Rules of Procedure and Evidence and accordingly, the concept has potentially a wide

27 ICC, *supra* note 13, p. 21.

28 ICC, *Rome Statute of the International Criminal Court*, opened for signature 17 July 1998, 2187 UNTS 90 (entered into force 1 July 2002) (ICC Statute), Article 30.

29 ICC, *supra* note 28, Article 31.

interpretation, meaning that there is no requirement that the disease or defect be officially or medically recognised. In addition, Article 31(1)(a) provides for a causative element in that the mental disease or defect must in itself destroy an accused's aforementioned capacity. The use of the term 'destroy' arguably raises the threshold for this Defence to a very high level. A mere impact or influence would not suffice but rather a complete destruction of an accused's capacity to either appreciate the legality of his or her conduct or his or her ability to control his conduct to conform to the requirements of the law.

2.2 *Duress*

Article 31(1)(d) of the Statute encompasses the defence of duress. Duress entails the situation where the accused commits a crime within the jurisdiction of the Court, however, he or she cannot be held criminally responsible, because they committed the crime due to threat of imminent death or serious bodily harm against him or her or another person. Essentially, the defence of duress is rooted in the notion that the accused's actions can be understood due to the circumstances that existed at the time that he or she committed the crime. Under Article 31(1)(d) of the Statute, in order to be successful in this defence, an accused must satisfy several cumulative elements. First, there must be an imminent threat of death or of continuing or imminent serious bodily harm. This threat can either be against the accused himself or against a third party. Second, the accused must have acted necessarily and reasonably to avoid the threat. In this sense, a reaction to a threat will be necessary in that it was the only possible means to deter the threat and that it was reasonable in the circumstances for the accused to react in this way. Third, the person must not intend to cause a greater harm that the one sought to be avoided. This phrasing introduces the requirement that the accused's actions must be proportionate to the harm threatened. It is not explicitly required that the accused causes less harm in fact, by rather that the person intended to cause no greater harm.[30]

The defence of duress has generated extensive legal discussion amongst academics,[31] yet there has been limited jurisprudential analysis at the international criminal level.

---

30 K. Ambos, 'Article 31: Grounds for excluding criminal responsibility', in *Rome Statute of the International Criminal Court: Article-by-Article Commentary* (Bloomsbury Collections, London, 2022), pp. 1347–1381, p. 1376, para 59, doi: 10.5040/9781509944064.0044.

31 C.F. Moran, 'A Perspective on the Rome Statute's Defence of Duress: The Role of Imminence', 18(1) *International Criminal Law Review* (2018) 154–177, doi: 10.1163/15718123-01801001; *See* also M. Joyce, 'Duress: From Nuremberg to the International Criminal Court, Finding the Balance Between Justification and Excuse', 28(3) *Leiden Journal of International Law* (2015) 623–642, doi:10.1017/S0922156515000321.

3 Culture as Part of the Evidence

In the *Ongwen* trial, the Defence tried to show that on the one hand, spiritual beliefs were widespread in Northern Uganda and, more importantly, that the LRA had its own system of belief.[32] It underlined that the horrific and transformative process that Dominic Ongwen went through from an early age left 'little room for moral development that would enable him to later take independent decisions.'[33] Intertwining culture into the legal submissions made before the judges would prove to be problematic. According to Anthony Good, culture becomes particularly challenging when is 'teleologized in courts of law, transformed from a conceptual tool of anthropological analysis into objective evidence,"[34] or perceived as a direct cause for actions or situations. Such issues become further complicated by the fact that in the courtroom there is no space to inspect the significant differences in how 'lawyers and social scientists are trained to think and reason.'[35] Culture can therefore produce 'the illusion of a self-evidence' and of meaning,[36] while this meaning can differ greatly from one individual to another.

While contemporary anthropology posits that culture 'does not cause behaviour, but summarizes and abstracts from it, and is thus neither normative nor predictive,'[37] the reverse is implied by the way in which 'culture' is oftentimes treated in the legal process.[38] In the debate between human rights versus cultural differences, and universalism versus cultural relativism, both sides 'take for granted an essentialist understanding of cultural communities as clearly bounded and internally homogenous.'[39] While the starting premise is that laws have universal applications, submitting real-life situations to the lens of the legal framework reveals that they are resistant to the essentialization of such categories.[40] Given that both 'legal facts' and the 'facts of the case' are social constructs, 'culture' is as performative as the legal arguments made by

---

32 Kristof Titeca called it 'the cosmological order of the LRA'. *See* K. Titeca, 'The spiritual order of the LRA', in T. Allen and K. Vlassenroot (eds), *The Lord's Resistance Army: Myth and Reality* (Zed Books, London, 2010), pp. 59–73.

33 ICC, *supra* note 13, p. 6.

34 A. Good, 'Cultural Evidence in Courts of Law', 14 *The Journal of the Royal Anthropological Institute: Incorporating Man* (2008) S47–S60.

35 Good, *supra* note 34.

36 Binsbergen, *supra* note 24, p. 461.

37 Good, *supra* note 34, p. 51.

38 *Ibid.*

39 Good, *supra* note 34, p. 52.

40 *Ibid.*

the trial parties.[41] The following section will thus provide an over-view of the ways in which culture was slotted into the legal framework of the Court and to what result.

3.1 *Spiritual Beliefs as Evidence*

> Tell me, if you encounter such things in your life, are you going to be normal? Are you going to remain normal for the rest of your life or are bad things going to happen to you?
>
> Dominic Ongwen, Appeals Hearing[42]

During its Opening Statement, the Defence argued that mental incapacity and duress are 'totally interrelated'[43] and that they share the 'common element of control.'[44] Applying the Rome Statute criteria to the reality of Northern Uganda, and more particularly of the LRA, the Defence linked the affirmative defences[45] to the supernatural powers of Joseph Kony, powers through which he could exert 'mental control over the minds of the soldiers.'[46] In relation to Dominic Ongwen specifically, the Defence argued that the impact of spiritualism led to the situation where 'Mr Ongwen's mind was not his own.'[47]

In probing whether during the charged period, 2002–2005, Dominic Ongwen had his mental capacity 'destroyed' and was acting under duress due to, in part, the intense spiritual indoctrination and surveillance he was under, several experts were brought in to evaluate him. They submitted reports and testified about the defendant's mental health during hearings on 18-29 November 2019. While the Chamber relied to a certain extent on the expert witness testimonies and reports, when it came to assessing whether the LRA soldiers believed in the supernatural powers of Joseph Kony, the judges seem to have placed more weight on the testimonies of former LRA soldiers themselves, although in several instances their statements were only briefly mentioned in a footnote.

---

41 Good, *supra* note 34, p. 52.

42 *Prosecutor v Dominic Ongwen*, Case No. ICC-02/04-01/15, Appeals Chamber, Trial Transcript, Appeals Hearing, 18 February 2022, p. 39.

43 ICC, *supra* note 13, 84.

44 *Ibid.*

45 ICC, *supra* note 13, p. 83.

46 ICC, *supra* note 13, p. 85.

47 ICC, *supra* note 13, p. 4.

P-0142 for example, a Prosecution witness, had stated in his cross-examination that Kony's predictions would often come true. He claimed that his own escape from the armed group was proof of this, as the LRA leader had foreseen it. Nevertheless, when the Defence asked the witness whether he believed that Joseph Kony had spirits, P-0142 responded: 'I could believe that *maybe* he has some spirit or in a certain way that the witch doctors would probably operate.'[48] Several witnesses, such as P-0023[49] and D-0049,[50] stated that Joseph Kony was able to read minds and predict whether someone would try to escape and that several of his prophecies had come true. Two witnesses mentioned in the judgment among 'some' of the persons who 'did believe in the spiritual powers of Joseph Kony',[51] namely witnesses D-0047 and D-0027, stated that 'everybody believed' in Kony's powers, that people had been 'working even without any payment because they know they are providing service to God,'[52] and that 'anybody who was a member of the LRA had the same belief that I did.'[53] D-0024 on the other hand added that from 'from the year 2000'[54] onwards the spirits had punished and abandoned Kony and some of his prophecies would not come true anymore.[55] Several witnesses similarly stated that while they believed at first, they later realized it was not true.[56] P-0379 testified:

48 ICC, *Prosecutor v Dominic Ongwen*, Case No. ICC-02/04-01/15, Trial Chamber IX, Trial Transcript, 8 May 2017, p. 20.

49 ICC, *Prosecutor v Dominic Ongwen*, Case No. ICC-02/04-01/15, Trial Chamber IX, Trial Transcript, 25 September 2017, p. 9.

50 ICC, *Prosecutor v Dominic Ongwen*, Case No. ICC-02/04-01/15, Trial Chamber IX, Trial Transcript, 23 September 2019, p. 22.

51 ICC, *supra* note 12, para. 2645, p. 930.

52 ICC, *Prosecutor v Dominic Ongwen*, Case No. ICC-02/04-01/15, Trial Chamber IX, Trial Transcript, 25 October 2018, p. 19.

53 ICC, *Prosecutor v Dominic Ongwen*, Case No. ICC-02/04-01/15, Trial Chamber IX, Trial Transcript, 25 February 2019, p. 15.

54 ICC, *Prosecutor v Dominic Ongwen*, Case No. ICC-02/04-01/15, Trial Chamber IX, Trial Transcript, 6 November 2018, p. 18.

55 ICC, *supra* note 58, pp. 17-19.

56 The witness statements of Simon Tabo and of Kenneth Banya, which are not open to the public, are referenced in the judgment, *See* ICC, *supra* note 12 paras 2653–2654, p. 932; P-0379 at ICC, *Prosecutor v Dominic Ongwen*, Case No. ICC-02/04-01/15, Trial Chamber IX, Trial Transcript, 27 March 2017, p. 81; *See also* P-0070 at ICC, *Prosecutor v Dominic Ongwen*, Case No. ICC-02/04-01/15, Trial Chamber IX, Trial Transcript, 18 September 2017, p. 19; *See also* ICC, *Prosecutor v Dominic Ongwen*, Case No. ICC-02/04-01/15, Trial Chamber IX, Trial Transcript, 2 November 2017, p. 33.

> We are told, we are told about these things. But later on I, I became wiser and I decided that the use of things like the holy spirit is done to brainwash the younger children so that they do not escape.[57]

While certain witnesses stated that that Kony's ability to read thoughts was merely guessing,[58] they had not completely discounted the possibility that 'there were spirits'[59] or that others believed.[60] Nevertheless, the answers were not always as straightforward as the differentiation in the judgment would make them seem. A linguistic analysis of the *Ongwen* trial reveals that the Judgment obscures the fact that testifying in the courtroom is a collaborative process, in which trial lawyers and judges not only elicit but also 'co-author' the evidence.[61] And more so, extracting only a few short extracts 'removes the broader canvas against which trial actors negotiate the meanings of such statements.'[62] Witness D-0019 for example is listed in the judgment as a 'non-believer,' predominantly because he stated that he had sufficient knowledge to know the spirits do not exist. However, as the following snippet from his examination shows, when he was asked whether he believed in spirits, his answer was not a clear no, or yes. But rather more ambiguous, indicating a sort of oscillation between moments of stronger and lesser belief:

> PRESIDING JUDGE SCHMITT: [12:19:24] Mr Witness, did you believe in these spirits?
> THE WITNESS: [12:19:45](Interpretation) Sometimes, just like any human being, you can actually be of disbelief. But again, when you see what happens and it happens according to how Kony would predict, again at

57 ICC, *Prosecutor v Dominic Ongwen*, Case No. ICC-02/04-01/15, Trial Chamber IX, Trial Transcript, 27 March 2017, p. 81; *See also* ICC, *Prosecutor v Dominic Ongwen*, Case No. ICC-02/04-01/15, Trial Chamber IX, Trial Transcript, 1 July 2019, pp. 44–46; *See also* ICC, *supra* note 51, pp. 17–19.

58 *See*, for example, P-0145 in ICC, *Prosecutor v Dominic Ongwen*, Case No. ICC-02/04-01/15, Trial Chamber IX, Trial Transcript, 17 January 2018, p. 58; P-0209 in ICC, *Prosecutor v Dominic Ongwen*, Case No. ICC-02/04-01/15, Trial Chamber IX, Trial Transcript, 28 February 2018, p. 52.

59 ICC, *Prosecutor v Dominic Ongwen*, Case No. ICC-02/04-01/15, Trial Chamber IX, Trial Transcript, 28 February 2018, p. 52.

60 Witness D-0134 stated 'people who believed in him are still in the bush because they still believe that Kony has a spirit, as he told them' at ICC, *Prosecutor v Dominic Ongwen*, Case No. ICC-02/04-01/15, Trial Chamber IX, Trial Transcript, 16 September 2019, p. 37.

61 *See* S. D'hondt, J.-P. Peréz-León-Acevedo, F. Ferraz de Almeida and E. Barrett, 'Trajectories of spirituality: Producing and assessing cultural evidence at the International Criminal Court', *Language in Society* (forthcoming).

62 *Ibid.*

> that point you believe. Before that he had, he had predicted that, for him, he will never ever be arrested, will just disappear in thin air. And up to now, unless I am mistaken, Kony has never ever been arrested. So sometimes as a human being, you can actually believe that probably this man's spirits worked. Now, for me, as somebody who has knowledge, a bit of knowledge, I don't believe in those spirits. But since things happened the way Kony had predicted, well, that is how it is.[63]

Two other crime-based witnesses explained that people did not have a choice but to believe, because they were not allowed to question it,[64] so they had to follow the rules.[65] As seen from the way in which witnesses oscillate and try to make sense of what guided their past behaviour, it can be seen that spiritual beliefs are not fixed constructs, which remain constant regardless of context or time, but that they are in constant fluctuation and transformation. Ultimately the judges rejected the defences of mental incapacity and the duress by conceptualizing 'beliefs' in a binary way which aimed to unveil that Ongwen and other commanders did not truly believe in the spiritual powers, but may have used the system of belief to manipulate the young and the naïve. However, this binary lens was 'not exclusively the outcome of the judges' recontextualization efforts,' but the foundations of such an approach had already been established 'at entextualization stage, in the questioning by the defence.'[66] The way in which the witnesses' answers are skilfully and subtly directed to follow a specific trajectory, reveal 'the underlying "grammar" of the legal language game.'[67] Additionally, a detailed reading of the testimonies reveals that a significant number of witnesses, most of which had underwent rituals and had to strictly obey certain regulations, when asked about Kony's supernatural powers or the spiritual system of beliefs within the LRA, stated that they were unaware of either.[68] These witnesses are not mentioned in the judgment. The process of 'co-authoring evidence' during trial proceedings and the Chamber's decisions reduces the issue of spirituality to the believers/

63 *See* D-0019 at *Prosecutor v Dominic Ongwen*, Case No. ICC-02/04-01/15, Trial Chamber IX, Trial Transcript, 16 August 2019, pp. 21–22.

64 Witness D-0092 at *Prosecutor v Dominic Ongwen*, Case No. ICC-02/04-01/15, Trial Chamber IX, Trial Transcript, 26 March 2019, p. 42; *See* also P-0205 in *Prosecutor v Dominic Ongwen*, Case No. ICC-02/04-01/15, Trial Chamber IX, Trial Transcript, 8 March 2017, p. 21.

65 P-0205 at *Prosecutor v Dominic Ongwen*, Case No. ICC-02/04-01/15, Trial Chamber IX, Trial Transcript, 8 March 2017, p. 21.

66 D'hondt *et al.*, *supra* note 61.

67 *Ibid.*

68 *See*, for example, the testimonies of witnesses P-0440, P-0309, P-0264, P-0218, P-0067, P-0138, P-0145, P-0209, P-0372, P-0026.

non-believers dichotomy, while overlooking the effect of certain rules on controlling the soldiers' behaviour. What was omitted was the fact that how the soldiers would obey these said rules would most likely benefit from, but would not be entirely dependent on the component of belief.

3.1.1 The Battle of the Experts

Towards the end of the trial and after all crime-base witnesses were heard, mental health experts for the Prosecution, Defence and Victim's Representatives testified. Out of all these experts, Ongwen agreed to meet only those for the Defence: Drs Dickens Akena and Dr Emilio Ovuga. Between 18 and 29 November 2019, the Courtroom became a battle of the experts. Tensions rose high as in one instance the Prosecution labelled an answer that it received from a Defence expert witness as 'nonsense.'[69] Similarly, the Defence called out the Prosecution's expert witness Weierstall-Pust for characterizing the report of the Defence experts as 'sloppy.'[70] This would culminate during the Appeals Hearings, when, referring to the way in which several testimonies on spirituality were dismissed by the trial chamber, Defence lawyer Ayena stated: 'I don't want to emphasise racism very much, but you could easily read it in this because all the evidence that was given by, you know, professors and experts who know better was completely ignored.'[71]

These exchanges and accusations reveal the contentious nature of such evidence, but also feed into the ongoing criticism that the Court faces in regard with its African bias.[72] Additionally, such disagreements between the parties can point to the fact that while looking at the same phenomena, the baseline of the actors engaged in this process is so fundamentally different, that there seems to leave not much room for common ground. Nevertheless, it should be also noted that these exchanges take place during adversarial proceedings and that the nature of the trial itself is generative of very opposing views. Irreconcilable differences between different worldviews might have been at play, but also the views concerning the methodologies employed. For example, one point of disagreement was the possibility of Ongwen malingering or faking symptoms, especially since he had been exposed to hearing a lot of information

---

69 ICC, *Prosecutor v Dominic Ongwen*, Case No. ICC-02/04-01/15, Trial Chamber IX, Trial Transcript, 22 November 2019, p. 31.

70 ICC, *supra* note 15, pp. 164-165.

71 ICC, *Prosecutor v Dominic Ongwen*, Case No. ICC-02/04-01/15, Trial Chamber IX, Trial Transcript, 14 February 2022, p. 20.

72 P. Clark, *Distant Justice: The Impact of the International Criminal Court on African Politics* (Cambridge University Press, Cambridge, 2018), doi:10.1017/9781108576260.

about himself during the trial.[73] The Defence experts nevertheless maintained that Ongwen had nothing to gain by pretending to be mentally ill.[74]

Another issue of contention was related to cultural differences and the potential misunderstandings arising from this. The Defence argued that because its expert witnesses were Ugandan, they were able to communicate with the defendant in his own language and local dialect allowing them to 'decode and decipher differences between what is culturally appropriate and what is not.'[75] In order to show what type of misunderstandings can arise in the context of not being sufficiently familiar with the patient's (cultural) background, the Defence pointed to one incident that occurred in detention: Ongwen had asked for termites or white ants for lunch and the request was perceived as a joke by the detention psychiatrist, who further reported that the defendant was in a good mood and did not present signs of depression. Defence experts explained that 'white ants' is a condiment in Uganda and that Ongwen's request was a legitimate one and not indicative of being in good humour.[76] The risk is that in the instances where practitioners 'draw on their own cultural expectations of how a traumatised person will present, they may not recognise trauma in someone who does not conform to their norms.'[77] This example is only one of the several put front by the Defence in order to highlight the way in which not having sufficient knowledge on the background of the person, in this case the defendant, can lead to misinterpretation and potentially misdiagnosis.[78]

Concerning the aspect of spiritual possession, while the two teams of experts broadly agreed that one phenomenon or the same symptoms can have on the one hand a cultural explanation (spiritual possession) and a medical one (dissociation) depending on the person describing them, the issue became contentious when it came to the evidence or the proof that Ongwen had indeed suffered from this affliction. The Defence experts maintained that during the battles, Ongwen was possessed by spirits or that he was dissociating

---

73 ICC, *Prosecutor v Dominic Ongwen*, Case No. ICC-02/04-01/15, Trial Chamber IX, Prosecution Closing Brief, 24 February 2020, p. 168.

74 ICC, *Prosecutor v Dominic Ongwen*, Case No. ICC-02/04-01/15, Trial Chamber IX, Trial Transcript, 21 November 2019, p. 32.

75 ICC, *Prosecutor v Dominic Ongwen*, Case No. ICC-02/04-01/15, Trial Chamber IX, Trial Transcript, 18 November 2019, p. 32.

76 ICC, The Prosecutor v Ongwen, Case No. ICC-02/04-01/15, Trial Transcript, 19 November 2019, p. 51.

77 A. Vredeveldt, Z. Given-Wilson and A. Memon, 'Culture, trauma, and memory in investigative interviews', 24(9) *Psychology, Crime & Law* (2003) 935–956, doi: 10.1080/1068316X.2023.2209262.

78 *Ibid.*

and this could be proven by the fact that numerous witnesses described him as extremely brave, which indicated something 'abnormal' about him.[79] They also underlined that 'if the patient was dissociating in the context of being spiritually possessed, in the context where everybody was controlled by the spirits,'[80] other people going through the same possession would not be able to recognize that because it affected their own judgment as well, especially in the context of 'shared delusions.'[81] Their assertion was therefore that other LRA members would not be able to notice this dissociative episodes because they were themselves under the spell of the spirits. On the issue of whether spiritual possession could be characterized as a mental disease or not, the Ugandan experts consider that his episodes of being possessed were beyond what would be 'normal' within the cultural framework and that he suffered episodes of dissociation.[82] The Prosecution highlighted that on the one hand, the Defence experts explained how in certain instances, Ongwen's spiritual possessions/dissociative states were involuntary, while on the other hand, the same experts had suggested that at other times the defendant could supress or hide these dissociative states from the others. According to the Prosecution experts, such explanations were self-contradictory.[83]

Moreover, the Prosecution also tried to show that the so-called 'miracles' that some of the LRA members had talked about, had been in fact not verified for their truth value. Therefore, when it came to the idea of a shared delusion, it criticized the fact there was no attempt to challenge the explanations given by the former LRA concerned the 'miracles' that they observed. On the other hand, the Prosecution took issue with the fact that the Defence did not corroborate Ongwen's self-reported episodes of spiritual possession. For example, in one instance, the Prosecution asked Dr Akena to explain whether 'chances are that it's valid, true, that Joseph Kony could turn stones into bombs'[84] to which the expert replied that 'is something that everybody else seems to believe in,'[85] an answer which was labelled as not helpful.[86] A similar approach was taken during the cross-examination of Defence expert witness, anthropologist and political scientist Kristof Titeca. The Prosecution also

79 ICC, *Prosecutor v Dominic Ongwen*, Case No. ICC-02/04-01/15, Trial Chamber IX, Trial Transcript, 28 November 2019, p. 24.
80 *Ibid*, p. 95.
81 *Ibid.*
82 ICC, *supra* note 81, p. 23.
83 ICC, *supra* note 78, p. 31.
84 ICC, *supra* note 79, p. 109.
85 *Ibid.*
86 *Ibid.*

challenged the witness by stating he should have verified the truth value of the beliefs held by the former LRAs. It implied that there is an objective baseline of reasonableness in establishing what is believable or not.[87] This approach suggests a failure on the part of the Prosecution to appreciate the "emic" nature of the anthropological endeavour (which focuses on the view from within the culture that is researched, or the insider's perspective), which is very different than the endevour of a lawyer. This points to what Anthony Good exemplified as a mismatch between how 'lawyers and social scientists are trained to think and reason'[88] when dealing with the same phenomenon. Simultaneously, such an approach does not account for the fact that what is deemed reasonable or believable is equally cultural dependent, and not based on universal and objective criteria.[89]

The judges would ultimately not rely on Kristof Titeca's evidence based on the fact that the expert had not challenged 'the statements made to him about the spiritual influence on LRA fighters and did not consider it to be his role to make a judgment about the truthfulness or falsity of the statements.'[90] The judges considered that 'his evidence is only of very limited value in the present proceedings, especially given the abundance of direct evidence of witnesses.'[91]

Both Prosecution and Victim's Representatives challenged the idea that the recruits, in particular commanders such as Ongwen, actually believed in the supernatural powers of Joseph Kony. The parties interpreted the fact that the defendant had defied Kony's order on certain occasions as *proof* of his lack of fear and belief in Kony's spiritual powers,[92] an approach that was ultimately adopted by the Chamber as well. The Defence and its expert witnesses offered a different explanation, suggesting that at one point, Ongwen 'really didn't care whether he would be alive or dead'[93] and that his behaviour was that

87 *See* ICC, *Prosecutor v Dominic Ongwen*, Case No. ICC-02/04-01/15, Trial Chamber IX, Trial Transcript, 19 November 2018, pp. 68–69, 71.; *See* also A. Nistor, A. Merrylees and B. Hola, 'Spellbound at the International Criminal Court: The intersection of Spirituality and International Criminal Law', in J. Fraser and B. McGonigle Leyh (eds), *Intersections of Law and Culture at the International Criminal Court* (Edward Elgar, Cheltenham, 2020), pp. 147–168.

88 Good, *supra* note 37, p. 47.

89 *See*, for example, Good, *supra* note 37, pp. 48–50.

90 ICC, *supra* note 12, para 597, p. 216.

91 *Ibid.*

92 *See*, for example, ICC, *Prosecutor v Dominic Ongwen*, Case No. ICC-02/04-01/15, Trial Chamber IX, Trial Transcript, Confirmation of Charges, 27 January 2016, pp. 25–26; *See also* ICC, *Prosecutor v Dominic Ongwen*, Case No. ICC-02/04-01/15, Trial Chamber IX, Trial Transcript, Prosecution Closing Statement, 10 March 2020, p. 10.

93 ICC, *supra* note 79, p. 107.

of a 'madman.'[94] While the parties offered diverging explanations on the correlation between behaviour and belief, they did not explain based on what criteria these inferences could be made. Determining a link between spiritual beliefs and behaviour seemed at times to rely on a presumed universal expectation on how an individual should behave in certain circumstances, and at others, through comparison with how other individuals have behaved in similar situations. When it came to the strength of the defendant's belief in the power of Joseph Kony, the Defence expert Dr Ovuga also conceded that Ongwen was not entirely under the leader's spell:

> I don't think he [Ongwen] was 100 per cent convinced, although to us in the clinical interview he did mention certain belief systems related to spirit protection of the soldiers when their bodies are smeared with oil, so that they don't get hurt. So I think with respect to Mr Ongwen, the influence he's – maybe 75/25, I'm just speculating, 75 being for and 25 per cent being against.[95]

But the main issue concerning the submissions on the role of spiritualism impacting the behaviour of the defendant was, according to the Prosecution, the fact that the Defence did not show 'any link between these [spiritual beliefs] and Mr Ongwen's crimes' and that this was because 'no such link can be found in the evidence heard in this case.'[96] Moreover, it faulted the Defence for not showing that a threat or harm coming from the spirits themselves had existed before each crime and each attack:

> No witness suggested that Mr Ongwen was visited by spirits prior to or during any of the charged attacks or the sexual and gender-based crimes and crimes against children. Moreover, despite many assertions about Kony's spiritual orders and rules, LRA commanders, including Mr Ongwen, frequently violated them.[97]

In his Unsworn Statement during the Sentencing Hearings, Dominic Ongwen would address some of the points raised by the Prosecution. He spoke in open

---

94 ICC, *supra* note 14, p. 8.

95 ICC, *Prosecutor v Dominic Ongwen*, Case No. ICC-02/04-01/15, Trial Chamber IX, Trial Transcript, 29 November 2019, p. 10.

96 ICC, *Prosecutor v Dominic Ongwen*, Case No. ICC-02/04-01/15, Trial Chamber IX, Trial Transcript, Prosecution Statement at Sentencing Hearing, 14 April 2021, p. 17 (brackets within quote added).

97 ICC, *supra* note 100, p. 18.

court about his own beliefs. He described how, at a very early age, he witnessed a stone fly off his hand 'like a bomb,' in what he described as 'magic' and the 'first miracle' by Joseph Kony.[98] He said that if he would have been able to, he would have stopped the spirits 'from possessing Kony and prohibiting him from committing all these crimes.'[99] He confirmed that the LRA leader indeed 'has the spirits.'[100] He said that there is 'no jail in the world which is tougher than that of LRA'[101] and that there has been a moment when he felt that he was going mad, so that he even sometimes refused the orders of Joseph Kony.[102] He pleaded with the Court to help him so in the future he could 'be a better human being.'[103] Having mentioned several times that he was a very religious man, he ended his statement with 'God bless you all.'[104]

4 The Judicial Assessment of Culture: Spirituality and the Rome Statute Criteria

At the end of the trial, in its Closing Statement, Defence lawyer Beth Lyons asked: 'But the bottom line is, look, whom do you believe? (…) So this is really – that's really a question at the end of the day.'[105] The word 'to believe' has been indeed used numerous times in the judgment, either referring to what the witnesses, the parties to the trial, or the judges believed 'to be true.' While the purpose of the trial is to reach legal truth, when it comes to something as intimate as spiritual beliefs and peeking into the minds of the people holding such beliefs, a court of law might not be best equipped to address such issues. The rigid nature of its purpose is to determine whether an individual is guilty or not of certain crimes, regardless of motives and personal circumstances.

In the trial judgment rendered on 4 February 2021, the Chamber stated that 'the fact that Joseph Kony acted also as a spiritual leader, building on Acholi traditions, is uncontroversial and well-attested in the evidence.'[106] However,

98 ICC, *supra* note 2.
99 *Ibid*, p. 17.
100 *Ibid*, p. 20.
101 *Ibid*, p. 26.
102 ICC, *supra* note 2, p. 35.
103 *Ibid*, p. 19.
104 *Ibid*, p. 37.
105 Full quote: 'But the bottom line is, look, whom do you believe? You have heard the witnesses. You have three experts from the OTP, two from us, and then you have Professor – the Court-appointed expert. So this is really – that's really a question at the end of the day' in ICC, *supra* note 14, p. 75.
106 ICC, *supra* note 12, para 2643, p. 929.

when it came to the Defence's argument that Ongwen had acted under duress while at the LRA, this 'was examined in the same legalistic manner'[107] in which the Chamber considered whether, 'regardless of Ongwen's past victimization, he could still be held criminally responsible.'[108] Guided by the Rome Statute, the judges' role was to determine only whether the LRA's spiritual indoctrination and brutality constituted 'a threat of imminent death or continuing or imminent serious bodily harm' against Ongwen, and in this way quoted 'verbatim the legal requirements for establishing duress.'[109] Once the Chamber determined that the facts presented by the Defence did not meet the stringent criteria laid out in the Rome Statute, 'their potential significance for shedding light on the system of indoctrination within which the defendant had been brought up appeared irrelevant.'[110]

Additionally, the judges summarily noted that 'there is evidence that *some* persons did believe in the spiritual powers of Joseph Kony.'[111] They then provided a more extensive overview on the testimonies of the witnesses who either never believed in the cosmological order of the LRA, or who had been initially indoctrinated in it, but later 'became wiser.' While the testimonies of the 'believers' are relegated to a footnote,[112] those of the non-believers are described in thirteen paragraphs spread over two pages in the judgment. While the judges deemed the testimonies of all these witnesses as overall credible, it is evident that they found the explanation of the former/non-believers much more compelling. The judges concluded that:

> All of this evidence leads the Chamber to the conclusion that LRA members with some experience in the organisation did not generally believe that Joseph Kony possessed spiritual powers. There is also no evidence indicating that the belief in Joseph Kony's spiritual powers played a role for Dominic Ongwen, and in fact the evidence of Dominic Ongwen defying Joseph Kony, discussed above, speaks clearly against any such influence. The Chamber therefore does not discern in the issue of LRA

107 L.G. Minkova, 'Expressing what? The Stigmatization of the Defendant and the ICC's Institutional Interests in the Ongwen case', 34(1) *Leiden Journal of International Law* (2020) 223–245, p. 242, doi: 10.1017/S0922156520000539.

108 *Ibid.*

109 *Ibid.*

110 *Ibid.*

111 ICC, *supra* note 12, para 2645, p. 930 (emphasis added).

112 ICC, *supra* note 12, footnote 7047, p. 930.

> spirituality a factor contributing to a threat relevant under Article 31(1)(d) of the Statute.[113]

It is relevant to note a few details concerning the evidence of the witnesses that testified to the fact that LRA soldiers believed in the spiritual powers of Joseph Kony. For example, in relation to witness P-0142 (a believer), through selecting a particular sentence from his testimony, the judges highlighted that the witness used the word 'maybe' when it came to the spiritual order within the LRA: 'maybe [Joseph Kony] has some spirit.'[114] About witness D-0056, they noted that the witness stated that he 'did have some kind of belief, but not a hundred per cent belief.'[115] When it came to evaluating the overall credibility of these witnesses, the Chamber found that in relation to six out of the eleven non-believers and one believer out of the seven, parts of their testimony were not assessed as credible. For their part, the areas of their testimonies that were discounted either had to do with the witnesses minimizing their own role in the commission of a crime or the role of the defendant in an attack. Moreover, concerning two of the 'believers' who had stated that 'everybody believed' in Kony's powers,[116] the Chamber noted that such assertions were 'proved false by the evidence cited in the following paragraphs,'[117] therefore finding these generalizing statements as not believable. Determining witness credibility is 'a balancing act' and 'a result of an interplay of various factors relating to each individual witness, assessed in the context of the evidentiary record as a whole.'[118] As such, inferring how the judges reach such conclusions by merely accessing transcripts of trial hearings and decisions remains therefore speculative. It seems that the judges found some explanations more plausible than others, weighing them against other evidence submitted on the record. The Chamber also added that there 'is also no evidence indicating that the belief in Joseph Kony's spiritual powers played a role for Dominic Ongwen, and in fact the evidence of Dominic Ongwen defying Joseph Kony, discussed above, speaks clearly against any such influence.'[119] This indicates that they found the Prosecution and Victim's Representative explanation the most convincing.

113 ICC, *supra* note 12, para. 2658, p. 933.

114 ICC, *supra* note 12, footnote 7047, p. 930.

115 *Ibid.*

116 ICC, *supra* note 56; *See* also ICC, *supra* note 60.

117 ICC, *supra* note 12, footnote 7047, p. 930.

118 G. Chlevickaitė, B. Holá and C. Bijleveld, 'Suspicious minds? Empirical analysis of insider witness assessments at the ICTY, ICTR and ICC', 20(1), *European Journal of Criminology* (2023) 185–207, doi: 10.1177/1477370821997343, p. 15.

119 *Ibid.*

The fact that the Defence mental health experts also asserted that Ongwen himself had some doubts about the supernatural powers of Joseph Kony might have also weakened the assertion that Ongwen did not 'have a mind of his own.' Concerning the fact that Ongwen defied Kony several times – an issue presented by the Defence as proof of his suicidal tendencies, and by the Prosecution as a lack of fear of and belief in Kony's powers, the judges determined that such behaviour indicated that Ongwen was not under the influence of the spiritual medium.[120] Concerning the role of culture in assessing the mental state of Dominc Ongwen, the Chamber underlined that: 'whereas Professor Ovuga and Dr Akena evoked cultural factors on several occasions, they did not provide any real explanation of what these factors were, how they impacted the analysis, and how their consideration was to take place according to the standards and practices of mental health expertise.'[121]

The judges considered the issue of Ongwen having requested termites for lunch and being misunderstood as a joke by the detention psychiatrist, and the fact that the word 'blues' (to have the blues; to be blue) does not exist in many African languages[122] as 'trivial and without serious link to the issue under consideration.'[123] Given the implications that such 'trivial' misunderstandings can have when it comes to misdiagnosing, it is surprising that the judges completely dismissed these suggestions. Moreover, they highlighted that the former LRAs that testified in Court were credible and coherent witnesses[124] and that none of them had noticed episodes of possession or disassociation in Dominic Ongwen. The chamber concluded that the defendant did not 'suffer from a mental disease or defect at the time of the conduct relevant under the charges. A ground excluding criminal responsibility under Article 31(1)(a) of the Statute was not applicable.'[125] Furthermore, in rejecting the spiritual or cultural aspect of the mental health assessment of Dominic Ongwen during the charged period, the judges stated that they were unable to rely on the reports submitted by the Defence expert witnesses. The reason for this exclusion

120 ICC, *supra* note 12, para 2658, p. 933.

121 *Ibid.*

122 During the Appeal Hearings, the Defence submitted that: 'Even the DSM-V acknowledges cultural factors. Dr Akena mentioned there's no word for feeling, quote, blue in Acholi so that the mental literacy, the communication of psychological distress within the Acholi culture and the other cultures that exist in Uganda need to be considered when this whole topic of eyewitness testimony, what was observed, what was said, is considered'. In ICC, *Prosecutor v Dominic Ongwen*, Case No. ICC-02/04-01/15, Appeal Chamber, Trial Transcript, 15 February 2022, p. 8.

123 ICC, *supra* note 12, para 2463, p. 871.

124 *Ibid*, para 2504, p. 885.

125 *Ibid*, para 2580, p. 909.

was based on concerns related to their methodology, the fact that it 'is not in the role of a forensic expert to sustain a relationship of trust and confidence with the person to be examined for the court'[126] and that their conclusions included 'contradictions' that are 'major and readily apparent.'[127] The judges noted also the insufficient triangulation of information and the heavy reliance on the defendant's own self-reporting of symptoms.[128] On a final note, while the judges did not explain how, the fact that the Defence relied on issue of spiritualism in order to raise the two affirmative defences, had an impact on the way in which the Chamber assessed this type of evidence, they indicated that:

> On the one hand, it may be observed that the two grounds for excluding criminal responsibility cannot coexist even in the abstract, given that one is premised on a destruction of the person's capacity to appreciate the unlawfulness or nature of his or her conduct, or capacity to control his or her conduct to conform to the requirements of the law, and the other on a conscious choice to engage in conduct which constitutes a crime based on an evaluation of the harm that is caused. On the other hand, the Chamber recognises that similar discussion of facts and evidence partly underlies the analysis of both grounds excluding criminal responsibility discussed in the present case, and to the extent that the Defence in fact aimed to make this point, the Chamber is confident that all relevant considerations have been made under each heading.[129]

The same aspect was brought up by the Prosecution in its closing statement.[130] This raises the question: how did the fact that spiritual beliefs were raised in relationship with two legal concepts that are diametrically opposed influence the way in which they were assessed?

For the Appeal Hearings, the Court invited various experts to submit amici curiae on several contentious matters of dispute between the parties, one of which, the issue of Dominic Ongwen's mental health assessment. Dominic Ongwen took the stand again and described being kidnapped by the LRA as joining a 'spiritual army'[131] as the 'the spirits sent them to abduct a young

126 ICC, *supra* note 12, para 2531, p. 893.
127 *Ibid*, para 2544, p. 898.
128 *Ibid*, paras 2551–2568, pp. 900–906.
129 ICC, *supra* note 12, para 2671, pp. 937–938.
130 ICC, *Prosecutor v Dominic Ongwen*, Case No. ICC-02/04-01/15, Trial Chamber IX, Trial Transcript, Prosecution Closing Statement, 10 March 2020, p. 55.
131 ICC, *supra* note 46, p. 36.

child.'[132] The rituals that were performed on him clouded his mind and he said that to this day he feels as if he were drunk, although he never had alcohol in his life.[133]

The Appeal Chamber nevertheless upheld the decision of Trial Chamber IX. However, Judge Luz del Carmen Ibáñez Carranza submitted a Partly Dissenting Opinion in which she held that the sentence imposed on Dominic Ongwen should have accounted more for his victim status. The judge highlighted submissions made by Erin Baines, Kamari M. Clarke and Mark Drumbl in their amici cuarae who submitted that: 'Mr Ongwen's mental and moral development were impacted by his experience as a child soldier, which 'resulted in a destruction of [his] ability to understand the immorality of his actions.'[134] She held that Ongwen's development within the 'coercive environment of the LRA had a long-lasting impact on his personality, the development of his brain and moral values, and future opportunities. These circumstances merit significant weight in mitigation when imposing a new sentence on Mr Ongwen.'[135] While the partly dissenting opinion has no bearing on the outcome of the trial, it might be of significance at a later stage, if Ongwen would submit a request for early release.

5 Conclusion

This article aimed to shed light into the potential complications that arise on the one hand from the way in which a concept derived from anthropology has been employed in a legal setting, an arena that functions according to a different epistemic framework than the social sciences. This analysis is therefore not set up to offer definitive answers when it comes to the role of 'culture' in international criminal proceedings, but to raise questions concerning the way in which it impacts the delivery of justice. Furthermore, the article offers an overview of various other dynamics that play a role into how spiritual beliefs were assessed. It reveals a mismatch between what the judges expected from the expert witnesses in terms of their methodology, approach, reports and their testimonies and what was submitted to them. Also, while the judges did

132 ICC, *supra* note 46, p. 37.

133 *Ibid.*

134 ICC, *Prosecutor v Dominic Ongwen,* Case No. ICC-02/04-01/15, The Appeals Chamber, Judgment on the appeal of Mr Dominic Ongwen against the decision of Trial Chamber IX of 6 May 2021 entitled 'Sentence', ANNEX 1: Partly Dissenting Opinion of Judge Luz del Carmen Ibáñez Carranza, 15 December 2022, paras 110–111, p. 41.

135 ICC, *supra* note 129, para. 196, p. 67.

not offer details concerning how it impacted their decision, the fact that they view the two affirmative defences as incompatible even in the abstract, might indicate the fact that they regarded certain Defence evidence as internally inconsistent and contradictory.

While speculative, an analysis of the judgment indicates that the Chamber seems to have considered that the extent to which LRA members in general, and Ongwen in particular, believed in the spiritual dimension of the LRA and in Kony's supernatural powers, could be rationally inferred. According to the judges, this behaviour was in contradiction to Ongwen's alleged beliefs in the supernatural powers of Kony. They appear to have considered that a direct and clear determinative correlation can be inferred between a person's belief systems and their behaviour. This approach has been criticized by social scientists who posit that the court did not grasp the role of spiritualism in the LRA.[136] Research into the belief system of the LRA seems to indicate that spirituality was a complex issue and that it played a central role in the way in which the soldiers perceived reality.[137] However, socio-anthropological and political science research differs greatly from the work of a criminal courtroom; the individual asking the interviewee questions, and the (perceived) purpose of the questions, might skew the answers greatly. Confronted with the fact that their past acts are (potentially) criminal, former LRA soldiers might rationalize their lived experiences in different ways. Trials capture only a snippet of a past event that is reinterpreted or explained for very particular reasons and one needs to approach their findings while factoring in their considerable limitations, in particular when it comes to establishing historical truth or advancing understanding on the profile of the perpetrators, their motivations.[138] Furthermore, the judgment does not present an exhaustive

---

136 K. Titeca, 'I testified at the trial of one of Joseph Kony's commanders. Here's what the court didn't understand', *The Washington Post* (17 January 2019), available online at www.washingtonpost.com/news/monkey-cage/wp/2019/01/17/i-testified-at-the-icc-trial-of-one-of-joseph-konys-commanders-heres-what-the-law-doesnt-seem-to-understand/ (accessed 03 October 2023).

137 *See* K. Anderson, *The Dilemma of Dominic Ongwen* (preliminary title, Rutgers University Press, New Brunswick, NJ, forthcoming); E. Baines, 'Complex Political Perpetrators: Reflections on Dominic Ongwen', 47(2) *The Journal of Modern African Studies* (2009) 163–191; K.D. Peel, *Abduction, Rebellion and Reprieve: The Narratives of Former Members of the Lord's Resistance Army* (PhD thesis, University of Cambridge, Cambridge, 2008), available online at https://summit.sfu.ca/_flysystem/fedora/sfu_migrate/17113/etd8850_KPeel.pdf (accessed 15 May 2023).

138 T.B. Bouwknegt and A. Nistor, 'Studying 'Perpetrators' through the lens of the criminal trial', in A. Smeulers, M. Weerdesteijn and B. Holá (eds), *Perpetrators of International Crimes: Theories, Methods, and Evidence* (Oxford University Press, Oxford, 2019), pp. 89–116.

overview of the testimonies of all the witnesses who were questioned on the issue of spirituality. Only the most 'contrasting' answers are selected to present an almost precise dichotomy of believers and non-believers, while the testimonies of the witnesses who claimed to be unfamiliar with the issue of the spirits or Kony's supernatural powers are not even mentioned. Analysing how the spirituals beliefs were assessed in this trial therefore needs to be based on a close inspection of the evidence on the record, which determines the parameters of how the parties 'co-created'[139] the evidence with the witnesses and how the judges evaluated these issues, and of the strict criteria that had to be met in order to exclude criminal responsibility for acts so grave that can be qualified as international crimes.

Thirdly, at a first glance, the judges seem to have taken an approach of quantifying the extent to which the LRA soldiers believed in the powers of Joseph Kony by giving an overview of the witnesses who proclaimed to be believers versus those who were former believers or non-believers. However, reading that section of the judgment alongside the individual assessment of each witness, it becomes apparent that the extent to which the judges found the statements of some witnesses more credible than others probably played a more decisive role.

Determining the role of 'culture' throughout trial proceedings is a complex task of untangling a myriad of threads, all so intertwined and embedded in each other, that it is hardly possible to find where one starts and where it ends. Or where and how they have merged. Submissions about culture more broadly, and spirituality in particular, have been fused with the legal criteria they had to measure up to, thus morphing into new concepts, specific to this trial. Definitions of local cultural concepts have been intertwined with the various legal, psychological, sociological understanding of them provided by various experts and legal practitioners or in their description as lived experiences of individual witnesses. Different views concerning the appropriate methodology to measure and analyse these cultural concepts also came into play, subjecting them to every participant's own frame of reference. And engaging with these concepts became a battle of diverging and sometimes heated arguments. The impossibility to find common ground is often the result of the adversarial nature of the proceedings. But it also reveals that this challenge to reach a consensus is based on what various actors, all with different vested interests in this trial, consider to be reasonable, believable, meaningful, not in legal sense, but in the very subjective interpretation of reality.

139 D'hondt *et al.*, *supra* note 61.

Acknowledgements

The author wants to thank A.M. for the feedback on the earlier drafts of this paper, in particular concerning the legal framework and its criteria, I.W. for insights in applying the anthropological lens, and to Barbora Hola for the insightful suggestions on the final draft. Many thanks to the anonymous reviewers for their valuable comments and suggestions.

CHAPTER 9

The Post-*Ongwen* Case Period and the Reconciliation Process in Northern Uganda: Local Communities as a Site of Knowledge

Christelle Molima Bameka

Abstract

By providing victims with more space in the *Ongwen* case, the International Criminal Court (ICC) has significantly contributed to the healing of the trauma and community reconciliation in northern Uganda. That said, this court has also raised issues that could affect local efforts to achieve peace, namely the positioning of victims of child soldiers *vis-à-vis* criminal child soldiers. Drawing on qualitative data collected through focus group discussions with some community members from locations under investigation by the ICC, this sociolegal study examines the victims' narratives about child soldiers and the different ideas of human rights that emerge. Then, it explores how these ideas may shape future transitional justice mechanisms designed in the global sphere. Finally, it discusses the extent to which they may impact the relevance of current justice initiatives. Overall, this paper analyzes the substantive effect of victim participation in the *Ongwen* case on local peacebuilding initiatives in northern Uganda.

Keywords

child recruitment – LRA – reconciliation – victims

1 Introduction

The International Criminal Court's (ICC) trial of Dominic Ongwen, a former commander of the Sinia Brigade of the Lord's Resistance Army (LRA), accused of crimes he himself suffered—he was abducted by the LRA at the age of ten—has been described by many legal scholars as 'both the ICC's success story and

 | DOI: 10.1163/9789004743380_010

the antithesis of what it stands for and fights against'.[1] Indeed, Ongwen is both the one who 'jeopardized the future of humankind'[2] by using children to participate in hostilities,[3] and a victim of this jeopardization of humankind who should have benefited from international legal protection.[4] That said, opening the door to discussions of Ongwen's dual identity as both victim and perpetrator[5] from the outset of the trial[6] gave the ICC the opportunity to address the issue of child recruitment in northern Uganda in a comprehensive manner. Indeed, during the trial, the ICC highlighted that the forced recruitment of children affected communities as well as the child soldiers.

The acknowledgement of communities' sufferings was rendered possible by the prominent presence of victims in and outside the courtroom. A total of 4107 people from the villages identified as the sites of Ongwen's crimes—Lukodi,

---

1 T.B. Bouwknegt and B. Holà, 'Dominic Ongwen: the ICC's Poster and Problem Child', *Justiceinfo.net* (2021), available online at https://www.justiceinfo.net/en/44014-dominic-ongwen-icc-poster-and-problem-child.html (accessed 18 November 2021).

2 Former ICC Prosecutor Luis Moreno Ocampo has described those who recruit children to take part in hostilities as individuals who have 'jeopardized the future of humankind'. *See* 'Statement by Luis Moreno-O'Campo, Press conference in relation with the surrender to the court of Mr Lubanga Dyilo', 18 March 2006.

3 In the Sentence Decision, the Chamber IX considered this crime 'to be of very high gravity ... in fact particularly striking', and 'not incidental or a result of disregard for the age of the recruits, but ... a specific and methodically pursued organisation-wide policy, which Dominic Ongwen shared and actively sustained'. *See* ICC, *Prosecutor* v. *Dominic Ongwen*, Case No. ICC-02/04-01/15, Trial Chamber IX, Sentence, 6 May 2021, para. 358. On this basis, the Chamber sentenced him to a prison term of 25 years (*See* para. 373). The sentence was confirmed by the Appeals Chamber. *See* ICC, *Prosecutor* v. *Dominic Ongwen*, Case No. ICC-02/04-01/15 A2, Appeals Chamber, Judgement, 15 December 2022, para. 374.

4 In its first decision on child recruitment, the Lubanga Case, the ICC embeds the portrayal of child soldiers as individuals whose trauma from the violence they experienced had left them devastated and damaged for life, requiring specific protection. *See* M.A. Drumbl, 'The Effects of the Lubanga Case on Understanding and Preventing Child Soldiering', 15 *Yearbook of International Humanitarian Law* (2012) 87–116; B. Holá and T.B. Bouwknegt, 'Child Soldiers in International Courtrooms: Unqualified Perpetrators, Erratic Witnesses and Irreparable Victims?', in M.A. Drumbl and J.C. Barrett (eds.), *Research Handbook on Child Soldiers* (Edward Elgar, Cheltenham, 2019), pp. 350–373. Some therefore question the applicability of this rhetoric once the child soldier has come of age in the armed group. *See* R.L.A. Pangalangan, 'Dominic Ongwen and the Rotten Social Background Defence: The Criminal Culpability of Child Soldiers Turned War Criminals', 33(3) *American University International Law Review* (2018) 605–635.

5 *See* A. Branch, 'Dominic Ongwen on Trial: The ICC's African Dilemmas', 11(1) *International Journal of Transitional Justice* (2017) 30–49; W. Nortje, 'Victim or Villain: Exploring the Possible Bases of a Defence in the *Ongwen* Case at the International Criminal Court', 17(1) *International Criminal Law Review* (2017) 186–207.

6 *See* ICC, *Prosecutor* v. *Dominic Ongwen*, Case No. ICC-02/04-01/15, Pre-Trial Chamber, Decision, 23 March 2016, paras 66–67.

Abok, Odek and Pajule—were registered as victims in the trial.[7] Those who were unable to participate in the trial physically had the possibility to make it virtually through the video screening of the trial (video screening session) sponsored by the Danish Embassy in Uganda[8] and the restitution sessions held by the ICC Outreach Team and the Office of the Prosecutor (OTP).[9] On the one hand, such participation allowed the victims to express their feelings in court and have their voices echoed outside the courtroom. On the other hand, it allowed the ICC to testify to the lasting impact of the LRA's crimes on communities in northern Uganda and acknowledge the victims of a war that for years has been described as the world's largest forgotten and neglected humanitarian emergency.[10] Furthermore, and most importantly, it gave the Court the opportunity to address child recruitment in this region both from the angle of child soldiers and the victims child soldiers left on their path.[11] By emphasizing victims' sufferings, the ICC went beyond its scope and brought to light additional elements that deserve due consideration by peace initiatives in northern Uganda.

The element this paper explores is how the LRA's policy of child recruitment has shaped some community members' views of LRA child soldiers and what these views tell us about the justice needs of some communities and the ideas of human rights these justice needs rely on. According to testimonies collected throughout the trial, people in northern Uganda experienced first-hand the forced recruitment of children by the LRA. Either they were abducted or one of their relatives was. Under these circumstances, one would expect them to support the Defence. Paradoxically, their proximity to this harsh reality has not prevented them from strongly supporting Ongwen's punishment.[12] This position is not a real paradox as many empirical studies from northern Uganda and other war-torn societies show that communities victimized by

---

7 Human Right Watch, *Who will stand for us? Victims' legal representation at the ICC in the Ongwen case and beyond* (2017).

8 Personal interview, ICC Outreach Team, Gulu, 3 November 2018.

9 *See* ICC, *Prosecutor* v. *Dominic Ongwen*, Case No. ICC-02/04-01/15, Trial Chamber IX, Judgement, 4 February 2021, paras 1172–2008.

10 P. Schulz, 'Tek-Gungu: Wartime Sexual Violence in Northern Uganda', in *Male Survivors of Wartime Sexual Violence. Perspectives from Northern Uganda* (University of California Press, Oakland, CA, 2021), pp. 48–73.

11 For the purpose of this paper, the concept 'child soldier' refers to every human being below the age of 18 years associated with armed forces or armed groups (*See* Article 2 African Charter on the Rights and Welfare of the Child).

12 Human Rights Watch, *supra* note 7.

child soldiers demand accountability before their social reintegration.[13] That said, this *paradox* is interesting to explore in the context of the Ongwen trial because it offers an opportunity to unearth and deepen existing knowledge about the victims of child soldiers. Particularly, it is an occasion to start a conversation as to what we know about the justice needs of victims of child soldiers in northern Uganda, how we know it and from whom.

Given that the recruitment of children by the LRA took place years before the period under investigation by the ICC, this paper suggests that the position taken in the *Ongwen* trial—supporting the prosecution of a former LRA child soldier—is one of many ways in which these communities view LRA child soldiers. In other words, there are likely to be other ways of viewing LRA child soldiers that need to be identified and analysed to assess the extent to which they might influence current and future transitional justice mechanisms. Therefore, this paper will explore how some community members construct their victimization vis-à-vis their perpetrators—child soldiers—and what notions of human rights they draw upon to do so, to identify these other ways of envisioning child soldiers and the crimes they commit. To this end, it asks the following questions: How do victims of child soldiers construct their victimization? What can this formation process tell us about the justice needs of victims of child soldiers, and the value and relevance of peace processes to be implemented in the post-*Ongwen* case era?

After presenting the context for this research and its methodological aspects, this paper briefly reviews the complex nature of the child soldier phenomenon in northern Uganda by looking at the history of child recruitment by the LRA. It then explores the extent to which it shapes the narratives on child soldiers developed by some community members and the different ideas of human rights that emerge. Then, it explores how these ideas of human rights may

13 G. Akello, A. Richters and R. Reis, 'Reintegration of Former Child Soldiers in Northern Uganda: Coming to Terms with Children's Agency and Accountability', 4 *Intervention* (2006) 229–243; E.K. Baines, 'The Haunting of Alice: Local Approaches to Justice and Reconciliation in Northern Uganda', 1 *International Journal of Transitional Justice* (2007) 91–114; K. Fisher, *Transitional Justice for Child Soldiers: Accountability and Social Reconstruction in Post-conflict Contexts* (Palgrave Macmillan, New York, NY, 2013); M. Schotsmans, 'No Return Home: The (non-) Reintegration of Youth Ex-Combatants in Sierra Leone as a Challenge to the Contextualisation of DDR and Transitional Justice', in I. Derluyn *et al.* (eds.), *Re-Member: Rehabilitation, Reintegration and Reconciliation of War-Affected Children* (Intersentia, Antwerp, 2012), pp. 215–241; C.K. Kiyala, 'Challenges of Reintegrating Self-Demobilised Child Soldiers in North Kivu Province: Prospects for Accountability and Reconciliation via Restorative Justice Peacemaking Circles', 16 *Human Rights Review* (2015) 99–122.

affect future transitional justice mechanisms to be designed in the global sphere and influence the relevance of current justice initiatives. It ends with a conclusion.

2 Research Context

2.1 *Aim of the Study*

This research aims to discuss the potential impact of the local coexistence of different meanings of child soldiers on justice initiatives in northern Uganda, thus contributing to the advancement of current knowledge about the justice needs of LRA child soldiers' victims from a bottom-up approach. Northern Uganda is a suitable case study for two reasons.

First, a former child soldier from a Ugandan armed group has been identified as one of those responsible for ordering the commission of crimes against civilians in the region, and has been prosecuted by an international court.[14] Second, northern Uganda has, in the process of reintegrating child soldiers, benefited from significant support from foreign humanitarian actors that brought with them a vision of the child soldier that many communities resist. Many communities in northern Uganda resist the *victim* paradigm mobilized by humanitarian actors[15] and demand instead the use of accountability and reparation processes before considering the return of children to the communities.[16]

Empirical studies exploring the challenges faced by child soldiers upon their return to communities provide valuable insights into how communities in northern Uganda respond to these two visions of the child soldier. However, they provide little information on the different choices these communities make in relation to child soldiers, particularly the evolving process of their formation. The *Ongwen* case therefore provides an opportunity to begin this conversation and to explore how child soldier-affected communities are likely to perceive and act upon their vulnerability in the face of disruptive knowledge about child soldiers. Given the geographical limitations of this research, it is not intended to be broadly representative. It could, however, pave the way for

---

14 *See* ICC, *Prosecutor* v. *Dominic Ongwen*, Case No. ICC-02/04, Pre-Trial Chamber II, Decision, 8 July 2005, para. 30.

15 G. Akello, 'Child Agency and Resistance to Discourses within the Paris Principles in Rehabilitation and Reintegration Processes of Former Child Soldiers in Northern Uganda', in M.A. Drumbl and J.C. Barrett (eds.), *Research Handbook on Child Soldiers* (Edward Elgar, Northampton, 2019), pp. 436–451.

16 Fisher, *supra* note 13, pp. 48–49.

more in-depth research in similar contexts to increase knowledge about the victims of child soldiers.

2.2 *The Conduct of the Research*

This research relied on qualitative data collected through semi-structured group interviews conducted with five groups of people in Lukodi, Abok, Odek, and Pajule from 2–27 November 2018. The focus group was chosen as the method for gathering data as this research was interested in: (1) accessing both individual points of view on LRA child soldiers and the collective perspective; (2) capturing the way in which the significance of the concepts *child soldier* and *victim* are negotiated and co-produced in these four locations to ascertain what ideas about human rights circulate within these communities and how these ideas shape some community members' position in relation to LRA child soldiers. The focus group is the appropriate method for collecting this kind of data because it takes into account both the dialogue with participants in the group and the interaction that occurs within the group, and it seeks to capture the ways in which meaning is co-produced and embedded in the group context.[17] Furthermore, it favors what Boyden calls 'a form of collective intelligence.'[18]

The focus groups took place at the end of the video screening sessions and the restitution sessions. The video screening session was structured in the following way. Before the screening, the ICC Outreach Team's focal point would briefly discuss the trial, the completed session, and provide a recap of the previous screening to the attendees. The video screening of the trial then followed, and finally, there was the question-and-answer session. I was allowed by the ICC Outreach Team in Kampala, Uganda, to attend these sessions. It was an opportunity to immerse myself in the trial's atmosphere and become familiar with communities' concerns before proceeding with the interviews. It was decided that at the end of the session, the ICC Outreach Team's focal point would select interviewees from the residents who had gathered for both sessions.

In each location, people between the ages of 20 and 60 were selected. An element characterized the sample obtained. The focus group participants had either been forcibly abducted by the LRA in their childhood/adulthood or had had their children abducted. This was both an advantage and a disadvantage

17 J. Sim and J. Waterfield, 'Focus Group Methodology: Some Ethical Challenges', 53(6) *Quality & Quantity* (2019) 3003–3022.

18 J. Boyden, 'Anthropology under fire: Ethics, Researchers and Children in War', in J. Boyden and J. de Berry (eds.), *Children and Youth on the Front Line: Ethnography, Armed Conflict and Displacement* (Berghahn Books, New York, NY, 2004), chapter 12, p. 243.

for the research. The disadvantage is that it could bias the 'community' dimension of this research, which would result in the research reflecting only the views of the parents of child soldiers and former child soldiers, rather than those of ordinary community members. In northern Uganda, one of every two people had been abducted by the LRA.[19] And some of them managed to escape and return in communities, which suggests that in the four locations studied, many people are former LRA abductees. Consequently, there is no clear delineation between abductees, including former soldiers, and other community members. Both identities apply to all in one way or another, as the abducted of yesterday are the community members of today, and vice-versa. This element was thus beneficial in that it led to a focus on the meaning which some community members in the four locations attach to key concepts of the research, namely *child soldier* and *victim*. Some of the interviewees had been abducted long before the period under investigation by the ICC, which did not affect the data collected as this research is unrelated to people registered as victims in the Ongwen trial. Five focus groups (ten people per group) were organized, two of which were held in Lukodi. A total of 50 people (nine women and 41 men) were interviewed.

Conducting interviews in a post-conflict context can, depending on the sensitivity of the topic, lead to a number of threats for the participants (e.g. risk of marginalization) and constraints for the researcher.[20] At the time of the data collection, there was a risk of clashes between two camps: those supporting Ongwen's trial and those opposing it. Although community leaders were working hard to de-escalate such tensions through regular meetings, a number of measures were taken to limit the risks with regard to this research. It was decided that the ICC Outreach Team Focal Point would make the initial contact with interviewees, introducing me and obtaining their consent beforehand. This decision was constraining as I was not the only one involved in the selection of the interviewees. That said, as the selection criteria were (1) residence before July 2002 in one of the four sites under investigation by the ICC 2) age (18 and over) and (2) a personal direct or indirect experience with LRA, the data were not significantly affected in the end. In addition, the involvement of the ICC Outreach Team Focal Point made the participants feel safe and comfortable talking to me about their experiences with the

19 Some estimate that the LRA abducted 54 000 to 75 000 people between 1986 and 2006. *See* P.N. Pham, P. Vinck and E. Stover, 'The Lord's Resistance Army and Forced Conscription in Northern Uganda', 30 *Human Rights Quarterly* (2008) 404–411.

20 *See* E. Apio, 'Ugandan's Forgotten Children of War', in R.C. Carpenter (ed.), *Born of War: Protecting Children of Sexual Violence Survivors in Conflict Zones* (Kumarian Press, Bloomfield, CT, 2007), pp. 94–109.

LRA. In Pajule, where it was obvious that expressing conflicting views would lead to people's marginalization and further fragmentation of communities, an additional measure was adopted. The focus group would take place in the school close to the screening area to ensure the safety and privacy of the participants. During the focus group in the three other locations, when conflicting views that would lead to the interruption of the discussion were expressed, I followed the strategy proposed by Kitzinger and Farquhar,[21] that is, to avoid the closing of sensitive possibilities or pushing them too far and instead keeping the discussion at an appropriate level. After encoding and analyzing the data, I cross-referenced them with textual analysis results of the literature review using the intertextual approach.[22]

3 The Complexity of Child Soldiering in the Northern Ugandan Armed Conflict

3.1 *The History of Child Recruitment by the LRA*

The LRA earned notoriety for its brutal method of abducting children and using them to carry out bloody attacks on civilians, and for using fear as a weapon to terrorize the people of Acholiland. While this non-state armed group is not the first to use children in such a way, the logic behind the LRA policy is interesting to note. Its goal was to recreate an Acholi society receptive to Joseph Kony's ideals, for he believed his community had become impure and needed to disappear and be replaced by the pure ones, the abducted children. As a result, some have described the massacres committed by the LRA against the Acholi community as *auto-genocide*.[23]

As the Ongwen trial judgement indicates, the LRA's objective was to overthrow President Museveni[24] who seized power in 1986. After him becoming the president of Uganda, many human rights abuses were committed, particularly against the Acholi community, by the victorious rebels and supporters of

21 J. Kitzinger and C. Farquhar, 'The analytical potential of "sensitive moments" in focus group discussions', in R.S. Barbour and J. Kitzinger (eds.), *Developing Focus Group Research: Politics, Theory and Practice* (Sage Publications, London, 1999), pp. 156–172.

22 L. Hansen, *Security as Practice: Discourse Analysis and the Bosnian War* (Routledge, New York, NY, 2006), p. 49.

23 R. Doom and K. Vlassenroot, 'Kony's Message: A New Koine? The Lord's Resistance Army in Northern Uganda', 98 (390) *African Affairs* (1999) 5–36.

24 *See* ICC, *The Prosecutor* v. *Dominic Ongwen*, *supra* note 9, paras 1084–1147.

Museveni's new government, especially when they invaded Acholiland.[25] Therefore, a succession of armed groups, among them the LRA of Joseph Kony, used military force to resist the government until Joseph Kony's armed group was defeated in 2006.[26] The LRA began fighting the central government and, by extension, the LRA's enemies, in 1988. The LRA saw anyone who collaborated with the Ugandan government as its enemy. The LRA initially gained the support of the Acholi community, which perceived Yoweri Museveni as hostile to their people.[27] In the early years of the rebellion, large numbers of Acholi children and adults volunteered to fight Yoweri Museveni's government.[28] In time, the LRA 'became so powerful that it roamed Acholiland almost without a military challenge from the NRA'.[29] But this euphoria was short-lived.[30] Tired of the war, many Acholi turned away from Kony and began to work with the government army, the Uganda People's Defence Force (UPDF).[31] And in the 1990s, some Acholi formed a militia to fight the LRA.[32] To Kony, the loss of interest in the LRA's cause was the result of the betrayal by his people after they aligned with the Ugandan government.[33] The ultimate betrayal was when the Acholi went to live in 'protected' government-run internally displaced persons (IDP) camps.[34] Therefore, they had to be punished. According to Doom and Vlassenroot,

> The most obvious change, in fact also the most terrifying one, was the change of conduct in regard to the Acholi people. Violence was from the

25 A. Bogner and G. Rosenthal, 'Rebels in Northern Uganda after their Return to Civilian Life: Between a Strong We-Image and Experiences of Isolation and Discrimination', 51(2) *Canadian Journal of African Studies* (2017) 175–197.

26 *Ibid.*, 179–180.

27 A. Borzello, 'The Challenge of DDR in Northern Uganda: The Lord's Resistance Army: Analysis', 7(3) *Conflict, Security and Development* (2007) 387–415; A. Branch, 'Uganda's Civil War and the Politics of ICC Intervention', 21(2) *Ethics & International Affairs* (2007) 179–198.

28 Baines, *supra* note 13, 95.

29 O. Otunnu, 'The Path to Genocide in Northern Uganda', 17(3) *Canada's Journal on Refugees* (1998) 4–13.

30 A. Borzello, *supra* note 27, 387–415.

31 A. Branch, *Displacing Human Rights: War and Intervention in Northern Uganda* (Oxford University Press, New York, NY, 2011), pp. 75–76; Doom and Vlassenroot, *supra* note 23, 23.

32 Baines, *supra* note 13, 100.

33 C. Dolan, *Social Torture: The case of Northern Uganda, 1986–2006* (Berghahn Books, New York, NY, 2009), p. 53.

34 Branch, *supra* note 31, p. 77.

> beginning a trademark of the movement, but now the people as a whole seemed to be declared guilty.[35]

From that moment, Kony 'used the people's refusal to back him as a justification for inflicting horrific forms of violence'.[36] Around 1994, the LRA began targeting the Acholi population, particularly those living in the government-sponsored IDP camps, killing or maiming them by cutting off their noses, lips, and ears.[37] The culmination of this intragroup violence was the mass abduction of children.

The abduction of children should have achieved Kony's plan to form the 'nucleus of a new Acholi identity' as they were 'supposed to be a blank sheet of paper that may be filled in with Kony's commandments', and to build an Acholi society in conformity with his ideology. According to Jackson, 'Kony views young Acholi as being the most susceptible to his own views—a blank sheet of paper. As such, they will form the nucleus of a new Acholi identity, the old one having proved unsuccessful.'[38] Then, children were used to exterminate the Acholi community Kony was seeing as impure.

3.2 *The Use of Children to Exterminate the Acholi Community*

The children forcibly recruited as soldiers were used to destroy the social fabric of the Acholi community and to fragment families that the LRA suspected of colluding with the Ugandan government. In other words, child soldiers were Joseph Kony's instrument to achieve his malevolent policy of destroying any link between the old Acholi, who were considered impure, and the new Acholi, the children who would come from the LRA. To this end, the abductions were accompanied by violence and fear. Children were forced to kill family members at the time of their abduction or to witness violence against their families.[39] This socialization into violence at the time of recruitment was reinforced in the bush. Children were forced to kill their comrades who did not adapt to

---

35 Doom and Vlassenroot, *supra* note 23, 25.

36 R. Jeffery, 'Forgiveness, Amnesty and Justice: The Case of the Lord's Resistance Army in Northern Uganda', 46 *Cooperation and Conflict* (2011) 78–95.

37 C. Blattman and J. Annan, 'Child Combatants in Northern Uganda: Reintegration Myths and Realities', in R. Muggah (ed.), *Security and Post-Conflict Reconstruction* (Routledge, New York, NY, 2008), pp. 103–126; P. Jackson, 'The March of the Lord's Resistance Army: Greed or Grievance in Northern Uganda?', 13 *Small Wars and Insurgencies* (2002) 29–52.

38 Jackson, *supra* note 37, 43.

39 S. Vindevogel, K. Coppens, I. Derluyn, M. De Schryver, G. Loots and E. Broekaert, 'Forced Conscription of Children during Armed Conflict: Experiences of Former Child Soldiers in Northern Uganda', 35 *Child Abuse & Neglect* (2011) 551–562.

the training and those who tried to escape.[40] These children were then sent into their communities during LRA attacks to kill their neighbors, relatives and other community members.[41] Between 30 000 and 60 000 children between the ages of eight and 16 were reportedly forcibly abducted by the LRA between 1994 and 2005 to serve as combatants in its ranks.[42] These stories have been brought to the international judicial arena through victim testimonies.[43]

This comprehensive review of LRA policy suggests that in the northern Ugandan context, there was collective intragroup victimization, resulting in 'multiple identity positions experienced by abductees'[44]:

> the shocking, brutal reality of this war is that those who have been forcibly recruited, and those who are killed, raped or themselves abducted, all come from the same communities.[45]

Ongwen was no exception to this socialization to violence, having been abducted by the LRA on his way to school in 1986 when he was under 15.[46] Like many children, Ongwen was exposed to the harsh living conditions of the Acholi community before his abduction. According to Baines, despite the suffering inflicted on LRA children, Ongwen had a strong capacity for resilience.[47] As a result, he rose to the leadership of the Sinia Brigade, a branch of the LRA, and became what she calls a 'complex political perpetrator'.[48] Stories vary about his motivation to take up positions in the LRA and become one of its leading figures. For some interviewees in Lukodi, Ongwen enjoyed and valued his various positions.[49] For interviewees in Odek, he had no choice since refusing Kony's orders would have put him in danger.[50] The latter view

---

40 K. Cheney, ''Our Children Have Only Known War': Children's Experiences and the Uses of Childhood in Northern Uganda', 3 *Children's Geographies* (2005) 23–45.

41 Akello, *supra* note 15, 447.

42 E.K. Baines, 'Complex Political Perpetrators: Reflections on Dominic Ongwen', 47 *The Journal of Modern African Studies* (2009) 163–191.

43 *See* ICC, *Prosecutor* v. *Dominic Ongwen*, *supra* note 9, paras 2312–2447.

44 A. Veale and A. Stavrou, 'Former Lord's Resistance Army Child Soldier Abductees: Explorations of Identity in Reintegration and Reconciliation' 13 *Peace and Conflict: Journal of Peace Psychology* (2007) 273–292.

45 Z. Lomo and L. Hovil, 'Behind the Violence. The War in Northern Uganda', *ISS Monographs* 99 (Institute for Security Studies, Pretoria, 2004), p. 87, cited by Veale and Stavrou, *supra* note 44, 276.

46 Branch, *supra* note 5, 38.

47 Baines, *supra* note 42, 170.

48 *Ibid.*

49 Focus group, Lukodi, 14 November 2018.

50 Focus group, Odek, 20 November 2018.

is based on Joseph Kony's alleged mystical power to control the minds of LRA soldiers and anticipate their conduct.[51]

The knowledge on which the focus group participants based their understandings of the *child soldier*, the *victim* and the *offender* came from various sources: their personal experience, the testimonies delivered in court and accessed during the video screening sessions, evidence gathered by the prosecution and the defence, and the stories from returnees.

4 Some Communities' Understanding of Child Soldiers

According to Barbot and Dodier, victims of collective tragedies are often confronted with three questions that will shape their meaning of the notion of *victim*: Who should be the target of the legal action (the individual or the organization)? What action should be taken against those responsible? How should they construct and adjust their relationship to the damages paid in money?[52] The definition of the targets of the legal action refers to making a choice between the individualization of the action (i.e., the prosecution of an individual) and the collectivization of the action (i.e., holding an organisation accountable).[53] The second question refers to choosing the suitable judicial mechanism (civil, administrative or criminal action) to convict those responsible for the damage suffered.[54] Finally, adjusting the relationship with the damage involves answering the question: 'How can we avoid focusing solely on compensation?'[55] How victims approach these questions structures their relationship with their own situation.[56]

Some community members were confronted with the same questions during the focus groups in Lukodi, Abok, Odek and Pajule. How they answered them structured their understanding of who is a LRA child soldier (including Ongwen) but also of their victimization, which LRA child soldiers essentially caused.

51 *Ibid.*

52 J. Barbot and N. Dodier, 'Se Confronter à l'Action Judiciaire. Des Victimes aux Carrefours des Différentes Branches du Droit', 223–224 *L'Homme, Revue française d'anthropologie* (2017) 99–130.

53 *Ibid.*, 107.

54 *Ibid.*, 116–117.

55 *Ibid.*, 118.

56 *Ibid.*, 107.

4.1 *The Target of the Legal Action in Case of Crimes Committed by Child Soldiers*

After the video screenings sessions, attendees in the four locations asked the following questions during the question-and-answer session:

> Is Dominic Ongwen responsible for all our misfortunes? Why are we blaming Dominic Ongwen who is a victim of the LRA like us? Doesn't Joseph Kony have any responsibility in all this? And the other members of the LRA, why aren't they worried?

These community concerns[57] about who is to blame for LRA crimes in these four locations reveal two trends in answering the question 'who the target of legal action should be'. In the first trend, the LRA is a homogeneous and interchangeable group of people. They are collectively and indistinctly responsible for crimes committed against their villages, whether they are adults or children.[58] As far as child soldiers are concerned, this trend sees them as Kony's soldiers, regardless of whether they have participated in military activities. Legal action must therefore target both adult and child members of the LRA.[59] We then have the second trend, for which a case-by-case assessment—and thus an individualization of the action—is required before a former member of the LRA can be targeted. This is evident both at the community level—with questions raised following the video screening sessions—and at the individual level through the dialogues within the group discussions, as Kony's role in the conduct of criminal activities in these locations was repeatedly questioned.[60] In this trend, being a member of the LRA does not automatically mean being a target of legal action for a number of reasons. First, some abductees refused to align themselves with the LRA's vision and managed to escape despite the violence of the armed group or returned after

57 Concerns were raised during the question-and-answer sessions following the screening of the trial in the four locations, which were attended by more than a hundred people. They were also echoed by religious and community leaders and traditional Chiefs, who were working on a model to be used to avoid another cycle of violence within communities between those who support the prosecution of Ongwen and those who oppose it. Personal interview, religious leader, Lukodi, 24 November 2018.

58 Participants also raised this point during discussions with traditional Chiefs in Pajule, Abok and Lukodi.

59 In Lukodi, 0/20 participants identified with this trend. In Abok, 3/10 participants identified with this trend. In Pajule, 6/10 participants identified with this trend. In Odek, 8/10 participants identified with this trend.

60 During the group discussion in Abok, Odek, and Pajule, the role of Kony in the commission of crimes in these locations occupied a large part of the discussion.

being granted amnesty by the government.[61] Second, some abductees did not participate in the commission of crimes. Thirdly, many of the children were successful escapees, proving that they never intended to embrace the ideology of this armed group.[62] Therefore, as all abductees did not align with the LRA's vision, the action must be individualized. This trend includes the following groups of interviewees: those who escaped, those who did not participate in the commission of crimes while in the bush, those who carried loots into the bush and were then released, and those whose children were abducted.

By calling for the individualization of legal action, the second trend implies that the association with the LRA should not be a prerequisite for being targeted by legal action. Nor should it be a condition for being labelled a child soldier. In other words, with regard to children, being associated with the LRA does not turn an abducted child into a child soldier.[63] Determining the level of *belonging* to the LRA should be the key to distinguishing between a *child abductee* (a child who refused to subscribe to Kony's ideology and managed to escape) and a *child soldier* (a child who embraced Kony's vision and remained in the LRA).[64] Two criteria must thereby be considered for any legal action. The first criterion should be the child's deliberate intention to subscribe to Kony's murderous ideology. The second criterion to consider should be the willingness to achieve Kony's agenda through attacks on civilians.

Consequently, there are in the second trend two categories of people who should be targeted by legal action: 1) those who caused the suffering of the Acholi people, namely Joseph Kony, and 2) those who helped Kony achieve his goal, namely the child soldiers who refused to escape and became consequently Kony's soldiers, such as Ongwen.[65] Within this trend, Ongwen symbolically represents the abductees who have embraced the LRA's ideology, have accepted to serve its agenda, have consequently become child soldiers, and who should therefore be punished. The following categories should not be

61 Focus group, Lukodi, 25 November 2018.
62 Focus group, Lukodi, Abok, 14, 15, 25 November 2018.
63 This vision of who is a child soldier differs from the definition promoted by international policy, which defines a child soldier as 'any person below eighteen years of age who is or who has been recruited or used by an armed force or armed group in any capacity, including but not limited to children, boys and girls, used as fighters, cooks, porters, messengers, spies or for sexual purposes'. *See* point 2.1 of The Paris Principles and Guidelines on Children Associated with Armed Forces or Armed Groups, February 2007.
64 These interviewees described themselves and their children as abductees, not as soldiers.
65 Focus group, Lukodi, 14, 25 November 2018.

targeted for legal action: 1) those who were abducted and managed to escape[66] and 2) those who did not participate in criminal activities.[67]

Overall, whether a child falls into the category of *abductee* or *soldier* depends on the type of relationship with the LRA. Furthermore, as we will see in the next section, escape is seen by many interviewees as a reason to absolve children of the crimes they have committed and as an additional indicator to distinguish between a child soldier *victim* and a child soldier *criminal*.

4.2 *Who Should Be Entitled to Victim Status?*

Before considering the target of the legal action, focus group participants wanted to define themselves in relation to the child soldiers, as many people were abducted by the LRA,[68] by addressing these questions: 'Who deserves the victim status: the child soldier, the community, or both?' Focus group participants in the four locations learned from their own experience or from other returnees (including their children) that life in the LRA was filled with unspeakable suffering.[69] As a result, communities expressed resentment towards LRA leaders, whom they saw as responsible for their children's suffering, and felt compassion for abducted children for years. When they were alerted to the case opened by the ICC, they welcomed the ICC's impending involvement in their situation.[70] After learning from Ongwen's legal team about his identity as a former child soldier,[71] interviewees took several—sometimes conflicting—positions.

A woman in Odek reported feeling confused when she heard Ongwen's story. Having had a child abducted who never returned, she expressed remorse for supporting the prosecution of someone who had experienced unspeakable suffering and who could have been her child. Three women in the focus group agreed by nodding their heads. However, this woman was quick to point out, as did the other nine interviewees, that Ongwen was prosecuted for crimes committed during his adulthood.[72] Participants in this focus group refused to answer the question: 'Would the answer be different if Ongwen was prosecuted

66 20 participants who were abducted identify themselves as abductees, not as LRA members. Focus group, Lukodi, Abok, 25, 15 November 2018.

67 Focus group, Lukodi, Abok, 25, 15 November 2018.

68 As a reminder, more than 200 000 people were abducted by the LRA in northern Uganda between 1994 and 2005.

69 Focus group, Lukodi, Odek, Abok, 14, 20, 15, November 2018.

70 Focus group, Lukodi, Abok, 14, 15, 25 November 2018.

71 Except for a young woman from Abok who lived with Dominic Ongwen in the same military camp, none of the focus group participants in the four locations knew Dominic Ongwen's story before the trial.

72 Focus group, Odek, 20 November 2018.

for crimes committed before his 18th birthday?', claiming that a focus on his past as a child soldier was now irrelevant. He should have stopped attacking people when he turned 18.The remorse expressed at the beginning of the group discussion was thus obscured by the OTP's decision to charge Ongwen for crimes committed after he reached 18. For these community members, therefore, Ongwen should be disqualified from the victim status because he committed crimes as an adult.

The Abok interviewees raised another set of issues. One young woman, who was abducted at the age of 12, reported living with Dominic Ongwen in the same military camp. She knew his story long before it was made public by the defence team. For her, even if people in the group discussion disagreed, Ongwen was merely subject to the treatment that all children were subjected to. It would thus be unacceptable to make him bear the burden of Joseph Kony's crimes. He should be seen as a victim.[73] Four participants in the focus group disagreed, saying that Dominic Ongwen should have done what other children did and run away from the LRA. If he had, he would have deserved to be treated as a victim. He refused to leave, even when President Museveni offered them amnesty. So he lost his status as a victim on his own.[74] This conversation suggests that, for these participants, members of their locations should be the only ones to be granted victim status. Child soldiers like Ongwen should be treated as criminals and punished.

This last point was echoed in discussions with interviewees in Lukodi, particularly a man abducted by the LRA at the age of 15 in the 1990s. For him, Ongwen lost his privilege as a victim when he chose to stay with the LRA. When I asked him if he saw a difference between himself and Ongwen, he replied:

> The difference between Ongwen and me is that I refused to stay in the armed group and to adapt to the LRA way of life. At my young age, I already had the knowledge of right and wrong. And I knew that killing was wrong. That's why I chose not to stay with the armed group and to run away despite Joseph Kony's mystical powers. And I am not the only one. Many children who had been forcibly enrolled managed to flee. And today the defence lawyer wants us to believe that Ongwen was unable to flee the armed group. He wanted to stay there, and that makes him different from the rest of us. Because of this difference, he should not be considered a victim because he finally refused that role.[75]

73 Focus group, Abok, 15 November 2018.

74 *Ibid.*

75 Focus group, Lukodi, 25 November 2018.

Lukodi's nine other focus group participants entirely agreed with him. To the question 'Would that answer be different if Ongwen was prosecuted for crimes committed before his 18th birthday?', their answers remained the same. Having been forcibly recruited or having had children who were forcibly recruited, they considered their children (and themselves) to be different from Ongwen because they refused to belong to the LRA. Therefore, they vigorously claimed that any child who did not want to escape from the armed group should be treated as a criminal and any child who fled the armed group should be treated as a victim. In other words, they see themselves or/and their children as the only ones to be entitled to the status of victims.

In summary, the different answers to the question 'Who deserves the victim status: the child soldier, the community, or both?' reveal that *escape* is seen by the interviewees as the key indicator to consider in distinguishing between a child soldier *victim* and a child soldier *criminal*. Together with the responses to the question 'Who should be the target of the legal action', these elements suggest that for some community members in the four locations, association with the LRA does not make an abducted child a child soldier, nor does it make him or her a criminal child soldier. And Ongwen corresponds to the meaning some community members give to the notion of *criminal child soldier* as he remained in the armed group and continued to contribute to Kony's project during his adulthood.

4.3 *Reparation Aspects in the Case of Crimes Committed by Child Soldiers*

Following the focus group discussions, another issue arose; Joseph Kony's alleged mystical power and its potential implications for reparations. During the video screening sessions, attendees repeatedly expressed concern about the likelihood that the ICC would consider Joseph Kony's spiritual power.[76] In fact, during the trial, the defence called several traditional Acholi doctors to demonstrate that Joseph Kony had spiritual control over LRA members. According to traditional leaders,[77] if Joseph Kony were found to have exercised mind control over LRA members, child soldiers would have to be treated as manipulated and bewitched persons within these four locations. No action, including claims for reparations, could therefore be taken against them by communities.[78]

76 Screening session, Lukodi, Odek, and Abok, 14, 20, 15 November 2018.
77 Personal interview, local Chief, Odek, 20 November 2018.
78 *Ibid.*

Interviewees from Lukodi unanimously had a different opinion.[79] For them, if Kony had the power to control people's minds, how could it be that many children managed to escape from the LRA without him being able to stop them through mind control or find them once they had escaped?[80] This question led them to the conclusion that, regardless of the issue of the trial, Kony has no mystical power. Therefore, regarding the success stories of escapees they presented during the group discussion, they emphasized that all child soldiers who did not want to leave the LRA pretending Kony had the power to control their mind should not be entitled to the status of victim. Rather, they must repair the damage caused by their actions.

As the discussions of the mystical power of Joseph Kony in Lukodi show, the will to defy Kony and his mystical power by running away is proof that a child has refused to embrace Kony's ideology. It is therefore a key to deciding which category of LRA child soldiers deserves the status of victim, and an additional indicator in distinguishing between a *victim* and a *criminal*. Children who have defied Kony and his power are, according to Lukodi's interviewees, the ones who deserve the status of victim. Former child soldiers like Ongwen must be treated as criminals.

Discussions in focus groups raised many points in answering these questions: Which of the child soldiers or the community should be considered a victim? Which of the child soldiers or Joseph Kony should be held responsible for the harm done to the Acholi people? and Which of the child soldiers or the victims of their criminal acts should be entitled to reparations? As the data suggests, the demarcation between child soldier *victims* and child soldier *criminals* is not constructed in a similar way by the interviewees—albeit the level of affiliation to the LRA seems to be the key condition—leading to different constructions of child soldiers and a lack of consensus among some community members on mechanisms to be implemented to ensure reconciliation in the region.

79 In Abok and Pajule, four and six participants, respectively, strongly believed that regardless of the ICC's consideration, Kony has mystical power that bewitched child soldiers. Therefore, child soldiers should be treated as victims as crimes they committed were not their fault. Focus group, Abok and Pajule, 15, 22 November 2018.

80 Six participants in the group discussion were abducted in the 1990s but managed to escape, and four women had their children abducted who successfully left the LRA. Focus group, Lukodi, 25 November 2018.

5 Implications for Peace-Making Processes in the Post-*Ongwen* Case Era

The use of restorative justice is highly recommended by scholars for its propensity to capture the victim–perpetrator identity of LRA child soldiers and to provide a space for child soldiers to ask for forgiveness and for their victims to forgive them. The different meanings given by some community members from Lukodi, Abok, Odek and Pajule to the concepts, *child soldier* and *victim*, as described in the previous sections, reveal three ways of approaching crimes committed by LRA child soldiers within these communities. These approaches are rooted in two different paradigms, namely *it's not your fault* and *unacceptable*.

The fact that community members rely on a diversity of paradigms suggests that the justice initiatives to be implemented in northern Uganda should creatively strike a local balance between child soldiers' needs and the needs of the communities they have victimized beforehand, to be a tool that effectively supports post-conflict reconstruction.

5.1 *Criminal Child Soldiers as the Unique Victims to Be Acknowledged*

The first approach to crimes committed by LRA child soldiers views criminal child soldiers as *exclusive victims* because they were destroyed by the life in the bush and used by Kony's mystical power as a tool to inflict harm among their communities. This approach is based on the idea of *it's not your fault,* whose meaning is different from the one deployed by humanitarian actors involved in the reintegration process of child soldiers in northern Uganda and elsewhere. The *it's not your fault* paradigm mobilized by humanitarian actors implies that, because child soldiers were necessarily forcibly recruited, they have been socialized into violence, so that any crimes they commit are not their fault. They cannot be blamed. Instead, adults must be held accountable because they forced the children to do harm.[81] This paradigm accompanies the reintegration of child soldiers in order to encourage families to accept

81 S. Shepler, 'The Rites of the Child: Global Discourses of Youth and Reintegrating Child Soldiers in Sierra Leone', 4 *Journal of Human Rights* (2005) 197–211; M. Utas, 'Building a Future? The Reintegration and Re-Marginalisation of Young Ex-Combatants in Liberia', in P. Richards (ed.), *No Peace No War: An Anthropology of Contemporary Armed Conflicts* (James Currey, Oxford, 2005), pp. 137–154; M.A. Drumbl, *Reimagining child soldiers in International Law and Policy* (Oxford University Press, Oxford, 2012), pp. 37–40.

them with ease.[82] As to the contemplations of certain participants in Abok, the foundation of their *it's not your fault* paradigm lies in Kony's mystical powers.[83] This means that, for this approach, child soldiers should not be seen as responsible for their crimes and should not be held accountable because whatever they did was not of their own volition and therefore not *their fault*. Their minds were controlled by Joseph Kony.[84] For this approach, therefore, child soldiers, including Ongwen, are the only victims to acknowledge.

This approach to crimes committed by child soldiers is also based on a specific meaning of the *unacceptable* paradigm. This specific meaning refers to the idea that the treatment children were subjected to during their life in the bush was the worst and was undeniably *unacceptable*. Child soldiers have become *animals* who are destroyed by life in the bush and the violence they have been constantly exposed to, not criminals. As a woman in Lukodi said:

> My son does not know anymore how to live in society. He has lost the sense of right and wrong. I don't know what to do with him. He gets angry every time I try to tell him he has done wrong. He drinks too much; he beats people when he is drunk. He is not bad. On the contrary, he has been destroyed by life in the bush. There are many in the village. We don't know what to do to help them and how to live with them.[85]

For this reason, this approach perceives the victimization of child soldiers as more critical than the suffering of those who remained in IDP camps, even if they were attacked by the LRA.[86] Therefore, it is of the view that child soldiers should not be prosecuted or held accountable; instead, something should be done to help them heal from the trauma. Regarding how to deal with criminal child soldiers, this first approach aligns with the *it's not your fault* paradigm mobilized by humanitarian actors, as it advocates for the healing of child soldiers rather than their prosecution, which it sees as an injustice.

5.2 *Criminal Child Soldiers as a Continuity of Community Suffering*

The second approach to crimes committed by child soldiers is based on the second variant of the *unacceptable* paradigm, which refers to the idea that

---

82 C. Ryan, *Children of War: Child Soldiers as Victims and Participants in the Sudan Civil War* (I.B. Tauris, London, 2012), p. 19; K. Hill and H. Langholtz, 'Rehabilitation programs for African child soldiers', 15 *Peace Review* (2003) 279–285.

83 Focus group, Abok, 15 November 2018.

84 *Ibid.*

85 Focus group, Lukodi, 25 November 2018.

86 Focus group, Lukodi, 14, 25 November 2018.

children were manipulated by malevolent adults who implemented the policy of terror that characterized the LRA. In other words, this approach sees LRA child soldiers as people who were used as tools to carry out the LRA's agenda, namely exterminate the Acholi community. They killed civilians because they were forced to and they had to survive, not because they agreed with the LRA's criminal ideology. The evil adult behind the misfortunes of the Acholi people, Joseph Kony, should be held accountable for these crimes, not the children, even if they have reached adulthood. For that reason, this approach perceives the victimization experienced by people in the four locations as an extension of the one experienced by child soldiers. As most of the children were forced to commit crimes in their neighborhoods,[87] this approach sees LRA child soldiers as *irresponsible criminals*. As a result, it disapproves of the prosecution of child soldiers like Ongwen and seeks to circumvent it by advocating for the use of traditional rites of reconciliation for children and the prosecution of adults who abducted children.[88] Interviewees supporting this approach are people whose children have been forcibly abducted or have experienced forced recruitment. This variant of the *unacceptable* paradigm is closer to the *it's not your fault* paradigm mobilized by humanitarian actors as it advocates for cleansing rituals instead of accountability for child soldiers.

5.3 *Criminal Child Soldiers as Individuals to Be Held Accountable*

We finally have the third way of constructing criminal child soldiers among interviewees from Lukodi, Abok, Odek, and Pajule, which corresponds to the third variant of the *unacceptable* paradigm. The *unacceptable* refers here to the idea that children should be considered criminals from the moment they have willingly embraced the LRA project by refusing to escape. Because they did not escape, it is unacceptable not to punish them, as this could promote a culture of impunity within communities. As noted above, some focus group participants have argued that many children have succeeded in escaping from the LRA. As a result, the mystical powers of Joseph Kony or the assumption that abductees might be killed if they failed to escape is an unacceptable ground to forgive those who remained in the LRA for years, such as Ongwen. Following these arguments, what is *unacceptable* for this approach is forgiving the actions of former LRA child soldiers who decided to stay in the bush. It therefore strongly supports the punishment of former child soldiers like Ongwen and sees Ongwen's prosecution as a reminder to all former child

87 Some focus group participants in Lukodi witnessed the violence inflicted on children to commit crimes. Focus group, Lukodi, 14, 25 November 2018.

88 Focus group, Abok, 15 November 2018.

soldiers that they will be punished. We have an example of how this approach is mobilized on the ground from one interviewee's personal story as a former abductee in Lukodi.[89] The LRA abducted him in Lukodi in the 1990s. After several years, despite Joseph Kony's alleged mystical powers, he escaped from the armed group. Because of his willingness to leave the armed group, this participant believes that it is unacceptable to treat child soldiers who chose to remain in the LRA as victims. Only those who refused to identify with the armed group and did everything in their power to escape should be considered victims and forgiven. In sum, for this approach, those who stayed in the armed group, held positions, and remained complacent should bear responsibility for their crimes. Forgiving them would be unacceptable.

5.4 *Lack of Unanimity over the Mechanisms to Be Implemented in the Post-*Ongwen *Era*

The diversity in the meaning some community members attach to the notion *criminal child soldier* leads to a lack of unanimity as to which mechanism to implement to ensure accountability of those considered as the target of legal action, and to promote reconciliation in northern Uganda. This element is consistent with previous observations that this lack of unanimity is due to the difficulty communities have in 'distinguishing the "collaborators" and "sympathizers" from those acting under duress'.[90]

Interviewees who rely on the second approach—the one viewing LRA child soldiers as irresponsible criminals—expressed dissatisfaction and concern about the injustice that Ongwen was facing in The Hague.[91] For them, child soldiers should go through traditional cleansing mechanisms, such as the *Mato Oput*, as they believed this is the only mechanism to heal the trauma they have experienced. At the same time, it is the only mechanism that can restore their trust in these former child soldiers. However, as trying Ongwen was the only way to access reparations, these interviewees were reluctant to mention his victimhood during the video screening sessions or advocate for its consideration by the judges.[92] One interviewee from Lukodi, however, highlighted the difficulties of using this traditional justice mechanism. *Mato Oput* is not a cleansing mechanism but primarily a dispute resolution mechanism.[93] As a result, victims are unlikely to use the *Mato Oput* for fear of getting into disputes with former child soldiers. On the other hand, if a

89 Focus group, Lukodi, 25 November 2018.
90 Jeffery, *supra* note 36, 85.
91 Focus group, Abok, 15 November 2018.
92 *Ibid.*
93 Focus group, Lukodi, 14 November 2018.

former child soldier who has become an adult confesses responsibility for the commission of crimes, he or she could see the confession used against him or her in criminal proceedings. Therefore, few returnees would be willing to go through such mechanisms, especially since the government has granted amnesty to all children who have returned or been released from captivity.[94]

Focus group participants who align with the third approach—the one that sees LRA child soldiers as criminals—do not believe that the criminal justice system should be used. They indicated in Lukodi that they do not trust the Western system because it will not bring out the full complexity of the crimes committed by LRA child soldiers like Ongwen.[95] They are of the view that criminal child soldiers should instead be held accountable through the *Mato Oput* and then ask for forgiveness according to Acholi culture. As such, they would have access to reparations and reconciliation under the guidance of paramount Chiefs. After the discussion with the OTP's representatives, these Lukodi interviewees took a more nuanced view. They started to see the ICC trial as the key to access reparations, and the *Mato Oput* as the starting point for the peace process after Ongwen's return to society.[96]

The Ongwen trial has made this lack of unanimity over the mechanism to be implemented in the post-Ongwen era invisible, due to community expectations of reparations. Indeed, whether or not they were convinced of the children's autonomous role in the commission of the crimes, interviewees who were registered as victims in the trial were expecting to receive reparations for the harm done. Accordingly, the need for reparations outweighed concerns about who should bear responsibility for the suffering of the Acholi people.

6 Conclusion

Discussions from focus groups in Lukodi, Pajule, Abok and Odek reveal that the meanings these community members give to the notions *child soldier* and *victim* are far different from the traditional definition provided by international law and policy. In this case, the level of *belonging* is the key condition to be called an *LRA child soldier* or a *criminal*, not the simple association with the armed group as international law and policy commonly approach child soldiering. These discussions also reveal that there are different approaches to the crimes committed by LRA child soldiers among these community members, as not all

94 *Ibid.*
95 *Ibid.*
96 Focus group, Lukodi, 25 November 2018.

villages were affected by the crimes committed by child soldiers in the same way, and not all interviewees experienced child recruitment in the same way. We have a first approach that sees them as *exclusive victims*, a second approach that sees them as *irresponsible criminals*, and a third approach that sees them as *criminals*. The Ongwen trial has hidden this complex reality behind the child soldiering in northern Uganda as those registered as victims in the trial will have access to reparations as Ongwen has been sentenced, and this shared expectation has apparently put them in the same box. Indeed, as this paper has shown, the Ongwen trial has masked the fact that some community members are far from reaching a consensus regarding how to deal with LRA child soldiers who have committed crimes or how to respond to communities affected by such crimes. The distinction between child soldier *victim* and child soldier *criminal*, and between *child abductee* and *LRA child soldier* is not made by focus group participants in the same way.

These elements suggest that peace initiatives in northern Uganda should not assume that all communities will support the criminal justice process or restorative justice to address crimes committed by child soldiers, or that all communities will see child soldiers in the same way. Instead, further research should be undertaken at the regional scale to collect all ideas of *child soldiers* and *victims* that circulate within these communities, keeping in mind that the child recruitment started long before the ICC investigation. Then, they will come with a comprehensive material composed of diverse local understandings of *unacceptable*, *child soldier*, *it's not your fault*, *belonging* and *accountability* that will constitute the starting point for assessing the justice needs of child soldiers' victims and tailoring genuine responses to each community. In other words, this paper suggests that peace initiatives should adopt a bottom-up approach that will be the most inclusive of various communities' needs and concerns. Under this condition, they will provide answers that will reflect those needs and concerns while remaining in line with the goals of global policies and transitional justice. As such, peace initiatives will be a valuable tool in supporting local chiefs to de-escalate violence between supporters of Ongwen's punishment and supporters of Joseph Kony's single punishment and prevent potential struggles in the Post-*Ongwen* case era.

CHAPTER 10

Children Born of War: The Recognition of Children Born of War as Victims in the *Ongwen* Case

Giovanna M Frisso

Abstract

This article explores the challenges associated with recognizing children born of war as victims within the framework of international criminal law. Focusing on the case of Dominic Ongwen, a former child soldier and senior commander of the Lord's Resistance Army (LRA), it analyses how the criteria established in the definition of victim in the Rules of Procedure and Evidence of the International Criminal Court have been applied to children born of war. This analysis brings to the fore conceptual challenges to the recognition of children born of war as victims and highlights the risks that the binary victim-perpetrator that characterises the international criminal narrative presents to a comprehensive understanding of the experiences and needs of these children.

Keywords

children born of war – ICC – victims – SGBC

1 Introduction

Dominic Ongwen, a former child soldier and former senior commander of the Lord's Resistance Army (LRA), was convicted in 2021 of some of the most egregious crimes in international law, including various instances of sexual violence, torture, recruitment of child soldiers, and crimes against people living

 | DOI: 10.1163/9789004743380_011

in internally displaced camps.[1] During his trial at the International Criminal Court (ICC), Ongwen admitted that he had committed the acts, but did not admit being guilty. He argued, among others, that his experience as a child soldier and the brutal regime of the LRA left him with *no other choice* but to comply with orders to commit such crimes.[2] Ongwen is the first known person to be charged with and convicted of war crimes of which he is also a victim.[3]

Like Ongwen, many children have grown up in war in Uganda. Estimates indicate that approximately 4000 to 6000 children have actually been born out of sexual and gender-based crimes (SGBC) committed during the armed conflict.[4] These children, it has been argued, were conceived with the intent of establishing a distinct Acholi nation within Uganda[5] and to sustain war as potential recruits for the LRA.[6] Their plight has been brought to the attention of the ICC in the opening statements to Ongwen's trial. The Legal Representative

1 ICC, *Prosecutor v. Dominic Ongwen,* ICC-02/04-01/15-1762-Red, Trial Chamber IX, Trial Judgement, 04 February 2021 (hereinafter, Trial Judgement). The Appeals Chamber confirmed the decisions of Trial Chamber IX on Dominic Ongwen's guilty verdict ICC, *Prosecutor v. Dominic Ongwen,* ICC-02/04-01/15-2022-Red, Appeals Chamber, Judgement on the appeal of Mr Ongwen against the decision of Trial Chamber IX of 4 February 2021 entitled 'Trial Judgement', 15 December 2022.

2 Duress and mental illness were the defences sought by Ongwen. Both were related to the coercive environment to which he was forcibly introduced when recruited as a child. See ICC, *Prosecutor v. Dominic Ongwen,* ICC-02/04-01/15, Defence for Dominic Ongwen, Public Redact Version of 'Corrected Version of "Defence Closing Brief", filed on 24 February 2020, 13 March 2020, Section X. See also K. Titeca, *Spirits on trial? The case of Dominic Ongwen in the International Criminal* Court, available online at www.blogs.lse.ac.uk/africaatlse/2019/02/19/spirits-on-trial-the-case-of-dominic-ongwen-in-the-international-criminal-court/ (accessed 16 November 2023).

3 M.A. Drumbl, 'Victims Who Victimise', 4 *London Review of International Law* (2016) 217–246. See also N. Grant, 'Duress as a Defence for Former Child Soldiers? Dominic Ongwen and the International Criminal Court', *ICD Brief 21,* available online at https://internationalcrimesdatabase.org/upload/documents/20161209T155029-ICD%20Brief%20Nadia%20Grant%202.pdf (accessed 16 November 2023), p. 3.

4 T.R. Kirabira and L. Choukroune, 'Uganda: how to bring justice for thousands of children born of war', *The Conversation* (2023) available online at www.theconversation.com/uganda-how-to-bring-justice-for-thousands-of-children-born-of-war-151121#:~:text=In%202018%2C%20JLOS%20carried%20out,sub%2Dregion%20of%20northern%20Uganda (accessed 1 July 2023).

5 E. Baines, 'Forced marriage as a political project: Sexual rules and relations in the Lord's Resistance Army' 51(3) *Journal of Peace Research* (2014) 405–417. See also A. Bunting, 'Women's law-making and contestations of 'marriage' in African conflict situations', 55(4) *Law and Society Review* (2021) 614–633.

6 E.O. Apio, *Children born of War in northern Uganda: Kingship, Marriage, and the Politics of Post-conflict Reintegration in Lango Society,* PhD thesis submitted to the University of Birmingham (2016), available online at www.https://etheses.bham.ac.uk//id/eprint/6926/1/Apio16PhD.pdf (accessed 20 November 2023), pp. 5, 9.

of the Victims (LRV), for instance, referred to a 'whole new generation born and raised in the camps' who had experienced a loss of cultural and traditional values as well as to the social stigma associated with being the children of LRA commanders.[7] The Office of the Prosecutor (OTP) drew attention to 'a whole category of other victims: the children born in captivity resulting from (...) forced marriages, who sometimes face hostility and taunts as a result of their parentage'.[8]

It has been anticipated that early references to children born of war in the *Ongwen* case could enable a better understanding of the unique hardship faced by these children, underscoring the necessary recognition of them as individual victims who have suffered unique harms and require redress.[9]

In fact, during Ongwen's trial, it was found that he 'fathered at least 13 children with the seven so-called 'wives'.[10] Ongwen was also found guilty of SGBC committed against girls and women within the Sinia brigade, of which he was a commander, crimes that could have led to the birth of children.[11]

In the literature, these children are referred to as children born of war.[12] The expression encompasses 'a child that has one parent that was part of an army or peacekeeping force and the other parent a local citizen'.[13] Reflecting patriarchal structures, the hardships faced by such children have been linked to their fathers' involvement in the armed conflict. As such, some definitions of children born of war already position the father as the combatant and the mother as the local citizen.[14] Within this perspective, studies aimed at better understanding how children born of war are affected by the circumstances of their conception and birth have led to their categorisation in accordance with their father's role in the armed conflict. They have been categorised

7 ICC, *Prosecutor v. Dominic Ongwen*, ICC-02/04-01/15-T-27-ENG ET WT, Trial Chamber IX, Transcript, 7 December 2016, 59.

8 ICC, *Prosecutor v. Dominic Ongwen*, ICC-02/04-01/15-T-26-ENG, Trial Chamber IX, Transcript, 6 December 2016, 35.

9 E. Dowds, 'Children Born of Sexual and Gender-Based Violence in Conflict: The International Criminal Court' 33(3) *Children & Society* (2019) 226–238.

10 Trial Judgement, *supra* note 1, para. 2068.

11 *Ibid.*

12 For the development of the terminology, see I.C. Mochmann, 'Children Born of War: A Decade of International and Interdisciplinary Research', 42 *Historical Social Research* (2017) 320–346.

13 I.C. Mochmann, 'Children Born of War', 2(2) *OBETS Revista de Ciencias Sociales* (2008) 53–61.

14 S. Lee, H. Glaesmer and S.A. Bartles, 'Editorial: Children born of war: Challenges and opportunities at the intersection of war and post-war justice and reconstruction' 6 *Frontiers in Political Science* (2023), available online at www.https://www.frontiersin.org/articles/10.3389/fpos.2023.1122280/full (accessed 25 November 2023).

as: (1) children of enemy soldiers, (2) children of occupation soldiers, (3) children of child soldiers, (4) children of UN peacekeepers[15] and (5) children of paramilitary soldiers and rebels.[16] This last category is particularly relevant to the recognition of children born of war as victims in the *Ongwen* case. In addition to that, one should also note that due to the large recruitment of child soldiers by the LRA, children might have been fathered by LRA child soldiers.

Children born of war, whether born of consensual or coercive relationships, face social stigmatisation and discrimination.[17] Additionally, they may find it challenging to define their cultural, ethnic, and national identity.[18] On a legal front, obtaining proper documentation, such as birth certificates, has also proven to be a challenge for them.[19] The lack of legal citizenship can deny them access to essential services and basic rights, such as education and health care.[20]

In addition to these challenges, children born of coercive relationships often encounter further difficulties.[21] Those born of wartime SGBC are often perceived as reminders of the conflict itself and of the violence suffered by their mothers.[22] They are affected by the social stigmatisation and discrimination directed not only towards them but also towards their mothers. In certain cases, they may face neglect or abandonment.[23]

---

15 *Ibid.*

16 Regarding the addition of the category children born of paramilitary soldiers and rebels, see S. Lee and H. Glaesmer, 'Children born of war: a critical appraisal of the terminology', in S. Lee, H. Glaesmer and B. Stelzl-Marx (eds.), *Children born of war: past, present and future* (Routledge, Abingdon, 2021), pp. 12–34.

17 Mochmann, *supra* note 13, p. 55.

18 On the different meanings of identity referred to in the debates regarding children born of war, see M. Goodhart, 'Children Born of War and Human Rights: Philosophical Reflections', in R.C. Carpenter (ed.), *Born of War: Protecting Children of Sexual Violence Survivors in Conflict Zones* (Kumarian Press, Bloomfield, CT, 2007), pp. 188–209.

19 M. Goodhart, 'Sins of the Fathers: War Rape, Wrongful Procreation, and Children's Human Rights', 6 *Journal of Human Rights* (2007) 307-324.

20 *Ibid.*

21 See R.C. Carpenter, *War's Impact on Children Born of Rape and Sexual Exploitation: Physical, Economic and Psychosocial Dimensions*, available online at www.charlicarpenter.net/childrenbornofwar/Carpenter-WP.pdf (accessed 25 November 2023). Discussing whether the category children born of wartime rape renders the category children born of war irrelevant, see Mochmann, *supra* note 12 and Lee and Glaesmer, *supra* note 15. In this article, reference is made to children born of sexual and gender-based crimes due to the relevant legal framework.

22 K. Theidon, 'Hidden in Plain Sight', 56 *Current Anthropology* (2015) S193–S200.

23 See L. Woolner, M. Denov and S. Kahn, '"I Asked Myself If I Would Ever Love My Baby": Mothering Children Born of Genocidal Rape in Rwanda', 25(6) *Violence Against Women* (2019) 703–720. Regarding the situation in Uganda, see Apio, *supra* note 6, 3.

The acknowledgement of the harm endured by children born of war, especially those born of wartime SGBC, has brought attention to their victimisation.[24] This article examines the challenges associated with the recognition of their victimisation within the context of international criminal law. It does so through the analysis of the definition of victim in the Rules of Procedure and Evidence (RPE) of the ICC and its application to children born of wartime SGBC in the *Ongwen* case. The focus on the *Ongwen* case aims to explore whether the expectations it has generated concerning children born of war were realised.[25]

This article argues that the challenges associated with the recognition of children born of war as victims by the ICC go beyond the application of the criteria specified in RPE Rule 85(a). Within the international criminal context, the focus on individual criminal responsibility develops a narrative that embraces simplistic opposing categories of victims and perpetrators, failing to recognise and address complex political realities. In relation to children born of war, this oversimplification, it is argued, has led to a narrative in which their victimisation has been overshadowed by the acknowledgement of their mothers' victimisation process and the need to create a cohesive discourse about the international criminal responsibility of Ongwen. Potential conflicts between the rights of children born of war and the rights of their mothers as well as the overall experiences of these children whilst in captivity have, therefore, been silenced throughout the proceedings. This silence not only constrains the potential recognition of children born of war as victims of SGBC but also perpetuates stereotypical associations portraying girls and women as pure, innocent, helpless, vulnerable victims and the perpetrator, Ongwen, as the incarnation of evil.

As such, this article contributes to a critical analysis of the jurisprudence of the ICC regarding victims' rights. It highlights the selectivity inherent to the ICC's legal framework and the conceptual challenges it presents to the recognition of children born of war as victims. Specifically, it challenges the oversimplified differentiation between victim and perpetrator, calling for comprehensive accounts of the complex victimisation of children born of war as well as of their mothers. Such accounts are essential for designing meaningful reparation orders.

---

24 In 2018, the International Day on the Elimination of Sexual Violence in Conflict was dedicated to the 'Plight and Rights of Children Born of War', available online at www.un.org/sg/en/content/sg/statement/2018-06-19/secretary-generals-message-international-day-elimination-sexual (accessed 1 July 2023). In April 2019, the United Nations Security Council passed Resolution 2467, recognizing for the first time children 'born of war' as a particular victim group, United Nations Security Council Resolution 2467, S/RES/2467(2019).

25 Dowds, *supra* note 9.

2 Victims in the International Criminal Court

The Rome Statute has been considered a progressive instrument concerning victims' rights in international criminal law.[26] Despite this, the term victim is not defined in the Statute but in the RPE. According to RPE Rule 85(a), victims are defined as 'natural persons who have suffered harm as a result of the commission of any crime within the jurisdiction of the Court'. Additionally, RPE Rule 85(b) extends victimisation to legal persons, stating that 'victims may include organisations or institutions that have sustained direct harm to any of their property which is dedicated to religion, education, art or science or charitable purposes, and to their historic monuments, hospitals and other places and objects for humanitarian purposes'. When related to Article 68(3) of the Rome Statute, which provides for the participation of victims in the proceedings, a judicial decision on whether a person is a legal victim is necessary. In this regard, victim status is determined in line with the definitions of RPE Rule 85.

The definitions of victims provided in RPE Rule 85, nonetheless, do not consistently inform who is a victim to the ICC. Analysis of the negotiation process of the Rome Statute reveals that various working groups considered the involvement of victims in the proceedings.[27] As a result, the term victims in the Statute refers 'to different persons at different times, as specific victims interact in distinct ways with different parts of the [c]ourt at different phases of the proceedings'.[28]

The ambiguity that characterises the status of victim in the Rome Statute has been furthered by the case law, which has, for instance, differentiated between victims who wished to appear directly before the Chamber, registered victim participants, and 'victims who choose not to register or who are, for practical

26 See E. Baumgartner, 'Aspects of Victim Participation in the Proceedings of the International Criminal Court', 90 *International Review of the Red Cross* (2008) 409–4410; C. Stahn, H. Olasolo and K. Gibson, 'Participation of Victims in Pre-Trial Proceedings of the ICC', 4 *Journal of International Criminal Justice* (2006) 217–238; C P. Trumbull IV, 'The Victims of Victim Participation in International Criminal Proceedings', 29 *Michigan Law Review* (2008) 777–826.

27 UN Doc Preparatory Committee on the Establishment of an International Criminal Court, *Working Group on the Composition and Administration of the Court, Draft Statute for the International Criminal Court* (UN Doc A/AC.249/1998/WG.4/DP 19), Part 4, Articles 36 and 37. Preparatory Committee on the Establishment of an International Criminal Court, Working Group on Procedural Matters, by France and the United Kingdom of Great Britain and Northern Ireland. On the negotiation process of the Rome Statute, in relation to victims, see also Baumgartner, *supra* note 26.

28 Assembly of State Parties, *Report of the Court on the Strategy in Relation to Victims* (ICC-ASP/8/45), 18–26 November 2009, p. 2.

or security reasons barred from doing so'.[29] As established by Trial Chamber V, this differentiation involves different actors in the recognition of the status of victim, with the relevant Chamber being responsible for granting the status of victim in the first category[30] and the common legal representative in the second and third categories. This differentiation also has an impact on the ability of victims to express their views and concerns to the Court, with registered and non-registered victims having their views expressed, in a general way, through common legal representation.[31] Although, as emphasised by Kendall and Nouwen, these developments may lead to the formation of a vague, abstract victim category[32] whose characteristics can be more conveniently tailored to fit an idealised victim profile,[33] they make a significant contribution to the analysis of victimisation processes. They underscore the idea that victimhood is a legal construct that is historically and politically contingent. As Christie pointed out, 'being a victim is not a thing, an objective phenomenon. (…) It has to do with the participants' definition of the situation'.[34]

In the context of children born of war, these developments suggest that the applicability of the term victim to refer to children born of war in the ICC might vary. This variability arises because, at different times, different actors are responsible for conveying and acknowledging the victimisation experienced by these children. The views of these various actors are, nonetheless, informed by the ICC legal framework, bringing to the fore the relevance of the definition of the term victim in RPE Rule 85(a).

To be granted the status of a victim by the ICC under RPE Rule 85(a), four criteria must be met: (1) to be considered a natural person, (2) the commission of a crime under the jurisdiction of the court, (3) to have suffered harm and (4) the establishment of the nexus between the harm suffered and the crime within the jurisdiction of the ICC. These criteria are assessed by the relevant Chamber against the information provided in applications for participation in the proceedings. The application process is provided for in RPE Rule 89, which establishes that 'to present their views and concerns, victims shall make written application to the Registrar, who shall transmit the application to the relevant

29 ICC, *Prosecutor v. Uhuru Muigai Kenyatta,* ICC-01/09-02/11, Trial Chamber V, Decision on Victims' Representation and Participation, 03 October 2012, paras 24, 51.

30 *Ibid.*, para. 24.

31 *Ibid.*, para. 38.

32 See S. Kendall and S. Nouwen, 'Representational practices at the international criminal court: the gap between juridified and abstract victimhood', 76(3) *Law and Contemporary Problems* (2013) 235–262.

33 N. Christie, 'The Ideal Victim', in M. Duggan (ed.), *Revisiting the 'Ideal Victim'* (Bristol University Press, Bristol, 2018), pp. 11–24.

34 *Ibid.*, pp. 11–12.

Chamber'. The defence and the prosecutor are allowed to comment on the application form. RPE Rule 89(2) grants the Chamber the power to reject the application, on its own initiative or based on the comments of the parties, if it considers that the person is not a victim or that the criteria set forth in Article 68(3) of the Rome Statute are not fulfilled.[35] RPE Rule 89(3) provides that an application 'may be made by a person acting with the consent of the victim, or a person acting on behalf of a victim, in the case of a victim who is a child or, when necessary, a victim who is disabled'. As such, even if the applicants are under the age of 18, they could be recognised as victims by the ICC.[36] It is, nonetheless, interesting to note that no information concerning applications submitted by or on behalf of children born of war is provided in Ongwen's trial.

In this article, each of the criteria outlined in RPE Rule 85(a) will be assessed against information available in the literature concerning children born of war, in particular children born of SGBC in Uganda, and the information provided in Ongwen's trial and articulated in the trial judgement and in Ongwen's sentence. Section 3.1 examines the criterion 'natural person' in light of the fact that the crime occurred prior to the conception and birth of the concerned children. Section 3.2 explores how the existing legal framework can enable the recognition of the victimisation of children born of war given the absence of a crime within which the ICC could hold an individual accountable for children born of war. Section 3.3 examines the criterion 'harm' to explore how the harm experienced by these children due to the circumstances of their of their conception and birth and the involvement of their fathers in the conflict has been articulated during Ongwen's trial. Section 3.4 considers how the relationship between the harm suffered by children born of wartime SGBC and the crimes for which Ongwen was found guilty has been established in his trial judgement and in the sentence decision.

35 As Article 68(3) of the Rome Statute relates the status of victim to the right to participate in the proceedings, ICC Chambers, when assessing participation applications, beyond the criteria outlined in RPE Rule 85(a), take into account factors such as the potential prejudice to the accused's rights, the risk of compromising a fair and impartial trial, the impact on the victim's personal interests, and the most appropriate stage for participation to grant victim status. This article will not address these aspects, as it points out that the fulfilment of criteria set forth in RPE Rule 85(a), a prerequisite for addressing concerns related to victims' participation, already poses substantial challenges to the recognition of children born of war as victims by the ICC.

36 It is, nonetheless, important to note that the application process has been used by the ICC to restrict participation, not only through the assessment of substantive information, but also by the imposition of a series of formal requirements. See, for instance, the discussions related to the Ugandan situation, ICC, Situation in Uganda, ICC-02/04-101, Pre-Trial Chamber II, Decision on victims' applications for participation a/001/06, a00064/06 to a/0070/06, 0/0081/06 to a/0104/06 and a/0111/06 to a/0127/06, August 2007, paras 16–20.

3 The Selectivity of the Definition of Victim in RPE Rule 85(a)

3.1 *Natural Person*

The concept of legal personhood has not generated much discussion in the jurisprudence of the ICC. The criterion 'natural persons' has been interpreted to refer mainly to human beings.[37] At first glance, the interpretation of this criterion does not appear to present any (conceptual) challenges. After all, the applicant, be it an adult or a child, certainly qualifies as a natural person, if the criterion 'natural persons' is considered at the point of the application for participating in the ICC proceedings or seeking reparations and its subsequent review by the ICC. In this regard, Lee and Glaesmer explain the term children in the expression children born of war should not be read from a chronological perspective, but from a generational perspective.[38] In other words, the term children born of war can be applied to individuals who are legally considered adults, as the terminology intends to bring to attention the impact that the circumstances of their conception and birth had on their life.

The analysis of the criterion 'natural persons' becomes more complex if it is undertaken when the crime occurred. This complexity arises because the relevant SGBC occurred prior to the conception and birth of the concerned children. In fact, these children came into existence through the violation of the rights of their mothers. This discussion is further complicated by the fact that, had it not been for the SGBC suffered by their mothers, the children said to be harmed by that crime would not exist.

As such, the recognition of children born of war as natural persons seems to raise challenges similar to those related to the recognition of the deceased as victims by the ICC. Whilst our common understanding does not deny that those who died as a result of a crime under the jurisdiction of the ICC are victims, in the *Situation in the Democratic Republic of Congo*, Pre-Trial Chamber I held that deceased persons do not fall within the meaning of natural persons under Rule 85(a) and, therefore, cannot be considered victims.[39] Pre-Trial Chamber

37 H. Olásolo and A. Kiss, 'The role of victims in criminal proceedings before the International Criminal Court', 81 *Revue Internationale de Droit Penal* (2010) 125–163.

38 Lee and Glaesmer, *supra* note 16.

39 ICC, *Situation in the Democratic Republic of Congo,* Pre-Trial Chamber I, Corrigendum à la « Décision sur les demandes de participation à la procédure déposées dans le cadre de l'enquête en République démocratique du Congo par a/0004/06 à a/0009/06, a/0016/06 à a/0063/06, a/0071/06 à a/0080/06 et a/0105/06 à a/0110/06, a/0188/06, a/0128/06 à a/0162/06, a/0199/06, a/0203/06, a/0209/06, a/0214/06, a/0220/06 à a/0222/06, a/0224/06, a/0227/06 à a/0230/06, a/0234/06 à a/0236/06, a/0240/06, a/0225/06, a/0226/06, a/0231/06 à a/0233/06,a/0237/06 à a/0239/06 et a/0241/06 à a/0250/06, ICC-01/04-423, 24 December 2007,para. 23.

I's decision emphasised the need to consider the criteria established by Rule 85(a) at the time of the application and its due consideration by the ICC in light of their ability to participate in the proceedings or to seek reparation from the ICC for the harm they suffered. In contrast, in the *Bemba* case, Pre-Trial Chamber III considered that as long as the applicant was a natural person whose death resulted from a crime within the jurisdiction of the Court and a written application has been submitted by their successor, the status of victim can be granted.[40] The relevant timeframe for the application of the criterion 'natural persons' can, therefore, have a significant impact on the ICC's ability to recognise victimisation processes.

In the context of the literature regarding procreative wrongfulness, the challenge related to the recognition of the victimisation of future children has been addressed through the need to develop a normative interpretation of personhood, one that enables its detachment from a person's identity. Such understanding requires interpreting the natural person criterion not as an existing identifiable human person but as a category that could be applied to a normative significant set of characteristics. These characteristics indicate what kind of beings natural persons are and the interests they have.[41] When applied to future children, this approach would mean that

> the non-identifiability of future children should not prevent us from thinking about them as rights-holders to whom particular duties are owed, for we still know the kinds of creatures they will become, and thus the kinds of interests they are likely to have. Regardless of their numerical identities, all children have certain interests qua children, the satisfaction of which is necessary for them to lead minimally decent lives. Thus, our procreative duties are owed to all the future children who we create, whoever they turn out to be.[42]

Within this framework, the 'natural person' criterion would be seen as a type-description that does not require an identifiable human existence at the moment in which the relevant crime under the jurisdiction of the ICC is committed. This approach would enable the ICC to acknowledge a child's right to be born into conditions that allow for the satisfaction of their basic welfare

---

40 ICC, *Prosecutor v. Jean-Pierre Bemba Gombo,* ICC 01/05-01/08-320, Pre-Trial Chamber III, Fourth decision on victims' participation, 12 December 2008, paras 39–52.

41 R. Kumar, 'Who can be wronged?', 31(2) *Philosophy and Public Affairs* (2003) 99–118.

42 E. Magnusson, 'Children's Rights and the Non-Identity Problem', 49(5) *Canadian Journal of Philosophy* (2019) 580–605.

interests during their childhood.[43] In Goodhart's view, this approach recognises the right to be born with human rights.[44] This view allows the ICC to consider children born of war as natural persons at the time of the commission of the crime. Nonetheless, if not carefully framed, it also reignites the discussion of the rights of non-born children and abortion, a discussion that, as will be seen below, has been considered one of the reasons for the lack of a crime for which the ICC could hold an individual accountable for children born of war.

3.2 *A Crime under the Jurisdiction of the ICC*

As with the provisions regarding victims' rights, the Rome Statute has been praised for its provisions regarding crimes against or affecting children, as well as the protection of children's rights and interests. Despite this, there is no international crime for which the ICC could hold an individual accountable for children born of war. As a result, children born of war are not referred to in ICC policy papers. In fact, not even the plight of children born of wartime SGBC is clearly considered by the ICC policy papers. In this context, it is interesting to note that the OTP policy paper on children refers in a footnote to the rape of female child soldiers resulting in pregnancy and to the impact on the education of those children who become pregnant from the rape,[45] but remains silent about the education of children born of wartime rape.

Carpenter relates the silence towards children born of war to conflicts in claims of rights. These conflicts surrounded the discussions regarding forced impregnation during the negotiation process of the Rome Statute. As she explains, throughout the negotiation of the Rome Statute, the term forced impregnation, used to describe conception, pregnancy, and childbirth, became conflated with the international abortion debate.[46] 'The language of abortion rights … focuses attention onto women's reproductive freedom and unborn children's rights, and away from the born child – she is reduced to a foetus whether she was in fact born or not.'[47] As such, the discussion of the rights of born children has given space to the discussion of the alleged rights of unborn children and the rights of women. Within this context, the

43 D. Archard, 'Wrongful life', 79(309) *Philosophy* (2004) 403–420.

44 Goodhart, *supra* note 19, p. 198.

45 ICC Office of the Prosecutor, *Policy on Children* (2000), available online at www.icc-cpi.int/sites/default/files/iccdocs/otp/20161115_OTP_ICC_Policy-on-Children_Eng.PDF (accessed 1 July 2023), footnote 6 and para. 87.

46 R.C. Carpenter, 'Surfacing Children: Limitations of Genocidal Rape Discourse', 22 *Human Rights Quarterly* (2000) 428–477.

47 *Ibid.* See also B. Bedont and K. Hall-Martinez, 'Ending Impunity for Gender Crimes under the International Criminal Court', 6(1) *Brown Journal of International Affairs* (1999) 65–85.

criminalisation of SGBC was achieved at the potential expense of addressing the harm experienced by children born of war.[48]

Despite that, SGBC has provided the main way to approach the victimisation of children born of war in the ICC. As such, in the *Bemba* case, the Expert Report on Reparations drew attention to the 'highly vulnerable' situation of children born of rape.[49] In the *Ntaganda* case, Trial Chamber VI stated that 'recognising children born out of rape and sexual slavery as direct rather than indirect victims, is an acknowledgement of the particular harm they suffered and may constitute an adequate measure of satisfaction, in addition to other forms of reparations that may be awarded to them'.[50] On the contrary, whenever the ICC has failed to address SGBC, the experiences of children born of war have been silenced. The experience of children born to the SGBC girls soldiers were subjected to could not be thematised in the *Lubanga Dyilo* case, as the OTP failed to include sexual violence charges in the indictment against Lubanga.[51] Also excluded from the discussion were the children born of sexual slavery in the case against militia leaders Germain Katanga and Mathieu Ngudjolo, as the OTP dropped the charges after the Pre-Trial Chamber I judge excluded the statements of witnesses supporting those charges on the grounds that the witnesses were not adequately protected.[52] Against this background, the *Ongwen* case, considered a milestone in relation to the prosecution of

48 Carpenter, *supra* note 46, p. 448.

49 ICC, *Prosecutor v. Jean-Pierre Bemba Gombo,* ICC-01/05-01/08-3575-Anx-Corr2-Red, Registrar, Public Redacted Version of "Annex, 30 November 2017, p. 40.

50 ICC, *Prosecutor v. Bosco Ntaganda,* ICC-01/04-02/06-2659, Trial Chamber VI, Reparations Order, 8 March 2021, p. 123.

51 Answering this criticism, the OTP explained the decision to suspend investigations on other crimes committed by Lubanga as being due to the lack of time to conduct the investigations necessary to collect further evidence to substantiate possible new charges. ICC, *Prosecutor v. Thomas Lubanga Dyilo,* ICC-01/04-01/06-170, OTP, Prosecutor's Information on Further Investigation, 28 June 2006. ICC, *Prosecutor v. Thomas Lubanga Dyilo,* ICC-01/04-01/06-399, Pre-Trial Chamber I, Decision on the Requests of the Legal Representative for Victims VPRS1 to VPRS 6 regarding 'Prosecutor's information on further Investigation', 26 September 2007. See also S. SáCouto and K. Cleary. 'Importance of Effective Investigation of Sexual Violence and Gender-Based Crimes at the International Criminal Court.' 17(2) *American University Journal of Gender, Social Policy & the Law* (2009) 3349–359.

52 ICC, *Prosecutor v. Katanga & Chui,* ICC-01/04-01/07, Pre-Trial Chamber I, Decision on Evidentiary Scope of the Confirmation Hearing, Preventive Relocation and Disclosure under Article 67(2) of the Statute and Rule 77 of the Rules, 25 April 2008.

SGBC,[53] has been deemed a relevant opportunity to articulate the experiences of children born of wartime rape and recognise their victimisation.[54]

References to children born of war in the *Ongwen* case can be identified in the SGBC charges for which he was held directly accountable[55] and in the charges for engaging in a coordinated and methodical effort to commit SGBC against women and girls in the Sinia brigade.[56] During Ongwen's trial, references to children born of war are found in the testimonies of the so-called Ongwen's 'wives' and in the testimony of the forensic expert Professor Kloosterman, who performed a DNA kinship analysis of children considered to have been fathered by Dominic Ongwen.[57] The OTP presented the DNA evidence as 'overwhelming proof' of the SGBC committed by Ongwen.[58] Three children born of war were used as evidence of the unlawful confinement of three women who were made pregnant, in this case, through acts of rape by Ongwen.[59] It was also acknowledged that 'as a result of rapes, some of the concerned victims became pregnant and gave birth to children fathered by Dominic Ongwen'.[60]

In the absence of a crime for which the ICC could hold an individual accountable for children born of war, these children have been presented mainly as evidence of the crimes committed against their mothers. As such, their existence, not their experiences, has been relevant to the proceedings. As pointed out by Apio, children born of SGBC are perceived as 'mere evidence of the consequences of sexual violence, the same way effects such as HIV/Aids and other STDs, physical, psychological and social wounds are discussed'.[61] The reference to children born of SGBC seems, therefore, to be an afterthought associated with the status of their mothers, the *concerned victims*.

---

53 S. Van Campen, 'A Legal First in International Criminal Justice: A Conviction for Forced Pregnancy in the Ongwen Case', *ILG* (2021), available online at https://ilg2.org/2021/05/18/a-legal-first-in-international-criminal-justice-a-conviction-for-forced-pregnancy-in-the-ongwen-case/ (accessed 16 November 2023).

54 Dowds, *supra* note 9.

55 Trial Judgement, *supra* note 1, para. 2271. Trial Chamber IX also noted that there was evidence that the so-called 'wives' in Sinia brigade bore children. *Ibid.*, para. 6216.

56 *Ibid.*, para. 2068.

57 *Ibid.*, para. 5690.

58 ICC, *Prosecutor v. Dominic Ongwen,* ICC-02/04-01/15-422-Red, Pre-Trial Chamber II, Decision on the confirmation of charges against Dominic Ongwen, 23 March 2016, 604–606.

59 *Ibid.*, 316–317. As pointed out by Trial Chamber IX, in its sentencing decision, their relevance, even as evidence of his crimes, is limited to whether they were born within the period of the charges. ICC, *Prosecutor v. Dominic Ongwen,* ICC-02/04-01/15-1819-Red, Trial Chamber IX, Sentence, 6 May 2021, 301 (hereinafter Ongwen's sentence), para. 226.

60 Ongwen's sentence, para. 301.

61 Apio, *supra* note 6, p. 15.

The analysis of proposals aimed at translating our moral intuition regarding the wrong committed against these children into a crime under the jurisdiction of the ICC illustrates how challenging it is to untangle the experience of children born of SGBC from those of their mothers. Birth-by-forced-maternity, a proposal put forward by Carpenter, can, for instance, lead to unwanted consequences when considering the availability of abortion. In Carpenter's words, birth-by-forced-maternity 'encompasses both forced impregnation and enforced pregnancy together (but not forced impregnation that results in an abortion)'.[62] As such,

> if abortion is available to a pregnant victim of forced impregnation who elects not to abort, the resulting birth cannot by definition constitute birth-by-forced maternity. As a result, if one woman had the option to abort and the other not, both children would be children of the enemy, conceived through the rape of their mothers, but only one would be considered a victim, even though both would be stigmatised. As a result, in these cases, it seems that, when available, abortion ends up being compulsory.[63]

Carpenter's proposal to criminalise birth-by-forced-maternity also seems to allow for the allocation of responsibility for the harm endured by children born of SGBC to be, if not shifted entirely from the father to the mother, at least jointly shared between them whenever abortion is available. Within this context, Carpenter's proposal appears to convey the problematic idea that 'the crime is in allowing the child to be born at all'.[64]

A different set of challenges is faced by Goodhart's proposal to criminalise wrongful procreation, i.e. intentionally causing conception or pregnancy calculated to result in the birth of a child likely to suffer human rights violations.[65] This proposal, he explains, shifts the focus from the mother to the child, as the crime 'lies less in the force involved in the conception than in the calculation regarding the wrongs the prospective child is likely to suffer'.[66] It is always wrong to cause conception or pregnancy with the intention that

62 According to Carpenter, it is "through forced maternity, not forced impregnation directly, that the child comes into being as a rights bearer and has claims to make on the community". Carpenter, *supra* note 46.

63 Goodhart, *supra* note 18, p.198.

64 This same idea, as pointed out by Carpenter, is implicit in Wing and Merchan's proposal to criminalise forced birthing. Carpenter, *supra* note 46, p. 463.

65 Goodhart, *supra* note 18, p. 198.

66 *Ibid.*

the resulting child will be unable or unlikely to enjoy its rights, regardless of whether that intention is realised.[67]

Departing from the violence suffered by the mother, Goodhart's proposal can expand the scope of the definition of children born of war that may be relevant to international criminal courts, allowing the inclusion of children born out of consensual intercourse. As such, it addresses the challenges related to the clear differentiation between consensual and coercitive relationships in an armed conflict context.[68] Despite that, Goodhart's proposal faces other challenges, such as the recognition of the rights of unborn children.[69] To the extent that the violation of such rights requires the analysis of the substantive content of such conditions, this proposal brings important normative implications to the fore. As explained by Wasserman, such approach could lead to the condemnation of 'parents of limited means and prospects, or in hostile or unstable social environments, from having any children, even children expected to have lives worth living despite their privations and hardships'.[70] As argued by the Defence in the *Ongwen* case, 'despite the difficult circumstances in which children born of war live, to be born is a gift, not a crime'.[71]

---

67 *Ibid.*

68 As pointed out by Stotz et al, the boundaries between violence, coerciveness and consensus are sometimes blurred during an armed conflict. L. Stotz, J. Rokke Elvebakken, I.C. Mochmann, I. Skjelsbæk, S.Á. Tobiasen and T.L. Tryggestad, 'Children Born of War Should be More Than an Afterthought' *PRIO Blog* (6 March 2022), available online at https://blogs.prio.org/2022/03/children-born-of-war-should-be-more-than-an-afterthought/. Consent was also raised during Ongwen's trial, as the conceptualization of consent to sexual intercourse is ambiguous in Acholi society. This, in accordance with Seymour et al., means that 'ICC pre-trial brief's representation of gender based crimes in relation to the charges of forced marriage and sexual slavery does not necessarily coincide with the abductees' perceptions'. E. Seymour, E. Apio and B. Rossi, 'Captive Wives or Conjugal Slaves? The Slavery-Marriage Nexus in Northern Uganda Since the Mid-Nineteenth Century', 43(2) *Slavery & Abolition* (2022) 414–443.

69 Archard, *supra* note 43. From this perspective, 'what is potentially wrong is not that the child is made any worse off than he otherwise would have been, but rather that he is made worse off than he is entitled to be'. D. Wasserman, 'The non-identify problem, disability and the role morality of prospective parents' 116(1) *Ethics* (2005) 132–152.

70 Wasserman, *supra* note 69, p. 138.

71 ICC, *Prosecutor v. Dominic Ongwen*, ICC-02/04-01/15-1991-Red-Corr, Appeals Chamber, Public Redacted Version of 'Defence Omnibus Response to the Submissions on Reparations', 7 March 2022, 34. According to Provost and Denov, this understanding has generally informed the findings of courts when considering whether a child born of harmful behaviour should be seen as a victim; R. Provost and M. Denov, 'From Violence to Life: Children Born of War and Constructions of Victimhood' 53 *New York University Journal of International Law and Politics* (2020) 1–70.

Due the challenges related to the potential development of a prosecutorial strategy based on these proposals,[72] the prosecution of SGBC seems to provide a less contentious approach to the recognition of the victimization of children born of war.[73] After all, the definition of a victim provided for in RPE Rule 85(a) is not limited to those against whom a crime has been committed. It embraces all those who have suffered harm as a result of a crime under the jurisdiction of the court. In this context, once SGBC are viewed not only as the origin of the lives of children born of war, but also as foreseeable causing harm to them, they enable the consideration of the victimisation of children born of war within the ICC existing legal framework. Whether children born of war can be granted the status of direct or indirect victims of SGBC depends, therefore, not only on the interpretation of the criterion natural person, but also on the consideration of the harm caused by SGBC from their perspective. The following section will, therefore, explores the extent to which the harm experienced by these children due to the circumstances of their conception and birth was elucidated during the Ongwen trial.

4 Harm

There is no definition of harm in the Statute of the ICC or in its RPE. According to the Appeals Chamber in the *Lubanga Dyilo* case, '[t]he word "harm" in its ordinary meaning denotes hurt, injury and damage [and] it carries the same meaning in legal texts, including in the RPE'.[74] Various ICC Chambers have interpreted the notion of harm broadly to encompass physical or mental injury, emotional suffering, and economic damage.[75] The determination of a

72 According to Goodhart, 'wrongful procreation has a strong affinity with the other crimes against humanity defined in Article 7 of the Rome Statute'. Goodhart, *supra* note 19, p. 322. To the extent that Carpenter's proposal aims to address similar acts, it could also be considered as 'other inhumane acts of a similar character intentionally causing great suffering, or serious injury to body or to mental or physical health'.

73 In this perspective, even if SGBC do not provide a legal framework for the prosecution of rapists or their superiors for harm suffered by children born of SGBC, they allow the recognition of children born of war as victims.

74 ICC, *Prosecutor v. Thomas Lubanga Dyilo*, ICC-01/04-01/06-1432, Appeals Chamber, Judgment on the appeals of The Prosecutor and The Defence against Trial Chamber I's Decision on Victims' Participation, 18 January 2008, para. 31.

75 See ICC, *Prosecutor v. Jean-Pierre Bemba Gombo*, ICC-01/05-01/08-320 Pre-Trial Chamber III, Fourth Decision on Victim's Participation, 12 December 2008; ICC, *Prosecutor v. William Samoei Ruto, Henry Kiprono Kogsey and Joshua Arap Sang*, ICC-01/09-01/11-249, Pre-Trial Chamber II, Decision on Victims' Participation at the Confirmation of Charges Hearing and in the Related Proceedings, 5 August 2011, para. 50; ICC, *Prosecutor v. Thomas*

single instance of harm suffered has been considered sufficient to fulfil this criterion.[76]

In addition, it has been understood that harm can be suffered directly or indirectly. In the *Lubanga Dyilo* case, the Appeals Chamber clarified the meaning of indirect victims, stating that the harm suffered by indirect victims must arise out of the harm suffered by direct victims, brought about by the commission of the crimes charged.[77] It was further established that close personal relationships, such as those between parents and children, were considered an effective means to prove both the harm and that the harm resulted from the crime committed.[78]

Despite no explicit reference to children born of SGBC in the groups of victims represented by the LRV or the Office of the Public Counsel for Victims (OPCV),[79] both the LRV and OPCV argued that children born of SGBC, of which Ongwen was found guilty, should be regarded as direct victims for reparations purposes.[80] In their view, the harm suffered by these children is the result of such crimes. In contrast, the Defense argued that the harm they suffered is the result of the harm suffered by the direct victims, in this case, their mothers.[81] The challenge related to the categorisation of children born of war as direct or indirect victims is evident in the Amicus Curiae brief, which advocated for their direct victimisation and the recognition of the intergenerational

---

Lubanga Dyilo, ICC-01/04-01/06-1432, Appeals Chamber, Judgment on the appeals of The Prosecutor and The Defence against Trial Chamber I's Decision on Victims' Participation of 18 January 2008, 11 July 2008, para. 32. The Booklet Victims before the ICC: A guide for the participation of victims in the proceedings of the Court, produced by the ICC, refers to these types of harm.

76 See, for instance, ICC, *Situation in the Democratic Republic of Congo*, ICC-01/04-101-tEN-Corr, Pre-Trial Chamber I, Decision on the Applications for Participation in the Proceedings of VPRS1, VPRS2, VPRS3, VPRS4, VPRS5, VPRS 6, para. 82; ICC, *Prosecutor v. Bosco Ntaganda*, ICC-01/04-02/06, Pre-Trial Chamber II, Decision on Victims' Participation at the Confirmation of Charges Hearing and in the Related Proceedings, 15 January 2014, para. 33.

77 ICC, *Prosecutor v. Thomas Lubanga Dyilo*, ICC-01/04-01/06-1432, Appeals Chamber, Judgment on the appeals of The Prosecutor and The Defence against Trial Chamber I's Decision on Victims' Participation of 18 January 2008, 11 July 2008, para. 31.

78 *Ibid.*, para. 32.

79 The confidentiality of the forms submitted by victims does not allow a clear identification of how many fit the category of children born of war.

80 See, respectively, ICC, *Prosecutor v. Dominic Ongwen*, ICC-02/04-01/15-1921, Trial Chamber IX, Victims' Preliminary Submissions on Reparations, 6 December 2021, 42 and ICC, *Prosecutor v. Dominic Ongwen*, ICC-02/04-01/15-1923-Red, Trial Chamber IX, Common Legal Representative of Victims' Submissions on Reparations, 7 December 2021, 21.

81 *Ibid.*

and transgenerational transmission of harm, a characteristic of indirect victimisation.[82]

The articulation of the harm experienced by children born of war is, therefore, essential to their recognition as victims in proceedings before the ICC. The literature has identified various types of harm suffered by these children, such as physical injuries, psychological trauma, socioeconomic marginalisation, statelessness, discrimination, stigma and legal barriers.[83] These categories of harm have been contextualised in the *Ongwen* case mainly through the expert testimony of Professor Musisi. Questioned about the harm experienced by children born of SGBV, Professor Musisi pointed out the lack of acceptance of these children by their mother's families, their lack of inheritance or land due to being born out of wedlock; the double burden of stigmatisation of being born out of wedlock and being a 'so-called rebel child'; the absence of 'socialisation' in traditional Acholi culture or society; and the gendered challenges facing boys who have no land ownership.[84] It is interesting to note that the language used by Professor Musisi moves beyond the violence suffered by their mothers to the harm these children experience due to their fathers' status as a combatant within the LRA. From this perspective, his testimony seems to allow the recognition of children born of war as both direct and indirect victims.

Focusing the discussion of the harm suffered by children born on war due to the perception of their fathers' enemy status, Kincoco relates the stigmatisation suffered by these children to Uganda's patriarchal and patrilineal societal systems, where children fathered by members of the LRA are perceived as proxy members of the LRA and considered symbols of misfortune. They are stereotyped as violent, unproductive, unequal members of society.[85] In this context, the acceptance of a mother who returned to her clan might not mean

82 ICC, *Prosecutor v. Dominic Ongwen*, ICC-02/04-01/15-1971, Other participants, Amicus Curiae brief pursuant to article 75 of the Statute and Rule 103 of the Rules of Procedure and Evidence, 04 February 2022 (hereinafter Amicus Curiae), para. 63. In their words, 'the rejection and stigma (children born of war) face sometimes started with the grandmothers, victims themselves of rape and who also gave birth to children, and cascaded to their children and grandchildren'.

83 See Mochmann, *supra* note 12, Carpenter, *supra* note 21, as well as the United Nations Secretary General, *Women and girls who become pregnant as a result of sexual violence in conflict and children born of sexual violence in conflict* (UN Doc S/2022/77), para. 1.

84 ICC, *Prosecutor v. Dominic Ongwen*, ICC-02/04-01/15-T-177-ENG ET WT, Trial Chamber IX, Transcript, 23 May 2018, from line 10 onwards.

85 A. Kiconco, 'Children born of rebel captivity: politics and practices of integration in Uganda', *Frontiers in Political Science* (2022) www.frontiersin.org/articles/10.3389/fpos.2022.823995/full (accessed 1 July 2023).

the acceptance of her children, resulting in their separation and, potentially, further hardships to the children.[86] In cases where these children are born of SGBC, Clark explains that they often acquire superimposed identities linked to that of the rapist that are difficult to shift.[87] To the extent that these children evoke memories of distress associated with conscription into the LRA and the endured sexual violence, they may be abandoned or neglected by their mothers.[88]

Children born in LRA captivity in the Democratic Republic of the Congo, Central African Republic, or the Republic of South Sudan also face the challenge of not having Ugandan birth certificates or national identification cards, as pointed out by Ocitti.[89] The lack of documentation has been brought to the attention of Trial Chamber IX by the Amicus Curiae brief pursuant to article 75 of the Statute and Rule 103 of the Rules of Procedure and Evidence (hereinafter, Amicus Curiae brief).[90] The violation of the right to a name and registration after birth leads to further violations of human rights, such as the right to vote or travel, to join a school or institution, to gain employment in Uganda, and the right to land and inheritance.[91] Missing or insufficient documentation might also hinder their eligibility as beneficiaries of an ICC reparation order.[92]

It is interesting to note that even though the lack of documentation has been brought to the attention of the ICC, the harm that could be derived from the given name of these children has not been considered. Nonetheless, the literature points out that, in cases involving SGBC, the stigmatisation of these children is at times facilitated by their given names. Names such as Koni, Olum, Rebel and LRA[93] 'compile all the bad experiences of a mother into a

---

86 C. Oliveira and E. Baines, 'Children 'born of war': a role for fathers?', 96(2) *International Affairs* (2020) 439–455. See the testimony of D-0110, ICC, *Prosecutor v. Dominic Ongwen*, ICC-02/04-01/15-T-231-Red-ENG WT, Trial Chamber IX, Transcript, 05 July 2019, 10.

87 J.N. Clark, 'A crime of identity: rape and its neglected victims', 13(2) *Journal of Human Rights* (2014) 146–169.

88 M. Denov and A.A. Lakor, 'When war is better than peace: the post-conflict realities of children born of wartime rape in northern Uganda', 65 *Child Abuse and Neglect* (2017) 255–265.

89 Children born in LRA captivity have been unable to register their birth in Uganda due to existing requirements. See J. Ocitti, 'Birth registration for children born in LRA captivity in Northern Uganda', *LSE*, available online at www.lse.ac.uk/africa/Assets/Documents/Policy-documents/Trajectories-of-Displacement/Policy-2-Birth-Registration-for-children-born-in-LRA-captivity-in-Northern-Uganda.pdf (accessed 1 July 2023).

90 Amicus Curiae brief, *supra* note 82.

91 Ocitti, *supra* note 89.

92 Amicus Curiae brief, *supra* note 82, para. 35.

93 Apio, *supra* note 6, 22.

name and give it a life in the nature of her baby'.[94] Other instances of harm channelled through their mothers have not been articulated.[95] In this context, it is interesting to note that the expert witness refers to the lack of acceptance of these children by their mother's families, but not to the lack of acceptance of these children by their own mothers. In addition to that no reference can be found to the fact that the stigma associated with SGBC can also lead mothers to conceal the identity of the fathers of their children,[96] impacting kingship ties and land use, as these are traditionally acquired through the father's side in Uganda. As such, the mothers' silence might have further consequences on the children's identity and feelings of belonging. From the children's perspective, these omissions are particularly serious when considering their potential involvement in the proceedings, particularly in relation to the submission of an application form on their behalf or in relation to common legal representation.

Our understanding of the victimisation of children born of SGBC is also limited by the silence towards the harm they experienced during their early childhood.[97] Carpenter explains that this silence reflects the current understanding of war-affect children, which is based on 'a notion of a normalized childhood "disrupted" by the onset and continuation of war'.[98] This frame focuses on the harms faced by older children already living at the outbreak of armed conflict. As a result, specific harms infants may experience remain unarticulated.

More broadly, the overall impact of the violent conditions in which they live in whilst in captivity remain unarticulated. Nonetheless, as explained by Apio, whilst in captivity, they might have directly experienced and/or witnessed severe and brutal forms of violence and cruelty.[99] In her words,

> As children fathered by the LRA army ranks, these children originally formed part and parcel of an outlawed group hunted night and day by the UPDF ... At the same time, other LRA enemies, including the SPLA and sometimes the Sudan government troops, poised a great threat to

94 Theidon, *supra* note 22.

95 Provost and Denov, *supra* note 71, p. 62.

96 It is important to note that, in some cases, the father's identity might be unknown. Denov and Lakor, *supra* note 88, p. 262.

97 The only exception was the testimony of witness D-0110, a child fathered by Kony. ICC, *Prosecutor v. Dominic Ongwen*, ICC-02/04-01/15-T-231-Red-ENG WT, Trial Chamber IX, Transcript, 05 July 2019. Most of the testimony has been redacted. In addition, Trial Chamber IX did not find her account directly relevant to the charges. Trial Judgement, *supra* note 1, para. 609.

98 Carpenter, *supra* note 21.

99 Denov and Lakor, *supra* note 88.

> the security of the children during confrontations. During such ventures, many children's lives were lost alongside those of the mothers and the LRA. Some children were stuck onto their dead mothers' bodies, and many may have been left undiscovered at the mercy of the wild; others sustained bullet wounds.[100]

As such, children born of wartime rape might have been direct and/or indirect victims of other crimes under the jurisdiction of the ICC. In addition to that, in cases where they lost their parents, had their mothers escape without them, or became lost during battles, these children might have faced further challenges in accessing their basic rights due to the lack of maternal care. It is not, therefore, only through proximity to their mothers that many children born of war experience (secondary) harm.[101]

Focusing mainly on their post-conflict experiences, the discussion of the harm suffered by children born of wartime rape in the *Ongwen* case has centred around their acceptance and recognition by their (maternal) communities or by the states of their birth. This approach, as explained by Goodhart, 'contradicts our commonsense intuition that it is the rapist-fathers who bear moral responsibility for the children's plight'.[102] As such, the next section examines whether Trial Chamber VI has been able to relate the few instances of harm briefly introduced in the case to the crimes for which Ongwen has been charged.

5 Legal Frames and Their Selectivity: The Nexus between the Harm and the Crime under the Jurisdiction of the ICC

As with the existence of children born of wartime SGBC, their experiences have been related to the consequences of sexual violence experienced by their mothers in the *Ongwen* case. When discussing forced marriage charges, for instance, Trial Chamber IX stated that 'the birth of children was considered to create even more complex emotional and psychological effects on the victim and their children, … beyond the obvious physical effects of pregnancy and childbearing'.[103] It considered that the continued association established between the women forced into marriage and Ongwen has been 'exacerbated

100 E. Apio, *Uganda's Forgotten Children of War*, available online at https://charlicarpenter.net/childrenbornofwar/Apio-WP.pdf (accessed 20 November 2023).
101 Provost and Denov, *supra* note 71.
102 Goodhart, *supra* note 19, p. 308.
103 Trial Judgement, *supra* note 1, para. 2748.

by the fact that, as part, and consequence of this imposition of forced marriage, children fathered by Dominic Ongwen were also born to P-0099, P-0101, P-0214 and P-0227'.[104] In the Trial Chamber's understanding, '[t]his circumstance further perpetuates the continuing bond between Dominic Ongwen and his *victims*, extending beyond the psychological and social pressure created by the (forced) 'marriage' itself'.[105] The terminology used by the Trial Chamber reinforces the idea that women and girls are the only possible (direct) victims of SGBC.

Apio points out that the birth of children whilst in captivity has indeed worsened the living conditions of their mothers due to the extra responsibilities associated with raising a child, such as: 'feeding, clothing, fleeing from enemies, tending to a sick child, having no access to pre- and post-natal services and as a result, the agony of watching one's infant struggle to overcome imminent death'.[106] Even though the challenges related to these responsibilities have a direct impact on the children, on the implementation of their human rights, such impact has not been addressed. The individuality of children born of war was denied, and they were treated as appendages to their mothers. As such, the emotional and material costs that children born of SGBC presented to their mothers ended up outweighing the analysis of the violation of these children's rights throughout Ongwen's trial.[107]

This approach seems to endorse a patriarchal understanding of motherhood that equates the feminine with the maternal and emphasises the responsibility of mothers in raising children.[108] Such responsibility is expected to be carried out with respect, patience, and unconditional love.[109] As such, the Trial Chamber IX has failed to acknowledge situations in which the interests of the

---

104 Ongwen's sentence, *supra* note 59, para. 292.

105 *Ibid.*

106 E. Apio, 'Uganda's Forgotten Children of War', in R.C. Carpenter (ed.), *Born of War: Protecting Children of Sexual Violence Survivors in Conflict Zones* (Kumarian Press, Bloomfield, CT, 2007), pp. 94–109.

107 Financial costs associated with the children have been raised in the sentencing decision, as the Trial Chamber IX assessed the statements of relatives of Dominic Ongwen as 'a plea for the Court to be lenient on Dominic Ongwen so that he can return home and provide for his many children, thereby reducing the economic pressure on his relatives'. Ongwen's sentence, supra note 59, para. 121.

108 T. Takseva, 'Motherhood studies and feminist theory: elisions and intersections', 9(1) *Journal of Motherhood Initiative* (2018) 177–194. Regarding the Ugandan context, Apio points out the gendered and generational ideas that have seen women as caretakers and children as minors in need of care. Apio, *supra* note 6.

109 T. Takseva, 'Mother Love, Maternal Ambivalence, and the Possibility of Empowered Mothering'. 32(1) *Hypatia* (2017) 152–168.

mother and the children are at odds with each other.[110] This silence denies not only the individuality and selfhood of the children but also of their mothers.

In addition, when establishing the nexus between the harm suffered and the relevant SGBC, the Trial Chamber IX has failed to consider the relationship between mother and children as multidirectional. As such, it acknowledged that the children might have increased the psychological harm experienced by the mother, but it did not consider the impact that the psychological harm experienced by the mother might have on them. In this context, not even the indirect victimisation of children born of war has been articulated during Ongwen's trial.

Within the international criminal law narrative, these silences contribute to the creation of idealized victims of SGBC. Women and girls, victims of SGBC, are helpless, fearful, young, and unexperienced, but still caring as potential mothers.[111] As pointed out by Schwöbel-Patel, such representation of victimhood is essential to justify and legitimise the efforts undertaken by the ICC in controversial cases.[112] In the *Ongwen* case, such controversies have been broadly linked to Ongwen's abduction whilst a child and to the Ugandan Amnesty Law.[113] Nonetheless, various other contentious issues can be identified throughout the case, as illustrated by the views of one of Ongwen's wife, who once asked about the forced marriage charges against Ongwen, explained that he had no choice. In her words:

> How they are living there is that when girls are caught and taken from villages Kony would order forcefully what man took what girl – you don't have a say – you are being given forcefully and you don't have a say in it ... he [Kony] would distribute these women to the men. There was a time in Sudan when he [Dominic Ongwen] was given another wife and he said 'no' and they threatened and said they would kill him and so he had to take that woman.[114]

---

110 E. Burman, 'Beyond 'Women vs Children' or 'WomenandChildren': Engendering Childhood and Reformulating Motherhood', 16 *International Journal of Children's Rights* (2008) 177–194.

111 Christie, *supra* note 33. See also C. Schwöbel-Patel, 'The 'Ideal' Victim of International Criminal Law', 29(3) *European Journal of International Law* (2018) 703–724.

112 Schwöbel-Patel, *supra* note 111.

113 See, for instance, Drumbl, *supra* note 3; E. Baines, 'Complex Political Perpetrators: Reflections on Dominic Ongwen', 47(2) *Journal of Modern African Studies* (2009) 163–191; Florence Ayot Interview, *The New Humanitarian* (14 June 2012), available online at www.thenewhumanitarian.org/report/95645/uganda-florence-ayot-my-children-are-always-reminded-their-father-notorious-rebel-commander (accessed 25 November 2023).

114 In Seymour et al., *supra* note 68, p. 418.

Within such a controversial context, children born of wartime rape played an important 'role in reinforcing social representations of their mothers – as victimised subjects – and their biological fathers – as the incarnation of evil'.[115]

On the contrary, the perspective of the children might risk the construction of their mothers as ideal victims. After all, even if limited, the agency of mothers can threaten the interests and rights of their children.[116] Once the potential victimisation of children born of war through their mothers is articulated, these women and girls become bad mothers who have failed to fulfil their parental roles. In fact, to the extent that women are reduced to caretakers and children to minors in need of care; these women become not only bad mothers, but bad individuals. This discussion certainly does not exclude the overall moral blamelessness of women and girls towards SGBC, but the complexity it brings to the fore is prejudicial to the construction of a clear opposition between idealised victims and perpetrators.[117]

In the *Ongwen* case, the underling understanding of motherhood that shaped the discussion of the victimization of women and girls has also contributed to shape the image of an ideal perpetrator. After all, the assumption that childcare is primarily a woman's duty overlooks the father's role in the raising their children. In this context, the silence towards the relationship between fathers and children throughout captivity and its aftermath during the *Ongwen* case is unsurprising. However, Denov and Lakor have pointed out that to some children born of war, captivity was better than peace due to a strong sense of family, including the presence of a caring and protective father.[118] Oliveira and Baines have drawn attention to circumstances in which men who fathered children born as the result of forced marriage during the armed conflict in Uganda assumed full or partial responsibility for their children's well-being after the conflict.[119] Within this context, the silence towards the paternal figure impedes the construction of a far more complex picture of the perpetrator(s)

115 Oliveira and Baines, *supra* note 86.

116 Christie, *supra* note 33, p. 31. Christie suggests that ideal victims must be strong enough to be listened to, or dare to talk and, at the same time, be weak enough not to be a threat to other important interests. *Ibid.*, p. 15.

117 As explained by Christie, the construction of ideal victims cannot be isolated from the construction of the ideal perpetrator, these roles are interdependent. *Ibid.*, p. 18.

118 Denov and Lakor, *supra* note 88, p. 262. See, for instance, the testimony of witness D-0110, ICC, *Prosecutor v. Dominic Ongwen,* ICC-02/04-01/15-T-231-Red-ENG WT, Trial Chamber IX, Transcript, 5 July 2019, lines 11–16.

119 Oliveira and Baines, *supra* note 86, 441. Oliveira and Baines have pointed out that the status of the father as a perpetrator has also impacted our ability to explore 'new ways of thinking about the victim status of children born of war and about how to promote their well-being' in light of their father's role.

of SGBC. In relation to Ongwen, such simplification is articulated by the Trial Chamber IX in the following words:

> that while Dominic Ongwen may harbour certain notions about his responsibilities as a father, it would be improper and even cynical, in the circumstances of the present case, to consider his fatherhood as a circumstance somehow warranting mitigation of his sentence. [...] It cannot be overlooked that while, as a result of his rapes, children were born in the bush to women and girls abducted into the LRA and forced to live with him as so-called 'wives', those children were then kept with their mothers in the same coercive environment. This was not inevitable, as Dominic Ongwen had a realistic possibility of escaping or leaving the LRA.[120]

As such, the efforts to create ideal perpetrators and victims have an impact on the potential recognition of children born of SGBC as victims, as significant aspects of their lives are neglected in the narrative. Within this context, it is not surprising that Trial Chamber IX stated that 'little is known about the children fathered by Dominic Ongwen'.[121] The lack of careful engagement with the harm suffered by Ongwen's children and, more broadly, by children born of SGBC in order to establish its nexus to the SGBC contributed to a narrative in which the individuality of the children has given space to the construction of women and girls as ideal victims of SGBC and of Ongwen and the men who fathered children through SGBC as ideal perpetrators.

Nonetheless, reliance on ideal victims, as explained by Bouris, is problematic as it fails to recognise more complicated images of victimised individuals as victims.[122] It fails, for instance, to acknowledge a woman, victim of SGBC who has abandoned her child, or a child born of wartime SGBC who, raised in the context of the armed conflict, has actively participated in the hostilities as a combatant. Such an approach holds the victim up to a nearly unreachable standard of pure good and pure innocence, denying her humanity.[123] From a practical perspective, any reparative order becomes either unavailable or ineffective for the engagement and healing of more complex victims as significant aspects of their lives are silenced.

---

120 Ongwen's sentence, *supra* note 28, 123.

121 Ongwen's sentence, *supra* note 28, 122. Trial Chamber IX seems to assign this fact to the defence, stating that 'they have been referred to as a category and by an approximate number'.

122 E. Bouris, *Complex political victims* (Kumarian Press, Bloomfield, CT, 2007).

123 Drumbl, *supra* note 3, p. 221.

6 Conclusion

In accordance with Provost and Denov, 'there is a constitutive dimension to the legal narrative, such that victims are in many ways created by their recognition in legal institutions such as the ICC. This constitutive process is far from the objective representation of an existing set of facts. Rather, through the selection and exclusion of relevant elements, the law creates the object it seeks to regulate'.[124] In the Ongwen, this selective process has excluded relevant aspects of the experiences of children born of SGBC, perpetuating a limited understanding of the harm they endure.[125]

The silence towards the experiences of children born of SGBC during their childhood, for instance, has enabled the construction of their mothers, victims of SGBC, as ideal victims. In this context, it is interesting to note that not even the harm indirectly experienced by children born of SGBC has been articulated during Ongwen's trial. As ideal victims, and ideal mothers, women and girls, victims of SGBC, protected their children from the impact of the harm they themselves experienced. Despite the children being constructed mainly as a reminder or, in legal terms, evidence of the SGBC in the trial, there is no space for the expression of conflicting emotions towards these children. No evidence of harm caused by their mothers has been introduced in the trial.

Trial Chamber IX's ability to establish the nexus between the harms experienced by children born of SGBC and SGBC seems to have been compromised by the sparce discussion of such harms. As a result, the Trial Chamber has directed its focus towards establishing the nexus between the harm suffered by women and girls and SGBC. The focus on women and girls has allowed the Trial Chamber to postpone the discussion of the nexus between a child's suffering and a crime predating their conception and birth. Consequently, the discussion of the natural person criterion has also been postponed.

One would have expected that, due to victims' participatory rights, a more significative discussion of the criteria established under RPE Rule 85(a) would have taken place in relation to children born of war. Until now, this has not been the case. Nevertheless, this silence seems convenient to the ICC as it contributes to the development of a coherent narrative, portraying their mothers as ideal victims and the perpetrator as the incarnation of evil. From the perspective of the children born of war, this approach not only negates their victimisation, but also denies their subjectivity.

124 Provost and Denov, *supra* note 71, p. 68.
125 Denov and Lakor, *supra* note 88, p. 256.

In any case, the legal claims related to the characterisation of children born of war as indirect and/or direct victims can, nonetheless, be seen as a step forward towards a better understanding of the tensions that define these children and how their interests can be legally represented. To ensure that this process is properly conducted, a more careful discussion of the applicability of the criteria established in RPE Rule 85(a) needs to take place. Without such discussion, it seems that the categorisation of children born of war as victims in the *Ongwen* case can, at most, be carried out as indirect victims. Even that, however, is open to debate.

Despite the lack of such discussion in the *Ongwen* case, one of its important contributions to the topic is the need to engage with these children to pursue a better understanding of the victimisation process they experienced and to develop adequate community-based reparations. This engagement might enable the articulation in the reparation phase of the proceedings of aspects of their experiences that have remained silenced until now. In a context in which these children are hardly listened to, this engagement can also be conceived as a form of satisfaction, as it acknowledges that they have rights of their own. More importantly, it acknowledges their subjectivity. As such, their lives, when engaging with the ICC, are not reduced to the harm inflicted on their mothers or to the embodiment of their fathers' wrongs. In this process, it might also be possible to restore the humanity of their mothers and fathers and, therefore, their fragility. The challenge related to the characterisation of children born of war as direct or indirect victims in such a context becomes, therefore, a challenge related to the acknowledgement and clear communication of the subjectivity and rights of children born of war to the relevant communities. Within the ICC, this communication involves a clear analysis of the applicability of the criteria established in Rule RPE 85(a) to children born of war.

Acknowledgements

I would like to thank Dr Juan Perez-Leon-Acevedo and Dr Fabio Ferraz de Almeida for the opportunity to present an initial version of this paper in the 'Lights and Shadows of the *Ongwen* Case at the International Criminal Court' webinar and for the feedback received. I am also grateful for all suggestions and comments received from the reviewer. As always, any remaining errors are my own.

CHAPTER 11

Epilogue: *Ongwen* and the Legitimacy of the ICC

Juan-Pablo Perez-Leon-Acevedo and Fabio Ferraz de Almeida

The discussions surrounding the *lights* and *shadows* of the *Ongwen* case set the grounds for a broader debate about the legitimacy of the International Criminal Court (ICC), a concept that is frequently invoked to evaluate (and often criticize) the court's fairness and efficacy in administering justice. Following Langvatn and Squartrito's[1] conceptualization, we understand that legitimacy involves the assessment of three dimensions: a) *origin, pedigree or source legitimacy*, i.e., the way in which the international criminal tribunal was created,b) *procedural legitimacy*, i.e., the process through which the court or tribunal exercises its power, and c) *result or outcome legitimacy*, i.e. the qualities of the selection of cases and decisions produced by the Court.

The book comprises contributions that illustrate how the *Ongwen* case could potentially impact (positively or negatively) the legitimacy of the International Criminal Court (ICC). The discussion presented herein is structured around three key dimensions previously outlined: i) origin, source, or pedigree legitimacy; ii) procedural legitimacy; and iii) source or outcome legitimacy.

1 Origin, Pedigree, or Source Legitimacy

At the origin level, the book explored the court's authority and credibility, scrutinizing its establishment, mandate, and legal foundation to gauge alignment with international law and founding principles. For example, Nortje and Quénivet's analysis allows us to conclude that the ICC legal framework and its legal instruments have proven partially insufficient to handle several complex issues such as grounds for excluding criminal responsibility, especially concerning claims of coercive environment—as it was the case in Ongwen. In this regard, the legitimacy of the ICC and, especially, its legal framework may be affected. Yet, it could be argued that the same legal framework provides

1 S.A. Langvatn and T.J. Squatrito, 'Conceptualising and measuring the legitimacy of international criminal tribunals', in N. Hayashi and C. Bailliet (eds.) *The Legitimacy of International Criminal Tribunals: Studies on International Courts and Tribunals* (Cambridge University Press, Cambridge, 2017), pp. 41–65.

 | DOI:10.1163/9789004743380_012

an avenue for the ICC to potentially enhance its origin or pedigree legitimacy. That is, under article 21(1)(c) of the Rome Statute, the ICC can and should rely on general principles derived by the Court from comparing national legal systems since there is no international treaty containing or fleshing out defences in international criminal law—other than the Rome Statute.[2]

Another example derives from Sanchéz-Mera's discussion about victimhood recognition and gender representations in the enslavement charges. It can be argued that the origin legitimacy of the ICC was arguably compromised because the Office of the Prosecutor did not charge the enslavement concerning the forced military training and fighting imposed on men and, thus, the manner in which the case and then the trial were brought into existence corresponded to stereotypes about or traditional representations of gender and war, which partially distorted the scope of perpetrators and victimhood regarding the enslavement charges.[3] All in all, the fact that the Office of the Prosecutor included enslavement charges for the forced labour imposed on civilians and for the forced labour inflicted on women and girls may plausibly enhance the pedigree legitimacy of the ICC regarding the scope of the *Ongwen* case and the subsequent trial.

Bases on Friso's discussion, one can argue also that the source legitimacy of the ICC was partially affected since the *Ongwen* case challenge linked to the recognition of children born of war as victims by the ICC exceeded the victimhood criteria crafted by the drafters of the ICC Rules of Procedure and Evidence and the subsequent related ICC's jurisprudence on victims. In this case, the source legitimacy of the ICC legal framework does not really help to strengthen the ICC's origin legitimacy as it poses conceptual challenges to acknowledging children born of war as victims of international crimes.[4] Nevertheless, unlike previous cases such as *Lubanga* and *Katanga & Ngudjolo Chui*, the *Ongwen* case arguably provided the ICC with additional source legitimacy through a broader range of charges, particularly sexual and gender-based violence charges.[5] This means that the *Ongwen* case from its very origin was

---

2 *See* chapter 2; W. Nortje and N. Quénivet, 'Fertile or Futile Grounds for Excluding Criminal Responsibility? A Critical Analysis of the *Ongwen* Judgment in Relation to the Claim of Coercive Environment', 23(5–6) *International Criminal Law Review* (2023) 675–704, pp. 690–691.

3 *See* chapter 6; S. Sánchez Mera, 'Fighters, Not Victims: On Victimhood Recognition and Gender Representations in the Enslavement Charges in the Ongwen Case', 23(5–6) *International Criminal Law Review* (2023) 782–803, p. 784.

4 *See* chapter 10; G. Frisso, 'Children Born of War: The Recognition of Children Born of War as Victims in the Ongwen Case', 24(1) *International Criminal Law Review*, p. 53.

5 *Ibid.*, pp. 66–67.

designed to more comprehensively capture the crimes perpetrated as opposed to other ICC cases.

Finally, Maloney, O'Brien and Oosterveld's analysis revealed that while the ICC provided clarity concerning forced marriage as a crime against humanity, the *Ongwen* case arguably revealed a normative gap: the lack of the said crime in the ICC Statute.[6] Such omission in the ICC legal instruments may be problematic for the ICC's source legitimacy.

2 Procedural Legitimacy

As for procedural legitimacy, the focus moves to evaluating the fairness and transparency of legal processes throughout the *Ongwen* case, including investigation, pre-trial, and particularly courtroom procedures. In most cases, the authors highlight problematic aspects of the trial, often associated with the unique cultural context in which the alleged crimes occurred and which could undermine the procedural legitimacy of the Court.

One strong example comes from Mushoriwa, whose work deals with the consequences of the refusal of the ICC Chambers to take into account the *mato oput* traditional justice mechanism of the Acholi people in the sentencing proceedings. By doing so, both the Trial and Appeals Chambers plausibly missed a great opportunity to shed some light on the function and suitability of traditional justice mechanisms at the ICC and discuss how this could be holistically considered and/or adapted into the ICC proceedings.[7] In any event, this procedural legitimacy deficit has arguably been (partially) mitigated by the ICC's explicit acknowledgment of not looking down on traditional customs as well as that the ICC Statute does not include traditional justice mechanisms.

The cultural context in the *Ongwen* case also lays the foundation for Nistor's analysis, which illuminates the issues that arise from intertwining culture into the legal submissions made before the judges at the ICC, that is, the difficulties to 'transform' and 'translate' spiritual beliefs into oral testimony and objective evidence through the legal process.[8] Nistor's powerful critique provides

---

6 *See* chapter 3; K. Maloney, M. O'Brien, and V. Oosterveld, 'Forced Marriage as the Crime Against Humanity of 'Other Inhumane Acts' in the International Criminal Court's Ongwen Case', *International Criminal Law Review* 23, 5–6 (2023) 705–730, p. 707.

7 *See* chapter 4; L. Mushoriwa, 'The Prosecutor v Dominic Ongwen: An Examination of the Role of Traditional Justice Mechanisms in International Criminal Justice', *International Criminal Law Review* 23, 5–6 (2023) 731–754.

8 *See* chapter 8; A. Nistor, 'Culture and the Illusion of Self-Evidence: Spiritual Beliefs in the Ongwen Trial', *International Criminal Law Review* 24, 1 (2023), p. 10.

insights for questioning the procedural legitimacy of the ICC by showing that the Court is not particularly well-equipped for assessing and evaluating matters of culture and spiritual beliefs. The critical view is shared by Viswanath and Li, but the authors offered an alternative explanation for the ICC's failure in adopting a culturally-sensitive approach to adjudicate the *Ongwen* case. For them, the purely textual format of the judgment creates singular and depersonalized narratives that obscure the socio-cultural contexts in which the events investigated happened and oral testimonies were produced. In this sense, the authors argue that the prevalence of textual format creates epistemic and procedural injustice, thus potentially damaging the ICC's legitimacy.

From a procedural standpoint, the *Ongwen* case was also problematic due to the way in which the ICC approached the analysis of the rights of children born out of sexual and gender-based violence. For example, Friso argued that the Court endorsed a patriarchal form of understanding motherhood, one that makes maternal and femininity synonyms and focuses on the mother's role to raise her children.[9]

Despite the complex procedural problems faced by the ICC in adjudicating Ongwen, the case has also contributed towards the procedural legitimacy of the Court. One example is highlighted Maloney, O'Brien and Oosterveld, for whom both the Trial and Appeals Chambers provided a straightforward answer for the nullum crimen question regarding forced marriage as a crime against humanity of inhumane acts.[10] By doing so, the ICC has further contributed towards the re-affirmation of the legality of prosecuting, trying, and convicting individuals based on forced marriage charges in the practice of international criminal courts and tribunals.[11] Another potential positive impact of the *Ongwen* case on the ICC procedural legitimacy involves the way in which the Court has dealt with the duress defence filed by Ongwen as a ground for excluding his criminal responsibility. As Nortje and Quénivet have demonstrated, duress is not a suitable defence for the exclusion of criminal responsibility in cases in which the accused grew in a coercive environment. As the authors' legal analysis of Ongwen have shown, this would also apply to cases in which duress is invoked to characterize continuing, implied, and/or latent coercive environment.[12] Yet, what slightly undermines the overall contributions to the

9 *See* chapter 10; Frisso, *supra* note 4, p. 78.
10 *See* chapter 3; Maloney, O'Brien, and Oosterveld, *supra* note 6, p. 727.
11 *Ibid.*
12 *See* chapter 2; Nortje and Quénivet, *supra* note 2, pp. 688–689.

ICC's procedural legitimacy is that the ICC did not apply all the requirements laid down in Article 31(1)(d) of the ICC Statute.[13]

3 Result or Outcome Legitimacy

Lastly, our discussion extends to issues of result or outcome legitimacy, which changes the focus to the quality of the judgment and sentencing in the *Ongwen* case, i.e. its perceived fairness and appropriateness. Following Nortje and Quénivet's argument, the Chamber's decision to reject a coercive environment-related defence can be considered to be an appropriate or correct outcome as a whole, which plausibly enhances the ICC's result legitimacy. This is because even if the ICC Chambers had been 'creative', the said defence could have not been seemingly derived from comparative national laws.[14]

Maloney, O'Brien, and Oosterveld point to potential positive contributions in the judicial findings related to forced marriage as a crime against humanity as the Chamber for example: i) clarified that forced marriage constitutes a sub-category of 'other inhumane acts', which is in turn an underlying criminal conduct within crimes against humanity; ii) acknowledged and confirmed the conduct and harms encapsulated by the expression 'forced marriage', differentiating it from other categories of crimes against humanity; and iii) confirmed that prosecuting forced marriage is coherent with the *nullum crimen sine lege* principle.[15]

On one hand, it can be said that the *Ongwen* case has contributed towards enhancing the ICC's result legitimacy by acknowledging that forced domestic labour constitutes enslavement and remarking its gender-related dimensions. On the other hand, while such jurisprudential development or finding is important for recognizing the differentiated impact of war on women, it may however reinforce the representation of women as victims by disregarding their fighting roles in non-state armed groups such as the Lord's Resistance Army, as demonstrated by Sanchez Mera.[16]

The evaluation of the results or outcomes of the Ongwe case includes also the sentencing stage. Sorvatzioti, for example, questions the quality of the

13 *Ibid.*, pp. 684–685.

14 *Ibid.*, p. 677.

15 *See* chapter 3; Maloney, O'Brien and Oosterveld, *supra* note 6, p. 705.

16 *See* chapter 6; Sanchez Mera, *supra* note 3, p. 800.

sentencing decision.[17] She argues that, in sentencing Ongwen, the Chamber did not sufficiently analyze the case's mitigating circumstances, i.e. how the social and cultural background in which the defendant operated affected his moral blameworthiness. By not addressing Ongwen's unique dual status as former child abducted soldier and perpetrator, the ICC failed to produce a proportional sentence, one which would be completely autonomous from the judgment, i.e. the conviction decision.

17 *See* chapter 5; D. Sorvatzioti, 'Proportionality and Moral Blameworthiness in Ongwen's ICC Sentencing Decision', *International Criminal Law Review* 23, 5–6 (2023), 755–781.

Index

www.ingramcontent.com/pod-product-compliance
Lightning Source LLC
Chambersburg PA
CBHW071247230926
51849CB00001B/258
9789004743373